A
MATTER
OF
HONOR

A MATTER OF HONOR

Don Kowet

MACMILLAN PUBLISHING COMPANY

NEW YORK

COLLIER MACMILLAN PUBLISHERS

LONDON

Don Kowet wrote A *Matter of Honor* without
the aid or involvement of *TV Guide*.

Macmillan Publishing Company
866 Third Avenue, New York, N.Y. 10022
Collier Macmillan Canada, Inc.

Library of Congress Cataloging in Publication Data
Kowet, Don.
    A matter of honor.
    1. Uncounted enemy (Television program)
2. Vietnamese Conflict, 1961–1975—Military intelligence
—United States.   3. Westmoreland, William C. (William
Child), 1941–   .   4. CBS News.   5. Journalistic
ethics—United States.   I. Title.
DS559.8.M44K68   1984   791.45′72   84-867
ISBN 0-02-566600-2

10 9 8 7 6 5 4 3

Printed in the United States of America

Macmillan books are available at special discounts
for bulk purchases for sales promotions, premiums,
fund-raising, or educational use. Special editions
or book excerpts can also be created to specifica-
tion. For details, contact:

    Special Sales Director
    Macmillan Publishing Company
    866 Third Avenue
    New York, New York 10022

To Begoña and Jack

Contents

Acknowledgments

For his tireless moral support and material assistance in the preparation of this book, I am indebted to my editor George Walsh. I also owe a debt of gratitude to Ilka Shore-Cooper and Dominick Anfuso for their efficient labors on my behalf.

Special thanks are also due my literary agent, Lois de la Haba, whose skill at representing me has been exceeded only by her sensitivity as a friend.

A MATTER OF HONOR

We must always remember that a significant viewpoint does not become less significant just because we personally disagree with it, nor does a significant and relevant fact become less relevant or significant just because we find it unpalatable and wish it weren't so.

Preface to the CBS News Standards
CBS News president Richard Salant
April 14, 1976

Prologue

ONE DAY IN DECEMBER 1981, *CBS Reports* producer George Crile was in an editing room on the eighth floor of the CBS News headquarters in Manhattan, working on the documentary he had been preparing for over a year. "The Uncounted Enemy: A Vietnam Deception" would charge that in the year leading up to the January 1968 Tet offensive the commander of the United States forces in Vietnam had engaged in a conspiracy to conceal the true size of the enemy from the president, the Congress, the Joint Chiefs of Staff, and the American people. Mike Wallace, the show's chief correspondent, would allege that Gen. William C. Westmoreland had blocked intelligence estimates of a larger enemy in order to prove that he was winning "the war of attrition" and to help Lyndon Johnson's reelection in 1968. This "conspiracy," Wallace would argue, had resulted in the United States' "setback" during Tet and President Johnson's subsequent decision not to seek another term. On this day George Crile was going to screen his film for Roger Colloff, CBS vice-president in charge of "soft" news (including the *CBS Reports* documentary department and *60 Minutes*). Colloff had already screened the finished film but had decided to review it again. He had been rereading crucial interview transcripts. Phyllis Hurwitz, the project's assistant editor, was rolling the documentary for Colloff when Crile suddenly heard in the film a faint comment that troubled him. The disturbing statement, barely audible, was in a Westmoreland interview on NBC's *Meet the Press* in November 1967.

Early in the course of his research Crile had learned that in the fall of 1967 Westmoreland's official infiltration figures (the number of regular North Vietnamese soldiers marching down the Ho Chi Minh Trail into South Vietnam) had never exceeded 8,000 a month. But Crile claimed he had spoken with several military intelligence analysts who said that during the five months before Tet their unit had been submitting infiltration estimates of approximately 25,000 *per month*. According to Crile, the analysts also believed that their superiors had suppressed these reports in an effort to keep enemy strength figures low to make it appear as if Allied troops were grinding down the enemy.

Mike Wallace had known about those allegations when he interviewed Westmoreland seven months ago. To Wallace's surprise, when he asked Westmoreland to recall the monthly enemy-infiltration figure just before Tet, Westmoreland replied, ". . . In the magnitude of about twenty thousand a month," apparently confirming the analysts' charges. Crile would juxtapose this statement to Wallace with one Westmoreland had made on *Meet the Press* on November 19, 1967, when the general had estimated enemy infiltration at only 5,500 to 6,000 a month. Crile regarded this discrepancy between the higher number Westmoreland told Wallace and the lower number Westmoreland had told a national TV audience fourteen years before as proof that in the fall of 1967 Westmoreland was deliberately deceiving the American people.

At the screening CBS News vice-president Colloff and the others saw the leaner, more youthful Westmoreland confidently confirming to *Meet the Press* moderator Lawrence Spivak that enemy infiltration, as of November 1, 1967, was "fifty-five hundred to six thousand a month." But the film clip did not end there. The NBC archivists had included several more seconds of film. Ira Klein, the CBS editor, had included the extra footage, without ever really listening to it, as "presence"—a background "extension" over which Crile could lay a line of transitional narration to seal the seam between this segment and the material in the show that followed it. Crile had already written a line that Wallace would record. The viewer would hear Westmoreland say "fifty-five hundred to six thousand a month," then see but not hear the general speaking, his voice muffled by Mike Wallace's as the correspondent introduced the next segment of the documentary. During those several seconds of extra film, after Westmoreland said "fifty-five hundred to six thousand a month," he added, "But they do have the . . ." When Crile realized that the film clip included Westmoreland's "But they do have the . . .," the producer became anxious. But Colloff did not seem to notice the half-uttered phrase.

As soon as the screening ended, Crile met with the editor, Ira Klein. "There's a line in the *Meet the Press* sequence that has to be removed," Crile said.

"I'll look into it," said Klein. Crile left. Klein made a mental note to obtain a copy of the *Meet the Press* transcript. Klein had not seen the complete transcript yet; he had not edited the segment of the show into which the *Meet the Press* clip had been inserted. Because the project had fallen behind schedule, he had convinced Crile to hire an additional editor, who had done the work on that one of the program's five "acts."

At 5:00 that afternoon Crile called Klein from a curbside telephone booth. He had just learned that Van Gordon Sauter, the newly named president of CBS News, wanted to screen the film the following morning. Klein and Crile agreed that Sauter should see the film not in an editing room but in the more technically sophisticated *60 Minutes* projection room on the ninth floor.

On the morning of the Sauter screening Crile was frenzied over the comment he had detected in Westmoreland's *Meet the Press* interview. Klein was sitting on a platform at the rear of the projection room. Crile approached him and reminded him over and over again to lower the sound track before the extra seconds of *Meet the Press* "extension" footage began.

Crile was on a couch right in front of the platform, behind the executives watching the show. As the Westmoreland quote from *Meet the Press* drew near, Crile stood up and turned toward Klein at the back of the room. He held his hand poised dramatically above his head like a symphony maestro. Then, just before Westmoreland uttered "But they do have the . . .," Crile sliced his hand through the air straight down— giving the signal for Klein, at the controls, to obliterate with silence Westmoreland's voice. Klein was puzzled by the whole charade—Crile's frenzy over that half-uttered sentence.

A few weeks later, on January 22, 1982, CBS placed a full-page advertisement in both the *New York Times* and the *Washington Post* alerting readers to the documentary scheduled the following night. The ad depicted a half-dozen faceless plotters huddling around a gray conference table. The word CONSPIRACY was emblazoned on the table in angry black letters. Then at 9:30 P.M. on Saturday, January 23, CBS broadcast "The Uncounted Enemy: A Vietnam Deception." In the days that followed, *Newsweek* magazine, a *New York Times* editorial, and columnists

William F. Buckley, Jr. (*Washington Post*) and Hodding Carter (*Wall Street Journal*) all accepted the program's central premise: that Westmoreland had deliberately hidden vital intelligence from President Johnson. However, the *Times* and the *Post*, respectively, also published responses from Walt Rostow and Gen. Maxwell Taylor, two former Johnson Administration officials, contradicting that premise.

It was an event three days after the broadcast that transformed the usual postmortem of charge and countercharge into a full-fledged controversy. General Westmoreland and Lt. Gen. Daniel Graham, a former military intelligence officer, held a two-hour press conference at the Army–Navy Club in Washington, D.C. They were joined by a quartet of former officials, all with firsthand knowledge, whose accounts had not been included in the show: Ambassador to Vietnam Ellsworth Bunker; CIA Director Richard Helms's special assistant for Vietnamese affairs, Dr. George Carver; Westmoreland's chief of intelligence, Gen. Philip Davidson; and Davidson's second in command, Col. Charles Morris. Each man in turn denounced the documentary. Both Westmoreland and Graham demanded an apology from CBS.

CBS did not apologize. Instead, that night on the *CBS Evening News*, anchor Dan Rather said that although CBS was not persuaded that the documentary had been "inaccurate or unfair in its reporting or its conclusions," CBS News would "give further study to the specific allegations made at the news conference." The next morning, January 27, CBS News vice-president Roger Colloff asked George Crile to submit to him a written rebuttal (standard network procedure whenever a documentary is seriously challenged). In early February, Crile obtained a set of video cassettes of the Westmoreland press conference. He was in front of a TV monitor in the office of Grace Diekhaus, executive producer of *Up to the Minute*, taking notes for his rebuttal.

Crile, thirty-seven, tall, slim, with thick brown hair, was handsome enough to have been allowed in front of the cameras to interview "friendly" witnesses while Mike Wallace grilled the "hostile" ones (with one exception: the show's paid consultant). He wasn't only physically attractive, he had a pedigree and was proud of it. He was George Crile III, son of a renowned surgeon. George's stepmother was the granddaughter of historian Carl Sandburg. These family connections had eased Crile's entry into exalted social circles: His ex-wife was the daughter of Washington political columnist Joseph Alsop.

Some at CBS considered Crile condescending. Others, especially the women, were charmed by his boyish good looks and rumpled elegance (white shirt, tie, and sagging corduroy slacks). In each of his previous

CBS Reports documentaries Crile had collaborated with an experienced woman producer. He had co-produced one such documentary, "Gay Power, Gay Politics," with Grace Diekhaus. "Gay Power, Gay Politics" had earned CBS a stern censure from the National News Council because of an unfair-editing violation.

Next to Crile in front of the TV monitor sat Sam Adams, a sallow-faced, Harvard-educated ex-CIA official—a self-styled "gentleman farmer" who had spent the past fourteen years crusading to convince skeptics that the military in Vietnam had participated in a conspiracy. Adams had served as the show's paid consultant and had appeared on camera in a crucial "friendly" interview with Mike Wallace. What Wallace still did not know was that, contrary to CBS's guidelines of fairness and accuracy, Adams had been thoroughly rehearsed before that interview.

At the left of Adams, Grace Diekhaus, in her mid-forties, was at her desk. Diekhaus, a former *60 Minutes* producer, had been present at many of Crile's interviews for the Vietnam show, providing counsel as well as encouragement. Directly behind Crile and Adams, on a rust-red couch, sat Ira Klein, the editor.

Klein would not be directly involved in writing the rebuttal, but it was more than curiosity that had brought him to Diekhaus's office that morning. In military parlance Crile had been the documentary unit's 1st lieutenant—the platoon leader who set the objective (to prove the conspiracy premise) and devised a strategy and the tactics to accomplish it. Klein had been the staff sergeant, helping to shape the raw, recruited data into a polished film. He was the one who had actually put the documentary together. Crile, the producer, would tell him which segments of interviews to include; Klein would decide how the effect Crile was aiming at could best be achieved and what editing techniques were necessary (say, an additional explanatory line of Wallace narrative) in order to bind these separate segments into a smooth-flowing film.

But providing technical expertise and advice was only one aspect of Klein's responsibilities. In television "hard news," with its breathless two-minute reports rushed on the air in time for each evening's broadcast, an editor's job often entails only cutting and splicing. In the long-form documentaries (and this one was of exceptional length—a full hour and a half), an editor assumed more serious obligations. The producer had to ensure that the network's stringent safeguards of fairness and accuracy were not violated. Edits had to reflect accurately each witness's statements—no quotes wrenched out of context, no answer to one question spliced to a question about a totally different topic. Thus the editor had to be concerned with the *appearance* of the film: Were "friendly" witnesses being allowed full explanations, while "hostile" ones were abruptly cut short?

In making documentary films, the roles of producer and editor can overlap. During the year or so that Crile and Klein had collaborated on "The Uncounted Enemy: A Vietnam Deception," Klein had felt compelled to raise a disconcertingly large number of questions—and objections.

The tape of the Westmoreland press conference continued on the monitor in Grace Diekhaus's office. ". . . Sam Adams's vendetta with regard to intelligence in Vietnam is well known to me and to most anybody associated with intelligence in Vietnam," the sixty-eight-year-old general was saying on the TV screen. "Only when I was on camera did I learn for the first time that the topic was specifically accusations made by Mr. Adams. I had done no research and had brought no documents to refresh my fourteen-year-old memory of events. . . ."

Klein shifted uncomfortably on the couch. The phrase "refresh my fourteen-year-old memory of events" was a virtual paraphrase of the one he himself had used a few days before Westmoreland's May 16, 1981, interview with Mike Wallace, when Klein had complained to other members of the documentary unit that Crile was not giving Westmoreland adequate time to prepare. Crile had waited until Westmoreland had already arrived in New York from his home in Charleston, South Carolina, before sending to Westmoreland's hotel the letter he had promised about a week before, confirming the topic of the interview. Klein had told his colleagues that sending the letter to Westmoreland so late would force the general to lean too heavily on his memory of events that took place fourteen years before.

". . . Realizing, upon reflection, that under pressure of Mr. Wallace's bombardment of questions I gave several imprecise answers," Westmoreland was saying, ". . . I wrote a letter to Mr. Wallace and Mr. Crile in which I enclosed several contemporary documents to correct my imprecisions. . . ."

Klein stiffened. A letter? What letter? At that moment Crile glanced over his shoulder at Klein. Klein mouthed silently: "What is he talking about?" Crile turned away and resumed watching the videotape of the press conference and taking notes.

Over the next two hours Klein kept growing more and more restless. Officials whose names had popped up time and time again during interviews, but whom Crile had dismissed as bit-players in the drama, suddenly were standing at center stage. There on the screen was Gen. Philip

Davidson, Westmoreland's chief of intelligence, whom Crile had never even interviewed.

Over six feet tall, with a glistening bald dome and a fierce brow, Davidson seemed the picture of health—robust and ruddy-cheeked. But George Crile had told his co-workers, including Mike Wallace, that Davidson (the most powerful intelligence officer in Vietnam during the period covered by the documentary) was "on his deathbed." Several times during Westmoreland's interview with Mike Wallace the general had said that Davidson was better equipped to answer a question.

"Why don't you ask Davidson? Haven't you interviewed Davidson?" the exasperated Westmoreland finally asked Wallace.

"General Davidson," Wallace replied, "is a very, very sick man."

And then there was Dr. George Carver—an ex-CIA official, small, with owlish glasses but a steely convincing tone—announcing that it was he and not Westmoreland who had proposed a key compromise over enemy troop estimates, a compromise the documentary had insinuated was a "cave-in," a ploy conceived by Westmoreland to twist the CIA's arm until it submitted.

Klein listened to witness after witness, none of whose accounts had been included in the film, credibly contradicting nearly every charge. His inner turmoil was increasing. Before today he had had doubts, a sense that something about the documentary he had edited was very wrong. Now the men on the screen were substantiating those suspicions. It was midafternoon before the videotape session ended. Klein walked out of the room with Carolyne McDaniel, Crile's secretary. They went into Klein's editing room. Klein closed the door.

"Westmoreland says he sent Mike and George a letter," Klein said.

Carolyne stared at him for a moment. "Do you want to see it?" Carolyne was plump, in her late twenties. She aspired to a career singing in the opera and had a habit of filling even the most trivial moment with the drama that usually precedes a desperate aria.

"Yes," Klein said, trying to conceal his irritation, "I definitely want to see it."

Carolyne left the room. Klein was sitting at his editing table when she returned a few minutes later. She dropped a thick packet of papers on the table. Klein started skimming the documents. There *was* a letter from Westmoreland to Wallace and Crile. Dated June 9, a full seven months before the program aired, the letter amended that crucial "20,000-a-month" enemy-infiltration figure Westmoreland had told Wallace during their interview, the number Crile had juxtaposed with Westmoreland's "5,500 to 6,000" statement on *Meet the Press*. Although the letter did not specifically ask for a correction to be made, it was clear to Klein that had been Westmoreland's intent. Why else would Westmoreland have included, along with that letter, a thick stack of official military intelligence documents, "proving" that his memory during the Wallace interview indeed had been faulty?

Klein began turning the pages of those documents. Suddenly he spotted a phrase that Westmoreland had underlined, and a missing piece of a jigsaw puzzle fell into place. The document was a partial transcript of the Westmoreland interview on *Meet the Press*. Now, for the first time, Klein read the rest of the unfinished sentence—"But they do have the . . ."—that had sent Crile into a frenzy. After Westmoreland had estimated the enemy-infiltration rate as 5,500 to 6,000 per month he had immediately added, "But they do have the capability of stepping this up."

The statement itself was relatively insignificant, a minor qualifier that easily could have been included in the documentary without damaging CBS's case. What was significant to Klein now were Crile's extraordinary efforts to keep even that minor qualifier hidden from the executives who had final approval over his program.

Klein left the CBS News building and plunged into the late-afternoon crowd spilling down 57th Street in Manhattan. He reached his apartment in Manhattan's Chelsea neighborhood. He agonized for a while. Then he decided: He had to meet with *CBS Reports* executive producer Andy Lack so that CBS would know there were serious problems with the broadcast. Before Lack's recent promotion to his present post, he had been senior producer of "The Uncounted Enemy" and thus Crile's immediate superior.

The next morning Klein was in his editing room with Phyllis Hurwitz and another CBS producer, Kent Garrett, when Sam Adams, wearing his trademark parka over his suitcoat, walked in. Klein greeted Adams warmly, embracing the show's paid on-camera consultant. Adams was an eccentric—plodding through the halls of CBS in his zippered parka, always carrying the conspicuous satchel that contained his precious "chronologies"—but a warm and intelligent one. Sam had a subtle sense of the absurd, poking fun at himself, at the ironies of life, at everything except the controversy over enemy-strength estimates that consumed him.

But today Adams was not smiling. "We have to come clean," he declared. "We have to make a statement. The premise of the show was inaccurate." Adams explained that he was now convinced Westmoreland had not been hiding the numbers from the president. He believed the documentary itself had proved that the conspiracy had originated in the White House. Westmoreland had been only a go-between.

Garrett and Klein exchanged looks of disbelief. It was Adams's "chronologies"—long, lined, yellow legal pads on which Sam had recorded every detail he had gathered, crucial or just curious—which had served throughout as the bible for the broadcast. It was Adams who had provided the list of eighty former officials from which Crile had selected his witnesses. It was Adams's comments penned beside each name on that list that had determined whether Crile ignored a potential witness or interviewed him. Effectively, George Crile did not unearth a single fact that was not exposed beforehand by Sam Adams—names, dates, places, interpretations of events. And now Adams was declaring that the premise of the show had been incorrect, that the conspiracy had originated not with Westmoreland but in the White House, that Westmoreland "wasn't the chief sinner but only a deputy sinner." Adams was standing the premise of the program on its head.

"Sam," Klein said, "don't you think it's a little late? Why weren't you telling George this all along?"

"I did, I did," Adams said. "I *was* telling him all along." Then he added, "George is writing his rebuttal of the press conference. I'll make sure he includes a statement admitting the premise of the show was wrong."

There was no longer a shred of doubt in Klein's mind: Something was drastically wrong with the broadcast. Right now, though, Klein needed someone to confide in. Kent Garrett, the producer, had already witnessed Sam Adams's bizarre about-face. Later that evening Klein showed Garrett the Westmoreland letter and the intelligence documents. Garrett skimmed the material and seemed as distressed as Klein had been. It was clear to Garrett as well as to Klein that Westmoreland had requested a correction. Klein told Garrett that he planned to talk to Andy Lack. Before he did, he would speak to Crile; protocol dictated that Klein speak to the show's producer first. But Klein learned that Crile had left on a trip to Washington, D.C.

The following morning at 10:00, Klein was working in his editing room when Garrett entered. Garrett looked disheveled and disturbed. "I haven't slept all night," he said.

"I'm going to go in and talk to Andy," Klein said.

Lack was busy with another producer. Klein waited in the corridor, leaning against the wall. Finally, the producer departed and Klein walked into Lack's office. He had never really spoken at length to Lack. With slick black hair and narrow-set eyes that stayed icy even when his lips were pulled back in a smile, Andy had been promoted to executive producer only a brief time before the Vietnam film had been completed. Howard Stringer, whom Lack had replaced as executive producer, had been the unit's real boss. Stringer had left *CBS Reports* a month or so prior to the broadcast to become executive producer of *CBS Evening News with Dan Rather*.

The conversation that day between Klein and Lack was a lengthy one. Klein had come determined to discuss only three items out of all the nagging inconsistencies that had troubled him these many months. By concentrating on three items he considered vital, he felt he could give Lack a yardstick to gauge the problem CBS faced. The first item was Adams's statement, "We have to come clean. . . ." The second item was the Westmoreland documents, the ones he had mailed to Mike and George, the ones Klein regarded as a request for a correction. Klein had not brought those Westmoreland documents with him. He did not want to place Lack in an awkward position. He knew that the proper course of action was first to confront Crile with the letter and documents. The third item was the assertion of the CIA's George Carver at the Westmoreland press conference that it was he, and not Westmoreland, as the documentary had indicated, who had proposed a crucial compromise at a 1967 conference in Saigon, a compromise the documentary had characterized as a CIA cave-in.

During their conversation that day Lack kept asking Klein questions: Didn't Crile talk to the CIA's George Carver? Why hadn't Crile interviewed the chief of military intelligence, General Davidson? As the chat wore on, Klein felt that Lack was growing more and more concerned, and that was important. As executive producer, Lack had the influence, the resources, and the authority to initiate internal action if he decided such a step was warranted. However, Lack told Klein that he did not want to see any documents—not, at least, until Klein had spoken to George Crile. The meeting concluded with Lack assuring Klein that "nothing will be suppressed." Klein was scheduled to begin a two-week vacation that coming Friday, February 26. He postponed his flight to Florida until Saturday.

The next morning, Thursday, Klein encountered Lack in an elevator.

"Have you spoken to George yet?" Lack asked.

"No, I still haven't been able to reach him," Klein said. They left the elevator at the eighth floor and walked together down a dimly lit corridor. "Look at the documents," Klein said. "All I'm asking is that you look. You tell me whether or not we were being asked to include a correction."

"Ira," Lack replied, "do it for me—talk to George first."

That afternoon Lack located Crile in Washington. Crile told Lack that Klein had been stirring up a "vendetta" against him. Then Crile telephoned Klein in the editing room. "What's the problem?" asked the producer. Klein explained his reservations about the film, his reaction to the press conference, his astonishment when he discovered that Westmoreland had sent Wallace and Crile a letter and documents that seemed to be a request for a correction. "All right," said Crile. "As soon as I get back, let's you, Andy, and I talk to Roger Colloff."

Klein had faith in the CBS system, faith that the guidelines of fair, balanced, and accurate journalism that had become the industry standard were more than rhetoric. He had revealed his misgivings to Andy Lack. It was up to Lack to initiate an investigation into his charges. "No," Klein told Crile on the telephone. "Lack understands my position. Let him follow it up." Klein gave Crile a telephone number where he could be reached while he was on vacation. The conversation ended.

Klein gathered up the Westmoreland documents. For the second time he walked into Lack's office. This time he laid the documents on Lack's desk. Lack scanned them. He picked up a telephone and requested a videotape of "The Uncounted Enemy." He also asked Judy Reemtsma, the senior producer of *CBS Reports*, to come into his office. For the next few hours the three discussed in detail the questions Klein was raising and the evidence in the documents, until suddenly the door burst open and Mike Wallace stormed in.

The sixty-four-year-old correspondent had made this same trek down from the ninth-floor offices of *60 Minutes* before when problems had arisen over the documentary and Crile had needed extra muscle to wrest a point from his superiors. Wallace had clout. He was the "point man" of one of the highest-rated and thus most profitable programs on television. Mike was widely regarded by his peers as the news division's "meal ticket"; each year he earned an estimated $60 million for CBS.

Mike sat down, and Andy Lack handed him the "correction" documents. Mike turned to Klein. He said, "You understand, I was only cosmetics in this show."

Wallace meant that his participation, apart from interviewing a few main targets of the conspiracy charge and the paid consultant Sam Adams, had been minimal. Not only his questions to witnesses but almost all of his follow-up questions had been written out for him in advance by producer George Crile.

Lack handed Wallace the Westmoreland documents. As he began turning pages, Wallace asked Klein, "Can you get me the Westmoreland transcript?" The transcripts of interviews were kept in an adjacent office. Just as Klein reached the door, Wallace added, "Why didn't you come forward sooner?"

"I didn't even know these documents existed," Klein said.

Wallace nodded noncommittally and continued thumbing through the official papers. Klein returned with the transcript of Wallace's interview with Westmoreland. Wallace began turning its pages. He spotted a passage on one page and said, "He lied there. . . ." He stopped a few pages later and said, "There, he was lying there, too. . . ." All the while the telephone kept ringing, always for Wallace. Mike was responsible for twenty-five 60 *Minutes* pieces each year, plus documentaries and speaking engagements. He was the caviar of correspondents, and CBS was spreading him thin. Wallace was late now for an important appointment.

Wallace stood up and dropped the Westmoreland documents on Andy Lack's desk. "I respect your opinion, believe me," Wallace told Klein without the abrasiveness that always clung to him on camera. As he moved toward the door he stopped and put his hand on the young editor's shoulder. "But don't worry," Wallace added soothingly, invoking the ultimate sanction of legitimacy at CBS News, "at 60 *Minutes* this kind of thing happens all the time."

On Saturday, Ira Klein left New York for his two weeks' vacation in Florida.

During the CBS evening news on the night of the Westmoreland press conference, Dan Rather had promised his national TV audience that CBS would study the charges raised by the documentary's critics. But CBS had not. Now a CBS employee had attempted to bring serious problems to the attention of his supervisors, submitting a set of documents that he felt cast doubts on the fairness of the program. Once again CBS took no action. George Crile wrote his "white paper," rebutting the testimony of the officials who spoke out at the press conference (without including Sam Adams's contention that the premise of the show had been incorrect). It gathered dust in a CBS News vice-president's desk drawer.

In its May 29, 1982, issue a *TV Guide* cover story entitled "Anatomy of a Smear"* accused the documentary of "massive distortions" and violations of CBS's own guidelines of fairness and accuracy, as well as accepted journalistic ethics. In response to *TV Guide*'s charges, CBS initiated an internal investigation, headed by senior executive producer Burton "Bud" Benjamin. On July 15, CBS News president Van Gordon Sauter released a memo to CBS employees admitting that Benjamin's investigation had uncovered "several" violations of CBS guidelines, but also insisting that CBS still "stands by the substance" of the broadcast. In a South Carolina federal court, lawyers for Gen. William C. Westmoreland filed a $120 million libel suit against Sam Adams, George Crile, Van Gordon Sauter, Mike Wallace, and CBS, Inc.

* Jointly written by the author of this book and Sally Bedell.

1

CBS
Gives the
Go-Ahead

IT WAS EARLY NOVEMBER 1980. A gusty wind was ruffling the tops of trees, thumbing through the leafless branches like a hurried browser in a bookstore. The wind soared onward over the rural Virginia countryside, stirring the grass in fallow fields, sweeping through cracks in a barn where goats and pigs and chickens coexisted in a harmony men rarely mimic. The wind skimmed the sloping roof of the sprawling, desolate farmhouse, deaf to the dim echo of history in a room below.

Sam Adams, the farm owner, was a direct descendent of an Adams who had caught a bullet at the Battle of Bunker Hill. George Crile, the CBS producer and Adams's guest, traced his lineage to historian Carl Sandburg. This Adams was in open rebellion *against* the American military; Crile was anxious to be his Boswell. Together, in that chill November night, the pair of old comrades was rekindling a fiery controversy, one still smoldering after more than a decade.

In 1967 and 1968 there had been a series of conferences in Washington and Saigon convened by the CIA to produce a National Intelligence Estimate (NIE) of enemy strength in Vietnam. During those meetings a battle had raged between the CIA and Gen. William C. Westmoreland's MACV (Military Assistance Command, Vietnam) over the enemy Order

of Battle—the strength, makeup, and disposition of the North Vietnamese and Vietcong armies. The central dispute was over whether a pair
of enemy organizations, Self-Defense and Secret Self-Defense units,
were sufficiently potent to be included, and quantified, in the monthly
military Order of Battle summary. The military had argued that these
organizations were poorly equipped and ill-trained, and thus should not
be counted as enemy soldiers. Adams had fought hard for their inclusion
and quantification in the Order of Battle.

Seven years later, in 1975, Adams had written an article about the
controversy ("Vietnam Cover-Up: Playing War with Numbers") for
Harper's magazine. In that explosive article Adams not only charged the
military in Vietnam with faking estimates and suppressing intelligence of
a larger enemy, he accused the CIA of caving in to the military cover-up.
Adams further chronicled his own extraordinary efforts to apprise his
superiors (up to and including Commander-in-Chief Richard Nixon,
who followed Lyndon Johnson into the Oval Office in 1968) of this
Vietnam deception. George Crile had been Adams's editor at *Harper's*.

"George had heard of me through a friend of mine," Adams recalled.
"He got hold of me and persuaded me to write the article on my experi-
ences in CIA."

Adams said he saw Crile "off and on for about a year or two" after the
piece in *Harper's* was published, but eventually lost contact with him.
Then, in November 1980, Adams telephoned Crile at CBS. Adams was
researching a book on Vietnam, and a hundred or so of his interviews
focused on the Order of Battle controversy.

According to Crile, Adams had uncovered new evidence, proving that
what had seemed a simple rivalry between the CIA and the military in
fact had been "a full-scale perversion of the intelligence-reporting process." Now Crile was at Adams's farmhouse in Virginia, reviewing Adams's
"chronologies" in search of the substance for a CBS documentary. Adams
had been taking notes on the details of the Order of Battle debate for
fifteen years. He estimated that if his 140 pages of OB chronology (handwritten on yellow legal pads) were typed out, they would total 500 to 600
pages. Recently, he had added a new element: allegations that Westmoreland and his intelligence command had suppressed higher estimates
of enemy infiltration during the five months preceding the enemy's Tet
attack. Adams was convinced that this deception had kept both the President and the U.S. armed forces in the field from properly anticipating the
enemy's sudden onslaught.

Adams and Crile discussed the chronology and other documentation
Adams had assembled. Crile agreed to write a proposal. Subsequently,

Adams read that proposal. He recalled that "it pretty well followed what these guys had said and what was in their letters."

Adams and Crile disagreed over only one word. "George liked the word 'conspiracy,'" Adams recalled later. "I slightly bridled at it. I was uneasy with the word 'conspiracy' in the sense that you have a bunch of villains sitting around a table conspiring together." Adams felt that while military intelligence had indeed faked official statistics in violation of the Uniform Code of Military Justice ("In a technical sense, if you get two people talking this over, it becomes a conspiracy"), his suspicion in November 1980 was that Westmoreland's ultimate superior, President Lyndon Johnson, "knew perhaps not the details but the overall thrust of what was going on. And if there were a conspiracy," Adams added, "I thought LBJ had to be in on it." However, Adams lacked convincing proof of Lyndon Johnson's participation in the plot.

George Crile shared Adams's suspicions about Lyndon Johnson's role in the Vietnam deception. But Crile did not share Adams's reservations about placing General Westmoreland at the pinnacle of the "conspiracy." On November 24, 1980, Crile delivered his "blue sheet" (the proposal a producer submits to get his documentary approved) to Howard Stringer, then the executive producer of the *CBS Reports* documentary department. While Stringer and *his* superiors (CBS News vice-president Bob Chandler and CBS News president Bill Leonard) considered Crile's proposal, Crile was busy attempting to convince Mike Wallace to be the program's chief correspondent.

Wallace had known Crile for two to three years; Mike had seen *CIA: The Secret Army*, an award-winning documentary that Crile had produced in collaboration with Judy Crichton. Crile's close friend and confidante, Grace Diekhaus, was a former colleague of Wallace's at *60 Minutes*. Wallace regarded Crile as "a sober man" and "a good reporter." Crile in turn admired Wallace both as a consummate professional and as a potentially powerful ally. Wallace's consent would be a definite asset in Crile's campaign to convince his superiors that the documentary was not only do-able but worth doing. Wallace was the star of *60 Minutes*, the most popular program on television. He was widely regarded as CBS News's meal ticket, his mere presence on a program a guarantee of sizable ratings.

But it was not only Wallace's clout with his superiors at CBS that made him invaluable to Crile. It was clear from the start that there could be no broadcast unless Gen. William Westmoreland, the focus of the conspiracy premise, agreed to appear on camera. Of all the CBS correspondents, Wallace was the one Westmoreland was most likely to trust. Wallace prided himself on being 60 *Minutes*'s "house conservative." Furthermore, he had already met Westmoreland "on several occasions." In March 1967 Wallace had traveled to Vietnam and actually spent a day in the field with Westmoreland. Wallace had letters in his file from Westmoreland commending him for work he had done on 60 *Minutes*. Wallace himself professed "great admiration" for Westmoreland. Although he knew Westmoreland only slightly, in Wallace's estimation Westmoreland was "an honorable man." As the chief correspondent of the program, Mike Wallace could assure Westmoreland's crucial participation in the project.

Crile summarized the premise of the show and gave Wallace Adams's 1975 *Harper's* article to read, but not the "blue sheet" proposal for the program. (Wallace wouldn't read any portion of that blue sheet until long after the documentary aired.) Crile told Wallace about the project, and asked him if he would be interested in participating. Wallace said yes.

Crile went back across the street to sell his blue sheet to his superiors.

For the most part, according to Adams, Crile's blue sheet was composed of "strung-together" quotes from officials Adams had already interviewed and excerpts from their letters home that Adams had managed to obtain. Because of Adams's formidable research, Crile was able to write a proposal far longer than the average one (often not more than a single page)—a full sixteen pages. In that blue sheet Crile proposed to document "how the United States military command in Vietnam entered into an elaborate conspiracy to deceive Washington and the American public as to the nature and size of the enemy we were fighting." Crile went on to suggest "that a number of very high officials—General Westmoreland included—participated in a conspiracy that robbed this country of the ability to make critical judgments about its most vital security interests during a time of war." The blue sheet used the word "conspiracy" a total of twenty-four times and used the word "conspirator" on five other occasions. The proposal's nine section headings included "The Conspiracy," "The Key Conspirator Takes Charge," "The Conspiracy Is Forced to Expand," and "The Conspiracy Continues." Later Crile stated that "conspiracy" was "the only word that worked for me to explain the pattern of events."

Crile's immediate supervisor was *CBS Reports* executive producer Howard Stringer. Stringer had known Crile for six or seven years. He had been introduced to Crile by a CBS vice-president when CBS was considering turning an article Crile had written for *Harper's* on the CIA into a documentary. Stringer had read Crile's article and had agreed that Crile should be hired, first as a consultant, then as a reporter, on that broadcast, *CIA: The Secret Army*. Crile became a producer a year later. During

Stringer's six-year reign as executive producer of *CBS Reports*, Crile had co-produced five documentaries.

Stringer felt that the use of the word "conspiracy" in the blue sheet twenty-four times "was George trying to sell an extremely reluctant executive producer. The length of the blue sheet reflected a massive amount of skepticism on my part."

It was not that Crile's superiors (in ascending order: Howard Stringer, CBS News vice-president Bob Chandler, and CBS News president Bill Leonard) doubted the blue sheet's premise of a Westmoreland-led conspiracy. They made no effort, then or later, to investigate the accuracy of Adams's story. What they were skeptical about was Crile's ability to confirm the story on camera.

"I was in on the earliest discussions with George. Bill Leonard was in on it," recalled Bob Chandler, then CBS vice-president in charge of all "soft" news (documentaries, *Magazine*, *60 Minutes*, etcetera). "Our only misgivings were: Could we actually do the show? Would these people actually say publicly what they were saying privately? These were solid citizens." Chandler added, "If they were anything less than solid citizens, we would have had grave doubts about the project. As it was, we had a fair degree of skepticism. We told George that if he could indeed get them to talk on camera, we would go forward."

"It was a conditional pass," said Crile. "The condition was: Go spend some time and see if you can bring in evidence, and show it to us."

Later, executive producer Howard Stringer would reveal that Bob Chandler's skepticism had not been limited to Crile's ability to record the whistle-blowers' charges. Stringer had discussed with Chandler more than five times whether Crile should be allowed to produce the documentary on his own. Several years before, in collaboration with Grace Diekhaus, Crile had produced a documentary called "Gay Power, Gay Politics." Stringer said that Chandler was "concerned" because "there had been complaints about one or two violations of CBS standards that were submitted to the [National] News Council. He wanted to be sure that they didn't happen again." Chandler had been the one assigned to defend "Gay Power, Gay Politics," before the National News Council, which ultimately found CBS guilty on three counts, including the insertion of applause into a politician's speech where in fact there had been no applause.

CBS made two other crucial decisions at this time. The first dealt with the role of Sam Adams. In his blue sheet Crile had written, "I had told [Adams] I would see if we could pay him for his research. . . . I made it clear to him, however, that this might not be possible—among other reasons because he is sure to be a key interview in the show." News vice-president Bob Chandler and his boss, CBS News president Bill Leonard, decided that Adams should be the program's paid consultant. (Adams eventually received $25,000 plus expenses.) Chandler said they further decided that if Adams appeared on camera, "we would have to make it clear on the show that Adams was a paid consultant as well as an inter-viewee—make it clear in the script and in the credits."

Chandler and Leonard also selected Mike Wallace to be the documen-tary's chief correspondent, although Crile would have to do the bulk of on-camera interviewing himself—Wallace was already committed to do at least twenty-five 60 Minutes segments a year. With Mike Wallace on board, Crile was set to venture out and prove that the officials named in his blue sheet would say in public what they had already told Sam Adams in private.

A week later, on December 1, 1980, CBS film editor Ira Klein was walking through the main concourse of editing rooms on the eighth floor of the Ford building (the massive glass-and-concrete edifice, across 57th Street from the main CBS Broadcast Center, in which CBS leased space for its soft-news units: CBS Reports, 60 Minutes, Magazine, Up to the Minute, etc.). As Klein walked by an editing room, an assistant editor called out to him, "George is looking for you." Klein knew that "George" meant George Crile; the assistant editor had worked on the controversial "Gay Power, Gay Politics" program which Crile had produced in collab-oration with Grace Diekhaus.

The thirty-year-old Klein had joined CBS Reports several years before. Technically he was a free-lance editor, moving from project to project, but he had never been out of work. He had worked as an editor at CBS for several years. Right now he was editing segments for the morning Magazine program.

Klein turned a corner in the corridor and glanced into his editing room. Crile was not there. Klein was en route to Crile's office when he met the producer coming down the hall. They walked back together into Klein's editing room. Klein sat on the edge of a table. Crile sat on a stool in front of Klein's editing machine.

When the news broke that the Three Mile Island nuclear reactor was in danger of meltdown, CBS had commissioned its entire documentary unit to generate an instant one-hour report. Virtually everyone at CBS Reports had been mobilized, with production crews scurrying around the country in search of information and pictures. Crile and Judy Crichton were the producers of the program; they and their peers at Reports would shoot segments that Crile and Crichton would assemble into the hour-long "special report." Although Klein had had only fleeting contact with Crile, he had heard complaints from field producers—that Crile was ripping the film out of their hands and reshaping it without consulting them. Klein knew there had been widespread dissatisfaction with Crile's stewardship. One angry producer had warned Howard Stringer, the executive producer, never again to leave him alone in a room with Crile.

However, Klein had taken the complaints about Crile with a grain of salt. The Three Mile Island project was, by the very nature of its immediacy, a chaotic one; it was understandable that nerves had been frayed and egos bruised: Someone had had to make final decisions about what the film would exclude and include, and that responsibility had fallen squarely on Crile's and Crichton's shoulders.

Today Klein met Crile in the hall. The two men walked together to Klein's editing room. "Are you interested in working on an hour-and-a-half-long documentary?" said Crile. Klein asked Crile what the focus of the film was. Crile told him it was about Vietnam but would not elaborate.

The following day, December 2, 1980, Klein was editing a film segment when Crile entered. He said that he definitely wanted Klein to be the editor of his broadcast. Klein accepted the assignment. "I'd like to see the blue sheet," Klein said. The blue sheet would tell Klein what the film was about. It would serve as a catalyst, sparking his own ideas and directing him toward outside reading material that could expand his understanding of the program's premise. But Crile did not want Klein to see the blue sheet yet. Crile told Klein that because the project was such a sensitive one, at that time he did not want to reveal the premise of the film.

Klein was not offended. He realized that if Crile had indeed uncovered a major story, there was a danger it might leak—the print media might get wind of it and publish an article that would dilute the impact of the CBS program. Investigative journalism on television was an unwieldy process. Print journalists were not burdened by the complexities of television production; they did not have to compete for camera crews, negotiate shooting schedules, lug around equipment, or convince reluctant witnesses to allow their faces on film. Television's logistics made investigative journalism both tedious and terribly expensive.

However, there was one item Klein did need to know then. Free lances who expected to survive in the business had to line up one job long before another was finished. Unlike full-time CBS staffers, when Klein didn't work he didn't get paid. He was always careful to ensure that he secured a

new assignment before he completed the current one. "What's your starting date?" he asked Crile.

"I'm in the process of getting approval," Crile said. Crile needed to get
the whistle-blowers' charges on film before his superiors would give him
the final go-ahead, but Klein did not know that. All he knew was that
Crile did not have a starting date. He told Crile he would continue
working on segments for *Magazine*. Crile said that he understood; he just
hoped Klein would not commit himself to any long-term projects and
thus be unavailable for Crile's own film. Klein agreed, they shook hands.
Crile and Klein—a study in contrasts. Crile, an ex-Marine, carried himself with the slouching, tweedy air of an Ivy League academic; Klein had
the supple ease of an accomplished ex-athlete. Crile was a bona fide
WASP, his father the renowned surgeon. Klein, from a middle-class
neighborhood in Queens, had never really known his father, who had left
the family before Ira was a teenager. Crile spent his evenings at sleek
upper-West-Side-of-Manhattan dinner parties. Klein could be found in
lower-Manhattan pubs. The only thing they had in common was an
uncommon verbal fluency. Ultimately, though, in the making of this
documentary, only George Crile's words would count.

While Klein kept on editing other CBS programs, Crile, usually accompanied by his paid consultant Sam Adams, began his attempt to
record on film the complaints against Westmoreland and his intelligence
directorate. Aside from Adams's voluminous chronologies, Crile's main
source in the search for interviewees was the list of eighty former officials
the consultant called "probably the most important single document I
supplied George." The document not only listed former officials knowledgeable about the events in Vietnam, it contained Adams's written comments summing up each official's likely testimony and thus his value as a
witness. For instance, beside the name of Gen. Maxwell Taylor (former
United States ambassador to South Vietnam, chief of staff of the United
States Army, and chairman of the Joint Chiefs of Staff) Adams had
commented: "I prepared for my interview [one prior to the CBS project,
for Adams's book] for upwards of a month and in our hour-and-a-half talk
got nothing save one usable quote. . . ." Of another United States ambassador to South Vietnam, Ellsworth Bunker, Adams had written: "Bunker
was in on all this, although it's problematical how much he knew of the
fakery. . . . But he's awfully old now, and CBS might look like it's hound-
ing an old man to his grave." Of Walt Rostow, the special assistant to
President Johnson who acted as the gatekeeper for information flowing
into the White House from Vietnam, Adams asked: "Would he finger

LBJ?" Adams wrote that Gen. Philip Davidson, Westmoreland's chief of military intelligence in Vietnam during the years in question, "is said to have cancer. . . . Deathbed confession? Doubt it but maybe worth a call."

Another name on that list of eighty was that of Col. Charles Morris, directly below Davidson in the military intelligence chain of command and his director of intelligence production. Morris, Adams wrote, was "resentful" of the success of his immediate subordinate, Danny Graham.

Finding former officials who would speak out about Lt. Col. (now, in 1983, Lt. Gen., retired) Daniel Graham's involvement in the conspiracy was vital. Crile had described Graham (in 1967–68 a lieutenant colonel and Westmoreland's chief of current intelligence and indications estimates) in his blue sheet as the "Key Conspirator."

As their first on-camera subject, Crile and Adams selected Lt. Col. David Morgan, who had served in 1967 as the deputy chief of the Order of Battle branch of Westmoreland's Saigon-based intelligence division. Morgan had been deputy to Col. Gains Hawkins, who had already agreed to go before the CBS cameras. Initially Crile and Adams were trying to document new information Adams had uncovered since his 1975 *Harper's* article: that in the fall of 1967 the reports of hordes of enemy infiltrators had been suppressed. Adams knew that Hawkins could offer nothing to substantiate that allegation. He believed that Morgan could.

In the November 1980 blue sheet Crile had written that "Colonel Morgan, who is now retired and living in California, is still haunted by his part in the conspiracy. 'We cut lots of units . . . ,' " Crile quoted Morgan. " 'It was terribly wrong. We had no criteria for dropping people. It was guesswork. There was nothing to back it up. Why did we do it? To make ourselves look good—to make Danny Graham look correct—so we could prove we were winning the war.' "

Adams telephoned Morgan on January 18, 1981. Two days later Crile and Adams flew to California to interview Morgan and attempt to convince him to appear in front of the CBS cameras. "When we started out CBS was really dubious we could get anybody to come on," recalled Adams. "We started out with a guy who I thought was easiest."

But Morgan proved more intractable than Adams had anticipated. "He was willing to tell me all kinds of stuff," said Adams, "but he didn't want to come on the tube. He said it was one thing to tell a guy like me, it's another to spill his guts in front of God knows how many million people."

Crile and Adams spent four and a half hours trying to convince Morgan, without succeeding. Morgan did, however, agree to telephone another witness, Lt. Col. Everette Parkins. Adams was convinced Parkins had been "fired" in 1967 when he attempted to submit to his superior an estimate showing a far larger enemy force. In researching his book several years before, Adams had persuaded Morgan to help arrange an interview with Parkins. But when Morgan telephoned Parkins this time on behalf of both Adams and CBS, Parkins indicated he wanted no part of any on-camera interview.

Next on Crile's list of whistle-blowers was a man whom Adams had characterized as "an old friend of mine." Ex-CIA analyst Joe Hovey could testify about the ultimate impact of the faked intelligence estimates and suppressed reports of dramatically increased infiltration: the United States' unpreparedness for the enemy's attack at Tet. In November 1967 Hovey had sent from Vietnam a report (commissioned by presidential adviser Walt Rostow) that seemed to foreshadow the enemy's all-out onslaught—a warning, Adams argued, that the military dismissed on grounds that the enemy force wasn't large enough "to carry off such an offensive with any hope of success."

To Adams's and Crile's relief, Hovey did agree to go before the CBS cameras. Crile interviewed him on January 21. Crile and Adams then interviewed Gen. Kao Ky, the South Vietnamese prime minister at the time of Tet who was now in exile in California. But talking to Ky they decided he was "too peripheral to the situation."

After spending three weeks attempting to persuade ex-officials to appear before CBS's cameras, Crile had succeeded in obtaining only one on-camera interview, with former CIA analyst Joe Hovey. "We were thrashing about, trying to get someone to come on," said Adams. "We'd fanned with Morgan, with Parkins—we figured, Jesus Christ, we've got to get somebody on here." It was time to absorb Mike Wallace, the program's chief correspondent, into the process. He would interview a former military intelligence officer named Marshall Lynn. Lynn was another young analyst whose totals of the enemy, Adams claimed, had been arbitrarily slashed.

Wallace was to interview Lynn on January 27, but given his hectic 60 Minutes schedule, Mike had scant opportunity to prepare beforehand. Crile was compelled to meet Wallace at the airport and brief him in a taxi on the line of questioning he should follow. "Wallace had had no background in any of this," recalled a CBS source. "It was the first interview he did. The only thing Mike knew about it was what George told him over coffee, so to speak."

Lynn had been a military intelligence analyst focusing on "service" troops—soldiers not normally engaged in actual combat but in supplying the front line with equipment, armaments, ammunition, and edibles.

Lynn opened his interview by recounting two anecdotes, both involving the same colonel whose name Lynn couldn't recall. In the first incident, in early fall 1967, the colonel had told Lynn that his estimates of some service units were too *low*; in the second incident, a few months later, the colonel had told Lynn his estimates of those same units were too *high*. There was a pause in the interview. When the cameras resumed rolling, Lynn repeated, in greater detail this time, only the incident when the colonel suggested that Lynn's estimates of service units were too *high*, and told him to lower them.

The interview was short, and none of it would be used in "The Uncounted Enemy." Later Adams would claim that the Lynn interview had been discarded because instead of massaging a reluctant whistle-blower, an overzealous Wallace had gotten Lynn in a verbal headlock, pressing Lynn on his own complicity in the "conspiracy." However, the actual unedited film footage of that interview contradicts Adams's explanation. Lynn seemed relaxed throughout; periodically he would erupt with laughter. He did not seem "reluctant"; the telling of his story did not seem to be causing him any stress. In retrospect, perhaps it was not Wallace's prosecutorial tone but Lynn's lighthearted one that caused CBS to discard the interview—Lynn's tone and the utter emptiness, evidentially, of his tale.

The Marshall Lynn interview, although never used, did have one long-term effect: Wallace in his initial foray had failed to corroborate the indignation and outrage Adams had attributed to Lynn in his chronology record of their earlier interview. The Lynn interview confirmed Sam Adams's growing concern about Mike Wallace's ability to conduct complex interviews on such a convoluted subject as the Order of Battle debate.

While Crile and Adams desperately scoured the country in search of convincing ex-officials willing to come forward and face the CBS cameras, Ira Klein was continuing to accept assignments from *Magazine*. Every so often he would encounter George Crile in the halls of *CBS Reports*. Crile would always inquire anxiously about Klein's schedule— had he tied himself to any long-range project since their last meeting? Klein had not; he was still editing features, working on an as-needed basis. Crile made it clear that he hoped Klein would keep his schedule free. Klein had a substantial reputation at CBS. Among the producers who admired his work was George Crile's close friend, Grace Diekhaus, who had asked Klein to work on *Up to the Minute* after he was done with the documentary.

In mid-January, Klein began a search of his own, for an assistant editor to work alongside him when and if CBS finally approved Crile's project. A friend recommended Phyllis Hurwitz, a young free-lance assistant editor who was then working at ABC. Klein interviewed Hurwitz and was impressed by her. Beneath her street-smart veneer, behind her Brooklyn accent were a shrewd intelligence and a steely forthrightness that Klein instantly admired. Hurwitz, like Klein himself, wanted to know exactly when Crile's project would start. Klein explained to her that the final go-ahead depended on Crile's getting people to be candid on camera. He did not tell her in detail what the project was about, in part out of cautiousness. Klein still had not been allowed to read Crile's blue sheet. All he knew was that the program would focus on Vietnam and the project was a sensitive and potentially controversial one.

In the weeks that followed, Phyllis Hurwitz called Klein often. Klein interpreted that as a positive sign; she seemed diligent and eager to work on the film. Klein told Hurwitz that he would telephone her when he heard a firm starting date, and that it was very likely she would actually begin working on the project before he did. Editors in the CBS Reports unit were under the jurisdiction of a different union than editors working in other areas of CBS soft news. Klein carried both union cards. But as long as he was still working for Magazine, say, and not officially assigned to CBS Reports, Klein could not handle even a foot of film belonging to the documentary department.

Periodically Klein would hear complaints muttered about Crile. But in spite of the criticisms Klein had heard during the Three Mile Island project and, more recently, the occasional bitter barb about the producer uttered within his earshot, he was looking forward to editing Crile's film. It would be Klein's first ninety-minute documentary (and Crile's first solo documentary, as well)—a chance to amplify and deepen his own film-making experience. Undoubtedly Crile's enemies were exaggerating his flaws and minimizing his assets. Jealousy and envy were the twin foods that fueled many TV careerists. The world of network television was rife with ambitious, aggressive go-getters who could not care less when they stepped on others, but whose own egos were as brittle as eggshells. Even if some disliked Crile, Klein reasoned, that did not mean the producer did not possess some special quality (why else would proud CBS have given Crile the job?) that would make their collaboration a stimulating and instructive one. Thus far, of course, Klein had not really been able to form his own impression of Crile's character. Their encounters had been brief, usually lasting no longer than five or ten minutes.

Crile and Adams were having better luck now. Two days after Mike Wallace's aborted interview with Marshall Lynn, Crile interviewed on camera Col. George Hamscher. Adams had spoken to Hamscher on three occasions in September 1978. From Hamscher he had learned of a meeting at the Pentagon chaired by Key Conspirator Danny Graham in the summer of 1967, six months before Tet. Crile had recapitulated in his blue sheet a portion of the story Hamscher had told Adams: ". . . Colonel Graham summons the two troubled MACV officers [Col. Gains Hawkins and Gen. George Godding] to a meeting at the Pentagon. There, in a small room adjoining the offices of the Joint Chiefs of Staff, he calls on them to openly falsify the estimates of specific enemy units. 'See, the Eighty-third Rear Service Unit,' Hamscher remembers Graham saying, 'there must be a lot of civilians in there. Let's knock it down. It's not 3,100, it's 1,900. The 516th Local Force Battalion. We all know it just got clobbered the other day. Let's lower it. . . .'

"In this manner," Crile concluded in his blue sheet, "Colonel Graham managed to march enough VC soldiers out of the Order of Battle to allow MACV's totals to conform with the ceiling that General Westmoreland had ordered. . . ."

Three weeks after Crile interviewed George Hamscher he filmed Lt. Richard McArthur. In the chain of conspiracy Crile was constructing, McArthur provided a crucial link with the post-Tet period. In his November 1980 blue sheet Crile had written: "*Feb. 13, 1968*—MACV's analyst in charge of VC guerillas, Lt. Richard McArthur . . . arrives at his desk this morning to discover that the wall chart on which he maintains his guerilla estimates province by province has been altered dramatically. Thirty-five thousand enemy soldiers have simply been removed from the total. Enraged, McArthur confronts his commanding officer, Lt. Col. Paul Weiler, demanding to know why his guerillas have been cut.

" 'Sorry, Mac,' Weiler responds, 'we had to do it.'

" 'That's no answer, sir. Why?'

"Weiler then ends the conversation with a plea for McArthur to stop making trouble: 'Lie a little, Mac. Lie a little.' . . ."

Adams had interviewed McArthur eleven times between December 5, 1975, and March 25, 1980, for a total of approximately twenty-four hours. In fact, almost every whistle-blower who loomed large in Crile's blue sheet had been previously interviewed by Adams in the course of researching his book. No one who had *denied* the charges of fakery and fraud was now being asked for an interview. At this early stage, CBS News president Bill Leonard, vice-president Bob Chandler, and executive producer Howard Stringer had commissioned Crile not to evaluate Adams's charges or examine them critically, but simply to document them. George Crile was telling Sam Adams's story, not testing it.

Early in February 1981 Alex Alben joined the project as a researcher, moving over from the CBS election-coverage unit. A veteran associate producer, Joe Zigman, had already been assigned to assist Crile.

Around the time Alben was arriving at CBS Reports, Bob Chandler was leaving his post as vice-president in charge of soft news. Chandler, who entertained doubts about Crile, was being shifted to the position of senior vice-president, administration. The move, which would make Chandler CBS News president Bill Leonard's deputy, was widely regarded as a career setback. Chandler had already served as the CBS News president's deputy from 1975 to 1977; besides, now he would be quarantined from the day-to-day decisions that had to be made about controversial news programs. Erroneous judgments might lead an executive into limbo, but correct ones could lift him toward the coveted presidency of the entire news division. (Bill Leonard was already past the age of mandatory retirement, retaining his job as news president only because of a special age waiver.) Bob Chandler couldn't earn his general's stars sitting outside Bill Leonard's office. Roger Colloff, Leonard's deputy till then, would replace Chandler as vice-president in charge of soft news. It was Colloff who would ultimately decide if George Crile's Vietnam project deserved final approval.

In the third week of February, George Crile finally told Ira Klein that in order to obtain that final approval he would have to screen segments of interviews for CBS executives, so that they could satisfy themselves that Crile had indeed captured on film the charges intelligence analysts had made privately to Adams. He told Klein that Roger Colloff would now be the executive who either issued the final go-ahead or ordered the project scrapped. For that Colloff screening Crile would prepare a rough cut, selecting compelling interview segments and splicing them together. Since Klein would not be able to participate in putting together this rough cut (CBS Reports editors paid dues to a different union than editors elsewhere in soft news), he and Crile agreed that Phyllis Hurwitz, the assistant editor, should be hired to help out.

On March 1, Hurwitz's first day of work at CBS Reports, Klein gave his new assistant an orientation speech. Its theme was loyalty—the importance of being loyal to George Crile and thus to the project itself. Klein told Hurwitz that he wanted the project to be insulated from office politics. He also warned her to be prepared for long hours, week after week, with only a few days off in between. Marathoning was Crile's work style. That was all the guidance Klein was able to provide. He could not disclose much about the film itself. Klein still did not know the project's intimate details. Klein had stopped asking Crile even superficial questions; he had learned that Crile was not interested in elaborating.

Hurwitz began preparing for the Colloff screening. Excluding Wallace's unusable session with Marshall Lynn, Crile currently had on film three interviews: Joe Hovey, the CIA analyst whose report to the White House foreshadowed the enemy's massive uprising at Tet; Col. George Hamscher, who claimed to have seen the Key Conspirator, Lt. Col. Danny Graham, arbitrarily slashing enemy troop totals in an illicit meeting at the Pentagon; and Lt. Richard McArthur, the guerilla specialist who claimed his estimates had been cut in half. Hurwitz began working with these "dailies"—the raw, uncut film footage. The cameramen would shoot "negative" film in 400-foot, ten-minute rolls. These ten-minute segments would be sent to an outside laboratory where two 400-foot rolls were combined into a twenty-minute one. The "negative" would then be processed on a printer, producing a "print"—and thus a roll of dailies. Crile would then screen the dailies, marking on his transcript of each interview the material he wanted to select. Hurwitz's task was to pull that material and create "select" reels. Each raw interview consisting of five rolls of film, 800 feet for twenty minutes on each roll, would be reduced to a single select reel, containing only those segments Crile felt might be useful for his film. From that select reel, in turn, Hurwitz (again at Crile's direction) would pull out the specific takes—a particular scene or an exchange of dialogue between correspondent and witness—Crile had chosen as being representative. Those takes, plus excerpts from interviews with Col. Gains Hawkins, the military Order of Battle specialist, and Gen. Joseph McChristian, a former chief of intelligence, would be assembled into the rough cut Crile had to show Roger Colloff in the last week of March.

It was painstaking work. Anxious to make a positive impression that first day, Hurwitz labored tirelessly, scarcely taking notice of the woman who kept popping in and out and conferring with Crile in hushed tones. During her first coffee break Hurwitz stepped outside her editing room and was pounced on by a passerby, who breathlessly began interrogating her: Was Crile working alone on this project? Why was Grace Diekhaus prowling around the cutting room? Was George going to co-produce this documentary as well with Diekhaus?

Hurwitz escaped. She went to the editing room where Klein was editing a segment for *Magazine*. "What," she asked, "is going on here?"

Klein had tried to prepare Hurwitz for the political ambience in which Crile was immersed, the resentment some felt because they believed he had climbed to the top astride the shoulders of a pair of powerful women. Now Hurwitz understood.

That Monday evening Crile and Adams boarded an airplane for London. Adams had interviewed Comdr. James Meacham, now the military correspondent of *The Economist*, for approximately nineteen and a half hours in November 1977, and again for two more hours in July 1980. Meacham was a crucial witness to certain events that Sam Adams believed occurred after the enemy's Tet offensive, when Lt. Col. Danny Graham had allegedly compelled one of Meacham's men to tamper with the historical record of the Order of Battle in the intelligence command's computer.

In his conversations with Bob Chandler, Crile had emphasized the activities of Meacham and his men—the tampering with the computer. Meacham's confirmation of the conspiracy would be crucial testimony.

Crile and Adams returned from London a few days later, adding the Meacham interview to the others being culled for scenes to show Roger Colloff. Again Crile resumed marking up interview transcripts so that Hurwitz would know what material to select from the dailies. When Crile was not supervising Hurwitz, he was usually in his office, listening and taking notes while Sam Adams conducted his chronology sessions.

Occasionally Klein would pass by Crile's office during one of those sessions (held daily whenever Crile and Adams were not off interviewing). He would glimpse Adams reading from the long, lined, yellow legal pads that contained the chronologies, while Crile and Alex Alben, the young researcher, sat mesmerized.

"Sam is one of the most meticulous note takers I have ever met," Alben recalled later. "In a two-, three-, or four-hour session, Sam was able to give a picture of what he was doing on any particular day and what everybody else was doing whom he had contacted." Adams's chronologies were convincing because of their vivid detail. "He was able to describe an officers' party in Saigon and the beryl-colored tiles of the swimming pool," said Alben. "In fact, he knew more about where everybody else was at any given time than they did. When he talked to someone he would say, 'Who else was in the room?' So when he contacted the next person, he could say, 'Don't you remember, you were beside the swimming pool at the officers' club right before Tet?' "

The problem was, Adams did not understand even the rudiments of proper journalism. Second- or third-hand reports of events, delivered to him with sufficient passion and tending to confirm his overall premise, were accorded more weight than first-hand accounts that contradicted his thesis. In the case of Lt. Col. Everette Parkins's "firing" by Col. Charles Morris, for instance, Adams had accepted the version of events of witnesses who only heard rumors over Parkins's own explanation.

When Alex Alben was not attending chronology sessions or telephoning the Lyndon Baines Johnson Memorial Library in Texas in search of declassified documents, he was mining the list of eighty names Adams had given to Crile. If there were any doubts about Adams's story, Alben said, those doubts disappeared when he found "people who had been incommunicado for the last fifteen years. You would find someone selling insurance in Arizona," Alben recalled. "They would say, yeah—and without even [your] asking a probing question, this person would just spill out his story."

Undoubtedly the ex-officials did have pent-up emotions about those long-ago events in Vietnam that caused their stories to come spilling out. However, it is also true that Adams had refreshed their memories of events when he had interviewed them—or most of them—in the course of researching his book. Col. Gains Hawkins, for instance, whom Crile interviewed on camera on March 9, 1981, had been Adams's confidant for years. Adams was convinced that Hawkins would testify Westmoreland had imposed an artificial "ceiling" on enemy-troop estimates, a ceiling Hawkins allegedly had been ordered to defend in the Order of Battle debate with the CIA.

A week later, after interviewing Hawkins, Crile flew to Florida to interview Gen. Joseph McChristian, who had preceded Gen. Philip Davidson as Westmoreland's chief of intelligence. Adams was convinced that Westmoreland had suppressed a report by McChristian of a far larger enemy. The McChristian interview was the last one Crile conducted before the crucial screening for the new CBS vice-president in charge of soft news Roger Colloff, in the last week of March 1981.

There was a special tension in Ira Klein's editing room on the morning of the Colloff screening. In part the tension stemmed from a natural anxiety over how the CBS executives (executive producer Howard Stringer would accompany Roger Colloff) would react to the material they were about to see. Along with the tension there was curiosity. While not unique, the screening was an unusual event.

It was clear, though, that Colloff's and Stringer's purpose in screening the film footage was not to question Crile's conspiracy premise. If they had been unsure or skeptical, the CBS executives would have asked to screen the raw, uncut interviews. Viewing these dailies, Colloff and

Stringer would have heard every interviewee's statement in its proper context. But Colloff and Stringer were busy men; they did not have time to sit through endless rolls of raw footage. The CBS system dictated that they trust their producer, and men who reach positions of power and influence in television are rarely the type to challenge the system. Instead, all Colloff and Stringer wanted to know was whether Crile had been able to capture on film the intelligence analysts' complaints. In his rough cut Crile had selected the segments from each interview which best buttressed those charges.

The screening began at 10:30 A.M. Crile sat at the editing console; Colloff sat on Crile's right, on an editing stool. Klein, due to the conflicting union policies, was still barred from working on the Vietnam project. He was sitting on the editing table behind Crile. Howard Stringer was sitting on another editing stool, beside Klein. Neither the assistant editor Phyllis Hurwitz, the researcher Alex Alben, nor the veteran associate producer Joe Zigman was in attendance.

Crile turned on the editing machine. One by one the whistle-blowers appeared on the screen, confirming in astonishing detail the scenarios and allegations Crile had mentioned in his blue sheet. The men spoke with obvious emotion. Sometimes they paused or stumbled, as if uttering such heinous charges (ones they knew would be used to convict on camera the commander of Allied forces in Vietnam) was almost too difficult a task. They seemed torn between conflicting inner imperatives; loyalty versus ethics, duty and honor versus country. At the completion of each terrible tale the screen would turn black. Crile would stop the editing machine and with his voice, weave these separate threads into the rich fabric of his tapestry, adding color and the larger context. Then he would restart the machine, and another somber ex-official would appear, with testimony of other dark deeds dreamed up by the cynical coven of colonels and generals. The rough cut of assembled takes was powerful.

Finally the reel finished. Roger Colloff was bursting with enthusiasm. He announced that he did not want CBS News president Bill Leonard, an experienced documentary maker, to see the rough cut. Colloff wanted Leonard to see, with fresh eyes, the entire film when it was completed. Colloff was convinced that Leonard would find the broadcast irresistibly persuasive.

It was evident that Howard Stringer was as impressed by the rough cut as Colloff. Klein was aware of Stringer's reputation as a documentary maker. Colloff was a novice in the field of broadcast journalism; when he had taken over for Bob Chandler in February, a CBS producer, Judy Crichton, had had to lead him by the hand out into the world to instruct him on how a documentary was actually done. Stringer, in contrast, was widely regarded as one of the most competent producers in all of television news. Furthermore, the subject of this broadcast—the war in Vietnam—was one he was only too familiar with. An Englishman and public school/Oxford graduate (he read Modern History), in 1965 Stringer had been in the United States only two months, working for CBS, when he was drafted into the United States Army. Although as a resident alien he was not obliged to serve at the time, he decided to enlist and was shipped to Vietnam as part of Westmoreland's army. Stringer stayed in Vietnam approximately ten months, from the fall of 1966 until May 1967. Assigned to the military police, he ended up as personnel sergeant of a battalion based at Bien Hoa, in charge of finances and administration. On several occasions he had been rudely reminded that a war was going on.

Twice he was accidentally fired upon by American troops: once when an MP machine-gunned the tent he lived in ("Luckily, we were lying down at the time") and again when Americans inadvertently mortared his compound one night. "I was at an ammunition dump one time when a sniper took a shot at us, hit a jeep," he recalled. "Was in a plane that was machine-gunned as it left Bien Hoa. Machine-gun bullets hit the tail. . . . Was shot at once on guard duty, when somebody lit a cigarette. I was at the ammunition dump at Bien Hoa when it was blown up. That set off a chain of explosions that lasted six hours." Stringer "had a friend, a close friend" who was killed in Vietnam. Clearly he realized exactly how sensitive this project was. He turned to Klein. He smiled and said softly, "You'd better hide the negative."

Colloff and Stringer seemed to feel relieved; Crile had fulfilled his promise to get the whistle-blowers' charges on film. Crile felt relieved because Colloff's approval meant he now had a firm commitment from CBS; for the first time he would be permitted to produce a long-form documentary on his own. Klein was satisfied, too. The months of waiting had paid off.

Klein's first official day working on the project was April 1, 1981. On that morning Crile finally disclosed to him the details of the film they were going to make together. The emphasis in documentary filmmaking *is* "togetherness." Long-form documentaries (and this one was to be a full hour and a half) require a collaborative effort among a small production crew embarking on an extended voyage into a vast sea of possibilities. The producer charts the journey; he is the one who conducts the investigation, directs the research. The editor depends on him to know where the submerged rocks and sandbars lie. The editor not only needs the producer's vision of the final destination, he needs accurate accounts of ports of call along the way.

After revealing the premise of the program, Crile explained to Klein his initial task. Using stock footage—material culled from the CBS film library and outside archival sources—Klein was to create the visual context in which the events were embedded. There would be the story of the conspiracy and the conspirators, which Crile was developing through his interviews. And behind it, in ghostly flickering images across the screen, there would be the bigger story, the texture of the times on a grand scale. Using stock footage Klein would resurrect the political turmoil in the United States, the anti-Vietnam War movement that had torn America in two. Splicing, say, a sequence showing soldiers trapped in a brutal firefight to a film clip of teenagers trapped in a demonstration, Klein could document visually why General Westmoreland had been anxious to underestimate the size of the enemy. (Historically, commanders had *overestimated* their enemies, as a ploy to get more troops.) Klein would be reconstructing in film the political climate of the times: Lyndon Johnson needed good news with an election upcoming in 1968; loyal to his commander-in-chief, Westmoreland was corrupted by political pressure into suppressing the true size of the enemy. What was Westmoreland's motive? By proving that there was "light at the end of the tunnel," Westmoreland could help reelect a president whose support he could count on in his prosecution of the war in Vietnam.

But listening that morning to Crile unravel his tangled tale of parallel themes, Klein began to have doubts. Crile was reaching for too much; the producer was asking him to reconstruct, in stock footage, the entire history of the Vietnam War.

Crile kept talking, expostulating, extemporizing, the tempo of his words escalating. He saw rioters pouring into the streets; "grunts" plunging into the darkening jungle; congressmen pounding their fists; President Johnson . . . Westmoreland . . . salvation . . . attrition . . . Chicago . . . Cam Ranh Bay . . . WhiteHouseSaigonsavagery . . . the images tumbling out in a torrent of embellishments. . . .

Klein interrupted him. "George," Klein said, "I think you're going to lose the focus of the film."

It was an innocuous comment. Klein had simply attempted to turn Crile's monologue into a dialogue between the editor and the producer collaborating on a project.

Crile reacted as if Klein had slapped him in the face. He said, "Wait. Don't cut me off."

Later that morning, Klein's first paid day as the editor of the Vietnam project, Crile invited him to attend a chronology session. It was a rite of initiation, a ritual as solemn as morning Mass, and just as obligatory. Crile would sit behind his desk with a legal pad in front of him. Alex Alben almost always attended, as did Joe Zigman. Day after day Adams would read aloud sections of his chronologies. He would remove one from the canvas bag in which he constantly carried the yellow legal pads. He would talk, the others would listen. Worst of all for a skeptic who had to endure those sessions, Adams's chronologies never stopped swelling.

"Almost every time I do an interview," Adams recalled later, "I write out a chronology beforehand of what the guy knows." For example, the chronology of George Allen, Adams's ex-boss at the CIA (who is not to be confused with George Carver, the senior CIA expert on Vietnam) was thirty-nine pages long *before* Crile talked to Allen for the first time in February 1981. "After the questions, I would add to the guy's own chronology," said Adams. "If he said anything really important, I would put it in either the master chronology or the Order of Battle chronology. I'm up to my ass in chronologies."

Klein sat there throughout the morning and into the early afternoon. Crile was at his desk, set perpendicular to the office window. Adams was on one side of the desk, Alex Alben on the other. Klein and Zigman were sprawled on the white couch, near the office door. The hours dragged on as Adams droned on, reciting in excruciating detail times and places—the anecdotal trivia of the military's original sin. After a while Klein stopped listening to the litany; he was concentrating his attention on Adams himself, on the man's morbid attachment to these moribund events, his monomaniacal fixation on the Vietnam War. Klein thought: Adams's entire life is wrapped up in that canvas bag teeming with chronologies. There were no copies; the shabby canvas bag contained the irreplaceable evidence of Adams's (irrelevant?) achievement.

At four o'clock in the afternoon Klein left Crile's office and returned to his editing room. He was leaning against his editing table when Crile entered. Klein knew Crile was nervous; Crile was flapping his tie with his hand. Klein stared at Crile for a moment. Then he said, "You realize that this man Sam Adams is totally obsessed. Can you trust a man who is obsessed?"

Crile returned Klein's stare. He said, "I know." He turned and left the room, feverishly flapping his tie.

2

The
Sam Adams
Saga

SAMUEL ALEXANDER ADAMS majored in history at Harvard University. He graduated in 1955, then attended Harvard Law School for two years. He left without obtaining a law degree. Adams spent "three years, four months, and eleven days" in the United States Navy. For approximately thirty months he served as a junior officer aboard the U.S.S. *George Clymer*, anchored off San Diego Bay. Adams joined the Central Intelligence Agency in 1963. He learned how to write intelligence reports; briefly, he was trained in "the nuts and bolts of espionage," too. But Adams was being educated as "a researcher and not a spy." His initial assignment, in January 1964, was as an analyst covering the Republic of the Congo, which at the time was in the midst of a bloody rebellion.

Day after day Adams sat behind a desk. On the desk there was a box with two shelves, the top one for incoming documents, the bottom one for outgoing ones. Each morning and several times during the day CIA employees would appear and place sheets of paper on the top shelf. These might be reports from the State Department or from CIA agents, or simply newspaper clippings about events in the Republic of the Congo. When Adams had collected a sufficient number of papers and clippings he considered important, he would write a report. During the days "when things were hot and heavy over in the Congo," he recalled, "I would be writing a report practically every day." Then, toward the end of 1965, the rebellion in the Congo started to sputter. Adams began to find fewer and fewer papers on the top shelf of his box, which meant that he laid his reports on the bottom shelf less frequently. He was feeling restive. He sought a more ambitious assignment, in the CIA's clandestine branch. When his petition was rejected, Adams cast his eye toward Indochina. In 1965, as the quarrel in the Congo was cooling down, the conflict in Vietnam was heating up.

Beginning in September 1965 Adams began writing for a CIA publication called *Situation in Vietnam*, "primarily concerning military matters in Vietnam." He discovered that there were areas of specialization: the South Vietnamese army, for instance, or the government or politics of South Vietnam. The component that intrigued Sam Adams was the Vietcong, who were regarded at the time as fully armed and trained South Vietnamese soldiers fighting alongside the North Vietnamese army (NVA) regulars. Adams would soon dispute that definition. " 'Vietcong' means Vietnamese Communists," he would argue, "whether they come from North Vietnam or South Vietnam." Years later both George Crile and Mike Wallace would absorb that explanation into their interviews, accepting Adams's definition of the Vietcong enemy without questioning it.

The special project that Adams undertook was a study of Vietcong motivation and morale. "I was trying to dope out what made these guys tick," he wrote ten years later in his *Harper's* article, "why they kept going in the face of what we were able to throw against them. I was trying to determine how long I thought they would keep fighting." He spent fruitless hours scanning sets of intractable statistics. Then he decided that, quarantined in Washington, he would never be able to plumb the deepest impulses of the Vietcong infantryman from a desk. In January 1966 he made his first trip to Vietnam. He began to read "captured documents."

From time to time, when American or South Vietnamese or Korean troops engaged in action in the field, they would find caches of official papers concealed in labyrinthine tunnels. Or else the captured document might be a diary or unsent letter home, retrieved from the cadaver of a single dead enemy soldier. Stacks of these captured documents were turned over to American military personnel in the field, who stuffed the letters and diaries and official papers into sacks and shipped them back to Saigon. In Saigon the sacks were deposited at the Document Exploitation Center. Vietnamese analysts skimmed the piles of paper, selecting items that seemed important and translating them into English. "We used to capture these things in the millions, millions of sheets," Adams recalled, "and only a small percentage of the millions of sheets of paper we would capture were translated."

Extracts were made of the small percentage of documents that the Vietnamese translated into English. Then certain of those extracts were published in a monthly MACV (Military Assistance Command, Vietnam) bulletin of anywhere from one to ten pages long. When Sam Adams said he was reading captured documents, he meant that he was reading that monthly bulletin—the monthly military intelligence bulletin published under the auspices of Westmoreland's army command in Saigon.

Adams returned to Washington in May 1966 with his captured documents. He began to "extrapolate": "I set up an equation which went like this: If A, B, and C units (the ones for which I had documents) had so many deserters in such and such a period of time, then the number of deserters per year for the whole VC army was X." Adams extrapolated the whole from fragments of its parts. His method was a valid one statistically as long as the documents from which he worked were reliable, timely, and representative. Often, though, the available documents were dated, and there was no way to verify the reliability and representativeness of captured documents unless their validity could be corroborated from other sources (POW interrogations, for instance), which was not always the case. This particular VC morale equation produced startling results: "No matter how I arranged the equation," wrote Adams in *Harper's*, "X always turned out to be a very big number. I could never get it below 50,000. Once, I even got it up to 100,000."

The implication was astonishing. Military intelligence's official estimate of enemy strength in 1966 was 270,000. Adding the killed, wounded, and captured to the 50,000 to 100,000 deserters a year Adams had extrapolated, it was hard to see how the enemy could endure more than another year or two. Adams briefed his superiors on his findings. Some at the CIA were skeptical, and the agency decided to test Adams's thesis further, forming a "Vietcong morale team" consisting of Adams as a consultant and four CIA psychiatrists. The team was sent to Vietnam to check Adams's results. Instead of studying captured documents, as Adams had, the quartet of psychiatrists spent their time actually in the field talking to CIA operatives who had regular contact with the enemy. The CIA officials in Vietnam regarded as ludicrous Adams's conclusion that the VC's morale was so low and their desertion rate so high that they could hold out only a year or two longer. Adams's equation was dead wrong.

Adams had an option. Either he could admit that his extrapolation from captured documents was in error, or he could argue that the enemy could sustain a high desertion rate because their actual number far exceeded the military's official estimate of a 270,000-strong army. Characteristically, he decided that the military estimate must be radically wrong. He began studying more captured documents, this time to extrapolate the true number of enemy the Allies in Vietnam were fighting. Beginning in the summer of 1966 Adams began writing reports on what he thought the Vietcong Order of Battle should be. He was, of course, the lone CIA analyst engaged full time on the VC Order of Battle, since the CIA had no official responsibility in that area. Until 1968 the mandate for developing Order of Battle estimates belonged to military intelligence's two hundred or so analysts actually in Vietnam.

Then, on the afternoon of Friday, August 19, MACV monthly bulletin 689 landed on the top shelf of the box on Adams's desk and utterly altered his life. Adams recalled the moment in his *Harper's* article: "It contained a report put out by the Vietcong headquarters in Binh Dinh province, to the effect that the guerilla militia in the province numbered just over 50,000," Adams wrote. "I looked for our own intelligence figures for Binh Dinh in the Order of Battle and found the number 4,500. 'My God,' I thought, 'that's not even a tenth of what the VC say.' "

The guerillas were not full-time, uniformed soldiers but part-time warriors, by day farmers and by night fully armed foes, ambushing Allied units behind their lines.

Adams, "in a state of nervous excitement," began rummaging through his file of monthly military intelligence bulletins in search of other discrepancies between the military's estimate of enemy strength and the numbers in extracts of captured documents. He found one for Phu Yen province that showed 11,000 guerillas. "In the official Order of Battle we had listed 1,100, an eighth of the Vietcong estimate," Adams wrote. "I almost shouted from my desk, 'There goes the whole damn Order of Battle!' "

Adams doubled his research effort over the weekend. By Monday morning he had "found further proof of a gross underestimate of the strength of the enemy we had been fighting for almost two years." That Monday a colleague gave him a year-old document from Vietcong headquarters in South Vietnam that claimed that in early 1965 the Vietcong already had 200,000 guerillas in the south and planned to increase that number to 300,000 by the end of the year. "It listed a figure of exactly 103,573 guerilla militia—in other words, half as many as the Vietcong said they had in early 1965, and a third as many as they planned to have by 1966."

There was a strange irony in Adams's easy, almost eager acceptance of the enemy's estimates of its own current guerilla strength. Unquestionably a patriot, a man who never publicly doubted the United States' mission in Vietnam, it was ironic that this descendant of *the* Adamses should be skeptical of the intelligence estimates of his countrymen, yet so naively credulous of the equivalent estimates of his enemy. Vietcong recruiters and political cadre and field commanders surely felt some of the same pressures to produce positive results as their American counterparts. The mere fact that the extracts Adams was dealing with were captured ones seemed to lend them a legitimacy that American ones lacked.

Adams was unable to contain his excitement over the discrepancies he had uncovered. That Monday afternoon, August 22, he wrote a memo to his superiors announcing that the current enemy-strength estimate of 270,000 "might be 200,000 men too low." He spent the remainder of that afternoon waiting for a response. "I imagined all kinds of sudden and dramatic telephone calls. 'Mr. Adams, come brief the director.' 'The president's got to be told about this, and you'd better be able to defend those numbers.' I wasn't sure that would happen," Adams wrote, "but I was sure it would be significant, because I knew this was the biggest intelligence find of the war—by far."

Sam Adams, the obscure CIA analyst, sat by his telephone waiting for an invitation to brief CIA Director Richard Helms or to defend his numbers before President of the United States Lyndon B. Johnson. No such call came. "Instead," Adams recalled, "on Friday the memorandum dropped back in my in box. There was no comment on it at all—no request for amplification, no question about my numbers, nothing, just a routine slip attached showing that the entire CIA hierarchy had read it." Adams was "aghast." Here he had uncovered "the biggest intelligence find of the war"—and his superiors were as blasé as if Adams had discovered how the Vietcong concocted their familiar conical hats. Angrily, he wrote a second memo, adding more ammunition. Still no call from Director Helms nor President Johnson. He went to the seventh floor of the CIA Langley Field headquarters, where the offices of his superiors were located. There, he claimed, he found his memo, in a manila folder marked "Indefinite Hold." He returned to his own fifth-floor office and wrote still another memo, appending even more documents. Instead of sending this memo upstairs in the usual way, Adams personally carried it to the seventh floor. "When I reached the office of the Asia–Africa area chief," Adams recalled, "he looked at me and said, 'It's that goddam Adams memo again. Adams, stop being such a prima donna.' In the next office," Adams added, "an official said that the Order of Battle was General Westmoreland's concern, and we had no business intruding."

That didn't deter Adams, nor did the fact that he was the CIA's only full-time analyst, sitting behind a desk in Washington reading extracts of selected documents, while Westmoreland had in his employ more than two hundred intelligence analysts in the field in Vietnam. Nor was Adams intimidated by the fact that he had virtually no training or experience in the art of military intelligence. What he did have was the Binh Dinh document; he accepted its calculations as if they had been revealed ex cathedra, by a pope.

Eighteen days after Adams had submitted his first memo, the CIA, in Adams's words, "let a version of it out of the building. . . ." But Adams was suspicious; this version of his memo was called a "draft working paper," meaning that it lacked official status. He became even more incredulous when he learned that only 25 copies were printed, instead of the usual 200; "it would go to 'working-level types' only," Adams wrote. However, one copy did travel to Saigon, to Westmoreland's Order of Battle section, headed by Col. Gains Hawkins.

Adams was so angry and exhausted, he "decided to take two weeks off to simmer down." When he returned to work he began to focus his energies on the Order of Battle itself; up to this time he had been relying on the monthly military intelligence bulletins. He discovered that although a new Order of Battle was issued monthly, the totals of three of the four categories listed—guerilla militia, service troops, and political cadres—never changed. He investigated and soon learned that military intelligence in Vietnam, then under Gen. Joseph McChristian, had inherited these estimates from the South Vietnamese and had never bothered updating them; the military intelligence command did not consider these enemy elements as a part of the "military threat." Adams took it upon himself to do the updating, by extrapolation. Taking a captured document he considered a key one, containing a VC estimate, say, of the number of guerillas in a particular province, he would multiply by forty-four—the total number of provinces in South Vietnam. "By December 1966," he wrote, "I had concluded that the number of Vietcong in South Vietnam, instead of being 270,000, was more like 600,000, or over twice the official military estimate." Over the next fourteen years Adams would never veer from a range of 500,000 to 600,000 as the accurate strength of the army Westmoreland's troops were fighting.

"Sam was a very imaginative and insightful, but not very disciplined, thinker," said George Carver, CIA Director Richard Helms's special assistant on Vietnamese affairs and Adams's ultimate superior. "Sam got very uncritical. If a Vietcong document said there were 6,000 Assault Youth, Sam took that as gospel. Sam tended to fasten on one province, figure out the error, and multiply by forty-four. I never realized the extent to which Sam was a true believer and had his mind made up," Carver added. "I had other work for him to do."

But Adams was not interested in "other work." He kept writing memos, and he kept getting them back with the notation that his superiors had read them. Then an opportunity arose for him to argue his case in front of a different audience. Gen. Earle Wheeler, chairman of the Joint Chiefs of Staff, convened a meeting of analysts from MACV (Westmoreland's Saigon-based intelligence organization), CIA, and DIA (the Pentagon's Defense Intelligence Agency) in Honolulu. The purpose was to reach a consensus on the Order of Battle. Adams traveled to Hawaii as a member of the CIA delegation. "I didn't trust the military and, frankly, I expected them to pull a fast one and lie about the numbers," Adams recalled later. To Adams's surprise, though, at the start of the conference he received support from an unexpected quarter. Westmoreland's Order of Battle chief Col. Gains Hawkins rose and astounded Adams by announcing: "You know, there's a lot more of these little bastards out there than we thought there were." Hawkins had received a copy of Adams's "draft working paper." He agreed in Honolulu to raise the estimate of enemy strength in the Order of Battle. Adams was elated; he thought he had won.

In May 1967 Adams again visited Vietnam, this time to make a study of the South Vietnamese security apparatus. When he returned he found a new CIA report had been sent to Secretary of Defense Robert McNamara. To his horror Adams saw that the strength of the enemy listed totaled 270,000—the number that had prevailed before the military's Order of Battle chief Gains Hawkins revised upwards his categories in Honolulu. Adams rushed into the office of George Carver, the CIA's top official on Vietnam. "George Carver supported my figures."

Carver, however, would dispute that contention. "Sam helped develop information that convinced a lot of us that the enemy's organized, administrative *manpower pool* was in the 400,000-to-500,000 range," Carver recalled. "But none of us was willing to say this was a half-million-man *army*, and Sam could never understand that distinction."

From June through August 1967 a series of meetings took place at CIA headquarters in Virginia, under the auspices of the CIA's National Intelligence Estimates Board. Again the purpose was to hammer out a consensus on the size of the enemy in Vietnam, which Adams had called into question. The dispute was not over the numbers of regular uniformed troops the Allies were facing; instead the arguments focused on "irregulars": How many South Vietnamese were guerillas? What was the size of the "political infrastructure," the political cadre in command posts of the enemy's hidden hamlet and provincial hierarchies? How many men, women, and children belonged to hamlet Self-Defense militias in Viet- cong-controlled territory and to Secret Self-Defense militias in hamlets located in areas controlled by the Allies? Adams argued that there were far more of these shadowy elements than Westmoreland's intelligence com- mand cared to admit and that they should be included in the Order of Battle as soldiers.

"They count them as soldiers when they're dead," Adams would say with compelling logic, "so why not count them when they're living?"

The military was prepared to admit that the guerillas were indeed a threat but considered the Self-Defense and Secret Self-Defense militias— a poorly armed collection of older men, women, and children—a mere nuisance. The main military threat, as far as the military was concerned, were the fully armed, uniformed North Vietnamese and Vietcong bat- talions and regiments.

In September 1967 the NIE debate shifted from Virginia to Saigon, resuming in Westmoreland's "Pentagon East" headquarters. There George Carver and Westmoreland privately reached a compromise: The disputed elements would not be included in the final NIE Order of Battle itself but would be explained textually in that report's final draft. The NIE of November 13, 1967, admitted that, "with the exception of the regular forces, we have previously underestimated the strength of" the admin- istrative service units supporting the regular troops, the VC guerilla forces, the Secret Self-Defense forces, and the Assault Youth (primarily composed of teenagers). It went on to say that the Vietcong and North Vietnamese regular forces were "now at least 223,000–248,000. It must be recognized, however, that this military force constitutes but one com- ponent of the total Communist organization." The National Intelligence Estimate suggested that the Vietcong "could recruit from a manpower pool of some 700,000–800,000 men, though less than half of this total are in VC-controlled areas." It provided estimated ranges for the size of each irregular category of the enemy and explained why some were not to be included in the Order of Battle. Adding up the numbers in the Order of Battle, plus the numbers in the accompanying text, the totals of the enemy did exceed 500,000. But that was not a 500,000-man army; Sam Adams had lost the argument. And he was not mollified by the fact that the military had not won either. He regarded the Carver-Westmoreland compromise as a "cave-in," initiated by CIA Director Richard Helms, capitulating under pressure from Westmoreland's military intelligence directorate.

"The Saigon conference was in its third day," Adams wrote in his

Harper's article, "when we received a cable from Helms that, for all its euphemisms, gave us no choice but to accept the military's numbers. . . ." ("That is completely wrong," George Carver said later. "I sent *Helms* a cable and said, 'I'll try to get an agreement.' Helms said he'd back me.") Adams was "extremely angry." It was then that his accusations against the military escalated. He wrote one last memo, nine pages long. The first eight pages told how the numbers in the NIE had been faked. "The ninth page," he wrote in *Harper's*, "accused the military of lying." He gave the memo to Carver to give to Richard Helms; he also submitted copies "to everyone I could think of in the research branch." He did not get any replies. "Two days later Helms signed the estimate, along with the doctored numbers." Adams walked into the office of George Carver and "quit Helm's staff." But he did not quit the CIA. He transferred to another branch where, he told Carver, "I hope to find somebody to listen to me."

He did not find a receptive ear anywhere among the leadership of the CIA, but Col. Gains Hawkins was willing to listen. His tour in Vietnam over, the military Order of Battle chief had been reassigned to Fort Hola- bird in Baltimore, Maryland. Adams visited Hawkins, who offered his assistance and encouragement in Adams's now-messianic mission: He must, at all costs, bring this matter to the attention of the highest au- thorities in American government.

"All along I had wondered whether the White House had had anything to do with fixing the estimates," Adams wrote later. "The military wanted to keep them low in order to display the 'light at the end of the tunnel,' but it had long since occurred to me that maybe the generals were under pressure from the politicians. Carver had told me a number of times that he had mentioned my Order of Battle figures to Walt Rostow of the White House. . . ."

On March 31 Lyndon Johnson announced his decision not to seek another term. Adams was convinced that "whoever the next president was, [he] needed to be told about the sorry state of American intelligence so that he could do something about it." On May 23, 1968, Adams filed formal charges with the CIA Inspector General, asking that those charges be forwarded to the president's Foreign Intelligence Advisory Board and to members of the White House staff.

"Sam wanted to get Richard Helms fired and Westmoreland court- martialed," said George Carver.

A review board was convened. When Adams decided that the CIA review board was not moving quickly enough, he petitioned the presi- dent's Foreign Intelligence Advisory Board, then headed by Gen. Max- well Taylor. He met with Helms, and he wrote letters to Walt Rostow and to General Taylor—he wanted them to intercede on his behalf to arrange a meeting between him and a member of the White House staff. In December 1968 Adams was granted an interview with J. Patrick Coyne, executive secretary of the influential and powerful President's Foreign Intelligence Advisory Board. According to Adams, Coyne "encouraged" him to write a full report. Adams wrote yet another memo detailing his charges, thirty pages long this time, and submitted it to Helms with a request for permission to forward it to the White House. "Permission was denied," recalled Adams, "in a letter from the deputy director, Adm. Rufus Taylor, who informed me that the CIA was a team and that if I didn't want to accept the team's decision, then I should resign." Adams was being told that his complaint had run its course; he had exhausted every review mechanism within the CIA.

Adams did not resign. Instead, he began arguing his case outside official CIA channels. He sent his thirty-page memo to John Court, a member of the National Security Council. "Three weeks later," Adams recalled, "Court told me that the memo had gotten around all right, but the decision had been not to do anything about it. So I gave up. If the White House wasn't interested, there didn't seem to be any other place I could go. I felt I'd done as much as I possibly could do, and that was that."

Not quite. Adams could do more, much more. He turned his attention again to the Vietcong intelligence apparatus. By May 1969 he had become convinced, again by reading captured documents, that the military had underestimated the number of Vietcong spies, too. But the head of the Vietnam branch of CIA Clandestine Services took no action.

By 1970 Adams's fortunes within the agency "had sunk to a low ebb." He was given an unfavorable fitness report that stated he had lost his "balance and objectivity on the war"; he was rated "marginal" as a researcher. He would be reassigned to a position where he would be "less directly involved in research on the war," writing a history of the Cambodian rebels.

Adams knew virtually nothing about Cambodia. He began his research the way he always had; by collecting documents. Predictably, by December 1972 Adams was back in the CIA inspector general's office, charging this time that the size of the Communist enemy in Cambodia may have been deliberately fabricated. It was a replay of his allegations about the American intelligence effort in Vietnam. There was only one difference: Now he was not accusing Westmoreland's military intelligence of falsifying estimates but the CIA itself. However, he was not quite ready to forget the military's Vietnam mischief either. He wrote yet another memorandum, this time to the army inspector general, summing up "what had happened to the VC estimate before Tet," almost five years before. In that memo Adams mentioned "the possibility of General Westmoreland's complicity" in a conspiracy to suppress the true size and strength of the enemy, "which might have implicated him in three violations of the Uniform Code of Military Justice." Adams asked the inspector general to investigate.

The army inspector general's office informed Adams that he "was in the wrong jurisdiction." The CIA inspector general's office did not find Adams's evidence of chicanery in Cambodia compelling either. "In a last desperate measure—desperate because my friends at the CIA assured me that congressional watchdog committees were a joke," Adams sent a new thirteen-page memo to committees in both the House and Senate responsible for keeping an eye on CIA activities. The chairman of the House Armed Services Subcommittee, Lucien Nedzi, thought Adams's memo was "pertinent." But, Adams added in his 1975 *Harper's* article, "he observed that the forthcoming elections obliged him to concern himself primarily with the question of busing. . . ."

Adams still would not quit his crusade. In January 1973 Daniel Ellsberg and Anthony Russo, former Rand Corporation employees whom Adams had met in Saigon in 1966, went on trial for releasing to the press stolen classified documents—the "Pentagon Papers." Reading a newspaper account of the trial in Los Angeles, Adams noticed that the prosecution was alleging that Ellsberg and Russo had violated national security by turning over to the press estimates of enemy strength in Vietnam. "I looked," Adams recalled, "and damned if they weren't from the same Order of Battle which the military had doctored back in 1967. Imagine! Hanging a man for leaking faked numbers!" Adams volunteered his services to the defense as an expert witness. "In late February I went to Los Angeles to testify at the trial and told the story of how the numbers got to be wrong."

At the Ellsberg-Russo trial Adams was compelled to reveal more than merely "how the numbers got wrong." Testifying under oath he was grilled by a federal prosecutor, Assistant U.S. Attorney David Nissen.

> NISSEN: Again, in January 1973, sir, you were of the opinion that Colonel [Gains] Hawkins had been under orders to keep the OB [Order of Battle] numbers artificially low, weren't you?
>
> ADAMS: I believed that Colonel Hawkins had been handed a piece of paper on which was written the number, and he was told to stay underneath that number.

NISSEN: In your opinion that constituted fabrication, did it not, sir?

ADAMS: Well, when you write a number on a piece of paper, hand it to a subordinate, and say, 'Stay underneath it,' I believe in the first instance the writing of the number on the piece of paper is a— could be a form of fabrication, yes, sir, making up the number to put on the piece of paper.

NISSEN: Also in January 1973, sir, you were of the opinion that General Westmoreland may have been ultimately responsible for the fabrication?

ADAMS: May have been, yes, sir.

NISSEN: Did you ever hear General Westmoreland order anybody to fabricate or retain figures at an artificially low level?

ADAMS: I have never met General Westmoreland.

NISSEN: He never attended any of the OB meetings that you attended?

ADAMS: No, sir.

NISSEN: Did you ever see any memoranda, statement, or writing from him that anyone should retain OB figures at an artificially low level?

ADAMS: No, sir. I have seen nothing with his signature on it like that.

NISSEN: Anything without his signature on it, sir, that you thought was his?

ADAMS: No, sir, I have not.

Nissen continued to probe Adams's relationship with Col. Gains Hawkins, which effectively dated from the Order of Battle conference in Honolulu in February 1967. It was then that Hawkins had stunned Adams by admitting that certain categories of the enemy should indeed be increased.

Adams told Nissen that he had been in contact with Hawkins from time to time since then; the last occasion on which he had seen Hawkins was "three or four days ago, a week ago."

NISSEN: Now, sir, when you say you saw Colonel Hawkins four days or a week ago—

ADAMS: Yes, sir.

NISSEN: —where did you see him, sir?

ADAMS: Right out in the hall here, sir.

NISSEN: In other words, in Los Angeles in the courthouse?

ADAMS: Yes, sir, that's correct.

Hawkins, it turned out, had been subpoenaed to appear as a defense witness at the Ellsberg-Russo trial! Later, in a November 14, 1982, article in the *Washington Post*, Hawkins explained that he "despised Ellsberg and his partner and considered the publication of the Pentagon Papers of enormous psychological benefit to the Vietnamese Communists." Shortly after Hawkins received the subpoena, he wrote, "two smiling agents of army counterintelligence showed up" on his front porch. " 'No,' I said, 'there was no hanky-panky [in the formulation of intelligence estimates] at all. None at all.' " Hawkins wrote in the *Post* that he "stuck by that position throughout two trips to Los Angeles before the trial collapsed. . . ." Why did Hawkins deny to army counterintelligence what he had been urging Adams to confirm? His excuse was that it "just didn't seem fair that one seamy episode [the faking of Order of Battle estimates] in an otherwise solidly successful intelligence effort should be cited in defense of an act which had caused irreparable harm to our own side." In that 1982 *Washington Post* article Hawkins admitted that in his two trips to Los Angeles, where he steadfastly refused to corroborate Adams's conspiracy story, he was "committing—or at the very least flirting with—perjury."

Adams returned to Washington from the Ellsberg-Russo trial in March. The CIA, he wrote, "once again threatened to fire me. I complained and, as usual, the agency backed down. After a decent interval I quit." In the very month that Adams resigned from the CIA, an official whom he had previously petitioned without result was taking renewed interest in his charges. Aroused by Adams's testimony at the Ellsberg-Russo trial, House Armed Services Subcommittee Chairman Lucien Nedzi privately informed the appropriate agencies of government that he planned to hold a hearing on the Vietnam Order of Battle controversy. The Pentagon's Defense Intelligence Agency (DIA) prepared a talking paper its director would use in discussions with Nedzi. The DIA memorandum was dated March 22, 1973, and was sent on to the secretary of defense on April 24. Its subject was "Differences in Enemy Order of Battle in South Vietnam."

The DIA memo challenged Adams's methodology. "The only source of data used by Mr. Adams to estimate guerilla strength was captured documents. . . . The captured documents, for the most part, gave only an indication of what the enemy wanted to do in a specific area, but did not necessarily show that he had been able to accomplish it. . . ." And then the memo dealt directly with the issue of Sam Adams's 600,000-man enemy army. "The basic correctness of the lower [military] figures was demonstrated," the memo insisted, "by the strength of the VC/NVA in the Tet offensive. All analysts agree that the Tet offensive was an all-out— if not desperate—effort on the part of the VC/NVA. The total number of enemy forces involved in the Tet offensive attacks was estimated at around 80,000 to include up to 15,000 hastily impressed villagers. This figure, which has not been contested by any intelligence agency, gives the lie to the numbers that Adams believed to be the case, that is, a force of 600,000 men. As a point of fact, it makes the lowest figure (240,000) then carried by MACV appear inflated." It would not be the last time this line of reasoning was used to challenge Adams's 600,000-strong enemy army.

Lucien Nedzi never did hold his hearings. Instead, four months later, in September 1975, the House Select Committee on Intelligence, chaired by Otis Pike, held hearings on "the risks and control of foreign intelligence." Sam Adams, of course, turned up as a key witness, peddling his conspiracy. This time the names of even more public officials, past and present, were entangled in his net. Alongside Westmoreland, Gen. Creighton Abrams, Jr. (Westmoreland's deputy in Vietnam), and CIA Director Richard Helms, Adams added Gen. Earle Wheeler (chairman of the Joint Chiefs of Staff), Ellsworth Bunker (former ambassador to South Vietnam), and Johnson Administration adviser Walt Rostow to those who "knew there was some kind of attempt going on to fool the press." And Daniel Graham had "apparently [been] involved in a lot of the chicanery that went on in Westmoreland's headquarters. . . ." Furthermore, Adams found it hard to believe that Secretary of Defense Robert McNamara was ignorant of these events, nor was Lyndon Johnson exempt from Adams's accusations: "When you have a Bunker sending a cable 'eyes-only-Rostow,' and Rostow is only one slot from the top," Adams told the committee, "the top must have known, too."

As General Graham said later, "If you were going to assemble all Sam Adams's 'conspirators' at the same time, in the same place, you'd have to rent a football stadium."

In this congressional forum, however, Adams's allegations would not go unchallenged. High-ranking CIA officials, including Adams's former boss at the CIA, George Carver, would publicly contradict Adams's assertions. In his statement to the Pike committee George Carver said that while the CIA had endorsed Adams's position, "that endorsement was not without qualifications." Carver said that Adams "frequently refers simplistically to an enemy of 600,000," and called this "lumping . . . of disparate types together . . . as unacceptable to most observers in the CIA as it was to those in military intelligence."

Then, exactly as the DIA had done in its memo, Carver dealt directly with Tet. In doing so, his argument against Adams mirrored DIA's own.

"Even if the only estimates of enemy strength were those of MACV—the lowest available—they were well within the numbers required for the Vietcong to mount the Tet offensive," Carver argued. He cited studies made after Tet by CIA and other intelligence branches, which demonstrated that "the Communists committed some 75,000 to 85,000 of their military forces in the Tet offensive. The capability to commit this many troops was well within existing estimates. This was true," Carver added, "whether one's perception of the strength of the VC/NVA military force was based on the lower figures held by MACV or the higher figures held by the CIA."

Carver's clinching conclusion had been an echo of the DIA's: If, as Adams contended, the actual military threat in the fall of 1967 was 600,000 men, why had only 80,000 or so turned up during the all-out attack during Tet? "*Double* the size of the enemy at Tet," Graham said later, "and you still don't have evidence of a 600,000-man army."

If CBS's executives had undertaken a little research, they might have been comforted by an excerpt of the committee's conclusions (although the hearings were public, the summary report of those proceedings was confidential and was never released), published in the February 16, 1976, issue of the *Village Voice*. ". . . The validity of most of the numbers was significantly dubious. Unfortunately, they were relied on for optimistic presentations. . . . General Westmoreland used such figures to support his contention in the fall of 1967 that the enemy's 'guerilla force' is declining at a steady rate. . . . In the context of the period it appears that considerable pressure was placed on the intelligence community to generate numbers, less out of tactical necessity than for political purposes. . . . Whether this was by conspiracy or not is somewhat irrelevant."

But reading the public transcripts of the Pike hearings, the CBS executives might also have found a litmus paper to put Sam Adams's allegations to the test in the testimony of George Carver, for instance, or of William Colby (who succeeded Richard Helms as director of the Central Intelligence Agency), or else the transcript of the Ellsberg-Russo trial, where a federal prosecutor had elicited from Adams a bizarre road map of his quixotic quest to prove—ultimately to the president of the United States—that he was right and everyone else was wrong. No one at CBS, outside of Crile and Adams, knew that Col. Gains Hawkins had been subpoenaed as a defense witness at the Pentagon Papers trial. No one knew that Hawkins, slated to be a star CBS witness in the Vietnam broadcast, was, in 1975, by his own admission, "committing—or at the very least, flirting with—perjury." No one at CBS, not the vice-president Roger Colloff nor the executive producer Howard Stringer, ever made any sincere effort to scrutinize the credibility of Sam Adams, the paid consultant on whose research the program's premise rested.

"I had met Sam Adams," said Mike Wallace later in a sworn deposition. "I read his *Harper's* piece. I did not read the Pike Committee hearings nor did I know about his testimony at the Ellsberg trial."

George Carver might have offered Wallace a balancing perspective. "Sam Adams," said Carver, "never understood the difference between a fascinating speculative hypothesis and something proved beyond a reasonable doubt."

Neither, as it turned out, did CBS.

3

Wallace
Grills
Westmoreland

LATE ON THE AFTERNOON of April 1, 1981, after Adams's chronology session, Ira Klein had one more brief meeting with Crile in Crile's office. They were discussing the film when Crile told Klein, "I don't want anyone else in the room while we're editing. I'd like us to work alone." Crile said that he was not going to allow anyone, including Sam Adams, the paid consultant, to be present in Klein's cutting room during the actual editing of the film.

"Phyllis has to be there," Klein said. "There are times when I'm going to *need* her to be there."

Crile was emphatic. "I'd like us to work alone," he repeated.

Klein was surprised. The collaborative effort involved in television documentary making had at its root the notion that there should be a free exchange of ideas. On a project of this sort, spending months on end together, a kind of loose, Leninist "democratic centralism" usually prevailed: Anyone working on the project might *propose* a fresh idea, as long as it was clearly understood by all that the ultimate authority to *dispose* rested squarely with the producer of the film. Yet Crile wanted to quarantine not only Adams and Hurwitz from the editing process, but Alex Alben, the researcher, as well. However, Klein did not ask Crile for an explanation. Every producer had his or her own idiosyncratic work habits. Klein dismissed Crile's concern about access to the editing process as another of the producer's eccentricities, like Crile's reluctance to permit him to read the blue sheet.

Over the next few weeks of April, Klein spent his time locating and searching through scores of rolls of stock footage in search of visuals he could use to tell about the Vietnam War on the grand scale. If he decided a roll of film contained a worthy sequence—exciting helicopter footage, for instance—he would mark it, and Hurwitz would place that roll in the pile they planned to keep. There was another stack of rejects. What Klein intended to do was attach these segments of news films to each other, building large 800-foot reels. Then he planned to have these stock-footage reels "slop printed"—a comparatively inexpensive printing process that avoided the necessity of making costly negatives. These cheap prints would be his cutting copies, each sequence on them bearing a code number that corresponded to the same segment on the original reel. It was an elaborate and tedious process—gathering the material, reviewing it, logging the sequences he wanted to keep, organizing and building his 800-foot reels.

Throughout April, Klein and Zigman concentrated on collecting stock footage from a variety of internal and external sources. Alex Alben stopped by periodically, helping to coordinate the schedules of Adams and Crile on the one hand, and Zigman and Klein on the other. While Klein and Zigman were concentrating on assembling footage to document the larger context of the Vietnam War, Crile and his paid consultant were pursuing their conspiracy premise. There were the chronology sessions, the questions Crile and Adams were composing for interviews. It was in April that Crile spoke on camera with another key witness. Alex Alben had tracked down Lt. Russell Cooley, a former military intelligence officer, in California. Cooley was particularly reluctant to appear on camera, but Crile succeeded in persuading him. Cooley had been the deputy of Comdr. James Meacham, who headed the Order of Battle Studies group, which made long-range estimates of enemy strength, and preserved the military's intelligence records; he could provide a crucial second source confirming the allegation in Crile's blue sheet that Danny Graham had forced Meacham's men to tamper with the historical record of the military's computer in the period after Tet. Then, toward the end of April, Crile made an announcement that took the members of his unit by surprise: CBS News vice-president Roger Colloff, for the second time in two months, wanted to screen excerpts of interviews. This time the rough cut would be even more elaborate. Crile could add the testimony of Lieutenant Cooley and Commander Meacham.

Early in the first week of May, Crile, Klein, and Colloff, accompanied by Howard Stringer, met in Klein's editing room. Crile turned on the editing machine. The witnesses whose "confessions" Colloff and Stringer had heard a month or so ago became even more compelling, buttressed now by the testimony of Lieutenant Cooley and Commander Meacham. Again, in between each interview the screen would go black. Crile would stop the editing machine and stitch these story threads into the fabric of the ever-expanding conspiracy. This presentation was even more powerful and convincing than the first one had been.

However, Roger Colloff did offer one suggestion. In George Crile's November 24, 1980, blue sheet, he had written: "Adams has chronicled [the] conspiracy with unbelieveable detail all the way to General Westmoreland's doorstep. It is for us to go beyond—to find out whether Westmoreland was acting on his own authority or whether, as seems more likely to me, he was receiving direct authorization or at least encouragement from above. The task will be to follow the trail of the conspiracy," Crile added, "to see how far up the chain of command it goes—first to the Pentagon, to the Joint Chiefs of Staff. Then to the Secretary of Defense, Robert McNamara, and finally to see what the White House knew about it." Colloff wanted to make sure Crile was keeping the promise he had made in the blue sheet, that he wasn't merely stopping at Westmoreland's doorstep.

It wasn't a directive, merely a reminder. Nonetheless, when Colloff uttered that casual remark, inexplicably Crile suddenly erupted: "We're trying to, we're *trying* to. . . ." Colloff and Stringer seemed stunned by the intensity of Crile's reaction. "It was only a suggestion," Colloff soothed. "I'm simply trying to help the project along." He continued to calm down the producer, and eventually Crile regained his composure. He turned on the editing machine and resumed his screening.

Klein was surprised that Colloff had retreated, becoming almost apologetic. But that was a difference between Roger Colloff and his predecessor, Bob Chandler. Colloff cultivated a more relaxed atmosphere, since he himself was still an apprentice, far less of an initiate than his rawest producer. Chandler, on the other hand, had earned a reputation for being an exacting critic of his producers' work. He never let a producer forget that *he* was the supervisor; a suggestion on his part might carry the impact of a command. He asked tough, probing questions and would not quit until he heard an answer that convinced him. Chandler knew a great deal about broadcast journalism. It is likely, although not certain, that the Vietnam broadcast would have been a different one had George Crile's overall superior been Bob Chandler rather than Roger Colloff. But political intrigues at CBS News had prevented that.

The screening ended. Crile's presentation, because it was more complete and included material from fresh interviews, was even more persuasive than the one he had delivered during the last week of March. "Have you made contact with Westmoreland?" Colloff asked. "Is Westmoreland going to come on and be interviewed?" Colloff seemed anxious; he understood that Westmoreland was the focus of the broadcast. Without Westmoreland, in fact, there could be no broadcast. Crile replied that he had not yet telephoned Westmoreland.

On May 7 Crile contacted Mike Wallace and Wallace telephoned Westmoreland at the general's home in Charleston, South Carolina. Westmoreland consented to be interviewed. "It was not difficult to reach him or get him to appear," Crile said later. "It was tough to get through to him what we were talking about—intelligence under him. He always had a cover story. . . . We told him we were doing the documentary on the role of intelligence, using Tet as a jumping-off point, and were we alert to enemy strength."

The following Thursday morning the entire Vietnam unit assembled to prepare for an interview equally as crucial as Westmoreland's: On Tuesday, May 12, Sam Adams would be interviewed by Mike Wallace at his farm in Virginia. That Thursday-morning meeting took place in researcher Alex Alben's office, which could accommodate more people than George Crile's. Alben recalled that there were two sessions that day, lasting up to two hours each. He, Crile, and Adams were present throughout; Zigman and Klein were in attendance for most of the time. Phyllis Hurwitz and Carolyne McDaniel were in and out. Klein's understanding at the time was that he and the others had been invited to provide "atmospheric presence"; Crile wanted to simulate an authentic interview situation. For the most part the actual questioning was done by Crile, with an occasional interjection, suggestion, or correction from Alex Alben. Crile was sitting at Alben's desk. In front of him he had a lengthy list of questions he had composed for Adams. Phyllis Hurwitz saw the list laid out in front of Crile when she entered the office and stood briefly beside Crile's desk. "I walked in on a session with Adams, Alben, Crile, and Klein," she said later in a sworn affidavit, "and saw sheets of questions on the desk. I later was in the room and read some of those questions." Crile's questions for Adams were arranged in chronological order; step by step he elicited Adams's story, from his earliest days as the CIA's Vietcong specialist, through his participation in the National Intelligence Estimate conferences in the summer and fall of 1967. After Adams answered a question, Crile would pause and give Adams feedback. Perhaps Adams had included in his answer information that Crile considered tangential; he would advise Adams to discard that material.

Perhaps Adams had discarded something in his response that Crile considered vital; he would suggest to Adams that he include that missing material in his answer. Crile also advised Adams on how to comport himself before the cameras.

"You want an individual who will project, have confidence in himself, and who can keep his responses succinct," Klein recalled later. "Because of Sam's intimacy with the story, over fourteen years, he was capable of talking for hours. I think that's what George was concerned about."

Crile confirmed that there was a ". . . special set of problems Adams presented to CBS. Those were first set forth in my blue sheet. . . . Once the decision was made to have Adams serve as our consultant, involved in our investigation, while also appearing in the documentary, it was no longer possible to deal with him as just another interview."

Researcher Alex Alben denied that Adams had been "coached," but did admit that Adams was afforded the opportunity to repeat anecdotes and information he had previously discussed.

"I went over with Adams those areas we intended to cover in the interview," Crile said. ". . . I did not even consider this process a rehearsal; in effect, I was serving as a traffic cop."

Whether or not those sessions with Adams did constitute a "rehearsal" was more than semantics. The official CBS News Standards of fairness and accuracy explicitly banned rehearsals of interviews: "Interviews which are not spontaneous and unrehearsed are prohibited unless specifically approved by the president of CND [CBS News Division]."

After Crile had spent two sessions with Adams—reading him questions, then giving Adams feedback not only on the content of his answers but his comportment—could Adams's interview with Wallace in Virginia still be "spontaneous and unrehearsed"? Clearly the answer depended on the questions Mike Wallace actually asked Sam Adams, questions written out for Wallace beforehand by George Crile. At least two people who attended those sessions with Adams believed the paid consultant had been rehearsed and that the questions Crile wrote out for Wallace were substantively the same ones Crile had used to quiz Adams. At the time, however, no one quarreled with Crile's ethics. Adams had become an integral member of the documentary team; he was ubiquitous—at virtually every interview Crile conducted or else in Crile's office chanting the solemn litany of his chronologies. Besides, surely, before contravening the clear CBS News Standard prohibiting rehearsals of interviews, Crile would have obtained the consent of his superiors. Crile kept telling members of the unit that Colloff and the others were scrutinizing the project closely, reading transcripts of interviews. Surely Crile must have cleared this "rehearsal" with Colloff and Stringer, who were aware of Adams's unique role as both a paid consultant and a crucial on-camera interview, and the conflicts those dual roles could cause.

On Sunday, May 10, Crile telephoned Westmoreland again. This time, Crile claimed, he read Westmoreland a letter he had drafted listing five topics to be covered in Westmoreland's upcoming on-camera interview in New York the following Saturday. Crile promised to mail Westmoreland this letter of confirmation so that Westmoreland could prepare himself. "We then spoke about the CIA," Crile recalled, "and he brings up the Adams story but never says: 'Is this the Adams theory?' "

Westmoreland's recollection of that conversation differed from Crile's. He did not remember Crile reading him a letter of confirmation. "The discussion on the phone was very vague," Westmoreland said.

Although Westmoreland did not specifically ask Crile during that conversation if he was setting out to document, or even to investigate, the charges Sam Adams had been making for over a decade, his mentioning "the Adams story" had offered Crile an opportunity to reveal Adams's role as the project's paid consultant; if Westmoreland had known of Adam's role, it is unlikely that he would have agreed to be interviewed by CBS. But Crile did not mention Adams's participation.

The following day, Monday, May 11, Crile sent Mike Wallace another memo:

Mike:

We're on for Westmoreland next Saturday morning. I read him the letter yesterday, and he didn't complain about any of our proposed areas of interest. He puzzles me—seems not to be all that bright.

I spoke further with him about the strength estimate controversy, and he repeated his earlier statement that it was only an argument between "the theoreticians—really statisticians—at the CIA who wanted to count every old woman and child . . ." and his "practitioners" at MACV, the people who had to fight the war and who really knew the enemy. He goes so far as to claim that Tet demonstrated to him that MACV itself had been exaggerating enemy strength estimates.

It is evident from the memo that, in this brief conversation, Crile had sensed Westmoreland might not have comprehended what CBS intended to discuss with him.

We have certainly covered our asses, technically at least. But I am a bit worried that he just doesn't understand that we are going to be talking to him about American intelligence, military intelligence during the Vietnam War. I just don't want to have him sit down and refuse to answer questions on the grounds that he can't remember certain things and that we hadn't told him what we were up to. So I think I will give him another call later in the week and try to bring him a little further along, without hitting him over the head with a sledgehammer.

Crile went on to discuss with Wallace Westmoreland's request for an honorarium. Then Crile closed with some comments about the questions Wallace would ask Adams.

I've redone the questions. There are now less of them and better focused with comments at front of each section. They're being typed now—will be sent up this morning. Would like to go over them with you when you can.

Crile and Alben flew from New York to Virginia to join Sam Adams at his farm and set up Wallace's interview, scheduled for Tuesday, May 12. Zigman arrived after Crile and Alben. By that time Crile was "redesigning the house," recalled one member of the project. He shifted paintings from one room to another, and he wanted to remove a door from its hinges, amid the protests of Adams's wife. Crile's aim was to create camera shots that were busy yet uncluttered. As producer it was his job to tell the cameraman exactly where and how he wanted Adams and Wallace filmed.

Crile particularly needed to avoid the unintentional parody of a previous interview. Crile had filmed Col. George Hamscher (who claimed he had attended a meeting at the Pentagon where enemy troop strengths were arbitrarily slashed) in Alex Alben's Manhattan apartment. The room in which Hamscher had been filmed was virtually bare of furniture. As a backdrop Crile had positioned directly behind the colonel a dead, stunted tree that Alben had not gotten around to getting rid of. Crile placed the leafless relic far behind Hamscher's back. But he didn't take into account one fact: in filming, foreground and background can appear to become compressed. When the film came back from the laboratory and was screened for the first time, those watching it were amused: Dead-branch antlers seem to be sprouting from Colonel Hamscher's bald dome. This time Crile's preparations for camera shots were even more painstaking. Nonetheless, in one sequence of the Adams interview a ceramic bird set on a windowsill would appear to be perching on Sam's left shoulder.

Wallace arrived the morning of the Adams interview. Crile spent the day filming the encounter between his chief correspondent and his paid, on-camera consultant. But even "encounter" is too adversarial; the inter-view of Adams by Mike Wallace was nothing more than a warm, ex-tended embrace. Wallace's usual querulous and abrasive tone was miss-ing; his questions were mostly soft ones—marshmallows that Adams had no difficulty regurgitating in pretty, pat phrases that Wallace had no trouble swallowing. It was a far different Wallace than the one who would interview White House adviser Walt Rostow and the targets of the con-spiracy premise, generals Westmoreland and Graham.

Wallace said that it never occurred to him to ask Adams probing questions. Wallace's understanding was that the interview would get on the record the charges of the whistle-blower. Wallace felt no need to cross-examine Adams. Subjecting Adams's story to scrutiny was not, said Wallace, "the method of operation."

Wallace acted as an on-camera coach instead of interrogator, interrupt-ing his questioning from time to time to beef up Adams's morale. When Adams did not come off well, Wallace gave him a chance to repeat. "This is perfect. . . . This is gonna be good," he told Adams. And later: ". . . We're saying this again, and it doesn't have the same flavor . . . 'cause you never said this before, Sam. I'll try and get it out of you in the same way. . . ." After Adams said, "I'm not doing this very well," Wallace replied, "Oh, no, no. You were perfect. Don't say that. You're doing it just right."

The Adams interview was a mockery; there was nothing spontaneous about it. Whether or not Crile and Wallace regarded Adams as a "special case" (Adams's own phrase) who deserved special treatment, viewers were bound to compare the coddling of Adams with the grilling of West-moreland. The implicit message would buttress the explicit one: Sam Adams wore the white hat.

With Adams on film, Crile began preparing for Westmoreland's on-camera confrontation with Mike Wallace. Crile wrote a rough draft of questions Wallace would ask, telling Wallace that by the following Friday he would "have them cleared up and brought down to size." Then he sent that list of questions to Wallace along with a memo that clearly enunci-ated Wallace's task.

Mike:

The Adams interview was not only a terrific interview. It looks beautiful. Now all you have to do is break General Westmoreland and we have the whole thing aced.

Crile went on to warn Wallace "at all costs" against "casting the inter-view as a Westmoreland vs. Sam Adams affair." Adams, Crile explained, "is the thread. He delivers the indictment to us based on his fifteen-year odyssey to find out just what happened. But this is now a joint venture of what we found out once we joined Adams's inquiry. And so anytime he does not have firsthand knowledge on an event, we have gone out and independently corroborated his reporting and expanded on it."

Crile concluded his memo by listing for Wallace "the areas where Westy seems to be guilty as hell and where you should direct your energies," before closing with a postscript that again warned Wallace against emphasizing the charges of Sam Adams. "If you do break Westmoreland at some point," Crile said, "then I think it's fine to fall back on Adams but not until [then]." Westmoreland, of course, had not been told that Adams was CBS's paid consultant on the project.

Crile returned to New York following the Adams interview to make final preparations for Westmoreland's confrontation with Wallace the next Saturday, May 16. But he still had not sent the letter he had promised Westmoreland the previous Sunday. Despite his concern over Westmoreland's apparent confusion, Crile had not followed up with a "call later in the week." On Friday, Klein learned that Crile still had not sent the letter of confirmation. He learned about it from Crile's secretary, Carolyne McDaniel.

Carolyne was about five-feet seven-inches, with black hair that hung to her shoulders, and glasses. Carolyne had moved from San Diego to New York. She was enamored of the opera. From time to time other members of the unit could hear her practicing her arias in a spare office. She lived in a hotel for women on 34th Street. She was warm, sensitive, and very emotional. But most of all she was a perfectionist. The longer Crile waited to send the letter to Westmoreland, the more anxious McDaniel became. That Friday she communicated her anxiety to Klein.

Klein became concerned as well. He searched for Crile but couldn't find him. It was then that he expressed his dissatisfaction to other members of the unit: How could they ask Westmoreland questions about events that had occurred fourteen years before without providing him an adequate opportunity to prepare himself?

It was not until Friday afternoon, shortly before Westmoreland registered at the Plaza Hotel, that Crile gave Carolyne McDaniel the letter of confirmation he had promised a week before and asked her to hand-deliver it. Even so, the letter Westmoreland received when he arrived was less than a frank discussion of the purpose of the upcoming interview with Mike Wallace.

"As promised," Crile wrote, "the following is a summary of the areas we will be considering in the broadcast and dealing with in the interview.

We talked over all of them on the telephone last Sunday, but let me run it down for you once again.

"Using the Tet offensive as a jumping-off point we plan to explore the role of American intelligence in the Vietnam War: How well did we identify and report the intentions and capabilities of the enemy we were facing . . .?"

Later Crile would argue that that lead-in was a clear explanation and warning of the purpose of the interview. But Crile's statement of his intent to "explore the role of American intelligence in the Vietnam War" was so broad as to be misleading. It was as if the Israeli government had sent a letter to Dr. Joseph Mengele, the "Butcher of Auschwitz" who perpetrated heinous experiments on prison camp inmates, inviting him to Tel Aviv to "explore the role of German medicine in World War II." The real purpose of the interview was buried fourth among the five topics of discussion Crile then listed.

Among the questions we will be considering:
1. Did American intelligence adequately predict the Tet offensive and the nature of the attack? Were those with a need to know adequately alerted? Were we surprised by the scope and timing of the attacks?
2. Was the Tet offensive an American victory or defeat? Why did so many Americans consider it a defeat when most military men claimed it was a major victory? How should we think about this critical event?
3. Did the press present a reliable picture of the enemy we faced and the state of the war?
4. What about the controversy between the CIA and the military over enemy-strength estimates?
5. What about the differing views of the enemy and progress in the war as seen by Lyndon Johnson, Dean Rusk, Robert McNamara, Richard Helms, Walt Rostow, and of course Gen. William C. Westmoreland?

We will, of course, want to discuss other areas as well, such as the antiwar movement and the pressures that antiwar sentiment placed on those responsible for making decisions about the war. But the focus will be on the performance of American intelligence during the war. . . .

The real subject was number four, "What about the controversy between the CIA and the military over enemy-strength estimates?" That, and that alone, was the topic CBS was bringing Westmoreland to New

York to discuss. The other points Crile catalogued were peripheral to the purpose of the interview. Crile was not obliged to run the risk of scaring off Westmoreland by telling him he was going to be accused of leading a vile conspiracy; he *was* ethically obligated to tell Westmoreland that the program was going to focus on the controversy over enemy-strength estimates, so that Westmoreland could prepare in advance.

For the Westmoreland interview Klein suggested to Crile that it might be wise to use two cameras. Normally, as a cost-saving device, television news interviews are shot using only one camera. The cameraman focuses on the subject, recording his answers. After the interview the camerman shoots "reverses," focusing on the correspondent, who repeats the exact questions asked during the interview in the order he asked them, with the same inflections of his voice. If the producer so desires, the cameraman can also at that time shoot "reaction" shots as the correspondent raises his eyebrows or grimaces or grins or merely seems soberly impressed. When the film of this one-camera interview is edited, the correspondent's separately shot questions can be wedded to the appropriate responses; the separately filmed "reaction" shots can be inserted so that during the broadcast a viewer sees the correspondent reacting to the subject's answers. These "reverses" fill one more crucial function: They serve as editing plaster, caulking the seams between separate sequences. In a television news interview, when the viewer sees the camera switching from the subject to the correspondent's face, it is often a sign there has been an edit.

Klein proposed to Crile that in the Westmoreland interview, instead of using only one camera, the producer employ a pair. The "A" camera would always be focused on Westmoreland; the "B" camera would never waver from Mike Wallace. When the common "clapstick" sounded, both cameras—the one focusing on Westmoreland and the one on Wallace—would start rolling simultaneously.

Because of the adversarial nature of the interview—Wallace was the chief correspondent and Westmoreland the ultimate target of the conspiracy premise—Klein felt it was crucial to capture their responses, verbal and facial, in real time. Doing so would not only enhance the power of the pictures (the spontaneous reactions of these two adversaries), it would also add to the interview's authenticity. No matter how careful a correspondent's "reverses," they are not, in fact, his actual questions nor his actual reactions. Klein was concerned that something might be lost. He reminded Crile that because this interview was such a sensitive one, its *appearance* was critical. Doing the interview with two cameras, simultaneously synced in real time, would preserve the actual tension between

Wallace and Westmoreland, and would also eliminate any appearance of manipulation. Crile agreed to use the A and B cameras.

On Saturday morning, May 16, the CBS crew convened at the Manhattan hotel in which CBS had rented a room for the Westmoreland interview. With Westmoreland were the two cameramen, the sound technician, plus Wallace, Crile, Joe Zigman, and Crile's confidant, *Up to the Minute* executive producer Grace Diekhaus. In the weeks preceding the latest screening for Colloff, she had been a frequent visitor, providing counsel to Crile. More and more Crile seemed to be relying on Grace for advice. In a sense, at the Westmoreland interview Diekhaus was standing in for Sam Adams, who had been present at almost every previous on-camera interview.

The reason Adams was not present at this interview was obvious: Westmoreland still had no idea that Adams was in any way involved in the project. "I was aghast after I heard Sam Adams was on the CBS payroll as technical adviser," Westmoreland said later. It was equally clear that Adams would have wanted to be present if he could have; Adams was still extremely anxious over Mike Wallace's ability to conduct such complex interviews. But this time Crile had prepared Wallace more thoroughly. Crile had not only written Wallace's questions in the order he would ask them but, anticipating Westmoreland's probable responses, Crile had written many of Wallace's follow-up questions, too.

Wallace began the interview by recapitulating, almost verbatim, the phrase from Crile's letter of confirmation about "using the Tet offensive as a jumping-off point for looking into the role of American intelligence during the Vietnam War." He then pointed out that "at the time of the Tet offensive it was perceived by the American public as a major defeat, and certainly it was a—a major turning point in the Vietnam War. How do you see Tet?" he asked Westmoreland.

Westmoreland agreed Tet "was a major turning point because Mr. Johnson, by virtue of public pressures—public pressures borne of false perceptions of the Tet offensive—begged the enemy to come to the conference table, and once he came to the conference table we were basically hooked. . . ." Westmoreland went on to discuss the role of the American press, the "false impression" of events it rendered to the American people. . . . He added, "So I would say, Mike, the bottom line was the—the Communist Tet offensive was defeated on the battlefields of South Vietnam, but they won a tremendous victory on the home front, here in the United States."

WALLACE: You say that thirty-five to forty thousand of them were killed, of the VC, North Vietnamese, were killed in the first few weeks of the Tet offensive.

WESTMORELAND: Yes. In accordance with—

WALLACE: And how many wounded?

WESTMORELAND: Well—we have no way of knowing that. But— usually the ratio is about three to one: three wounded for every one that is killed.

WALLACE: So you have thirty-five, forty [thousand] killed, then conceivably you could have as many as a hundred thousand more wounded.

WESTMORELAND: Well, conceivable, but I—I think that's probably an overstatement. Probably an overstatement.

WALLACE: At three-to-one, it's an understatement.

WESTMORELAND: [emphasis added] *Well, the three-to-one is not a precise calculation, and you cannot extrapolate that the way you have.*

Indeed, the official military intelligence figure was 1.5 to 1. Westmoreland himself had used the ratio in his official biography, *A Soldier Reports.* George Crile said later he had read that book. CBS also had in its possession other official military documents confirming that ratio of wounded to killed. The 1.5-to-1 formula had also been explained in detail in the November 13, 1967, final NIE. George Crile had read that document, too.

Subsequently, Westmoreland denied again, in the most specific language, that the 3–1 ratio was a valid one.

WESTMORELAND: I don't go for those numbers, no. I think that the three-for-one ratio is a very specious ratio, as I mentioned to you in the other part of this—I mean, we just don't know what it is. That is one that has been used, yes.

WALLACE: It's used all the time, as a matter of fact. Kill one, wound three.

WESTMORELAND: Well, we—we did not—that was not an official ratio that we adhere to.

And moments later:

WESTMORELAND: I don't—I don't recall our ever making any official estimates that there were three men knocked out of action for every one killed. . . .

But it was too late. Westmoreland had offered the 3–1 ratio at the start of the interview—no matter that he was now denying it, no matter that the official military intelligence number was 1.5 to 1. In this star-chamber proceeding, the witness would never be allowed an opportunity to modify or explain or correct himself. Interview was the wrong word.

"Wallace was grilling me—grilling, grilling, grilling," said Westmoreland later. "It was like a torture chamber."

> WALLACE: You thought McChristian was absolutely first rate. [Gen. Joseph McChristian had preceded Gen. Philip Davidson as chief of intelligence.]
>
> WESTMORELAND: I thought McChristian—I still do. I still do. But you have indicated some unhappiness by McChristian that was never made known to me. Now those—those young—
>
> WALLACE: It was not a matter of unhappiness. McChristian believes that the figures were being cooked.
>
> WESTMORELAND: And—but—he—he—well . . .

Wallace whipped Westmoreland mercilessly. Westmoreland was stuttering, biting his lips and licking them, his face red with rage. During a pause Westmoreland rose and walked up to George Crile. He stuck his chest out and thrust his face an inch or so away from the producer's. "You rattlesnaked me," he hissed.

The inquisition resumed. Wallace kept interrupting, punishing Westmoreland, prefacing his comments with a scathing "Sir" that only emphasized his utter contempt. Wallace was not a journalist; he was not on a quest for fresh information. He was both prosecuting attorney and judge. The CBS jury had already seen the plaintiff's witnesses in the rough cut, and Westmoreland had been found guilty *in absentia*. Now, in the best tradition of vigilante journalism, Wallace was meting out his particular brand of justice: a nationally televised character castration. All Wallace really wanted to get on camera were Westmoreland's stammering denials.

There was no cross-examination, no witnesses for the defense. No smoking gun was necessary for a conviction, not even the echo of one being fired. It was enough for Mike Wallace that a group of junior officers felt wounded; he was willing to accept George Crile's word as to "who done it" and why. Wallace was ruthless, clever, sharp—he was everything that day except a journalist. A journalist allows the target of his inquiry to make his best case. At least ten times throughout the interview Westmoreland replayed variations of one theme: If there had been a faking of enemy-strength estimates in the months prior to Tet—if his military intelligence had lied to the world about the enemy army that Sam Adams claimed to be some 600,000 strong (more than twice the military's estimate of about 240,000 regular VC/NVA fighting men)—where were they at Tet?

> WESTMORELAND: The proof of the pudding is in the eating: After the Tet offensive was over, and we assessed the—the number of Vietcong indigenous combatants that were involved, and this was an all-out effort, go for broke, it proved to be less than our estimate, considerably less. Less by a—order of magnitude of ten percent.

It was the argument with which George Crile was already familiar. The 1973 Defense Intelligence Agency memo had adopted the same reasoning to refute Sam Adams's estimate of a 600,000-man army. Westmoreland's words were also an echo of the 1975 testimony of the CIA's George Carver before the Pike Committee. The comparatively small number of enemy soldiers who turned up during Tet was a weak link in the CBS conspiracy theory, and Westmoreland hammered at it again and again.

> WESTMORELAND: But the fact is that after the Tet offensive was over and the dust had settled, even the estimate that we had was in excess of what was surfaced during this all-out attack.
> WALLACE (trying to change the subject): Let me take you back to 1964, if I may, General. . . .

Later again:

> WESTMORELAND: Well, all I can say is that this did not turn out to be an accurate appraisal because when they went for broke during the Tet offensive, and presumably they surfaced most of their forces, the Order of Battle after the dust had settled was, at that time, the first estimate was about eighty-four thousand, it was the order of magnitude. . . .

Wallace changed the subject. Seven times more Westmoreland revived the same theme and expostulated on it at length. If indeed the enemy army had been twice as large as the military said it was, where was that larger army at Tet? The evidence was, Westmoreland argued, that the military had *overestimated*, not *underestimated*, the size of the enemy.

Each time, Mike Wallace changed the subject. Apparently George Crile had not included the answer to that question in the chronologically ordered list he had scripted for Wallace.

Crile was kneeling on the floor behind Westmoreland's back as Wallace interviewed the general. Once, Westmoreland spun his head around. He was startled to see Crile holding up a large piece of paper with something written on it. The producer was flashing cue cards at Wallace.

> WESTMORELAND: Well, in the final analysis—the Order of Battle was in excess of what had been forecasted, after the Tet offensive. The day of reckoning was the Tet offensive. And the day of reckoning brought out the truth, that the Order of Battle had been— that had been developed was in the ballpark—as a matter of fact, it was in excess.

Now, finally, after Westmoreland's ninth "proof of the pudding is in the eating" response, Wallace could no longer evade an answer. He directly addressed the issue:

> WALLACE: I put that to Sam Adams, the young man from the CIA. I said, "General Westmoreland had told me this. He [Westmoreland] said that not only was Tet a great military victory, but it proved that [the military] had been overestimating enemy strength all along. How do you answer that? He still thinks you're nuts, Adams. He still thinks that you're dead wrong. Were and remain dead wrong."
>
> Forgive me, sir, for what I'm about to say. Adams said, "He's a liar. I know so much about what General Westmoreland has done behind the scenes that I know General Westmoreland is lying." I say, "What do you mean, what do you know?" "I know about all that he said to his Order of Battle subordinates." "What did he say?" "He told them, for example, to keep a ceiling on the Order of Battle, to count as many Vietcong as you want to, but just don't count anymore than three hundred thousand. He told them . . . he was behind that little slip of paper which says, yeah, I'll give you fifteen thousand extra guerillas if you allow us to march the Self-Defense militia out of the Order of Battle. He wrote the cable which says: The reason we want to have an Order of Battle that is under three hundred thousand is . . . a desire to keep our image of success."

Mike Wallace never mentioned that Adams was employed as the show's paid consultant, nor had he answered Westmoreland's repeated assertion that the size of the enemy at Tet proved the military's estimates were closer to the reality than Sam Adams's.

After three hours Mike Wallace's interrogation of Gen. William C. Westmoreland was over. George Crile was still sitting on the floor behind Westmoreland, his friend Grace Diekhaus beside him. For a moment there was an ominous silence as Westmoreland, stifling his anger, stood up. Wallace started unclipping his microphone. Wallace broke the tension, saying, "Have you got a car for . . ?" He nodded toward Westmoreland. When his gaze met Westmoreland's fierce glare, Wallace turned away, still fiddling with his microphone. "Jeez," he mumbled under his breath, "that was hard work."

Westmoreland stalked off. George Crile telephoned Ira Klein in his editing room at CBS. Klein asked about the interview. Crile replied that the interview had gone "really well—we got everything we needed."

Two days after the Westmoreland interview, on Monday, May 18, Crile wrote a congratulatory memo to Mike Wallace:

> Mike: The interview was a classic. It keeps growing in my mind. I don't think you could have possibly done a better job; I certainly know no one else could have. It was wonderful having you as our champion. . . .

The film of the Westmoreland interview was sent to a laboratory to be processed. By midweek Crile had the developed rolls. A few days later Klein screened the Westmoreland dailies. He was impressed. Wallace was absolutely dazzling. His questions were precise, surgically sharp; he was relentless, never losing the thread of his argument, never letting Westmoreland wriggle out from under his thumb.

"God," Klein exclaimed after a particularly incisive response by Wallace, "Mike did a great follow-up on that. This," he added, "is the consummate Mike Wallace interview!"

Crile started laughing. "It's the most uncanny thing I've ever seen," Crile said. "Mike was just following a script." He added, "Even Mike's follow-ups were written out for him." Crile explained to Klein how he had prepared every question and had anticipated almost every one of Westmoreland's answers. "It's the most uncanny thing I've ever seen," the producer repeated, elated over the way Wallace's questions and follow-ups so neatly coincided with the answers Crile had predicted.

Klein had had no idea that Crile was scripting Wallace's interviews, that Mike Wallace, America's most feared investigative reporter, had merely been a puppet propped on George Crile's knee.

4

The Plotters' Motive

THE LARGE WHITE COLONIAL squatted several yards away from the curb, dwarfing its ramshackle neighbors in this quiet, decaying section of Charleston, South Carolina. The front yard was partly cement bordered by neatly trimmed grass. An aging auto slumbered in the driveway, the summer sun peeling its metallic-silver paint. At intervals along the tree-less street there were other large houses like this one—some more impressive, porticoed in the antebellum style, but all gasping for breath, choking amid the architectural weeds (narrower and shabbier dwellings) clogging every inch between them. With its sleepy large houses next to the slatternly little ones, the neighborhood seemed too prosaic to be the refuge of an American Caesar.

But walk up the flagstone path, past the fading family sedan, and you enter an arbor of sweet-smelling magnolias surrounded by shade trees hovering overhead like watchful, towering sentries. The "front" door of the Westmoreland home was here, on the side, shyly hiding behind this rampart of lush foliage. Through the screen door, in the darkened living room, shafts of sunlight met mahogany. But a visitor's eyes did not linger there for long, lured further back by an antique gem. Between the main house and a small fenced-in swimming pool sat a perfect Georgian mini-ature: a pink-stucco and tile-roof building dating from the nineteenth century. Westmoreland rented the top floor to a young married couple; the ground floor served as his office and study. Since his retirement in 1972, this haven had been the embattled general's bunker.

Occasionally he abandoned it to commiserate publicly with some starched audience of conservatives, cowering under the shadow of their darkening Communist cloud. Often Westmoreland talked to these friendly audiences about the wartime role of the press. He had been the first American general ever to have to fight a war without censorship; he argued that the press had tailored events in Vietnam to fit its own liberal bias. He seemed particularly obsessed with CBS anchor Walter Cronkite, whose pessimistic on-air "commentaries" may have hastened Lyndon Johnson's decision to reduce American involvement.

More often than not, though, his speeches were not delivered to gatherings of sympathizers but to hostile crowds on college campuses. Eager to defend his record in Vietnam, Westmoreland rarely refused an invitation. His friends regarded these forays into the enemy camp as reckless. They advised him to devote his retirement years to his wife, Kitsy, their three children, and his grandchild. They warned him to cultivate a low profile and leave the defense of his reputation in the hands of historians. In private, officials who had served with him in Vietnam mockingly reminded listeners of his nickname, the Eagle Scout. To them Westmoreland's quixotic compulsion to argue his case in any forum was proof of his naivete. With his rigid definition of "duty," his authoritarian principles, the jut-jawed general seemed as archaic and out of place in this cynical plate-glass modern world as the gingerbread Georgian office where he spent hours marshaling his counterattack.

For almost a decade now he had been engaged in this self-appointed mission: attempting to justify his role in a war without fixed front lines, without censorship; a war in which tactics took precedence over strategy, a politicized war, without any clearly enunciated goal, run by a pork-barrel president; a war in which blasted hills barren of everything but human blood were traded back and forth like poker chips, while the "players" in Washington and Hanoi eyed each other for signs of failing nerve.

Westmoreland believed that he had acted honorably, carrying out the orders of his commander. He insisted he could have won that war if, after the enemy's rout during Tet, Lyndon Johnson had sent him the additional troops he requested and permitted him to pursue the enemy into Laos and Cambodia. Initially the reaction of his college audiences had been jeers; more recently, on the complacent campuses of the late seventies and early eighties, his monologues had begun to evoke stifled yawns and even some polite applause.

The most common off-the-record response a reporter heard when questioning ex-government officials was that Westmoreland simply "was not smart enough" to have engineered a conspiracy. In contrast, no one ever accused Lt. Gen. Danny Graham of being "dumb."

In mid-May, as soon as Westmoreland returned to his pink-stucco sanctuary in Charleston, he telephoned Graham, whom he had mentioned several times to Wallace as someone more qualified to answer a particular question than he was. "Westy said he'd given my name to Wallace, and would I go before the CBS cameras," Graham recalled, "because they'd caught him flat-footed on a bunch of numbers." No one had ever caught Danny Graham "flat-footed." Solidly built, with a chiseled face under slick white hair, mentally he was always on his toes, lulling his opponent with a disarming boyish grin, then suddenly lashing out with a scowling barrage of facts and four-letter words. In 1981 this leathery, pugnacious champion of the military's hardest line was president of his own private company, based in Washington, D.C., and dedicated to exploring the future of sophisticated computerized weapons systems in space.

In the period being scrutinized by George Crile, General Graham (then a lieutenant colonel) had headed the military's Current Intelligence, Indications and Estimates Division, one of a pair of Saigon-based parallel intelligence units under the command of Westmoreland's chief of intelligence, Gen. Philip Davidson. Col. Charles Morris, Graham's immediate supervisor, had been chief of the other intelligence shop, Intelligence Production. There had been no love between Graham and Morris. Morris's organization produced long-range estimates, the kind eventually included in the monthly Order of Battle. His "shop" also housed the computer, where the ongoing historical record of enemy and Allied killed and wounded was stored. Meanwhile, Graham's analysts generated the vital day-to-day intelligence used by American troops in the field. They had access to more sensitive sources. A rivalry had arisen between the two intelligence units, mimicking the mutal antagonism between their respective leaders. It is significant that George Crile could not find even a single analyst from Danny Graham's shop willing to go before the CBS cameras and testify to Graham's "misdeeds." Every one of the intelligence analysts who did appear on camera had reported not to Graham but to Charlie Morris. Morris, a full colonel in 1967, was Graham's superior, but Danny had made a mockery of that organizational chart.

Beginning in 1967 as a lieutenant colonel, within a year Graham had become a full colonel. His precipitous rise was a product not only of his own brilliance (some of CBS's own witnesses against Graham cited him as the most able intelligence officer in Vietnam) but his political instincts. Early in his Vietnam tour he began shuttling back and forth between Saigon and Washington, briefing top politicians on the progress of Westmoreland's war and simultaneously paving his own upward path. Graham would later become chief of the Pentagon's Defense Intelligence Agency before retiring as a lieutenant general. Charlie Morris, his immediate superior in Vietnam, would never be able to budge beyond the rank of colonel.

In the blue sheet Crile had called Graham the Key Conspirator. It was Graham's political nature that provided, in Crile's view, the motive for his participation in Westmoreland's plot. Just as Westmoreland had suppressed estimates in order to further Lyndon Johnson's career, thus ensuring continued presidential support for Westmoreland's war, Graham had collaborated in the "conspiracy" in order to further his own, tampering with intelligence in Vietnam so that his pals in Washington would be able to brag about "progress" in the 1968 presidential election. Sam Adams, in particular, held Graham in contempt. It had been Danny Graham who, in one final Order of Battle conference after Tet, in April 1968, had belligerently brushed aside Adams's estimate of an enemy army twice as large as the one the military was officially fighting. Adams had never forgiven him.

If Westmoreland had known beforehand that Adams was intimately involved in the CBS project, it is unlikely he would have consented to be interviewed. When Mike Wallace telephoned requesting an on-camera interview, Danny Graham did not know about Adams's participation either. But even had he known, he probably would not have cared. Graham was arrogant, tough, and utterly confident of his own abilities; he had not been scarred by the constant criticism which, over the years, had eroded Westmoreland's self-esteem. Danny Graham did not give a damn what CBS said, as long as Wallace gave him the opportunity to issue an opening statement. In the June 3, 1981, interview, Mike did:

> WALLACE: All right, the point that you want to make—about Tet. Why don't you make it right off the top so that we can more fully understand?
>
> GRAHAM: . . . The fact of the matter is that when Tet occurred, the biggest figure that anybody's ever estimated for the attacking force was eighty-four thousand people. And that included people that they had scraped out of hospitals and kids that they'd just thrown

in from the villages who didn't even know how to fire their weapons, and this meant [emphasis added] *that the MACV estimate, which I made, was too high. We were too high.*

By then the refrain should have been a familiar one to CBS—the same "proof of the pudding is in the eating" argument offered in the 1973 DIA memo, then reiterated by the CIA's George Carver (and, in fact, by Danny Graham as well) at the 1975 Pike Committee hearings, and advanced time after time by Westmoreland in his interview with Wallace. But Wallace dealt with Graham the way he had with Westmoreland. Instead of attempting to rebut or even understand his adversary's strongest argument against the existence of a 500,000 to 600,000-man enemy army, Wallace ignored it. He shifted topics. "As you know . . . as you know, General Graham," Wallace responded, "one of the areas that we want to explore is the dispute between the CIA and the military over intelligence estimates during the Vietnam War. . . ." It was as if Wallace had gone selectively deaf, afflicted with some bizarre auditory dysfunction that edited out any answer which did not conform to George Crile's script of questions. Wallace interviewed Graham for ninety minutes. Crile would allow Graham, in the broadcast, only twenty seconds to respond.

While Graham and Wallace were butting heads in Washington, Westmoreland was busy laboring in his pink-stucco office. The ground-floor suite of rooms was cool, dark, and cluttered, teeming with memorabilia of his years in the military. There were the nineteen United States military decorations (plus scores of foreign ones) he had earned while leading seventeen battle campaigns in three different wars. There were five honorary doctoral degrees and the *Time* magazine cover portrait crowning him "Man of the Year" in 1965. On a wall were the gold leaf of a four-star general and a pair of plaques from the United States Military Academy at West Point, one commemorating his graduation in 1936, the other his term as the military academy's superintendent. Both bore the official West Point seal, circumscribed by the motto: "Duty, Honor, Country."

Believing he had done his duty for his country, Westmoreland was prepared to accept the judgment of current history that he had "lost" the war in Vietnam. Now, however, Mike Wallace had accused him of being something far more dishonorable than a loser; Wallace was accusing him of being a liar. As soon as Westmoreland had returned to Charleston from New York, he began to do what he told Wallace he would in the closing moments of their interview: He was reviewing the actual totals of enemy infiltrators the military had tallied in the fall of 1967. He had to explain the discrepancy Wallace had pointed out between Westmoreland's statement on *Meet the Press* of 5,500 to 6,000 a month, and his memory early in the interview of 20,000 a month. On June 9, 1981, he wrote a letter to Wallace and Crile:

Dear Mike and George:

The session with you in New York City on Saturday, May 16, was interesting, but I must frankly say it turned out to be more of an inquisition than a rational interview.

After fourteen years (1967 to 1981) have gone by, I was unable to speak with precision on the details of items presented to you by your researchers. But now I have gone through my files in Washington and am enclosing several papers from my files that might be helpful to you. These are enclosed. As a general statement, it seems to me that your researchers perceive intelligence as a much more precise matter than it is in fact.

If it is your purpose to be fair and objective during your quest, which I must assume you intend to be, I suggest that you interview:

Ambassador Ellsworth Bunker
Mr. Robert Komer
Lt. Gen. Daniel Graham
Gen. Walter Kerwin, Jr.
Mr. George Carver (former) CIA and
Mr. William E. Colby

Another individual is a colonel who was associated with Colonel Hawkins whose name I believe was Morris. General Graham may be of help in identifying him.

Sincerely,
W. C. Westmoreland

Accompanying that letter was a packet of official documents: cables confirming that Westmoreland prepared in advance of the enemy's Tet attack, plus actual military intelligence infiltration reports. Westmoreland also included one other item. "Attached," he wrote, "is an extract from the *Meet the Press* program by Larry Spivak with Ambassador Bunker and me. You brought one question up during your May 16 session with me, specifically: infiltration as of the month of the program—November 1967. Please note my answer, 'I would *estimate* between 5,500 and 6,000 per month, but they do have the capability of stepping this up.' "

Westmoreland went on to say that "there was always a time lag of several months between actual infiltration and that confirmed by the MACV intelligence office." Then he referred to a military intelligence infiltration report dated August 1968 that he had enclosed. "As of November 1967, infiltration . . . was carried on the running tabulation as 5,900. Hence my estimate given to Larry Spivak [moderator of *Meet the Press*] was generally correct. You will note in the tabulation that infiltration did not reach the 20,000 mark until January 1968."

Later Westmoreland would argue he had regarded the letter (and packet) as a request for a correction; he had been wrong when he told Wallace the infiltration rate during the fall of 1967 was 20,000 a month; enemy infiltration had only reached that rate in January 1968.

Wallace received the Westmoreland packet, glanced at it, and turned it over to George Crile. Crile said he did not regard the letter and documents as a request for a correction since Westmoreland had not specifically asked for one. Time after time in the interview, Crile insisted, Westmoreland had confirmed the 20,000-a-month infiltration figure for the fall of 1967. Crile believed that during the interview with Wallace "Westmoreland remembered the facts and forgot the cover story." Besides, Crile said, the document Westmoreland was relying on was not relevant because it was not "contemporaneous": Westmoreland was basing his contention that infiltration only escalated to 20,000 per month in January 1968 on a document dated August 1968, six months after Tet. Westmoreland, in turn, would argue that infiltration estimates were updated for six months, and only then became official. It was only after six months had elapsed that the figures were actually entered on a permanent basis into the military's computer.

Crile wrote a memo to Wallace stating: ". . . As far as I can make out Westmoreland doesn't bring anything to our attention that is particularly relevant. Certainly nothing that causes concern and requires a new look at anything we have been asserting. . . ." Crile did not describe to Wallace what the Westmoreland packet contained, nor did Wallace ask to review its contents. Later, long after the broadcast, when Wallace did learn more about the documents at which he had only cursorily glanced, he said that "with 20/20 hindsight" CBS might have included a sentence in the broadcast confirming that Westmoreland, after his interview, had submitted a letter and documents. "It would have been a sentence that answered his concern," Wallace said, "and yet would not have diminished the basic thrust of the documentary, which was that there was a calculated cover-up."

On June 25 Crile answered Westmoreland's letter. His response said in part: ". . . Thank you very much for your suggestions and documents.

Mike is off on vacation now, and so we have gone into a summer lull. We'll be getting in touch with more people soon. . . ." However, aside from Danny Graham, whom CBS had already interviewed, Crile would not ask any of the ex-officials Westmoreland listed in his letter to appear before the CBS cameras.

George Crile kept collecting interviews. Meanwhile, Ira Klein was busy selecting stock-footage "takes," culling reel after reel of news film for sequences he could include in his reconstruction of the Vietnam War on a grand scale. Then suddenly, in June, George Crile made a startling announcement: It was possible that CBS might want to air the documentary as early as September. Everyone started working longer hours. Days off became a luxury. Klein doubled his efforts at re-creating on film the ebb and flow of the Vietnam conflict.

One day Alex Alben, the researcher, handed him a white box. When Klein opened the container, pieces of film popped out. He had to retrieve dozens of them from the floor. The tiny bits of film—all intertangled— were "trims," outtakes (material never aired) from a pair of exclusive CBS News interviews with Lyndon Johnson in 1969, the year after Tet. Alben had obtained a transcript of those CBS broadcasts; he had it under his arm. He told Klein that Crile wanted them to search through the trims to see if they contained any useful material. Crile, of course, was arguing that Westmoreland might have kept crucial data from the president.

Alben and Klein studied the trims for days but found nothing. Klein assumed that Crile and Alben had not found anything relevant in the transcript of those 1969 CBS interviews either, since no segments were given to him to edit into the Vietnam broadcast.

A corollary of Crile's conspiracy premise was that Westmoreland's plot to fool the American public, the Congress, and perhaps even the president had led to America's unpreparedness for the Tet attack. In those 1969 CBS News interviews Johnson had said: "We were ready for Tet. My advisers told me in the late fall that a substantial move by the North Vietnamese was underway. The troop deployments, captured documents, information available to us said it was coming, but we did not think they would do it exactly at Tet, a religious holiday. . . . Westmoreland cancelled leaves so as to be prepared."

Johnson went on to say that he had warned the Australian cabinet that the enemy in Vietnam was preparing to launch an all-out "kamikaze" attack; that Tet was a military victory for the United States; and that General Westmoreland had rightly predicted the United States victory. Ira Klein never knew what Johnson had said since all he had reviewed were the outtakes of the broadcast. Executive producer Howard Stringer knew what Johnson had said because he had been the young researcher assigned to those 1969 CBS interviews. Apparently, though, Stringer never questioned whether Crile was familiar with the broadcasts or whether he planned to include LBJ's comments from Johnson's own lips (critical in determining how much Westmoreland had revealed to him during the crucial months prior to Tet) in his documentary.

As soon as Klein had edited a stock-footage sequence, Crile would come in and discuss it with him. It was then that a pattern began to emerge. One of Bob Chandler's objections to allowing Crile to produce this broadcast had been, he said later, Crile's "overreliance on other people and the waste of time and resources this dependence on others had cost CBS." As a precondition to authorizing the project's preliminary budget, Chandler had made Crile promise that this time he would produce a broadcast entirely on his own. But more and more often Crile was relying on Grace Diekhaus for support. For instance, after Klein edited a sequence showing Westmoreland visiting the LBJ ranch in April 1967, Crile decided that another element should be included. Klein suggested that the added element "wouldn't work." Crile said, "I'm not ready to let go of it yet." Enter Grace Diekhaus. "It doesn't work," she said. "Yeah, it doesn't work," Crile said. This give-and-take between producer and editor was the normal kind that always arose in a collaborative endeavor. Crile and Klein did not have an actual argument until they jointly "cut" the crucial scene in Act 1 of the broadcast—the "McChristian/Hawkins briefing."

Before Klein began working on the documentary (on April 1), Phyllis Hurwitz had "pulled" from the interviews both of Gen. Joseph McChristian and Col. Gains Hawkins the takes Crile intended to use in this sequence. They had been stored on reels which were stacked in three-deep tiers on a long shelf in Klein's editing room. Now, under Crile's direction, Klein began to assemble the "briefing" sequence, integrating the takes Crile wanted from the McChristian, Hawkins, and Westmoreland interviews. Since Klein had not screened the dailies (the raw uncut interview footage), nor read the full interview transcripts (absorbed in compiling his stock footage, he hadn't had time), he was totally dependent on Crile's interpretation of the event they were historically re-creating. Klein's perception at that time was only a piecemeal one; only Crile, the producer, knew what was correct and what was not.

The sequence they were going to cut would document Westmoreland's first illicit act: his suppression of a report of a much larger enemy, delivered to him at a briefing in the spring of 1967 by his then-chief of intelligence General McChristian and his Order of Battle expert Colonel

Hawkins. Crile was going to charge in the broadcast that Westmoreland had "blocked" this report, fearful of its political repercussions in the media and in Washington. The initial problem in constructing this sequence was how to introduce McChristian and Hawkins to the viewer.

"Why don't we introduce them together?" Klein suggested. His idea was to use still photos of each officer side by side on the screen. Later Crile could write narrative that Wallace would read, explaining who the two officers were.

"It's very vague as to whether McChristian was actually with Hawkins at that briefing," Crile replied. "It's very vague."

So Klein dropped the notion of introducing the men simultaneously, with side-by-side still photos. They settled on another method. First Hawkins would speak, then McChristian. Klein included, in order, all the comments Crile wanted from each officer's interview. Then it was time to insert the responses Crile had selected from the Westmoreland interview—and Klein became concerned. Crile, he felt, was "cutting Westmoreland short," allowing him only brief denials of the serious charges the two officers seemed to be lodging against him. Klein was particularly troubled by the Hawkins segment of that sequence. It began with Hawkins recalling how he had "briefed" Westmoreland on the new strength figures for two categories of irregular forces, the Vietcong's political bureaucracy and the guerillas. The sequence, as Crile wanted it, was:

WESTMORELAND: I remember such a report, yes.

HAWKINS: I don't want to read anybody's mind, George, but there was a great deal of concern about the impact that this new figure would have. And General Westmoreland appeared to be very much surprised [at] the magnitude of the figure.

WALLACE: According to Colonel Hawkins, he said that "the general seemed to be taken by surprise." He remembers your first words after listening to that briefing were, "What am I going to tell the press? What am I going to tell the Congress? What am I going to tell the president?" True?

WESTMORELAND: I—I do recall a session with Hawkins, yes.

HAWKINS: There was no mistaking the message.

CRILE: They didn't want higher numbers.

HAWKINS: That was the message.

Klein suggested to Crile that he allow Westmoreland an opportunity to *explain* his reaction to Hawkins's briefing. After Westmoreland had said

"I—I do recall a session with Hawkins, yes," he had added, "but I was very, very suspicious of—of this particular estimate. And the reason was that you—you come to a shade of gray. You get down at the hamlet level, and you've got teenagers and you've got old men who can be armed and can be useful to the enemy, and who are technically Vietcong—"

WALLACE: Right.
WESTMORELAND: —but they don't have any military capability of consequence.

Klein wanted Crile to include this complete statement in the McChristian-Hawkins briefing sequence, but Crile was adamant. He insisted on making the cut after Westmoreland's "I—I do recall a session with Hawkins, yes." Klein said that he warned Crile he was "destroying our credibility by not permitting Westmoreland to present his point of view. Give your viewers a role," he said he told Crile. "Let the viewer decide between right and wrong." Crile defended his editing as being honest and fair. The debate between the producer and his editor turned into a lengthy one. Ultimately Crile exercised his authority and ended the argument. They went on to edit the rest of that "briefing" sequence, concluding it with the following exchange between Westmoreland and Wallace, in which Westmoreland offered a different explanation of why he had not accepted the numbers put forth by Hawkins.

WESTMORELAND: I did not accept his recommendation. I did not accept it. And I didn't accept it because of political reasons. That was a—I may have mentioned this, I guess, but that was not the fundamental thing. I just didn't accept it.
WALLACE: What was the political reason? Why would it have been a political bombshell? That's really—
WESTMORELAND: Because the people in Washington were not sophisticated enough to understand and evaluate this thing, and neither was the media.

Crile screened the completed McChristian-Hawkins briefing alongside Ira Klein in Klein's darkened editing room. Crile sat there in silence until Westmoreland uttered his damning "admission" that political considerations had caused him to reject his subordinates' briefing. Then Crile, talking to Westmoreland on the screen, said, "I got you, I *got* you, I *got you!*"

Crile had an edited sequence in which Westmoreland seemed to be saying that he had not accepted the McChristian-Hawkins "briefing" because of "political reasons." Now he wanted to enlarge upon that theme. He needed a witness who could illuminate the political reasons for suppressing not only that single report but the entire spectrum of military intelligence strength figures. He needed George Allen, who had been Sam Adams's immediate supervisor at the CIA. Allen had been the CIA's number-two man on Vietnamese affairs. Number *two* because Allen was George Carver's deputy. It was Carver, not Allen, who had orchestrated the compromise with Westmoreland at the September 1967 National Intelligence Estimates conference in Saigon. It was Carver, not Allen, who dealt on a daily basis with CIA Director Richard Helms. Why not interview George Carver instead of George Allen? Crile explained later that he "called Carver initially, and he was out of town when I called." Besides, Crile added, "Carver's record was documented; we had Carver in cables." In any case, according to Crile, Allen was "really the leading expert [on Vietnam] at that point."

Allen, however, said that by 1967 his role was peripheral to the Order of Battle dispute. He said that he was not one of the principal players: He had not played a role in the Langley conferences; he had not traveled to Saigon. His information about the details came secondhand, from Carver and Adams.

Nevertheless, Allen offered advantages as a witness that George Carver did not. In the first place, Allen was a longtime defender of Sam Adams. Secondly, he might, with his testimony, mollify Mike Wallace. "Mike was very skeptical," recalled Crile, "in that he wanted to know: Why would a commander want to downgrade the enemy? It didn't make sense to him. Ordinarily," Crile added, "a commander, if anything, wants to upgrade it, to get more troops."

In the "Prospects" list (the list of eighty ex-officials Adams had prepared for Crile), under Westmoreland's name Adams had penned the following comment: "Note obvious fact: *Normally*, commanders in the field *exaggerate* enemy strength to get more troops. Why did Westy deviate from the norm? Note Anderson col[umn] of November 30, 1967." In the margin Adams summarized that Jack Anderson column: "Anderson column notes alleged suspicion by [Secretary of Defense Robert] McNamara that Westy was exaggerating VC strength to get more troops."

During Wallace's interview with Westmoreland, the general himself had argued on at least seven occasions that a field commander would have no possible motive to underestimate the size of the enemy he was facing. Indeed, Wallace had reminded Westmoreland that in 1966 the general had been accused of *overestimating* the strength of the Vietcong and North Vietnamese. George Allen could resolve that contradiction—and dispel Mike Wallace's doubts.

In 1962, as a Defense Intelligence Agency analyst, Allen had been an important member of the task force assigned to draw up the first Vietnam enemy Order of Battle. Soon, however, he had become disillusioned with Gen. Paul Harkins (Westmoreland's predecessor in Vietnam), who, Allen would claim, had been told by his superiors "to accentuate the positive." Frustrated, Allen had left the DIA and joined the CIA, but had never ceased being a critic of the military's estimates of enemy strength. Allen had encouraged Sam Adams to devote his time to "this problem that I had felt for a lot of years was the one we had to overcome." Allen "wanted the estimates to reflect reality. And I was taking advantage of Sam's interest and enthusiasm toward this end."

Allen had an explanation of the contradiction (a commander underestimating the enemy when historically commanders had always overestimated the size of their foe) which was confusing Mike Wallace. Allen felt he knew the motive behind Westmoreland's crime.

By late June, Crile had already interviewed Allen for three hours on camera. In sharp contrast to the grilling Wallace had given Westmoreland, Crile had coddled Allen. When Allen did not respond with clarity to a particular question, Crile soothed: "George, let me—don't worry about it. I know exactly what you're doing as I recall the way you told it first. . . ." Meanwhile, Allen was trying to be as helpful as possible. "What do you want me to say, George?" he asked Crile. Several times Crile mentioned Sam Adams, who was at the interview.

Crile said, "George, would you please help your old protégé, Sam Adams here, in some way. . . ." And again: "Come to the defense of your old protégé, Sam Adams. . . ."

Nevertheless, Crile was dissatisfied with that Allen interview. "Allen had been camera-shy, nervous because he was trying to walk a tightrope," Crile explained later. "He felt loyal to the CIA and wanted it made clear he wasn't trying to take a swipe at the CIA as an institution." He decided he had to redo that Allen interview.

By the end of June, with a September air date still in the offing, Crile and Klein were collaborating daily as they jointly edited sequences to be inserted into the actual broadcast. Crile would appear in Klein's editing room, his arms bursting with transcripts. Crile was constantly taking notes on small CBS memo pads. At the end of a day, Klein said, he would find pages from Crile's notepads "sticking to the bottom of my shoes." He found a thin black looseleaf notebook in which Crile could keep all his notes intact. But it was an issue of far more substance than their disparate working habits that sparked their next confrontation.

One morning Klein was working in his editing room when Crile entered. Klein was standing by the door beside his editing table. Crile said, "I'm bringing George Allen here, into the editing room."

Klein stared at Crile in disbelief. He said, "You're compromising me. You're jeopardizing the project by bringing him into the room."

Crile reassured him. "Don't worry," he said and quickly walked out.

Klein stood there, astonished and angry. He knew it was not only a violation of CBS official guidelines to bring an interviewee into an editing room, it was a violation of common sense and common decency. Klein realized why Crile wanted to bring Allen into his editing room. Unhappy with Allen's first interview, Crile wanted to show Allen the rough cut on which the charges against Westmoreland by other CBS witnesses were already recorded.

Later Crile would explain that he brought Allen into Klein's editing room "to help [him] speak with the dignity he did off camera." Crile "was trying to reassure me that these intelligence people had already covered a number of points," said Allen, "and to minimize the inhibitions I had about discussing them. He wasn't trying to load me up or pressure me."

Nonetheless, by affording Allen an opportunity to compare his views with those of interviewees already on film, Crile was allowing Allen to screen some of the accusations against "conspirators" Westmoreland and Graham, without offering these generals any opportunity to hear the words of their accusers before the interviews or to redo their own interviews.

Crile returned to the editing room with George Allen. He closed the door behind him and introduced Allen to Klein. Allen and Crile sat down. Crile said to Klein, "George Allen is an old CIA man. This won't go any further." Allen sat there, nodding his head affirmatively. There was no mistaking it; Klein knew Crile was deadly serious. Crile was telling him that Allen was a man who knew how to keep a secret.

Crile then showed Allen segments of several interviews, filling the gaps between "takes" with rich detail, just as he had at the Colloff-Stringer screenings. And just as Colloff and Stringer had been, Allen was moved by what he saw and heard. After the screening Crile and Allen stood up. They thanked Klein and left the cutting room. Klein was still sitting there, stunned. He decided then that George Crile was "out of control." That same day he sought out the associate producer Joe Zigman and told Zigman about Allen.

Zigman was in the twilight of a long career at CBS; a few months after the broadcast he would opt for early retirement, give up his house in Brooklyn, and move to California. In theory, a documentary's associate producer should be intimately involved as a collaborator in all facets of the production. But Zigman had worked with Crile before and was familiar with the producer's habits. Thus, he did not complain when Crile invited Grace Diekhaus along on interviews in his place. He did not complain when his role in the production was reduced to a perfunctory one. Zigman's lined, weathered face would simply curl up in an ironic grin. "Ziggie" was blue-collar to the bone. He did not make waves; he had learned, over the course of his career, just how quickly a tide can turn. But it was Zigman's responsibility as the associate producer to report to his superiors that a serious violation of the CBS official guidelines had occurred. According to executive producer Howard Stringer, however, Zigman never uttered a word to him about the Allen incident..

On June 29 Crile interviewed the CIA's George Allen for the second time on camera. On this occasion, instead of interviewing Allen again at a hotel, Crile did so in the far more convivial ambience of Grace Diekhaus's midtown Manhattan apartment. At one point in the raw unedited film footage the camera pulls back, and the viewer can see Allen gripping in his fist a glass full of melting ice cubes. Meanwhile, George Crile kept applying his own kind of heat:

> CRILE: . . . We're going to keep at this until we get it right—until we feel comfortable. . . .

Again:

> CRILE: There was more to it than that, as you have explained it. Remember?
> ALLEN: No, I don't remember. Refresh me.
> CRILE: I'll refresh you. . . .

Time after time Crile kept on repeating the same questions, coaxing Allen to include fresh details. Even Allen became concerned over the ethics of all this repetition. "Is it really kosher to go over this?" he asked Crile. "Oh, this is what we do," Crile reassured him.

Three times Crile asked Allen about Westmoreland's statement that the enemy's irregular forces were not a threat. Three times he asked Allen about CIA Director Richard Helms and Allen's boss George Carver submitting to the military. Seven times in that second interview Crile asked Allen to recount the same anecdote, involving Gen. Danny Graham.

"In a documentary," Crile would explain later, "the producer can only deal with what is on film. I need to find a way to get in the clear that person's perceptions of what we are dealing with. . . . To get to that right moment you go another route to get it out. . . . It's like a dance, an art form. You're moving toward a moment. You're trying to get the essence of truth on film."

"They wanted to get something they might use in the way of an answer," said George Allen. "So, being aware of that, I would try to answer it differently the next time and try to say something that would be worthwhile."

With several answers to each key question at his disposal, Crile could select exactly the one that suited his purpose.

Now Crile had two George Allen interviews. He told Phyllis Hurwitz which takes to pull from each one; Phyllis assembled those segments onto a reel. Crile was preparing a special screening for Mike Wallace so that Allen could satisfy the chief correspondent's doubts over why a commander would want to underestimate the size of his enemy. As soon as the reel was ready, Crile telephoned Wallace. Minutes later Mike barreled into the editing room, said hello to Crile and Klein, and sat down, switching on Klein's editing machine.

There was George Allen, the CIA's "leading expert on Vietnam," revealing that the CIA's decision to compromise with the military "was strictly a political judgment, a political decision. . ." on the part of CIA Director Richard Helms, who "didn't want the agency to be perceived as persisting in a line which was contravening the policy of the Administration."

CRILE: If the military had accepted the CIA's new position, if the National Intelligence Estimate had come out with a claim that the Vietcong army was almost twice as large as we'd previously thought, what would the consequences have been? What would the reaction be?

ALLEN: Well, it would have scuttled entirely the effort that had been going on that summer to convince the people that the Administration's policy was on the right track. It would have meant that Vietnam would be a very important issue in the election—in the coming year, 1968—and would have produced all sorts of congressional inquiry and reaction to the war, and would have fed the popular opposition to the war.

In other words, Westmoreland had underestimated the size of the enemy in order to prove the U.S. was winning the "war of attrition," thereby stymieing those who wanted a stalemate or withdrawal, and helping Lyndon Johnson get reelected in 1968.

"Holy shit," Wallace exclaimed, "*that's* what it's all about."

5

What the President Knew

W HEN A MARRIAGE ENDS IN DIVORCE, in retrospect the disenchanted partners tend to magnify the disillusionments—the bickering, the broken promises—and minimize the delights. So it was with Crile and Klein, wedded by CBS to this Sam Adams-endowed documentary. Over the course of a year this Jack Sprat and his wife (a producer who preferred his facts thick with fat, and an editor who liked his history lean) shared occasional moments of levity, the tension between them temporarily unsprung by laughter.

By the beginning of July, for instance, it was clear to both men that, in order to be ready for a possible September air date, they needed to work weekends on a regular basis. As a final hiatus before plunging into the six- or seven-day work week, however, they agreed to pause over the upcoming July 4 holiday. They would not work on Saturday or Sunday; the question was, should they resume on the holiday Monday or relax on that day as well? Klein left the decision to Crile; if the producer wanted to work on Monday, he would telephone Klein sometime on Sunday afternoon. Both producer and editor intended to spend what would probably be their last extended respite at their respective vacation houses near the Long Island seashore.

Klein did not hear from Crile on Sunday afternoon; he assumed the producer had decided to take off Monday. Then, early Monday morning, Klein was awakened by the telephone. It was Crile.

"*I'm* in the cutting room," Crile said. "Where the hell are *you?*"

"Oh, shit," Klein stuttered, "I thought . . ."

"I'm kidding," said Crile.

He was still at his beach house. The telephone call was simply a prank. The producer and editor shared a laugh. The following day, however, they were back at CBS, their light mood turning leaden: That weekend away from the pressures and tensions of producing this ambitious documentary would be one of their last. Over the next few days they quickened their pace of collating, cutting, and assembling—and, on Klein's part, *dis*sembling, to conceal from other members of the unit his deepening agitation over Crile's mysterious disappearances. Crile's work habits were becoming more erratic than ever. He would materialize in Klein's editing room late in the afternoon, his arms bulging with flapping transcripts and bits of note paper wafting off as he walked, seeming harried and hurried, as if impelled by some personal breeze at his back that only he could feel. Klein ignored Crile's tardiness at first. Their relationship was already strained. He hesitated to say anything. But day after day Crile's behavior, as far as Klein was concerned, became more unpredictable. He would pop into Klein's room, chat with the editor for a few minutes, then turn on his heels and stride toward the door, calling over his shoulder, "I'll be right back." He might not come back for hours. He might not return until the following afternoon. Klein's own working habits started to alter. He found himself working late into the night because Crile had vanished during the day. Worse, Crile's disappearances were impeding progress; Klein did not want to edit the interviews (as opposed to the stock footage) without Crile being present. But he kept busy, adding a new element to his crowded work agenda. For the first time he began reading the transcripts of Crile's on-camera interviews.

Klein started with the transcript of a star CBS witness, Col. Gains Hawkins, the military Order of Battle specialist who had stood up at a conference in Honolulu in February 1967 and defended Adams's numbers, and who had subsequently encouraged Adams in researching his "conspiracy," while telling army counterintelligence (and the Ellsberg defense lawyers) that no such conspiracy ever existed. Klein knew from viewing the Hawkins takes on the select reel, and from hearing Crile's own supplementary comments during screenings, that the producer intended to use this witness's testimony to substantiate three central charges against Westmoreland (and Graham): first, that Westmoreland had blocked "for political reasons" the report of a larger enemy Hawkins had presented at the briefing in the spring of 1967; second, that Hawkins had been ordered, at the National Intelligence Estimates conference at CIA headquarters in the summer of 1967, not to allow the Order of Battle to exceed a ceiling imposed by Westmoreland; and third, that Hawkins, during the course of those conferences, indicated to Adams that military intelligence in Vietnam had been deliberately underestimating the size of the enemy.

Klein started skimming the interview, scanning segments piecemeal. As he read he became more and more curious about an official whom he had never heard Crile mention but whom Hawkins seemed to regard as pivotal. According to Hawkins, when he gave a second briefing to Westmoreland, Robert Komer had been present. Komer was Lyndon Johnson's special ambassador to Vietnam. (Along with William Colby, Komer would head the "Pacification" program, whose aim was to neutralize the Vietcong political cadre in the countryside by exposing and sometimes killing them.) It was Komer who had rebuked Hawkins after that second briefing. "He described the briefing as 'Byzantine,' " Hawkins told Crile. Later in the interview Crile reminded Hawkins that he had not believed the military's official estimate of enemy strength but had defended it anyway.

CRILE: Now, those figures were eventually going to be going to the president of the United States.

HAWKINS: That did not bother me in the least, George. The president of the United States had his own special ambassador in Saigon, Mr. Robert Komer. Mr. Komer was intimately familiar with all the details of all the strength figures which had been briefed.

CRILE: And he was one of the people that participated in the decision to block your increased estimates at that meeting when you briefed him?

HAWKINS: He was at the briefing. And . . . the strength figures were not accepted—blocked—

CRILE: So you felt that you knew what the command position was, and you also felt the president had access to the controversy?

HAWKINS: Certainly. He [Komer] had the most sophisticated communications facilities at his disposal. . . .

CRILE: So at least Mr. Komer knew. Ambassador Komer.

HAWKINS: That's correct.

And again, later in the interview, Crile revived the theme, asking Hawkins, "Why should we think that President Johnson knew about this controversy?"

HAWKINS: Because President Johnson had his special representative in Saigon, Mr. Robert Komer, who was at—
CRILE: Ambassador Komer.
HAWKINS: Ambassador Komer, who was acutely aware of every figure that was being presented, every figure that was being accepted, every figure that was being rejected or not approved. Thoroughly, completely aware. And you must assume that he was reporting—
CRILE: Back to the White House.
HAWKINS: To the White House. Else why was he there?

In his blue sheet Crile had revealed that he, like Adams, believed President Johnson had known about the faking and the suppression of enemy-strength figures, and promised to find out. At Colloff's second screening, the CBS vice-president had reminded Crile to take the investigation, if possible, into the White House. And here, in the unedited official transcript, Col. Gains Hawkins, CBS's primary military witness against Westmoreland, was telling Crile in no uncertain terms that Lyndon Johnson knew *everything*—had to know, since his special envoy Robert Komer did. Klein could not wait to talk to Crile, to ascertain whether indeed Komer had revealed what the president knew.

"What did Komer say?" Klein asked Crile, reviewing what he himself had read in the Hawkins transcript.

"We're talking to Komer's assistant," Crile replied, then changed the subject.

Klein persisted, asking Crile over and over whether and when he intended to interview Komer. "I was totally ignored," Klein recalled later.

Klein kept on reading transcripts, a portion of an interview here, a segment of another there. The more he read, the more disturbed he became. The premise of the broadcast was that Westmoreland had led a *conspiracy*. In the blue sheet, which Klein had finally obtained and read, Crile said that, in the course of Adams's research, Sam had become "a kind of father confessor" to the whistle-blowers. "Many wept when they told him their stories. . . . They all spoke on the record and acknowledged their part in the conspiracy. And most of them," Crile added, "spoke of it in just those terms—as having participated in a conspiracy."

Yet no CBS interviewee ever used the word conspiracy, nor did Crile ever ask whether the word was an appropriate description of the events being scrutinized. The testimony on camera to CBS was usually that reports or estimates were "not accepted." Nevertheless, Klein had to trust Crile's judgment. It was the producer who was conducting the research, not Klein. Klein did not know the details of the investigation; perhaps knowledgeable off-camera sources were confirming the conspiracy premise in spades. Ira Klein was relying on George Crile as an airplane passenger relies on a pilot.

Besides, Crile was constantly telling him that Executive Producer Howard Stringer and Vice-President Colloff were reading the transcripts. Surely Colloff and Stringer would discover the contradictions and the omissions, and the scattered references to Robert Komer, Director of Intelligence Production Col. Charles Morris, his boss Gen. Philip Davidson, and the CIA's George Carver. Even if his faith in George Crile was wavering, Klein could still trust Crile's superiors. What Klein did not realize was that Colloff and Stringer were as utterly dependent on the producer's judgment as he; they, too, were passengers on this blindly plowing plane.

George Crile never did interview Robert Komer for his Vietnam broadcast. But on July 24, in New York, Mike Wallace met another high-ranking ex-Johnson Administration official. Walt Rostow had been Lyndon Johnson's gatekeeper, controlling the flow of information to the president from Vietnam. Rostow assured Wallace that Johnson was fully informed about the debate over enemy strength. He told Wallace that Johnson "knew that starting in the autumn of 1967 . . . the North Vietnamese regulars were infiltrating at a higher rate." The president, Rostow said, "was following the number of the particular North Vietnamese units that were coming down, which he got straight from communications intelligence" that Rostow characterized as "of an unimpeachable kind."

On the Order of Battle controversy Rostow told Wallace: "The point is [Johnson] did understand that . . . there was a debate, and it was a debate essentially about whether they had underestimated in the past the scale of that category that you just described to me [guerilla militia and political cadre]." Rostow told Wallace that the president "was fully informed" over the higher estimates held by the CIA. He told Wallace that Johnson was fully apprised of the forthcoming all-out enemy attack, and that Johnson committed a critical error by not forewarning the American public.

> WALLACE: And conceivably—conceivably—he [Johnson] didn't know how much heavy fighting lay ahead because he was—be-

cause the books had been cooked. Because the bad news had not been sent forward.

ROSTOW: Now, there you are wrong. He absorbed all of this intelligence—

WALLACE: This intelligence didn't come to him!

ROSTOW: You're quite wrong. It did get to—you're wrong, Mike. Don't keep saying things that are not so. Because—let me nail it down. I sent out early in December of '67 a cable saying evidently we're going to see a maximum effort.

WALLACE: Early in—?

ROSTOW: December of '67.

WALLACE: Right.

ROSTOW (recalling the cable he sent): I want your evaluation of the nature of the offensive, and I want [an] estimate also [of] whether it's going to result in possibility of negotiations afterwards.

WALLACE: [Indistinct.]

ROSTOW: Saigon sent back a cable saying this is a maximum effort. We will never have seen anything like it before. The CIA—said no, it's more—rather more the same. This is a matter of record, and I'm going to give you the documents.

Rostow did not have to give Wallace the Saigon reply to his request for an "evaluation of the nature of the offensive" he had anticipated. CBS already had it. That reply from Saigon was the memo submitted by Joe Hovey, Sam Adams's old pal and CBS's first on-camera interview for the broadcast. The "Hovey memo" had been written at Walt Rostow's behest. Hovey had not been a lonely voice "predicting" the Tet offensive; he had been fleshing out and confirming a thesis already being advanced in the White House. The Johnson White House, Rostow was arguing, was fully informed that the enemy was marshaling its forces for an all-out assault, and was anticipating an opportunity for negotiations that might result after the enemy's inevitable defeat.

Rostow lectured Wallace as if the correspondent were a schoolboy who had not studied his lesson. "You must take this seriously," Rostow told Wallace. "You are going to damage the country and get it wrong." Rostow insisted that the Order of Battle debate consuming CBS's time and money was a tempest in a teapot since Johnson and the White House had never depended on the military's Order of Battle as the sole source of intelligence on enemy strength. He told Wallace that the raw materials flowed directly into the White House: provincial reports from the CIA, State Department, and AID officers; day-by-day battle reports; National Security Agency (NSA) communications intercepts; captured documents; assessments by Australians and other knowledgeable foreign observers in Vietnam; POW interrogations. All this raw unexpurgated data flowed directly into the White House. "The president," said Rostow, "was a voracious reader and absorbed this flow. . . ."

Early in the interview, between camera rolls, Wallace had promised Rostow: "When you see the evidence we have collected, you will be amazed, angered, and convinced that you and the president were 'had.' " Clearly, Rostow was not convinced. His tone became more and more condescending, in the face of what he obviously regarded as Wallace's utter ignorance of "the facts." Wallace became more and more frustrated. He stopped following Crile's question script. Afterwards, Klein recalled, "George told me that by jumping around and not following the questions in chronological order, Mike had 'made a mess of it.' "

Three days after the interview Rostow sent a letter to Crile and Wallace giving them his "reflections on our joint three-hour seminar." The opening point Rostow made was, "I believe it essential that you try to get [Ambassador Ellsworth] Bunker and Komer on tape. Bob was at the center of the reconstruction of affairs after Tet."

After the Rostow interview Wallace returned to his summer retreat on Cape Cod's Martha's Vineyard, then embarked on a trip to China. "I kept asking, 'Let me see the assembly on Rostow,' " he recalled later, "[but] I never saw it. I was under the impression Stringer, Lack, and Colloff had screened it."

None of the executives "screened" the assembled Rostow takes. However, Colloff and Stringer would read the Rostow transcript—Colloff the document in its entirety, and Stringer segments.

It was also during July that Crile revealed the premise of his documentary to an old family friend—Paul Nitze. Nitze was a former secretary of the Navy, and deputy secretary of defense from 1967–69 under Robert McNamara. (In 1981, he became head of the U.S. negotiating team at the Geneva arms-control talks.) Nitze had been intimately familiar with the details of the Order of Battle dispute. Later, in a sworn affidavit, Nitze recalled his encounter with Crile, and his reaction to Crile's "conspiracy."

"I told Mr. Crile," said Nitze, "that I believed that his thesis was incorrect and tried to discourage him from doing the documentary."

The Rostow interview was the final one filmed for the broadcast. Through July the Vietnam unit kept laboring long hours, with Crile and Klein working on weekends as well. Meanwhile, Crile's appearances in the editing room were becoming even more unpredictable. At the beginning of August, Klein learned why: Crile had been assigned the correspondent's role in a CBS evening news segment. Around August 1 Crile departed for Miami to pursue that story. It was obvious to the members of Crile's Vietnam unit that there would be no September airing of their broadcast.

For the next month Crile was shuttling back and forth between Miami and New York. And even when Crile was in New York, with two current CBS projects to juggle (and a third, a Miami drug trade documentary, pending), his work habits—never a paragon of orderliness—fell into further disarray. On one brief visit back to CBS, for example, Crile asked Klein to screen some cassettes for him containing material from *CIA: The Secret Army*, the documentary he had co-produced with Judy Crichton. Klein screened those tapes for Crile; then, together, they left the editing room.

"Thanks for taking the time," Crile said.

"Aren't you leaving something behind?" Klein said.

Crile had forgotten his precious cassettes.

Crile's momentary amnesia that day was not an isolated event. In order to achieve some progress on the Vietnam project, Klein suggested to Crile that he take back to Miami with him the interview transcripts so that he could study them in his spare time. Crile did so. One day he returned to New York from Miami; Carolyne McDaniel, Crile's secretary, rushed into Klein's editing room. "George forgot all the transcripts," she told Klein breathlessly. Crile had left behind in a Miami motel room the transcripts of this sensitive show. Luckily, Carolyne was able to locate them and arrange for their shipment to New York.

Carolyne, in particular, was bearing the brunt of Crile's absences. More and more she was being forced to assume the role not just of secretary but of surrogate mother. There were occasions at CBS when Crile did not want to suffer the solitude of a lonely nighttime vigil, catching up on work that had accumulated during a trip to Miami. He would tell Carolyne: "I don't want to be alone; just sit here while I work." Carolyne would keep him company, comforting the producer as a mother would her child, passing time by straightening up his cluttered office.

During the same period that Crile was assuming new obligations, immersing himself in two other CBS projects in addition to the Vietnam broadcast, and Carolyne was becoming more and more harassed at having to keep those conflicting commitments untangled, another member of the unit was confronting a critical career decision. In the course of his work on the broadcast Alex Alben, the twenty-three-year-old researcher, had become friends with Sam Adams. From time to time Alben would visit acquaintances in Washington, D.C., and then drive farther south to

Adams's farm nearby in Virginia. Alben admired Adams; for a while he was even considering a career in the CIA. But Alben was more interested in exploring the possibility of a career in television news. He was bright and well read. He was growing dissatisfied with the menial nature of his job as a researcher—telephoning the LBJ Library in Texas in search of photos and compiling data that could be included in chronologies. Alben's status in the production pecking order was summed up by a cartoon he had pinned to the wall of his office. It showed a harried flunky, overburdened with documents, attempting to satisfy an implacable superior. Alben was being run ragged confirming Crile's and Adams's conspiracy premise.

It was during this period that Alben expressed to Crile his interest in becoming an associate producer in the CBS News organization. He had decided that if he could not further his career at CBS, he would leave and attend law school. He met with Crile in the producer's office. Alben told Crile he was thinking of writing a letter to Howard Stringer revealing his ambition of a more responsible assignment in the CBS production hierarchy after the Vietnam project was completed. Alben wanted Crile's counsel on how to approach Stringer about becoming an associate producer. Crile reminded Alben that he lacked the necessary apprenticeship.

"You have a problem," Crile told him, "because you don't have any experience in the editing room."

"Well," Alben replied, "hopefully I'll gain that experience during this project."

Crile then informed Alben that he was "banned" from the editing room. Alben soon afterward decided to enroll in Stanford University Law School. He would be leaving CBS at the end of August.

Adams was not allowed to be present when Crile and Klein were editing. Now Alben had been quarantined from the process of putting together the film. Crile could not effectively bar Joe Zigman from the cutting room. However, the veteran associate producer refused to adapt his decades-long nine-to-five routine to suit Crile's arbitrary schedule. By the time Crile turned up in Klein's editing room, Zigman was usually subway-bound toward his sanctuary in Brooklyn. Ironically, though, at the very moment that Crile was narrowing access to the editing room, he was ushering in someone who was not even a CBS employee. One weekend the woman who lived with Crile stopped by. Sue Lyne worked for a Manhattan film company.

At first Sue would show up at CBS on a weekend, meeting Crile at the end of his working day. She would sit in the editing room as Crile and Klein toiled over a film segment. Then occasionally she began to offer her opinions. Klein was cordial and polite to her. She seemed intelligent and amiable.

It was in the middle of August that Crile, back from a visit to Miami, found a lengthy memo from Walt Rostow in his mail. In that "Memorandum for the Record," Rostow reviewed what he and Wallace had discussed in their interview, reiterating several points he felt were important. Attached to the memorandum was a cover letter, which concluded with this postscript:

"P. S. While this letter was being typed I was given a copy of Sam Adams's article in *Harper's*, May 1975. I find it astonishing that Adams seems wholly unaware of the Saigon-CIA estimates of December 1967 of the coming [Tet] offensive, Westmoreland's pinpointing of Tet as the time for the offensive and redisposition of United States forces before the event, etcetera. He is, quite simply, wrong, so far as the White House is concerned, that the Tet offensive was the 'biggest surprise to American intelligence since Pearl Harbor.' "

Wallace received Rostow's Memorandum for the Record, and immediately submitted it to Crile. Crile read the document and sent Mike a memo, concluding:

"I don't see anything to worry about in the points he raises. I think he's worried and trying to build a record to draw on later. We are trying to locate his cover letter to LBJ (which he denied having written in his interview with you). If we do find it, he won't have any credibility at all. What it will prove (would prove) is that Rostow was purposefully distorting intelligence going to LBJ. . . ."

A week or so later Crile sent another memo to Wallace summarizing a telephone conversation he had initiated with Rostow on August 25, ". . . to tell him that his summary of our position was way off base. . . ."

Crile had still made no effort to insert any Rostow takes into the sequences he and Klein were editing for the broadcast. In fact, during this period Crile was not really contributing to the progress of his documentary, his commitment having been splintered by the conflicting demands of the CBS hard-news segment and the *CBS Reports* investigation into the Miami drug trade. Until then Klein had only to concentrate on cutting the stock-footage sequences and the film itself. Now along with worrying about the film he would have to worry about the people who were making it. The more frequent Crile's trips to Miami and the less that was accomplished on the Vietnam broadcast, the lower the unit's morale plummeted. Joe Zigman would sit in Klein's editing room saying over and over, "How are we going to get this thing done?" Carolyne was growing more and more distracted, serving as Crile's travel agent/mother/nurse along with her secretarial duties. Without the glue of the producer's presence to bind them together, the core group was fragmenting. And all the while Klein was reading interview transcripts. He had never seen the raw uncut interview footage, which had been pulled by Crile and Hurwitz before he joined the project. Only now, reading those full interview transcripts, was he beginning to comprehend the contradictions between what some witnesses seemed to be saying in their selected takes and what they in fact had told Crile and Wallace during the course of their actual interviews. Klein was beginning to feel that something was wrong with the broadcast—and starting to wonder what he should do about it.

Klein would vent his doubts to Zigman. Zigman would smile and caution him, "Ira, don't do anything without first talking to Ziggie." The line became a running refrain between them. "Ira, don't—" "I know, don't do anything without first talking to Ziggie."

It was in late August, when Klein had finally decided that the documentary was in serious trouble editorially, that he received a telephone call from a close friend who used to work for the *New York Times*. "Where in hell have you been?" the friend said. He had been trying to telephone Klein at odd hours but had never found him at home. "I know you're working on some project," the friend added.

Without revealing the actual nature of the broadcast he was editing, Klein confided to his friend that he felt there was something desperately wrong. He was reading the transcripts, and they simply did not make sense when compared to the sequences Crile was cutting. He was also reading a book called *Tet* by Don Oberdorfer. Three years after the event Oberdorfer had written that "it is clear that the attack forces . . . suffered a grievous military setback. . . . The Vietcong lost the best of a generation of resistance fighters. . . . The war became increasingly a conventional battle and less an insurgency. Because the residents in the cities did not rise up against the foreigners and puppets at Tet—indeed, they gave little support to the attack force—the Communist claim to a moral and political authority in South Vietnam suffered a serious blow." In contrast, the implication embedded in the documentary was that, as a result of the suppression and fakery of enemy-strength estimates, the United States military had narrowly averted defeat and at best had achieved a Pyrrhic victory.

By the end of August Crile's hard-news segment had aired. Even though he was now usually to be found in New York, he still was devoting only part of his time to the Vietnam broadcast. Klein was in his editing room one evening cutting a sequence when Crile turned up. The producer sat down on an editing stool next to Klein. Klein was fed up with the delays and the disappearances. Unable to control his tongue, he turned to Crile and said, "Why are you doing this? Why, *why* are you doing this to all these individuals who have supported you, the executives you've made believe in the project?" Forget about CBS's money, Klein told him. "How can you be so inconsiderate to these individuals who've really stuck out their necks? How could you do this to them?"

Crile was sitting with his head against the wall, eyes locked on the ceiling. "I'm sorry," he said again and again.

"You've betrayed our relationship," Klein said.

Crile's voice grew smaller, his face taking on a forlorn look. He was like a child being punished. "I was just unrealistic," he replied. "I was being unrealistic."

At this juncture, of the broadcast's six proposed acts three were in decent order, one hardly organized, and the other two still nonexistent. Although a September broadcast date was now out of the question, there was no way of knowing exactly when CBS would order the program on the air, or with how little notice. Klein wanted to quit, to get out, drop this damned documentary in George Crile's lap. But he could not leave the other members of the unit in the lurch. "Okay," Klein said, "let's do the best we can."

Klein could have laid the broadcast's problems in the laps of Crile's superiors. But he was not going to usurp Crile's authority, since doing so would only levy additional anxiety and pressure on a producer already overextended beyond his strength and his ability. So Klein continued editing the stock-footage reconstruction of the Vietnam War. It was evident by now that one of CBS's lengthiest interviews, and one conducted by the chief correspondent Mike Wallace, was doomed to be discarded completely. Crile had decided that not a single moment of Wallace's interview with Walt Rostow merited air time in his documentary.

"I agonized over whether to use Rostow," Crile would say later. "I finally had to drop him for time. . . . The problem was Rostow was contradictory and in some places unresponsive. . . . The Rostow interview was a colossal problem for us to cope with."

Wallace supported Crile's decision to "kill" the Rostow interview entirely. "Rostow and LBJ were not our story," said Wallace. "Our story was that the 'books were cooked.' "

Indeed, LBJ and Rostow *were* the CBS story, or at least a crucial aspect. Rostow had assured Crile that Johnson was aware of the specifics of the debate between the CIA and military intelligence over enemy-strength figures, which was the subject of the broadcast. Rostow had argued that the president was fully aware of the fact that the military and the CIA had a serious disagreement over how to count the enemy. If both sets of figures reached the White House, from whom was Westmoreland concealing intelligence?

"The point is," CBS soft-news vice-president Roger Colloff would explain later, "that Rostow says LBJ knew there was a debate between [the military] and the CIA, but Rostow basically consigned this to a technician's dispute. . . . Never does he say in the interview that LBJ was aware of the scope, of guys within [military intelligence] not being given a chance to express dissent."

"The one thing I asked Rostow, and very specifically," Crile said later, "I said, 'Did anybody ever grab the president by the lapels and say: The base of the enemy is much, much bigger than we previously said?' Rostow simply said to me that he did not know of that." Crile added that "the real issue was . . . whether evidence of a larger enemy than had been previously acknowledged and whether evidence of a massive infiltration buildup in the fall of 1967 had been suppressed or manipulated. Rostow basically absented himself from that."

The truth is, though, Rostow did not "absent himself"; he expressed again and again skepticism over whether any such faking or suppression had occurred. Crile's logic was more appropriate to a journalist Alice might have met in Wonderland: He had discarded the Rostow interview because Rostow was unable to shed any light on a conspiracy he was convinced never occurred.

Rostow had offered overwhelming evidence that Lyndon Johnson was familiar with the military–CIA debate and the raw intelligence both sides had marshaled in their favor. Unless Rostow's testimony was seriously challenged (something CBS never accomplished, before or after the broadcast), it was clear from his interview that Johnson was so fully cognizant of the events in question that he could not possibly have been ignorant of the "conspiracy" itself. But despite Roger Colloff's exhortation to Crile to take his investigation into the White House, CBS decided to leave Rostow on the cutting-room floor. Perhaps it was only the special demands of the television business itself—a broadcast's need for both ratings and current relevance—that hoisted a living general rather than a dead president to the apex of CBS's conspiracy.

6

The
Stringer
Screening

IN THE EARLY WEEKS OF SEPTEMBER Crile began to channel his energies into the documentary being produced for *CBS Reports* by Maurice Murad. Its focus was the drug trade in Miami, which had swelled after an influx of Cuban immigrants who landed in south Florida in response to President Jimmy Carter's open-house invitation. Crile was useful to Murad because of his contacts among Cuban emigrés, a relationship forged during his research for the *Harper's* article, the seed of his first project at CBS, *CIA: The Secret Army*. The Murad drug show was important to Crile because in this full-hour broadcast he would serve as the correspondent. In the course of his visits to Miami he had also discovered the nucleus of a documentary he might produce after the Vietnam program aired. He had met a man named Ricardo Morales, an ex-operative of the CIA, the FBI, and the Venezuelan intelligence service. Crile felt that Morales's "story would make an interesting documentary." Morales agreed to a series of taped interviews. Eventually Crile would record Morales's tale, using both sides of thirty-eight audio cassettes.

Klein was still unaware of Crile's involvement in the Murad drug trade project. He did not know that when Crile disappeared during this period he was usually merely a few doors away, in Murad's office. He did not know that Murad had been given orders to start filming his broadcast by November 1, only two months away. Crile and Murad were meeting regularly to set up a shooting schedule and to discuss the nature of the film they were going to make, a program that would give Crile another opportunity to earn the on-air credit as a correspondent that he craved. All Klein knew was that too often when he needed Crile the producer was nowhere to be found.

From time to time when Crile *was* present, Grace Diekhaus would come into Klein's editing room. Klein welcomed her visits. Diekhaus was a CBS veteran, her work well respected. She provided reinforcement for Crile, who did not seem fully secure about his own judgments as a filmmaker. Diekhaus seemed to relieve the producer's anxiety and helped resolve his fits of indecisiveness. Even when Crile was not present Diekhaus would enter Klein's editing room, not to offer any comments on the work in progress but merely to use the cutting room as a sanctuary. In early September she was starting a new CBS News program, *Up to the Minute*. She was working long hours under enormous pressures, assembling a large staff. One day she came into the room and flopped onto an editing stool, obviously exhausted. Grace began telling Klein about her problems: the headaches of inventing a brand-new program under the weight of a rapidly approaching deadline.

"You think *you* have problems," Klein said. "I've given up. I can no longer get through to George."

In recent weeks Diekhaus had been assuming a more and more prominent role in Klein's relationship with Crile. She was becoming both a buffer and a conduit, her presence relieving the growing estrangement of the editor and the producer. Klein regarded her fundamental understanding of filmmaking as a timely asset to help overcome what he felt was Crile's inexperience in putting together a film. Later, Bob Chandler would sum up Crile's weaknesses as a filmmaker. "I think he tended to be more concerned about the content, which is fine, than the technical aspects of the production, of how one sets up the cameras and shoots scenes, the visual look of a broadcast," said the CBS vice-president. Diekhaus had competence in that area of filmmaking, and Klein had come to rely on her as a positive influence on Crile.

"I've had it," Klein told Diekhaus that day in his editing room. "I'm at the end of the line. I can't do anything with him." Buried in Klein's words was a coded plea; he was asking Diekhaus to intercede not only on his behalf but to benefit the entire Vietnam unit. Subliminally he was saying: Listen, try to talk to him. The project is falling apart.

Grace stood up. "Listen, Ira," she said, "your reputation here is what it is. You have nothing to be concerned about."

"I'm not concerned about my reputation," Klein said. "I'm only concerned about getting this project completed, done, over with."

By the second week in September the relationship between producer and editor had grown even more strained; it was clear that Crile was aware of Klein's disenchantment. One afternoon Klein entered Crile's office and sat down. Crile said, "You must have worked with a lot of weak producers."

"Not exactly," Klein replied cautiously. Klein understood what Crile was insinuating: Klein was being too assertive, asking too many questions.

Crile then launched a discussion about another editor with whom he had worked, Joe Fackovec, who had been associated with CBS for more than a decade. A towering bear of a man, congenial and charming, Fackovec was beloved by all those who collaborated with him. He had the reputation of being dependable, reliable, technically proficient, and always *there*. Crile raised his hands, palms outward, waving them at Klein. "Joe Fackovec," Crile said, "is just a pair of hands."

Klein sat there trying to fathom Crile's drift. Obviously the discussion about Fackovec was a preamble; Crile was preparing him for something, but what? Moments later Klein found out: Crile told him he had decided to cut a lengthy section of the stock-footage sequence Klein had constructed to open Act 1 of the broadcast. The purpose of that stock footage at the start of Act 1 was to reintroduce the viewer to the Vietnam War. Using bits and pieces of film, Klein had created an elaborate opening— helicopter gunships lifting off, their bellies brimming with ashen-faced American soldiers grimly embarking on some jungle foray against the enemy. The helicopters rose, resting momentarily on a cushion of dust clouds before disappearing into the distance. Landing at the edge of the jungle, they opened their hatches to spill out troops with weapons primed to fire at the invisible enemy lurking under cover perhaps only yards away. And then other soldiers disembarked, trudging fatalistically toward the dark, dangerous foliage, penetrating the jungle and being instantly swallowed by it. Still the cameras pursued them. A viewer could feel the tension as the men stopped to listen to the eerie sounds, then plunged further and further into a mystery mined with death. This was the guerilla war.

In order to cut that sequence Klein had had to locate shots that matched in tone and texture, creating out of stock footage a film segment that subtly shifted from light to darkness. It was a complicated task and a painstaking one. Diekhaus had seen the sequence and had called it "extraordinary"; Crile had also expressed his enthusiasm. Now Crile wanted to eliminate the sequence.

It was the producer's prerogative to make whatever changes he wanted, but Klein felt that the neglect and inconsideration Crile had shown—his disappearances, his erratic working schedule—were now having an impact on the broadcast itself. CBS might set an air date at any time. Now all Crile could really do was tell the story in its most simple terms, sacrificing some of the filmic subtleties that Klein and others had labored over so diligently. And Crile was making that decision unilaterally, without first consulting his editor. "Take it out," Crile told Klein.

Klein suspected that Crile expected him to show his anger. Instead Klein said, "If that's your decision, I'll take it out."

Klein walked back to his editing room and told Phyllis Hurwitz. "You're kidding," she said.

Klein and Crile were not the only ones concerned over the Vietnam film's lack of progress. Zigman kept saying to Klein, "How are we going to get this project done?" The unit was now without a researcher. Alex Alben had left before September 1 to matriculate at Stanford University Law School in California. And Carolyne was leaning ever closer toward the edge of hysteria. During that whole second week of September, at Crile's direction, she was running back and forth between the Ford building, where the CBS Reports department was located, and the Broadcast Center on the far side of 57th Street. Crile had to write opening narration to introduce the film. There was a library in the CBS Broadcast Center, and Carolyne, forced to assume duties that Alex Alben would have performed, was searching for articles on the Vietnam War. Crile had instructed her to write paragraphs from ancient magazine reportage, using as many superlatives as she could. Crile wanted something sensational he could rehash into something exciting to initiate his broadcast.

When Carolyne was not scurrying between the Broadcast Center and the Ford building, she was often in Klein's editing room attempting to convince him to listen to a conversation Crile had taped with a high-ranking government official. On several occasions from September through October, according to Klein, she tried to entice him into listening to Crile's tapes of interviews with ex-Secretary of Defense Robert McNamara. Klein was surprised when Carolyne told him that Crile had succeeded in talking to McNamara, who had avoided commenting on the conduct of the Vietnam War since his days as a Johnson cabinet member. Carolyne revealed to Klein that she had actually heard the tapes. At least four times, Klein recalled, Carolyne came in and told him that he *had* to listen to them. Carolyne knew by then that Klein was skeptical about Crile's conspiracy premise; from what Carolyne told him, Klein concluded that those McNamara tapes were "going to confirm the fact that McNamara was telling George that he's making a big deal out of nothing." However, Klein refused Carolyne's offer each time. He realized that Crile did not know that Carolyne had listened to those tapes. Carolyne kept on insisting. "I know where the tapes are," she told Klein. "They're in the bottom left-hand drawer of George's desk." But Klein never did listen to the McNamara tapes.

Klein heard that executive producer Howard Stringer was beginning to ask to see some of the film. "We've got to get this film prepared to be screened at some level by October first," he told Crile. Zigman was in the room when Klein added, "And what we have to do to get it done by then is hire an additional editor."

"If you want to go into Howard and explain to him why we need another editor," Crile replied, "feel free to do it."

Klein ignored the suggestion; he felt that Crile was just testing him to see if he indeed was so dissatisfied with the project's progress that he might be considering talking to Stringer. But it was not his responsibility to go to Stringer, it was Crile's. "The thing to do," Klein said, "is hire Joe Fackovec and have him cut the interviews on the last two acts with you. I'll cut the film sequences, and I'll hand them over to Joe to put in the film," he added.

Crile agreed. He left the room. Zigman looked at Klein. Zigman was leaning over an editing table, supporting his weight with his hands. He said, "All George wanted to know was whether you were going in to Howard. And that," Zigman added emphatically, "was *all* George wanted to know."

If Klein had gone to Stringer the executive producer might have become concerned over the progress of the program and immediately demanded to see what Crile had completed. And at that moment, two weeks into September and more than a year after the project had been initiated, there was absolutely no polished film that Crile could have screened for him. Instead, as Klein had anticipated, Crile himself went to Stringer and obtained permission to hire another editor. Joe Fackovec would begin working on the project after Stringer's early-October screening.

A few days later Crile convened his unit—Klein, McDaniel, Hurwitz, Zigman—in Klein's editing room. Crile was sitting on the edge of one of the editing tables. He began to address the unit, apologizing profusely for having to take time off, apologizing because the program had fallen so far off schedule. . . . And now a rough cut had to be completed by October 1 so that Stringer could screen it. Zigman, Klein, and all the members of the Vietnam project sat there listening to their leader. They realized what it would take to ready the film for a screening. It meant two weeks of nonstop effort with no weekends off.

Crile detailed what had to be done—the marathon task ahead of them to finish a draft of this film in two weeks. When he stopped speaking, Zigman walked over to a wall and yanked off a calendar. Zigman began trying to compute a definite schedule: Act 1 had to be completed by such and such a date; to stay on schedule, Act 2 would have to be finished three days later. . . . Zigman was calculating a schedule on the spot and kept encountering the same obstacle. No matter how he divided the two weeks, assigning a number of days to each act, *he could not find enough days*. Zigman would say, "Okay, you've got three days for Act One, that's the eighteenth of September; four days for Act Two, that's the twenty-second. . . ." Each time he would run out of days and have to revamp his calculations. Zigman was growing more nervous, a note of desperation coloring his voice. . . . Klein sat there. He did not say a word. Although in his view it was absurdly and ludicrously late, Crile finally seemed to be making an honest effort to get the broadcast done. Klein knew that, working together, the unit could accomplish the objective.

The decision was made to prepare three of the five acts for Executive Producer Howard Stringer. Those three acts would be sufficient for Stringer to develop a "feel" of the entire broadcast. The unit would keep on assembling the other acts but would concentrate on the first three. But Zigman, clutching the calendar in his hands, still kept running out of days, and in his near panic he was exacerbating an already difficult situation. Zigman had been internalizing his uneasiness about the program. Now it seemed the concerns consuming him were shattering his outward shell of complacency.

During the next two weeks the unit worked tirelessly, preparing something that could be screened for Howard Stringer at the beginning of October. Grace Diekhaus was coming into the editing room even more frequently now. Exhausted from her grueling *Up to the Minute* schedule, she would nevertheless find time to pop in at night to give Crile counsel and support. Soon Grace was visiting on Saturdays, too. On Sundays, however, Grace never appeared in Klein's editing room. Sundays belonged to George's friend, Sue Lyne. Around the halls of *CBS Reports*, people called Grace and Sue "Clark Kent and Superman," because no one ever saw them in the same place at the same time.

Sue would show up, pull out a CBS note pad, and interject herself into whatever discussion was taking place between Crile and Klein. She would offer suggestions—what in the film "worked" for her, which elements did not. Klein was not happy about Sue's visits; he did not need to work by committee, especially when a third of that coalition was someone not employed by CBS, someone who did not understand the standards of documentary filmmaking. Lyne was not a CBS journalist.

On those Sunday visits Lyne would compose paragraphs with Crile for the narrative that Wallace would eventually record. There were three available editing rooms; Klein used two, Lyne and Crile would sit in the third, working. At one point Klein and Crile were cutting a scene of a 1960s demonstration at the Pentagon. When Klein left his editing room to speak to Crile, he found Lyne with the producer, typing away. Klein ran some footage on an editing machine; Crile read aloud the narrative passage he and Lyne had composed. "It doesn't work," Klein suggested. "Yeah," Lyne agreed, "it doesn't work." More and more Crile was doing what Bob Chandler had warned him not to do: He was leaning on others as a crutch. Klein was growing more and more resigned. If the screening for Stringer was not a success, it was the producer who would have to pay the piper.

The two-week marathon finally ended. The night before the Stringer screening, Klein worked late. It did not matter. In the morning, finally, Howard Stringer would review a significant segment of the broadcast. Stringer, who had certainly been reading the transcripts all along, would be able to see for the first time how Crile, in Klein's estimation, had perverted their content. Klein was leaving the eighth-floor bathroom when, at the threshold, he encountered Crile.

"I've decided that we're not going to screen for Howard," Crile said.

Klein stared at him for a moment. Then he shook his head in disbelief and walked out the door. Like Klein, Crile was thoroughly fatigued. But that was the nature of the television-news business, a vocation in which there were always deadlines that had to be met. Klein accepted the marathoning and the pressures. What Klein could not accept, after all that suffering and toil and turmoil, was Crile's decision to arbitrarily postpone Stringer's screening. He walked into his editing room. Joe Zigman, the associate producer, was standing there along with Phyllis Hurwitz, the assistant film editor. Klein said, "Joe, you're not going to believe this. George has just told me that we're not screening for Howard."

Zigman became upset. He went to the elevator bank searching for Crile, who had gone for coffee to the ninth floor. Zigman was waiting for him when he got off the elevator. Zigman was more than merely disturbed; he was nearly incoherent. He kept telling Crile, "We have to screen for Howard, we have to, don't you understand? We have to screen for Howard. . . ."

Klein was sitting at an editing table when Crile entered. "What's wrong with Zigman?" Crile said.

"What's wrong with *Zigman?*" Klein said.

Crile walked out and went to see Howard Stringer. Stringer insisted on seeing the film. Crile came back. He told Klein that the screening would indeed take place. However, he added, he did not want Zigman to be present during the screening, and he wanted Klein to tell him.

"Zigman is the associate producer of this film," Klein said, fighting to keep his voice controlled "and he's going to expect to be present at the screening. He's *expected* to be here. If you don't think he should be here," Klein added, "*you* go and tell him."

Crile did not tell Zigman, nor is it likely that Zigman would have obeyed such an order from Crile anyway. Zigman was worried; he was reaching the end of his tether, the far side of his tolerance.

That morning Crile, Klein, and Zigman would join Howard Stringer for the screening. Klein felt relieved that Stringer would be seeing at least a portion of the assembled documentary. Stringer had been intimately, if occasionally, involved in the project since its inception. It was to Stringer that Crile had brought the idea of his broadcast sometime in the summer of 1980. It was to Stringer that Crile had submitted preliminary paragraphs before actually writing the blue sheet. It was Stringer who had convinced Bob Chandler that Crile should be allowed the opportunity to produce this program, overcoming Chandler's own reservations about Crile's readiness to work alone. Klein had been told that Stringer was reading the transcripts; he was confident that Stringer would be able to identify the broadcast's problems.

At about 10:30 A.M. Stringer arrived—graying, handsome, wearing a dress shirt and loosely knotted tie. There was a certain strangeness in Stringer's overseeing this documentary about a conspiracy engineered by a general of Westmoreland's historical stature. In other circumstances, given Stringer's own grasp of history and the tricks it plays, he might have been the first to appreciate the irony. Although few of his colleagues knew it, Stringer had grown up as the English equivalent of an American "army brat." The son of a career Royal Air Force officer, he said later, "I spent my entire childhood into early adulthood living on military bases." His father's friends "were the equivalent rank of general." As a teenager he had spent five years in the British ROTC, rising to the highest rank, regimental sergeant major of the entire corps. "In that capacity," Stringer said, he had "entertained generals ranging from field marshal rank all the way down to vice-marshal. And since I had a happy childhood," he added, "many of these individuals are still friends."

Nevertheless, it is clear that Stringer's positive attitude toward the general class of officers had been modified by close contact with the American breed, in his role of executive producer of CBS's five-part *The Defense of the United States* series, which CBS had begun airing that past

June. Stringer had become intimately involved in that project, helping to turn it into a successful one. He had not been impressed by the forthrightness of the generals he had met during the production of that program.

It was that ambitious series that had occupied much of Stringer's time during the first half of 1981. The last two months before the *Defense* series went on the air, Stringer would say later, "I did not give this broadcast [the Vietnam program] the attention I should have." During that period the possibility of a career plum had also first been dangled. Dan Rather, a *CBS Reports* correspondent before moving to *60 Minutes*, had assumed sole anchor duties on the CBS evening news, replacing the retiring Walter Cronkite. Rather had discussed with Stringer several times the possibility of his becoming that broadcast's executive producer.

Crile screened for Stringer the first three acts and then told Stringer that the fourth act was almost completed, although, in fact, it had not even been assembled yet. Stringer said very little in response to the film. "How much more have you got?" he asked Crile. Stringer added that it would be difficult for him to provide much feedback until he saw the entire film.

One of the elements Stringer had screened was the McChristian-Hawkins sequence at the close of Act 1—the briefing about which Crile and Klein had argued, with Klein accusing Crile of "cutting Westmoreland short" by limiting his responses and thus preventing him, in Klein's opinion, from adequately explaining why he did not approve Hawkins's briefing. Stringer had read "large portions" of that Hawkins transcript; he had been reading transcripts since early 1981, shortly after the initial batch of interviews had been filmed. However, it was Crile who effectively set the agenda of transcript material that Stringer read; Stringer had been concentrating primarily on the text surrounding the takes that Crile selected to screen for him. "The process of screening excerpts from the interviews enabled me to read extended portions of the transcripts around those excerpts," Stringer explained later. At the same time, though, Stringer's "process" prevented him from encountering those portions of an interview that might contradict or qualify the statements from whistle-blowers that Crile had selected. For instance, Stringer could not recall ever having read those portions of the Hawkins interview that dealt with Lyndon Johnson's special ambassador to Vietnam Robert Komer.

Whatever reservations Stringer had had at the time of this early October screening (and later it would become evident that he indeed had some), he held in check. He wanted Crile to finish the film so that he could review it in its totality.

After the screening Crile said he felt relieved. At least Stringer had not offered any serious objections. One imposing obstacle had been hurdled, but there was a larger one looming a week away when Stringer would again screen footage of the film, this time including the few changes he had requested. Then, during the third week in October, the film would be screened for vice-president Roger Colloff. Whatever changes Colloff requested would have to be inserted before the final and most crucial screening of all. In the first week of November Bill Leonard, the CBS News president, was scheduled to review the entire completed broadcast. It would be the first time Leonard saw any portion of the film; only Leonard could issue the final approval Crile required before the broadcast could be aired.

Shortly after that Stringer screening, at the start of October, Joe Fackovec (the additional editor Klein had asked Crile to hire) joined the Vietnam unit. Klein would concentrate on cutting the stock-footage sequences in acts 4 and 5 and the entire first three acts. Fackovec would lay out and cut all the interview material belonging to the final two acts, 4 and 5, which would be included in the next scheduled screening, again for Howard Stringer. Klein was using a pair of adjoining editing rooms in a cul-de-sac at the end of a corridor. Fackovec, the new editor, would be working in his editing room beyond a bend in that corridor in the main concourse of editing rooms. Early on Fackovec's first morning he had come to Klein's editing room to remove his "trim barrels," a contraption on wheels from which the "trims" (outtakes) were suspended. Fackovec took the trims, and he took the select reels relevant to acts 4 and 5. He particularly made sure that he removed all the material relating to Crile's and Adams's charge that military intelligence in Vietnam had suppressed reports of a large number of infiltrators coming down the Ho Chi Minh Trail in the months before Tet. The infiltration story was going to be told in Act 4, and Crile wanted Fackovec to begin with that act.

The entire first day that Fackovec was on the job, Klein did not see Crile at all. The producer was collaborating with his new editor. At the close of Fackovec's second day, Klein was working in his editing room when he began to hear a familiar sound. There were no carpets on the corridor floors, only linoleum. Klein could hear the sound of wheels squeaking across the linoleum, louder and louder. They were the wheels of the trim barrel heading back toward his editing room. Klein turned off his editing machine and sat there listening; the squeaking of the wheels across the linoleum was growing louder and louder, nearer and nearer. Klein had finally levered Crile into what he regarded as the proper working situation: editing Act 4 with Fackovec and thus leaving him alone. And now Crile was coming back, after less than two days away.

Crile entered Klein's editing room, pushing in front of him the trim barrel with strips of film hanging down and Crile's transcript books piled on top. He started telling Klein how much he had missed him, missed the creative interaction between them, missed—"No way, George," Klein said, interrupting him, "no way. The only way we're going to get this thing done is for you to get back in that room."

Crile's face turned glum, his shoulders sagged. He did not say another word. He turned the trim barrel around and began wheeling it back toward Fackovec's editing room, the trim barrel's wheels squeaking softer and softer over the linoleum like a child's muffled complaints.

After Crile hired Fackovec as an additional editor, Klein began pressuring him to add a researcher to replace Alex Alben, as well. Carolyne was harassed enough servicing Crile's other needs without attempting to assume Alben's researcher role—a position for which she was not qualified. Eventually Crile did "borrow" a researcher from CBS News. His name was Igor Brobowski, an ex-soldier who had actually been in Vietnam during the time of Tet. Crile's reinforced regiment plunged ahead toward the screening scheduled for Howard Stringer.

Crile's friend, Sue Lyne, began to turn up with even greater frequency. Now she was coming into the editing room not only Sundays but at night during the week, too. She was becoming involved more intimately with the actual writing of the narrative that Wallace would record. Lyne was not working with Klein but with Joe Fackovec on acts 4 and 5 of the broadcast. One weekend an editor working on a piece for *Up to the Minute* stopped Klein in the hallway. Her editing room was next to Fackovec's. "Who in hell does George have in that room working on his film?" she asked. The editor could hear Lyne discussing the script with Crile and Fackovec.

It was during this period that Alex Alben was brought back from Stanford University Law School to "sign off" on the film. Crile wanted Alben to signify, as the researcher, that he was satisfied with the broadcast's content. Alben was mailed a ticket by CBS and arrived in New York on a weekend. Adams was in New York at the time, too. They screened the program—acts 1 through 3 virtually completed and acts 4 and 5 in a rough-cut stage. Crile exited the editing room after the screening, leaving Alex Alben, Sam Adams, and Ira Klein behind. Sue Lyne was visiting CBS at the time, wandering around the corridors. The three men began discussing the film, exchanging frank but constructive criticisms and suggesting improvements Crile might make. During their discussion Sue Lyne walked into the room and approached Klein's editing table. She stood there fumbling with some papers. The following day was a Sunday.

Klein had arranged to meet Crile at CBS at 10:00 that morning. Klein was in his editing room waiting for the producer when Crile telephoned.

"Don't listen to Alex and Sam," he told Klein. Crile said he had tried to reach Klein at home the previous evening; he had heard that Alex and Sam had been "bad-mouthing" the broadcast.

Klein was angry. He felt he knew from whom Crile had learned of the discussion. "In the first place," he told Crile, "it's healthy to have this kind of dialogue about the film—that's what filmmaking is really all about. In the second place," he added, "Sue had no business being in the editing room. And I do not want her there anymore!"

The telephone conversation ended. Crile arrived later that day alone, although Sundays were traditionally Sue Lyne days (with Saturdays still reserved for Diekhaus). Crile was very, very angry. "You are totally inflexible," he told Klein. "You are rigid."

Klein defended his decision to bar Sue Lyne from his editing room; he argued that Lyne had no expertise in making documentaries, had not been hired to work on the project, and did not belong in a CBS editing room, especially when members of the project who did belong—Adams and Alben, for instance—already had been quarantined from the editing process. Crile kept insisting that Klein was rigid and inflexible. But Sue Lyne did not turn up in Klein's editing room again, not, at least, until immediately before the second Stringer screening. This time Stringer would be accompanied by the CBS Reports newly appointed senior producer (there previously had been no such position), Andy Lack, who was Stringer's ex-collaborator and personal friend. But before Crile screened his finished film for Stringer and Lack, he was going to show it to his chief correspondent, Mike Wallace.

7

Mike Wallace: Hired Hand

IN ITS INFANCY television news was collected and delivered by men and women who had apprenticed as print journalists. It was only natural that these pioneer broadcasters should appropriate their job descriptions from the print media. Thus, decades later, the credits of a 60 *Minutes* or a CBS documentary would call Mike Wallace a "correspondent," as if he were a newspaper reporter who rooted out a story, wrote it, then (after filtering it through the rewrite desk) was able to point proudly to the published product bearing his by-line as irrefutably his own. Nothing could be farther from the truth.

In television hard news (mainly the scheduled daily broadcasts of the three networks and their independent over-the-air and cable competitors) the correspondent does mimic the method of his newspaper or magazine counterpart, ferreting out a story and then recording it. However, in a 60 *Minutes* magazine format or in a documentary more often it is the producer who is the real reporter. The producer and his staff research the story in the field, tracking down leads, actually interviewing on camera some witnesses, and pre-interviewing others. The correspondent, if he or she has achieved star status, arrives later to conduct a critical, clinching interview or two. Some correspondents immerse themselves more deeply in the production of a piece than do others; some stories *require* a correspondent's continuing presence. But there is an inevitable progression: The more successful a television news correspondent (as a magnet attracting audiences), the more projects he will be assigned, assuring that his involvement in any particular project can only be superficial. Wallace, specifically, tended to be assigned by CBS the "correspondent" role on those complicated and convoluted stories called investigative ones. His busy CBS schedule precluded his becoming committed to a particular story, whether a 60 *Minutes* segment or a documentary.

This is not to minimize Wallace's talent as a broadcaster. He was an exceptionally skilled interviewer. His Achilles' heel was a schizophrenia, unresolved since he began in the broadcast business, between his desire to be a journalist and his destiny as an entertainer.

"Mike" (Myron Leon) Wallace was born in Brookline, Massachusetts, a suburb of Boston which for years prided itself on being the richest town per capita in the United States. Once the fortress of Boston millionaires—the Kennedys, the Larz Andersons—who built sanitized estates safely quarantined from tainted Boston's immigrant alleys, the town eventually absorbed a class of nouveau riche newcomers, many of Jewish descent. Alongside the Kennedys lived the Walters (Barbara), the Susskinds (David), and the Wallaces. Mike left Brookline for the Midwest after high school, enrolling at the University of Michigan with the goal of becoming an English teacher. However, he found his vocation in radio, beginning at station WXYZ in Detroit. When he was not announcing the news or writing it, he was serving as the "voice" on entertainment programs such as *The Green Hornet* and *The Lone Ranger*. Wallace was at radio station WMAQ in Chicago when he married actress Buff Cobb, the blonde, willowy granddaughter of humorist Irvin S. Cobb. Soon the Wallaces were hosting a daytime New York talk show called *Mike and Buff*. There were no signs that Wallace regretted surrendering news gathering for gossip and gab.

Mike and Buff ended its radio run when the co-hosts ended their marriage. Meanwhile, Mike was moving even farther afield from journalism. By 1954 he was an actor in a Broadway comedy called *Reclining Figure*. When the producers of *The Big Surprise*, a popular television quiz show, decided they needed a new host, Wallace was selected from a field of forty competitors. It did not take Wallace long to unveil a big surprise of his own: an interview program on local New York television called *Night Beat*. On Tuesday nights, on *The Big Surprise*, Wallace was NBC's solicitous Dr. Jekyll. Then, in the dead of night on independent television station WARD, Mike metamorphosed into Mr. Hyde. On *The*

Big Surprise, Mike greeted Francis X. Bushman, the silent-movie star, with a gushing: "Now, Mr. Bushman, tell us how you met your charming bride." On *Night Beat*, Mike welcomed John P. John (the milliner, Mr. John) with: "Is it true that most of the men in the fashion business are effeminate?" The set of *Night Beat* was a stark one—a few chairs and a spotlight. Mike sat on one of the chairs; the guest squirmed under the spotlight. If the heat of the light did not get him, Mike's questions did. "Psychiatrists say," he told Arctic explorer Peter Freuchen, "that a man who risks his life many times is not a brave man but one who doubts his own manhood. Does this apply to you?"

By today's standards Wallace's interrogations seem tame; in 1980, on national television, a sober newsman named Roger Mudd was quizzing presidential candidate Ted Kennedy about his sex life. However, in 1957 Wallace's bullying, badgering style aroused passions. Most television talk shows up to then had been bland and bleached. Wallace tossed tabu subjects into his viewers' living rooms: birth control, religion, prostitution, alcoholism, and homosexuality. And some of his "defendants" were characters who rarely got to mug in front of a camera: Fascists, Communists, racists, and hoodlums. In New York, arguments raged in saloons and beauty parlors, with some viewers calling Wallace vicious, a "sadist." The television executives at the struggling ABC network perceived in him one other quality. Viewers loved him or they hated him, but they were never indifferent to him. ABC signed Wallace for $100,000 a year (a king's ransom at the time) to broadcast a weekly national half-hour version of *Night Beat* entitled *Mike Wallace's Profiles*.

"The essence of *Night Beat*," TV *Guide's* Edith Effron wrote later, "was conflict—conflict between Mike and interviewee, conflict within the interviewee, and conflict between Mike and his public over both the form and the content of his show." Soon Wallace was adding a third ingredient to that volatile mix: conflict with his superiors at ABC when Mike's prosecutorial zeal clashed with the caution endemic in those days. When guests kayoed on *Mike Wallace's Profiles* started throwing haymaker hooks in the courts, ABC management grew timid and fearful. The image of being a distant third in the ratings among the three networks was embarrassing enough. ABC did not need the reputation of being the network of the third degree as well. Any grudging support Wallace received from ABC management dissolved after Mike's disastrous interview with mobster Mickey Cohen. Before the interview, which was to be live and ad lib, an ABC news executive said to Wallace, "Be careful. No leading questions."

"Don't worry," Wallace replied. Then, almost as soon as Cohen sat down, Wallace said, "And what do you know about Commissioner Parker?"

Cohen, residing on the West Coast in alleged "retirement" from the rackets, thought he knew plenty about the Los Angeles police chief. Everything Cohen thought he knew fell into the category of libel or slander. The television network was able to avert a law suit by issuing a public apology. However, the damage to Wallace's career at ABC was irreparable. The critics who initially had praised him for his boldness now panned him for his boorishness—his "sensationalism." Wallace had turned from the prophet of a new broadcast journalism into a pariah. At the end of its second network season, Wallace's interview program was cancelled. By 1960 he was covering the presidential conventions and election for the Westinghouse Broadcasting Company. Meanwhile, he was toning down his controversial, and thus unmarketable, image. Soon he was again the bland television host of a nighttime variety show called *PM*, and supplementing his income with television commercials for Parliament cigarettes, an avocation unlikely to endear him to the purists among his ex-colleagues in journalism. Wallace's *PM* variety show was luring a sizable audience. He might have persevered to become, some suggest, a slightly more savage Ed Sullivan had not a cathartic personal tragedy altered his life. During a camping trip in the summer of 1962, Mike's eldest son, Peter, nineteen, tumbled to his death in the mountains of Greece.

"Peter's death had a devastating effect on Wallace not only in the usual sense but also in terms of the direction his professional life had taken," Gary Gates wrote later in *Air Time*, a history of CBS News. Peter had "expressed journalistic aspirations of his own" and had been a desk assistant for CBS News during the 1960 political conventions. "Wallace had encouraged his son's interest in journalism, telling him it was both a stimulating and an honorable profession. That, he knew," Gates added, "was a lot more than he could say for what he was doing with his own life."

Wallace walked out of his *PM* variety show, leaving behind his lucrative salary. He was determined to resolve his career schizophrenia definitively, in favor of journalism. But there was little interest from network news executives, who viewed him strictly as an entertainer. After a winter-long series of rejections, he accepted the job of local anchorman at KTLA in Los Angeles. To emphasize his renewed dedication to news over entertainment, he volunteered to buy out his contract from the manufacturers of Parliament in order to keep those unseemly cigarette commercials off the air. CBS News president Dick Salant heard about

Wallace's proposal and was impressed. He telephoned Wallace and offered him a job at CBS News in New York. In the spring of 1963 Wallace was selected to anchor a new morning news broadcast called *Calendar,* which soon proved lively and stimulating, earning a thirty percent larger audience than its predecessor by draping the news with the trappings of melodrama. Wallace summed up his philosophy for *TV Guide:*

"Have you ever looked at a cauliflower on your dining room table? It looks anything but dramatic! But when you see a crate of cauliflowers being examined under klieg lights at three in the morning at a loading dock by white-coated men haggling about price . . . When you see the battle between profit and loss that is going on . . . When you see one man pitting his business understanding against that of his competitors—*this* is dramatic. This is *conflict.* This is how we shoot a cost-of-living story." Wallace believed that "news is drama. If you look closely, every interesting news item is built around a value conflict."

Calendar, despite its cauliflower journalism, restored Wallace's reputation as a legitimate broadcaster. Later he left that anchor slot to become a general-assignment reporter covering Richard Nixon's campaign in the 1966 midterm election; he continued to cover Nixon's efforts throughout the primaries and Nixon's nomination in 1968. Wallace might have been CBS's prime candidate as chief White House correspondent during the Nixon presidency; however, that summer CBS offered him an opportunity to star with Harry Reasoner in a brand-new broadcast. Wallace leapt at the chance to appear regularly on the fledgling *60 Minutes.* Initially the program was designed to showcase the wry writing talents of Reasoner, featuring clever (rather than controversial) lead stories paced to the gentle rhythm of Reasoner's casual style. Wallace's role was secondary; he delivered the run-of-the-mill hard-news segments. It was not until 1970 when Reasoner was replaced by Morley Safer that *60 Minutes* began to remold itself around the combative posturing of *Night Beat's* "Mike Malice." The program grew in prestige and popularity; Wallace's own reputation swelled, too. By the mid-1970s Wallace was outranked among CBS correspondents only by the venerable Cronkite himself.

With Wallace leading the charge, more and more *60 Minutes* became a newsroom Western in which good (CBS) always triumphed over evil: Mike barging into a hotel room in pursuit of some purported malefactor; Mike being tossed out of an office by some bamboozling businessman. The ratings of *60 Minutes* (abetted by its early Sunday evening time slot) skyrocketed. Wallace became the vivid symbol of investigative reporting—with the boldness, the brashness, and the courage to unmask a villain on national televison. Vigilante journalism became not only respectable but profitable as well. And the more successful Wallace became, the more CBS needed his by-line to sanctify other news broadcasts. Somehow television news—hooked on its ratings habit—had managed to reverse the "Peter Principle." Stellar correspondents such as Wallace were being promoted not one rank *above* their levels of competency but several ranks *below*. In return for their inflated seven-figure stipends, some of America's most renowned broadcast journalists had been transformed, becoming no more essential a part of the news-gathering process than the slick paper on which a magazine article is printed.

The afternoon Wallace arrived for his screening, sandwiches were ordered for everyone. Wallace saw the film and was satisfied. "This film is really a morality play," he said afterwards. Wallace did, however, offer the criticism that the events described in the documentary after Tet (focusing on the military's alleged cover-up of the large number of attacking enemy) were anticlimactic. He felt that after those Tet sequences the film lost its momentum. Wallace offered that reservation about the last act of the broadcast, but Crile was intent on keeping that section of the film intact. He made no changes based on Wallace's recommendation.

It was, of course, only the second time during the production of the documentary that Wallace had even been in an editing room. "I don't think I spent more than two to three hours in total in the cutting room," Wallace recalled later. Wallace was far less involved in the details of the Vietnam project than if the piece had been a 60 *Minutes* segment. "I have said it a thousand times: 60 *Minutes* is a producer's broadcast. *CBS Reports* is even more a producer's broadcast for the reason that they may stay on a given piece six months, eight months, even a year, whereas as a 60 *Minutes* correspondent I had twenty-five new pieces to do during the course of that time." Cumulatively, Wallace added, if the number of days he worked on Crile's project was totaled, "I would be surprised if it added up to two weeks. It was George's broadcast. I was in effect a hired hand. The information that I got from talking to various people led me little by little to believe that the information I was being fed by George was accurate. . . ." Wallace had "certain sources" of his own, "people from those Vietnam days whom I would have conversations with. . . . They said, 'Keep going, you'll find more.'"

Wallace revealed that there had been "some very serious arguments . . . very serious skeptical arguments by me to George, to Joe Zigman. . . . Very serious, skeptical questioning of why, why, why. What's the point? Are we sure? What would be the motive of these individuals? Why would a man like Gains Hawkins, for instance, a true blue—I never met the man, but one gets the impression of a true-blue, solid character. Why would he say these things? I needed to have this thing proven," he added. "There was a big knockdown with Crile, Zigman, Alben—*prove* it to me. George answered these questions for me. . . ."

Crile got *his* answers from Adams. Colloff's and Stringer's understanding was limited by the agenda of evidence that Crile chose for them. And Wallace, a victim of the star system, was busy assimilating so many fragments of so many different projects that he did not really know very much about anything at all. Later, during the CBS internal investigation that followed the broadcast, Senior Executive Producer Burton "Bud" Benjamin would write: "Is the star system here cutting Wallace so fine he can't participate?" There was something missing from the CBS fail-safe mechanism; no one outside the producer and his paid consultant had sufficient knowledge to effectively act as devil's advocate.

Following Wallace's screening, the next obstacle Crile had to clear was the screening of the full film for Stringer, who would be accompanied by the new *CBS Reports* senior producer, Andy Lack. The night before that Stringer-Lack screening, Klein telephoned Crile, who was working with Joe Fackovec on acts 4 and 5 in another editing room. Klein knew that the producer was feeling fatigued. Now, the night before the Stringer-Lack screening, Klein was telephoning Crile to see if he and Fackovec needed any assistance.

"How are you doing?" Klein said.

"At this point," Crile said, "I'm only trying to make it respectable."

The next morning Klein arrived at CBS at 8:00 A.M. If Crile decided any last-minute changes were necessary, Klein would have time to make them before the screening. He walked by room 210E and saw Crile in the room at an editing machine with Sue Lyne sitting behind him taking notes on a pad of paper. Lyne departed after an hour or so. The entire unit assembled at 10:00 A.M. for the screening. Crile was sitting on the edge of an editing table. He looked haggard, his complexion sickly, bloodless, and pale. At the moment Lack and Stringer entered, Crile was quipping that he was ready to be committed to a sanitorium for a long rest cure. Crile could not sit still. He kept bouncing up and down, nervously toying with his tie; his fatigue turned him somehow hyperactive.

The screening itself went smoothly until the close of Act 1 when Mike Wallace reminded Westmoreland that his first words after hearing the McChristian-Hawkins briefing were: "What am I going to tell the press? What am I going to tell the Congress? What am I going to tell the president?" Westmoreland replied, "I—I do recall a session with Hawkins, yes." That was the segment which had sparked an acrimonious debate between Crile and Klein, with the editor insisting Crile had to let Westmoreland explain why he did not accept the briefing. After screening that section of Act 1, Howard Stringer echoed Klein's earlier complaint, telling Crile, "George, we've got to give Westmoreland an opportunity to present his point of view." Not including Westmoreland's explanation, Stringer added, might damage the film's credibility; the interview sequence might appear manipulated.

Crile responded with an elaborate defense of his position, but neither Stringer nor Andy Lack would budge; Crile had to allow Westmoreland a fuller explanation. The discussion went back and forth until suddenly Crile turned on his heels and stormed out of the editing room. Stringer, Lack, and the others were left sitting there. All of a sudden Crile returned with Mike Wallace in tow. Klein was asked to rerun the film to where Westmoreland said, "I—I do recall a session with Hawkins, yes." Then Klein added into the film the extension of Westmoreland's comment that Stringer wanted: ". . . but I was very, very suspicious of—of this particular estimate. And the reason was that you—you come to a shade of gray. You get down at the hamlet level, and you've got teenagers and you've got old men who can be armed and ha— can be useful to the enemy, and who are technically Vietcong—"

> WALLACE: Right.
> WESTMORELAND: —but they don't have any military capability of consequence.

Now Wallace became entangled in this discussion over whether or not Westmoreland's statement should be extended to include his full explanation. Over and over the sequence was screened until finally Crile turned to Wallace and asked him for his opinion. It was an awkward position for Wallace; he did not know the details of the briefing sequence since he had not read the transcripts of either the McChristian or the Hawkins interview. "Howard is correct," Wallace said. The debate was over. Wallace departed. Klein was told to "extend" Westmoreland's answer.

The screening proceeded with no serious disagreements until Wallace, in the program, introduced the so-called August 20 cable.

> WALLACE: . . . Isn't it a possibility that the real reason for suddenly deciding in the summer of 1967 to remove an entire category of the enemy [the Self-Defense forces] from the Order of Battle, a

category that had been in that Order of Battle since 1961, was based on political considerations?

WESTMORELAND: No, decidedly not. That—

WALLACE: Didn't you make this clear in your August twentieth cable?

WESTMORELAND: No, no. Yeah. No.

WALLACE: I have a copy of your August twentieth cable—

WESTMORELAND: Well, sure. Okay, okay. All right, all right.

WALLACE: —spelling out the command position on the Self-Defense controversy.

WESTMORELAND: Yeah.

WALLACE: As you put it in the cable, you say the principal reason why the Self-Defense militia must go, quote, was "press reaction."

"That cable, dated August 20, 1967," Wallace would tell the CBS television audience, "spelled out General Westmoreland's predicament: 'We have been projecting an image of success over the recent months.' The Self-Defense militia must be removed, the cable explained, '. . . or the newsmen will immediately seize on the point that the enemy force has increased.' The cable went on to say that no explanation could then 'prevent the press from drawing an erroneous gloomy conclusion.' "

The August 20 cable sequence ended there. "And so went the intelligence war," Wallace would resume, segueing into the next segment of the documentary. . . .

What was missing from Wallace's quotations was the explanation the cable offered for the recommended action. The sentence Wallace quoted beginning "We have been projecting an image of success over recent months . . ." concluded with "and properly so," which Crile chose to omit. The cable argued, in segments that were not quoted by Wallace, that "from the intelligence viewpoint, the inclusion of SD and SSD [Self-Defense and Secret Self-Defense] strength figures in an estimate of military capabilities is highly questionable. . . . They are no more effective in the military sense than the dozens of other nonmilitary organizations which serve the VC cause in various roles. . . ."

The cable was arguing that progress *was* being made and that including categories of the enemy that the military did not regard as part of the "military threat" might be misconstrued.

Again, after this sequence was rolled, Stringer insisted that Crile give Westmoreland an opportunity to explain his actions. All Crile was allowing Westmoreland to do, as the August 20 cable sequence was then structured, was issue stammering denials to Wallace's allegations. Crile defended his editing; Stringer insisted on the change. Suddenly, again, Crile left the editing room and returned with Mike Wallace. In the Westmoreland interview, after Wallace had said, "As you put it in the cable, you say the principal reason why the Self-Defense militia must go, quote, was 'press reaction,' " Westmoreland had replied to the charge.

> WESTMORELAND: Well, sure. They would have drawn an erroneous conclusion because it was a non-issue. It was a false issue. It would have totally clouded the—the situation, which would have been detrimental. But the fact is that since it was wrong, since it was not accurate, since it was not sound, [it] would have brought about that impact, yes.

Stringer wanted his producer to include that explanation in the sequence; Crile disagreed. Klein showed the sequence again and again, with the extension, without it, with it. . . . Finally Crile turned to Wallace and asked Mike's opinion. Wallace said he agreed with the executive producer; in fairness to Westmoreland, the explanation should be incorporated into the broadcast. The issue was decided in Stringer's favor. Wallace departed. Twice Crile had called upon him for support, and twice Wallace had sided instead with the CBS executives. But Crile was setting a precedent. From then on whenever he needed extra leverage to wrench a point from his superiors, he would use Mike Wallace's muscle.

The screening was over. Stringer and Lack seemed very impressed. The extensions that Stringer wanted would have to be inserted; otherwise, except for minor word changes, there would be no alterations. Stringer and Andy Lack left the room; the unit members began to disperse.

After the others had gone, Zigman mentioned to Klein his astonishment at Crile's behavior during the screening; his attempts to use Wallace as a power broker, creating a potentially explosive confrontation with the CBS executives.

"You know," Zigman said, "I don't think Crile wants to work here anymore."

8

CBS
Approves
"Conspiracy"

IN A WEEK the broadcast had to be screened for CBS vice-president Roger Colloff. Then two weeks later, in the first week of November, CBS News president Bill Leonard would see the film for the first time. The extensions that Stringer had ordered were inserted into the film. Additional minor alterations were made, as the unit worked tirelessly, polishing their film into a finished program. One morning Klein was incorporating some script changes when Zigman entered the editing room. During the many months they had collaborated on this project, Klein had grown fonder of the veteran associate producer. He had penetrated Zigman's brusque protective shell, finding within an incurable worrier. Every ragged detail added to Zigman's anxiety. The less caring he appeared the deeper his inner dread. Zigman sat on an editing stool. He said to Klein, "If I don't come in tomorrow, if I don't make it to work, don't forget that this pile has to go back to Third World Films, that pile has to go back to the United States Navy. . . ." He was pointing at stacks of unused stock footage which he had readied for return to their sources.

Klein was puzzled by something eerie and ominous in Zigman's tone. "Joe. . . ." he started to say, then became silent. Zigman looked pale. "Joe, come on," said Klein. "Remember? You promised you'd never leave me alone." They both laughed.

The following afternoon Zigman was standing in front of Carolyne McDaniel's desk. Carolyne was typing and talking to Zigman while she concentrated on the memo in her machine. After a while she realized that the conversation had turned into a monologue. She looked up. The color was drained from Zigman's face. Quickly she rose and led him by the elbow to the chair beside her desk. Zigman sat down. The next thing Carolyne knew, Zigman had slid off the chair onto the floor. Someone dashed into Klein's editing room, shouting, "Zigman collapsed." Klein ran out. The *CBS Reports* unit manager, Gene Gary, a longtime pal of Zigman's, was kneeling alongside Joe's inert body. Howard Stringer was holding Joe's hand. Zigman was conscious but in obvious pain. Crile arrived and stood there in shock. Someone called an ambulance. Zigman was wheeled out and rushed to a midtown hospital. He would have to undergo an operation and a lengthy convalescence.

The unit's strength was again reduced, with Igor Brobowski (whom Crile borrowed from CBS News after researcher Alben had departed) having to assume some of Zigman's routine responsibilities. Brobowski had already deposed Carolyne as Crile's chief comber-of-back-*Newsweek*-issues, seeking superlative-laced passages about the Vietnam War that Crile could plug into the narrative of his broadcast.

Anxious over Zigman's health, the unit plunged onward toward the screening scheduled during the last week of October for the vice-president, Roger Colloff. It was Colloff, of course, at an earlier screening who had encouraged Crile to take his investigation into the White House.

On the day of Colloff's screening Hurwitz and Klein mounted the reels of film and lugged them up to the *60 Minutes* projection room on the ninth floor. Colloff was joined that morning by Executive Producer Howard Stringer, the Senior Producer Andy Lack, and Marjorie Baker, a vice-president of public affairs.

Colloff was overwhelmed by the power of the program. But he did discern a problem in Act 5. Colloff seemed skeptical of the scenario Crile had edited "proving" that Danny Graham had engineered a cover-up by coercing the keepers of the military's computer to alter its data base after Tet. The charge was vague: Who did what to which numbers? A debate started, with Crile using the testimony of a witness who did not appear in the broadcast, Lt. Bernie Gattozzi, to dispel Colloff's skepticism. Colloff had asked Klein to roll the entire Act 5 over again, so uncertain had he been about its accuracy. In the end, though, Colloff relied on the judgment of his producer and agreed to let Act 5 remain as Crile had constructed it. Now a final obstacle remained: the screening for CBS News president Bill Leonard around November 1.

Klein could not understand why Leonard had to see the program at the beginning of November and not, say, a few weeks later. Then one day he was present in Crile's office when Maurice Murad, the producer of the Miami drug trade documentary, walked in and said, "Remember, George, you have to be in Miami by the first of November."

Thus there would be no delaying Leonard's screening. The film had to be polished by the first week in November so that Crile could obtain the CBS News president's approval. And for that Leonard screening, one totally new element would be added to the broadcast—the opening "tease."

The "tease" of a broadcast is an introduction—either an intriguing scene or a montage of highlights summarizing the premise of the program. As Howard Stringer would say later, "A tease is brief—it provides a brief sense of the broadcast for the viewers in order to stimulate their interest before getting into the substance of the whole broadcast." The tease was a tactical hook intended to anchor viewers' interest during the commercial break that followed it. After the commercial break, the body and substance of the broadcast would begin.

Mike Wallace had drafted the initial tease, writing an opening sentence that read: "This is a mystery story . . . about Duty, Honor, and Country. . . ." Stringer remembered Wallace "discussing that as a way of getting the broadcast started." But Wallace's tease was discarded. Why? ". . . I don't remember anything more than a discussion of 'mystery story,' " said Stringer. "I only imagine it felt clumsy or the writing didn't have the same sense of introduction that we needed."

Wallace's "mystery story" might have led viewers to anticipate a program with a built-in ambivalence. His tease promised no conclusive verdict. It suggested pros and cons, with the viewers themselves, instead of the CBS cameras and correspondents, acting as their own judge and jury. The tease CBS ultimately selected relieved the audience of that onerous burden. Calculated to keep viewers glued to their armchairs, their gypsy fingers far from the channel buttons on their remote-control modules, the tease CBS chose had far more muscle than Wallace's wavering "mystery story." Vigilante journalism did not need men and women making rational judgments, it needed a mob. The "conspiracy" that George Crile had splashed, in one form or another, twenty-four times across his blue sheet was going to be trumpeted in the marquee of the broadcast itself.

Crile wrote the tease that would ultimately be used in the broadcast the night before Leonard's screening. He completed this introductory passage early in the evening. Wallace had to record it. But Klein was informed that Wallace intended to go out for dinner first. Klein was concerned. He walked into Howard Stringer's office—Crile was there, as well. Klein told Stringer, "I'll get the machine prepared to record Mike. But," Klein added, "he's got to come down here. You have to make him understand that we have a time problem." If Wallace insisted on recording the tease after dinner, what time would that be—11:00 P.M.? And there were still more wrinkles to be ironed out before the next day's crucial screening.

Wallace arrived wearing his trench coat. He recorded the tease, and then Klein began incorporating it into the program. Klein kept on working. Crile departed at about 9:30 P.M. and did not return again.

Klein mounted the acts on reels. CBS News president Bill Leonard would review the film in the ninth floor 60 *Minutes* screening room. The film projector there could accommodate the entire broadcast continuously and fluidly, whereas editing machines could show only twenty or so minutes of film at a time. It was important that Leonard view the broadcast in conditions as closely resembling an actual airing as possible.

At ten o'clock in the morning Klein went up to the screening room. Stringer was there, along with Senior Producer Andy Lack, Vice-President Roger Colloff, Crile, and Wallace. Fackovec, Hurwitz, and Klein sat behind the editing console which was set on a platform at the rear of the room. The CBS executives were below, sitting between the console and the screen. There was only one person missing: the film projectionist. Strict union policy barred anyone but the projectionist from operating the machine at a screening. Stringer was becoming agitated. He tried to telephone Bill Leonard in his office at the Broadcast Center across 57th Street but could not reach him. Stringer wanted to warn Leonard that the projectionist had not arrived so that the CBS News president would not waste his time waiting.

The clock on the wall read 10:05, 10:10—no sign of the projectionist—10:15. . . . Still no trace of him. Everyone was milling around, nervously awaiting the technician.

Finally the projectionist arrived, soon followed by CBS News President Bill Leonard, who took a seat alongside his subordinates. For a producer this was by far the most important screening of all. Whatever the critics conclude about a broadcast, the grade a producer gets from the news president is the one that can make or break his career. Leonard screened the entire film, and he seemed pleased with it. Of course, Leonard had to depend on what he was being told by his subordinates. Colloff had been able to "sell" the film to Leonard without screening any portion of it for the CBS News president. Leonard, an experienced documentarian, had been peripheral to the production. He might be able to spot minor inconsistencies embedded in the finished film but had no way of deciphering what evidence contrary to the conspiracy premise might have been overlooked or ignored. Leonard had to depend on Stringer and Colloff, whose own agendas of evidence had been set by Crile, who in turn had leaned on Adams. Level of authority propped up level of authority, without anyone ever testing the foundations of this film to find out whether its building blocks were made from concrete or wet sand.

In the course of that screening, all Bill Leonard requested were several word changes near the close of the broadcast. Afterwards Crile and Klein met on the eighth floor and walked side by side down the hallway toward the elevators. "We got through with the inside," Crile said. He finally had the ultimate approval he needed to put his program on the air. "You have to understand how controversial this film is going to be and the impact it's going to have. It's going to have to stand on its own," Klein added. "And if it can't, you're the one who will have to defend it."

A short time later Crile *was* defending his film in Bill Leonard's office where a meeting had been convened to discuss, among other topics, the opening tease of the broadcast and the controversial word it contained.

The second paragraph of the tease that Mike Wallace recorded for the Leonard screening began, "The fact is that we Americans were misinformed about the nature and the size of the enemy we were facing, and tonight we're going to present evidence of what we have come to believe was a conscious effort—indeed, a conspiracy at the highest levels of American military intelligence—to suppress and alter critical intelligence on the enemy in the year leading up to the Tet offensive. . . ." CBS wanted viewers to watch its program; that is why Wallace had been assigned the role of chief correspondent, his by-line usually a guarantee of sizable ratings. Likewise, viewers who might be turned off by a tease that promised a "mystery story" might be tempted to sit through the subsequent commercials, convinced that a military conspiracy was going to be revealed over the next ninety minutes.

The question was, did Crile's evidence (the testimony of his on-the-record, on-camera witnesses) justify the use of so explosive and damning a word as "conspiracy"—a court-martialable charge when levied against high-ranking military officers? After Leonard's screening, the use of that word engendered a debate among Crile and his superiors. "We talked about it [conspiracy] at my and Bill [Leonard]'s screening," said Roger Colloff. "Is the use of the word justified? We concluded that it was. It wasn't done haphazardly."

It is unclear who at that meeting actually questioned the appropriateness of the conspiracy charge. Whoever did question the use of that controversial word (perhaps Leonard himself), he was soon overwhelmed by the arguments of its partisans. Howard Stringer, in particular, would defend the use of the word conspiracy vehemently after the broadcast aired, in the course of the litigation sparked by that conspiracy charge. Later, in unpublished notes used to prepare their report, the CBS internal investigators would sum up their conversations with CBS executives about the use of "conspiracy":

"Chandler—these were very serious charges . . . fits definition of conspiracy.

"Crile—absolutely proper.

"Lack—feels wrong.

"Colloff—bothers me. Use not decided haphazardly.

"Adams—agrees conspiracy."

However, while Sam Adams had "no doubt" in his mind that "there was a legal conspiracy," he also said to a reporter that he did not intend to use the word in his book. "It was unlawful," he added, but "no one was being a traitor. I thought early on that conspiracy was too strong a word. . . ." Again, later, Adams added, "I'm not knocking George's judgment [in using the word conspiracy]. It is not something I normally use. To me it's a much more tragic story."

Adams would claim, of course, that he had attempted to dissuade Crile from using the word, beginning in the fall of 1980 when Crile was composing his blue sheet. In the course of the CBS internal investigation that followed the broadcast, senior executive producer Burton "Bud" Benjamin asked Adams, "did you see the blue sheet?"

"I must have," Adams replied.

"Conspiracy was used twenty-four times," said Benjamin.

"At one point," said Adams, "I said, 'Oh, for Christ's sake, George, come off it.'" Apparently, though, when the tease containing the premise of the program was written, no one consulted the man on whose research the broadcast rested. And evidently no one consulted CBS's own interview transcripts either. While the CBS *executives* might believe Westmoreland was guilty of leading a conspiracy, several of CBS's own star "pro conspiracy" *witnesses* did not. Needless to say, none of their statements contradicting that word were used in the broadcast.

Commenting on the memorandum he had sent to the White House two months before Tet (a memo CBS neglected to mention had been commissioned by Walt Rostow), CIA analyst Joe Hovey had told Crile in their interview: "I can't claim any kind of conspiracy to suppress this report."

George Crile told Col. George Hamscher: ". . . It sounds like a full-fledged conspiracy to fake intelligence reporting." Hamscher replied, ". . . Faking intelligence reporting is a different thing entirely. . . ."

> CRILE: It sounds like a full-fledged conspiracy.
> HAMSCHER: If there were a conspiracy—which I don't think it was—it probably had a good purpose. . . .

Comdr. James Meacham did not accept Crile's premise either. ". . . We quite clearly didn't agree with the figures that we were having to use, but it's not a question of honesty or dishonesty, and I think it's wrong of you to try to use those words," Meacham told Crile in their interview.

Nor did Gen. Joseph McChristian offer any evidence to support the "conspiracy" charge.

> CRILE: Can I ask you to confront the rather ugly fact that in November 1967 your old commanding officer [Westmoreland] publicly accused you of either incompetence, unreliability, untrustworthiness—in any event, he made it seem, and he did it publicly, that your operation was not to be respected.
> McCHRISTIAN: The only knowledge I have of that is what I have read in the papers. Never did he or Ambassador Bunker or anybody else ever question my intelligence or ever return it to me or ever tell me to redo it; under no circumstances.

The CIA's George Allen believed that the military's tendency to "accentuate the positive" began with the earliest days of America's entanglement in Vietnam.

Thus, although none of CBS's on-camera interviewees was ever asked if he subscribed to the characterization of events as a "conspiracy," clearly the testimony of at least five—Hamscher, Meacham, McChristian, Hovey, and Allen—indicated that with regard to events about which they were testifying, "conspiracy" was not an appropriate description. Again it bears repeating: None of these statements contradicting the charge of a conspiracy was included in the broadcast.

Later CBS would argue that the "word was only used once in the broadcast." Indeed, "conspiracy" *was* used only once: to state the premise of the program. The balance of the broadcast documented that conspiracy charge.

Early in November, George Crile departed for Miami to begin his role as correspondent on Maurice Murad's drug trade documentary. At this juncture Crile knew his air date would definitely not be in December. The best estimate of CBS executives was that the program would not be broadcast until some time in January 1982. Crile was going to be gone the month of November and return in December. While he was in Miami, Crile would write the final narration that Wallace would record and polish his script. In Crile's absence Klein began working on another documentary.

Two months before, Klein had agreed to edit Kent Garrett's program, "A Time to Live, A Time to Die." He worked on that program throughout November, never mentioning to Kent his distress over the Vietnam documentary. Klein needed to distance himself from it physically. But the problems of that project could not be contained; they started seeping into the new working environment.

9

The "Prospects" List

B Y THE START OF DECEMBER 1981 "The Uncounted Enemy: A Vietnam Deception" was a completed film. CBS News President Bill Leonard had approved the broadcast, including, of course, the tease, titillating viewers with "a conspiracy at the highest levels of military intelligence." Nevertheless, a full two months after Crile and Wallace had ended their on-camera interviewing, CBS still had not sought out a number of officials pivotal to the controversy. The CBS News official standards of proper journalism stated that ". . . the principle of fairness and balance is the cornerstone of our news and public affairs policy. . . ." That "cornerstone" had started crumbling the day in 1980 that Sam Adams gave Crile the list of eighty potential interviewees.

Adams's "Prospect" list (a document slightly longer than twenty-five pages when typed on paper fourteen inches by eight-and-a-half inches) was a catalogue of men (and one woman: the wife of Comdr. James Meacham) who might support the program's conspiracy premise. The names were arranged in alphabetical order along the left-hand margin of each page. Under each name Adams had provided an address and telephone number (whenever possible). Beside the name Adams had written comments, evaluating each ex-official's promise as a potential witness.

Adams had interviewed many on the list during the research for his book. His own bias in favor of the conspiracy premise drenched this germinal document. Hostile witnesses—those who had refused to accept Adams's version of events—were assumed to be concealing evidence. Of Gen. William DePuy, an aide to Joint Chiefs of Staff chairman Gen. Earle Wheeler, Adams wrote: "Hostile. Knows me and doesn't like what I'm up to. However, he knows a lot and would have a tough time defending himself on the tube." Col. Lewington Ponder had been deputy to Westmoreland's chief of intelligence production, Col. Charles Morris. Adams wrote: "United States Army colonel at MACV in the chain of command between Morris [head of research] and [Col. Paul] Weiler [head of OB]. Otherwise a nerd, he wrote Parkins's bad fitness report, doubtless at the behest of Morris. See immediately below:

> —Note: he [Ponder] retired from the army to Blowing Rock, North
> Carolina, where Morris lives. . . . Interesting coincidence.
> —Probably won't talk. *But* he has a bad conscience about ruining
> Ev Parkins's career in the army. . . ."

Adams does not explain how he knew about Ponder's "bad conscience" without ever having spoken to him. Neither DePuy nor Ponder would be interviewed for the broadcast. Nor would two other ex-officials, each of whom might have been able to offer firsthand testimony to contradict the premise of the program. On page one of the Prospects list the name George Carver [head of the CIA's Vietnam Affairs branch] and a telephone number appeared near the *right-hand* margin after comments about a "Colletti, James," as if added as an afterthought or to correct an oversight. No comments about Carver were included.

"Should we talk to Carver? George and I discussed it," Adams recalled. "We said, 'Goddam it, we've got Carver's deputy [George Allen].' " The fact is, though, that Allen was a committed Adams advocate while George Carver was a critic.

Another key official was Robert Komer, Lyndon Johnson's special ambassador to Vietnam. Two of the witnesses CBS held in highest esteem had portrayed Komer as a man of ominous influence intimately involved in the events being examined by the broadcast. Col. Gains Hawkins, the military's Order of Battle specialist, stated that Komer "was acutely aware" of the alleged dispute within military intelligence over enemy strength; he told Crile, "You must assume that he was reporting to the White House." Gen. Joseph McChristian (General Davidson's predecessor as chief of intelligence), when pressed by Crile, said he suspected that Bob Komer was the one who dislodged him from his post in May 1967. Clearly Sam Adams also regarded Komer as crucial; in his Prospects list Adams devoted more commentary to Komer than to any other ex-official:

KOMER, ROBERT

[Address]
[Telephone number]

An adviser on Vietnam to LBJ until May 1967 when he moved to Vietnam to become Westy's deputy in charge of pacification. My own suspicions about Komer include:

—A key role in the overthrow of McChristian, who hates his guts. (Interestingly, an interview with Komer—who might well talk—might get a rise out of McChristian.)

—A moving force behind such phenomena as the imposition of the 300,000 ceiling, the removal of the Self-Defense from the OB, and ups and downs in political cadre figure.

—Note: He was source of Reston's column of November 22, 1967.* God knows what Komer knew about lowering of infiltration statistics at this point, but it might be interesting to confront him with the firing of [Ev] Parkins on November 15, 1967.

—Note: He also ran the meeting to rebut the *Times* OB story of March 19, 1968. The meeting resulted in Meacham putting together the press briefing . . . which led Meacham to write on March 21, 1968: "Never in my life have I assembled such a pack of truly gargantuan falsehoods. . . ."

Then Adams concocted a "possible sequence" Crile might capture on film in an on-camera interview:

—Read Komer *Times* piece of March 19, 1968: "United States Undervalued Enemy Strength Before Tet," emphasizing CIA position. Ask him to comment.

—He'll say: "CIA full of crap" or "Honest disagreement."

—Recall Komer conference to rebut the *Times* piece (the one which Kelly Robinson attended).

—Ask him about it, including briefing which resulted. Make it clear the briefing done in OB studies.

*This column in the *New York Times* insinuated General McChristian had been removed from his post in Vietnam because of incompetence. Crile read portions of that column to McChristian during their interview, attributing its sources as Westmoreland and Komer.—AUTHOR

> —Read Komer the Meacham letter. "Never in my
> life . . ." CLOSEUP of his face. Maybe Komer'll
> pull it off. He's an impressive man. . . .

Adams was not finished with Komer yet. He went on in his Prospects
list to add further "Thoughts re Komer":

> —He's denounced me in the *Times* and *Post* as
> embarking on a vendetta. Still mad.
> —He'd probably talk, but expect fireworks. He
> might say, for example, "Of course we had to fudge
> the statistics. The goddam press was out to get us."
> Watch out! Half of the audience would believe
> him. . . .

The television audience never got the opportunity; Komer was not
interviewed for the broadcast. (Interestingly, though, Crile did interview
Carver's *deputy*, George Allen, and Komer's *deputy*, Richard Holbrooke.)
Nor was Ambassador to Vietnam Ellsworth Bunker interviewed. In West-
moreland's March 16 interview with Wallace he said, "I didn't report
directly to Mr. Johnson. I never talked to him a single time between
Washington and Saigon, not once. My chain of command was to the
ambassador, who had responsibility for all activities in Vietnam. . . ."
Several months later Johnson adviser Walt Rostow told Wallace, ". . .
The most important part of the intelligence network, which everyone has
missed—were the weekly cables that came from the ambassador in
Saigon—"

WALLACE: Ellsworth Bunker.
ROSTOW: Ellsworth Bunker—using all the resources that he had in
the field. These were the country-team assessments—but with his
own personal staff— And I must say historians are going to find
them [the weekly cables] superb, accurate sources of—for their
reconstruction of the period.

But the most startling omission from the broadcast was testimony from
Westmoreland's actual chief of intelligence in Vietnam during the period
being examined. Gen. Philip Davidson served in that capacity from May
27, 1967, until May 10, 1969. He had firsthand knowledge of events
about which his predecessor, Gen. Joseph McChristian, could only spec-

ulate. Davidson, whose name was well known to the CBS researchers, was one of the most important ex-officials that CBS overlooked. "If the figures on enemy strength were going to be manipulated, I had to do it," Davidson would tell *TV Guide* after the broadcast. Davidson, in fact, was the single most powerful military intelligence officer in all of Vietnam.

During Mike Wallace's interview with Westmoreland, the general grew weary of trying to answer questions that might have been more properly directed at his intelligence chief. Finally, Westmoreland asked Wallace why CBS had not interviewed Davidson. "General Davidson is a very, very sick man," Wallace answered. That exchange was not included in the CBS broadcast.

Adams said that two years before, when he was about to contact David-son in the course of researching his book, he had encountered a friend, Col. John Lanterman, who told him not to bother Davidson, who was dying of cancer. In the Prospects list Adams gave Crile he had included Davidson (incorrectly identifying Davidson's first name as Buford), along with Davidson's current address and a telephone number. But Adams added the comment that Davidson "is said to have cancer," mentioned the possibility that, although he doubted it, "a deathbed confession" might be worth a call, and said, "I plan to check with him prior final draft." Adams never contacted Davidson.

Researcher Alex Alben said it was his understanding that CBS was desperately attempting to contact Davidson. Wallace said that when he asked, he was told Davidson was a terminal cancer patient and not an-swering phone calls.

CBS had pursued witnesses who might support its conspiracy premise with an unrelenting zeal and with remarkable enterprise. What efforts had CBS undertaken to verify the availability of the most powerful mili-tary intelligence figure in Vietnam during the events CBS intended to document? The first step had been that Adams conversation with Col. John Lanterman, who allegedly informed Adams that Davidson was ter-minally ill with cancer. After the broadcast, when CBS senior executive producer Burton "Bud" Benjamin investigated charges leveled against the program by *TV Guide*, CBS telephoned John Lanterman. According to the "Benjamin Report," Lanterman told CBS that he "had not seen Davidson since the early 1970s . . . and never said he was ill because he had no contact with him."

George Crile later wrote that "CBS wanted very much to interview Davidson. The transcripts are filled with accusations made against him and his intelligence operation which CBS would have liked to put to him directly." Crile went on to point out that "Mike Wallace mentioned

Davidson's extreme condition to General Westmoreland in the course of their interview, and Westmoreland did not challenge this." (Apparently in the CBS court anything a witness *did not* say might be used against him.) Crile recalled that he had also mentioned Davidson's terminal condition to Gen. Danny Graham. "Wallace was present when Graham confirmed that Davidson was critically ill."

There is no record in the transcript of the Graham interview of any such exchange. However, even had Graham mentioned Davidson's illness off camera, if CBS were so anxious to interview this crucial military intelligence officer, would the word of Graham, whom both Crile and Wallace considered untruthful, be sufficient? What further steps to ascertain Davidson's availability did CBS take on its own? Adams had provided CBS with Davidson's address and telephone number. In Crile's first public comments on the matter to *TV Guide*, he said he did telephone Davidson.

Crile told *TV Guide* that he tried to telephone Davidson once, no one answered, and he "didn't go any further."

Later, in his "White Paper" rebutting the *TV Guide* article, Crile wrote that he and his assistant, Carolyne McDaniel, "put in no fewer than seven telephone calls and received no answer." Later still he told the CBS internal investigators that "he turned over the job of contacting General Davidson to Carolyne McDaniel, his secretary. McDaniel says she tried to phone him many times during the normal work day but could not reach him. She never tried him at night. She told Crile, who said Davidson was in a hospital dying but did not tell her what hospital."

Whatever misconception CBS had about the state of Davidson's actual health, however, one key document demonstrates that by December 15, five weeks and four days before the broadcast, Sam Adams knew that indeed Davidson was well enough to be interviewed on camera by CBS. According to Adams's own chronologies, on December 7, at a luncheon at the Fort Meyers (Texas) Officers' Club, Adams was introduced to a friend and ex-West Point classmate of Davidson's, a retired army colonel named Edward Hamilton. Eight days later, on December 15, at 3:30 P.M., Adams telephoned Hamilton and talked to him for approximately fifteen minutes. Hamilton told Adams (according to Adams's own contemporaneous account of the conversation) that he had seen Davidson the previous September, that Davidson was "doing fine," had remarried, and "was living down in Texas." Hamilton said that Davidson was "writing a book on General Giap," the commander of North Vietnamese forces. Hamilton added that although Davidson had had cancer of the prostate many years before, "he looked pretty good." Davidson was "bouncing around fine."

Davidson said that as far as he knew, CBS had not attempted to contact him, either by telephone or in writing. "In 1981," he added, "I remarried. Certainly not the action of a dying man."

No CBS executive could recall being informed in December that Davidson was indeed well, nor was any effort made to interview him at that time. While CBS did not interview Davidson, soon after Hamilton told Adams that Davidson was "bouncing around fine," Crile suddenly decided to interview one of Davidson's subordinates, Col. Charles Morris. "Morris," Crile wrote later, "was a powerful witness confirming the accounts of [the military's] infiltration analysts. . . ." Crile sent a memo to Colloff after the telephone interview, including selected segments of the conversation. "More than anyone else," Crile told Colloff, "Colonel Morris spelled out the political dynamic that caused [the military] to suppress intelligence on the enemy. . . ."

Later Morris would claim that the comments Crile included in his summary of the telephone interview were "taken out of context." If Crile's record accurately reflected the thrust of his conversation with Morris, why didn't Crile ask Morris to appear before the CBS cameras? Later Crile admitted that "CBS did have adequate time to include a Morris interview had it chosen to do so." Why didn't CBS choose to do so? Crile wrote that he "seriously considered asking Morris to participate. . . ." In the end, however, Crile decided that "Morris's testimony, while impressive, was largely a restatement of what Colonel Cooley had already said in his filmed interview."

That explanation is a bewildering one. In the military intelligence hierarchy Cooley ranked *at least five levels below Morris*. Although Morris did not have direct access to Westmoreland, except in the presence of Davidson, he was privy to the military intelligence command's most sensitive decisions. All Cooley knew about the decision-making process at Westmoreland's headquarters was rumor and scuttlebutt.

One thing is evident: If CBS had included on-camera interviews with Morris and Davidson in the program, the broadcast would have been radically altered. In his Prospects list several times Adams had drawn for Crile charts of the military intelligence chain of command. There was one such diagram in the section dealing with Col. Charles Morris (see top of page 134).

Morris would reiterate after the broadcast what his superior Davidson said in relation to his own role in any conspiracy. "A conspiracy," said Morris, "could not have occurred while I was there without my participating in it." Yet Morris was never mentioned by name in the program. Davidson's name was mentioned once, by Westmoreland, but since viewers had not encountered Davidson's name previously, nor did

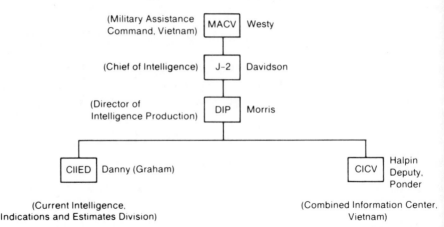

(Current Intelligence,
Indications and Estimates Division)

(Combined Information Center,
Vietnam)

Wallace follow up, viewers would remain unaware that Davidson and Morris had to have played pivotal roles. Indeed, after the broadcast a Vietnam observer as astute and experienced as Frances Fitzgerald, in the *Nation*, would write that *Lt. Col. Danny Graham* was the chief of intelligence who replaced General McChristian, instead of Gen. Philip Davidson.

Sam Adams explained the omission of officials such as Morris and Col. Lewington Ponder, Morris's deputy, as "too many names." By oversimplifying, however, CBS was distorting the reality of the military intelligence command structure. To begin with, only Davidson (aside from special ambassador Robert Komer) had direct access to Westmoreland; any military intelligence subordinate who wanted to speak—let alone conspire—with Westmoreland had to do so in the presence of the chief of intelligence. It is inconceivable that Davidson was not a plotter in any "conspiracy" that occurred. Indeed, as Crile wrote later, witness after witness provided testimony that Davidson was central to virtually every scenario of "suppression" or "fakery" CBS was alleging. Yet on every occasion when CBS could have placed Davidson at the crux of its conspiracy, it demurred from doing so. Consider Act 5 of the documentary when Wallace said, ". . . Several weeks after Tet, Colonel Daniel Graham, General Westmoreland's chief of estimates, asked [Col. Russell Cooley and Comdr. James Meacham] to alter MACV's historical record. In effect they [Cooley and Meacham] then accused Graham of personally engineering a cover-up. First, Commander Meacham."

> CRILE: There comes a time when Colonel Graham asked you and Colonel Weiler to tamper with the computer's memory, to change the data base in some way.

COMDR. JAMES MEACHAM (RETIRED): Yes, that's it.

CRILE: You said no.

MEACHAM: Well, we—we didn't say no. I mean, this thing wasn't our private property. It belonged to the intelligence directorate. We were the custodians of it. We didn't like what Danny Graham proposed to do. We didn't want him to do it. At the end of the day we lost the fight, and he did it.

CRILE: What was so wrong about going back into the memory? What got Meacham so distressed about it?

COOLEY: I would—a little bit of the 1984 syndrome here, you know, where you—you can obliterate something or you, you know, can—can alter it to the point where it-never-existed-type logic.

MEACHAM: Up to that time, even though some of the current estimates and the current figures had been juggled around with, we had not really tinkered with our data base, if I can use that jargonistic word. And—and Danny Graham was asking us to do it, and we didn't like it.

Then came Graham's twenty seconds of air time in the film: "Oh, for crying out loud. I never asked anybody [to] wipe out the computer's memory. I don't know what he—I honestly haven't got any idea what he's talking about."

WALLACE: We stress that Colonel Graham denies the allegation and insists that he never falsified nor suppressed any intelligence reports on the enemy. But Commander Meacham and Colonel Cooley insist that Graham did alter the record. And they suggest that because of this we may never be able to go back and understand exactly what happened.

That was the scenario: Graham asks Meacham and Cooley to tamper with the data base of the computer; he gets his way. But Crile ignored several important elements. To begin with, neither Meacham nor Cooley was in Danny Graham's chain of command. Adams diagramed that chain of command for Crile twice in his Prospects list (see top of page 136).

Thus, Meacham reported to, in ascending order: Paul Weiler, Edward Halpin (in charge of an intelligence branch unrelated to CBS's accusations), and Col. Charles Morris; Graham also reported to Morris. The differentiation between the two chains of command served a twofold

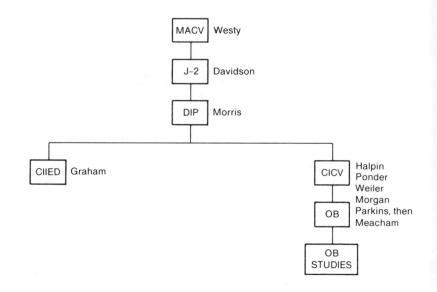

purpose: (1) CICV (Combined Intelligence Center, Vietnam) developed long-range research, while CIIED (Current Intelligence, Indications and Estimates Division) developed information for day-to-day use by American military forces in the field, and (2) CIIED was cleared for more sensitive intelligence sources, since some personnel in CICV worked side by side with the South Vietnamese, always suspect of being infiltrated by the enemy. OB studies was a unit within CICV.

"While OB studies, which was under my command, performed mostly an historical and accounting function," Meacham explained, "Current Intelligence had the job of providing the best information on what was going on that very day. It was always my belief," he added, "that there was intelligence available to persons in Current Intelligence that was not available to me." Meacham also said that his unit was not in Graham's chain of command and that, therefore, Graham was not in a position to order Meacham and his men to do anything.

Then how did Danny Graham manage the "cover-up," coercing men who were not under his command to act contrary to their consciences? Meacham recalled the real circumstances surrounding Graham's asking him to alter the computer's data base. "He didn't order us," said Meacham. "We had a great meeting up there [at MACV headquarters]. This was a proposal that was made to General Davidson. Davidson was there, Graham was there, I was there, Russ Cooley, a boy named Bernie Gattozzi. There were any number of hangers-on; must have been fifteen or twenty people in the room. And Danny Graham said, 'Look, General,

I think we ought to do this for this reason,' and I got up and made what I thought was a pretty stalwart, logical defense of why we should not do this—and we lost the fight. . . . There was nothing surreptitious about it, it was all out on the table." Davidson, said Meacham, listened to both sides of the argument and then said, "Let Danny do it."

Crile knew about that meeting chaired by Davidson. He mentioned it to Meacham in their interview in London.

> CRILE: . . . you were called to a meeting in General Davidson's conference room; it was a meeting attended by all the key people in the intelligence section. And at that meeting Colonel Graham called on—on you and Colonel Weiler to help him erase the computer's memory.

Crile mentioned that same meeting in his subsequent on-camera interview with Russell Cooley:

> CRILE: Do you remember that at that meeting in General Davidson's conference room, according to Commander Meacham, the argument was being carried by Meacham, Weiler, and Gatozzi—all three trying to prevent Colonel Graham from prevailing?

Thus, if there had been a "cover-up," as the documentary charged, it was not Graham (at least not alone) who engineered it but Gen. Philip Davidson, who had heard both opposing arguments and decided in Graham's favor. And George Crile knew that it was Davidson, not Graham, who had made that critical decision.

Neither Davidson nor Morris was ever blamed by name in the program. Morris could have been interviewed by Crile at any time; even if Davidson had been too ill to appear on the program (which, by December 15, CBS knew was not the case), testimony about his role could have been included, thus relieving Danny Graham of the burden of being the Key Conspirator. CBS had not hesitated when Lt. Col. Everette Parkins refused to go before its cameras to simply flash a photo on the screen, in order to tell the story of his alleged "firing." However, by revealing to the audience the importance of Davidson and Morris in the military intelligence hierarchy, CBS would have shattered the tenuous link between the targets of its conspiracy: Westmoreland and Graham.

Unlike Davidson and Morris, they were controversial figures: Westmoreland was the general who "lost" the Vietnam War; Graham's abrasive personality, combined with his political savvy and quick intelligence, had earned him enemies in the military establishment—ex-officials who might be willing to step forward and air their grievances against him. In fact, it is clear from Adams's Prospects list that finding men who detested Danny Graham was a priority. In the section of the Prospects list devoted to Col. Charles Morris, for example, three of Adams's four comments dealt with Morris's relationship with Graham:

POINT 1: He [Morris] dislikes Danny, his rival for Dave's ear.

POINT 2: He was the pessimist . . ., as against Danny, the optimist. . . .

POINT 4: A heart attack, occurring shortly after Tet, knocked him out of the . . . running and made Danny the uncontested #1. Morris resentful.

Adams looked with favor on other ex-officials who found Graham's personality offensive:

Lanterman, John	—Dislikes Danny, thinks he's a crook. . . .
Overcash, Robert	—. . . Dislikes Danny. . . .
Storey, Robert	—*Hates* Danny Graham. Thinks he [is] dishonest, etcetera. . . .
Heon, Leon	—. . . Told Danny he was full of crap. . . .

Only one ex-official out of the eighty (eighty-one including George Carver) on Adams's list thought highly of Graham.

Delpricio, Michael, Jr.	—Interesting as an admirer of Danny, but he didn't know about fakery.

There is no record of Crile ever contacting Delpricio. In fact, Crile did not interview any of the four ex-officials on the Prospects list who Adams said had no knowledge of "the fakery." Of course, that was the reason presidential adviser Walt Rostow had been excluded from the broadcast, too, despite the fact that Rostow could hardly "know" about a crime he doubted had ever been committed.

Rostow was the only ex-Johnson Administration official actually filmed for the CBS broadcast. However, George Crile did interview other ex-officials off camera, including U.S. representative to the United Nations Arthur Goldberg, former Under-Secretary of State George Ball, senators William Fulbright and George McGovern, Gen. Matthew Ridgway, and even former Secretary of Defense Robert McNamara. Crile would later cite these and other supplementary sources as proof that he "had actually relied on a large number of interviews beyond those included in the broadcast" and had not selected interviewees solely on the basis of whether their testimony might support his conspiracy premise. Again, though, it is clear that whenever remarks made by such officials contradicted the premise of the program, they were ignored. Consider the statements of the man who knew more about President Johnson than anyone except Rostow: Robert McNamara.

Mike Wallace made the first telephone call to McNamara while Crile listened in on an extension in Wallace's office. Several days later Crile interviewed McNamara by telephone. (This and subsequent interviews were "off the record.") According to Crile's notes, McNamara told him, ". . . My memory is so damn hazy, it's so long ago, I am not entirely sure, but I knew CIA and Defense differed on estimates. . . ." McNamara agreed to an in-person interview ("But it's got to be totally off the record. . . . I do not remember these things, and I don't have any access to files, and I am not a good source. . . .") on Tuesday, June 16, at 6:00 P.M. Only Mike Wallace knew that Crile had spoken to McNamara and had arranged to interview him in person. But not even Wallace knew that Crile had taped this off-the-record conversation with McNamara. Taping telephone calls without prior permission of CBS executives was a violation of the CBS News Standards.

Crile met McNamara at the World Bank, of which McNamara was president. "To my surprise," Crile wrote in a memo summarizing their encounter, "the interview lasted only thirty minutes and a car ride to his house. He had dinner guests waiting," Crile added, "and thus was able to cut short the interview before I could present him with all the evidence and ask him the questions I had in mind. . . . He was clearly uncomfortable having to deal with this information and kept interrupting right from the beginning," Crile continued in his summary, "almost as if he hoped he could keep me from going into it. . . . Despite the fuzziness of the session," Crile concluded, "certain key McNamara assertions did surface which," Crile added, "are all very significant—all supportive of our story and some critically supportive—but they were not delivered with great force. . . ."

Was McNamara supportive of CBS's conspiracy premise? The opening "point" in Crile's summary of the conversation confirmed that McNamara told him he knew nothing about any faking of intelligence; Rostow's similar statements were cited by Crile as the main justification for *excluding him entirely from the broadcast!* The truth is, McNamara was anything but supportive of the CBS premise.

"He explained that he had already made up his mind in the fall of 1966 that we couldn't win militarily," Crile wrote. "That was based in part on the OB which was (according to our findings) much too low. So if he heard that the enemy was bigger, then it would only have reinforced his convictions. In this manner he tried to dismiss the issue and get to his dinner. . . ."

In effect, by George Crile's own account McNamara was telling him what George Allen said he had: that CBS was making a mountain out of a molehill. Nor did a subsequent telephone interview with McNamara produce more useful results. On July 2 Crile memoed Wallace:

> Mike:
>
> Second interview with McNamara. He continues to be very odd—very detached from the accusations we are making about the faking of intelligence by his officers. . . .
>
> He says he refuses to give any observations about Vietnam. "I'm not going to give any evaluative judgments about Vietnam at all. Reason one—my memory is very bad, and secondly, I was a participant, and I don't believe that participants should evaluate their own roles."
>
> He says this after I reviewed our findings. He says he is not going to give any evaluations or judgments.
>
> He then tries to say that it doesn't matter that much because even after Tet the war went on for five years. . . .
>
> He doesn't know about suppression of infiltration estimates. Doesn't know why they did it if they did it.
>
> He said he was not told about massive infiltration but with hindsight it doesn't surprise him because he did not believe bombing was effective. . . .
>
> Double-talk about interpreting all estimates broadly. . . .
>
> Strength figures in his books—he used them as a beginning point in his thinking about the war but only as a beginning.

And then Crile revealed that McNamara did directly contradict at least one central prop of the conspiracy premise:

> McNamara says Wet. [Westmoreland] not under stress to deliver good news on war. . . .

Nothing McNamara told Crile supported the premise of the documentary; indeed, some of what McNamara said, in Crile's own summary of their conversations, directly contradicted parts of the program. George Crile took those tapes of his off-the-record telephone conversations with McNamara and put them in the back of his left-hand bottom drawer. No one who contradicted the premise of the program—with the exception of the targets of the conspiracy premise, Graham (allotted twenty seconds of air time in total to issue his denial) and Westmoreland—was allowed to appear in the broadcast. The purpose of this CBS "investigation" from the start was to confirm Sam Adams's interpretation of events. The penalty for contradicting Adams was immediate disqualification as a CBS witness or the guarantee, at least, that those confounding statements would not reach viewers' ears.

10

The
Documentary
Is
Completed

SOON AFTER THE SCREENING for CBS news president Bill Leonard, CBS announced the air date of George Crile's broadcast: Saturday, January 23, 1982. The tentative title of the program was: "A Legacy of Lies." In early December executives from CBS's advertising department reviewed the program. Their interpretation of the premise was clear: The copy they created portrayed faceless uniformed plotters around a conference table, whose surface shouted the word CONSPIRACY. Meanwhile, from Miami, Crile was telephoning Klein in New York, telling him that the script was completed. When Crile returned he made some minor changes in the script. Wallace recorded the narration that Crile had written for him. Now Klein could add to the film the sound-effects track and other technical touches necessary before the program could air.

Klein was working in producer Kent Garrett's editing room when Crile informed him that vice-president Roger Colloff was going to read all the transcripts, apparently to ensure that witnesses' statements in the broadcast had not been yanked out of context. Colloff spent several hours with Crile and Phyllis Hurwitz scrutinizing every detail of the film. Over and over again the CBS vice-president reviewed each sequence. It was then that Crile first heard Westmoreland's *Meet the Press* extension: After Westmoreland said that the infiltration rate as of November 1, 1967, was "5,500 to 6,000 a month," he added, "but they do have the capability of stepping this up." Crile asked Klein to remove that phrase; late that afternoon Crile telephoned Klein to inform him that the newly installed president of CBS News, Van Gordon Sauter, intended to screen the film the following morning. At that Sauter screening Crile enacted his elaborate charade, signaling Klein to kill the sound so that none of the assembled CBS executives could hear Westmoreland say, ". . . but they do have the capability of stepping this up."

When the film finished, the lights were turned on in the ninth-floor *60 Minutes* projection room. The CBS executives—Sauter and his deputy, Ed Joyce—seemed impressed. (Howard Stringer did not attend; earlier in December he had left *CBS Reports* to become executive producer of the *CBS Evening News with Dan Rather.*) However, Sauter did have one question.

"How do you think Westmoreland is going to react to this film?" he asked Crile.

The producer did not reply. Soon after the Sauter screening the title of the program was changed from "A Legacy of Lies," to "The Uncounted Enemy."

Colloff kept on reading transcripts throughout the month of December. Klein was still working on Kent Garrett's documentary, preparing a rough cut of that broadcast that could be screened for the new executive producer of *CBS Reports*, Andy Lack. Then, on New Year's Eve, Klein "mixed" the Vietnam broadcast, blending the various elements—sound tracks of narration, special effects, background "presence"—to create a polished program. The only elements now missing were the epilogue and closing credits. Klein decided to leave that three-minute section for the following week. It was growing late; everyone had plans for New Year's Eve celebrations. Klein departed with Crile, who kept telling the editor that he was going to be very proud of their film. "Everything will work out," Crile kept on reassuring Klein. The editor was silent. They wished each other a happy New Year and went their separate ways.

The film negative had been cut; aside from some minor tinkering, the only task that remained was to transfer the program from film to videotape, the medium used in almost all television broadcasts. That transference from film to videotape would take place at the "co-ord," a week before the program aired.

Early in January, CBS began the process of "selling" its show to the critics. "Viewing copies" were made of the broadcast so that selected members of the press could review it. In conversations with reporters,

CBS executives seemed enthusiastic. Crile carried a copy of the program with him to Washington, D.C., where he had arranged a screening at the *Washington Post.* (Crile landed in Washington, disembarked, and discovered he had somehow misplaced his review cassette. He telephoned Carolyne McDaniel in New York and asked her to rush another copy of the cassette to him. Carolyne told Crile she would call him back. By the time she did, Crile had located his missing copy.) Among those who screened Crile's program were Peter Braestrup and Don Oberdorfer whose books on Vietnam (*The Big Story* and *Tet,* respectively) were landmark accounts.

Then, on January 11, twelve days prior to the actual broadcast and long after the program had been "locked up," George Crile interviewed in Washington a pivotal figure in the controversy that had raged between the CIA and the military throughout 1967. For the first time George Crile interviewed George Carver, the superior of star CBS witness George Allen and the CIA's number one official specializing in Vietnamese affairs during the period in question.

"Crile was supposed to come at 10:30 A.M.," recalled Carver, a small man with owlish glasses. "He was delayed, and arrived at 11:00. I had a luncheon appointment at 12:00, so we talked for an hour."

It was, of course, Carver who throughout 1967 had orchestrated the CIA's efforts to resolve the dispute with the military over Order of Battle estimates. Carver was the one who had sent Sam Adams to the OB conference in Honolulu in February 1967. Carver was the one who had devised the CIA's negotiating strategy at the National Intelligence Estimate conferences beginning at CIA headquarters in Langley Field, Virginia, in the summer of 1967. Carver himself had led the delegation to Saigon in September 1967, at which the final NIE draft had been written. On September 14, 1967, Carver met in private with Westmoreland. At that meeting the two men resolved their differences and achieved a mutually acceptable compromise. Crile had not interviewed Carver for the broadcast, he said later, because "we had cables, internal memos, and reports which explicitly documented Carver's actions throughout the period."

According to Crile's summary memo of that January 11 conversation, Carver made three main points that supported controversial allegations contained in the program.

Later, in his June 3, 1982, "White Paper," Crile would argue that in his interview ". . . Carver in fact offered no information to counter anything that we stated in the documentary. . . ." But Crile's own page-and-a-half record of that hour-long interview contradicted that assertion.

Carver explained to Crile, in Crile's own words, "that Sam Adams and Danny Graham were both true believers coming from opposite extremes, each off, and he [Carver] was the one who took the middle ground. . . . On balance, he says he came out about right, and Tet demonstrated this. Graham was proven wrong because if his estimates were right, the enemy couldn't have mounted such an offensive. But if Sam were right, the enemy should have been able to mount a second offensive." In other words, Carver told Crile that both Graham *and Adams* had incorrectly estimated the size of the enemy. Graham's estimate was too low, Adams's was too high. Nowhere in the CBS broadcast would there be the slightest hint that Adams might be fallible, nor that *reasonable* men might differ with his judgment and still not be *treasonable* men.

Even more important, from Crile's notes it is clear that the ultimate NIE compromise between Carver and Westmoreland was initiated by the CIA. The documentary, in contrast, would charge that the CIA, in agreeing to that compromise, had caved in to pressure from the military. Here is how the program portrayed that crucial sequence of events:

WALLACE: . . . The battle between MACV and CIA went on for weeks. Before it was over it would become the most bitterly fought battle in the history of American intelligence. But in the end the CIA suddenly, without explanation, reversed its position and gave in to all of General Westmoreland's demands. George Allen explains why the CIA gave up the fight.

ALLEN: It was strictly a political judgment, a political decision to drop CIA's opposition and to go along with the modified set of figures.

CRILE: But once you make that decision, once you officially say that the enemy is a size you don't believe in, how do you go about making in—intelligence reports on the enemy subsequently?

ALLEN: That—that was my source of frustration.

WALLACE: CIA Director Richard Helms declined to talk to us for this broadcast. But without his authorization, MACV could not have prevailed. It was on Helms's authority that the CIA finally accepted Westmoreland's figures as the official estimate to be sent to the president.

ALLEN: As I say, I didn't talk to Mr. Helms about why he thought we should drop our opposition to the MACV figures. But the feeling was, naturally, that it was a political problem, that he didn't want the agency to be persisting—to be perceived as persisting in a line which was contravening the policy of—of the Administration.

Later George Allen was asked for the evidence underlying "the feeling" that the CIA had caved in because of political pressure. Allen had admitted he had not talked to Director Helms. Had he spoken with Carver about the events leading up to the NIE compromise? "No, no," said Allen irritably, "it was a *perception*. It was our *impression*—what else could we conclude? It was sort of a logical deduction—not a logical deduction but a plausible deduction. That's all I was saying there."

By his own admission George Allen was on the periphery of events during the summer and fall of 1967; he had no firsthand knowledge of CIA policy decisions regarding the Order of Battle debate—decisions that George Carver made in direct consultation with Director Richard Helms. In the documentary Wallace had said that "the CIA suddenly, without explanation, reversed its position and gave in to all of General Westmoreland demands. . . ." Twelve days before the broadcast, in the interview with George Crile, George Carver provided the explanation Wallace said was missing. Crile quoted Carver in the notes of their conversation:

> CARVER: There was a good deal of fiddling going on. Finally I went to Helms and said, "We can't get an agreement with Westmoreland if we keep going like this. I'll meet with him and see what we can do, but I'm not optimistic."

Crile wrote that Helms said he would "back Carver whatever course of action he takes." Crile continued, "Carver sees Westmoreland. Tells him he is being badly served. President not being well served. Can we work something out."

> So [Carver told Crile] he and I hammered out what to me was a fairly sensible agreement:
> 1. We would use hard stats when we could count—like main-force regulars.
> 2. We would use ranges where intelligence was soft—like guerillas.
> Where we couldn't really determine how many, we would just stop counting them.

Thus it was Carver, not Westmoreland, who initiated the move toward a compromise. Furthermore, CBS had in its possession convincing evidence that the compromise plan itself was suggested by Carver and not Westmoreland as the documentary intimated. Among those Carver "cables, internal memos, and reports" which Crile insisted "explicitly documented Carver's actions throughout the period" was a cable stamped SECRET, from Carver (code name "Funaro") to CIA Director Richard Helms (code name "Wren"). It began:

1. On July 9, Roger L. Scorburg and I had long, amicable, and thorough discussion of SNIE 14.3 draft and whole Order of Battle statistics problem with General Davidson [Westmoreland's chief of intelligence] and General Peterson [head of the higher CINCPAC intelligence agency]. After sketching nature and background of current Washington impasse and reviewing relative merits of estimative projection approach to OB as opposed to traditional data base approach, *I offered following proposal* [emphasis added] to resolve disagreements which had arisen during production of 14.3:
   A. Split analysis and presentation of Communist personnel assets into two major categories: military and nonmilitary.
   B. Under military category, show VC/NVA combat force at 116,000, administrative support at 75,000, and guerilla strength with range figure around 100,000, producing military force total in 291,000 range.
   C. In nonmilitary category, show political cadres at about 80,000, and Self-Defense [militia] with range figure around 125,000, producing nonmilitary total in 205,000 range, and thus showing total of at least partially trained and indoctrinated manpower pool to be in half-million range. . . .

This formula of separating military from nonmilitary forces, suggested by Carver over two months prior to his culminating mid-September Saigon meeting with Westmoreland, turned out to be the prototype of the ultimate National Intelligence Estimate draft. Clearly it was the CIA and not Westmoreland, as the documentary charged, that initiated the compromise. And Sam Adams had this crucial cable in his files.

Crile's record of his hour-long talk with Carver on January 11 totaled a page and a half. Later Carver would flesh out the remainder of that interview, adding his recollections to Crile's:

1. I pointed out to Crile . . . there was no evidence of a conspiracy. . . .
2. I said there was not suppression of evidence. Everyone had the

same [intelligence] pool, even those opposed to MACV. Their support was drawn from [the military's] own evidence and developed at considerable length. The suppression of evidence doesn't wash because even *Sam* was using [military intelligence's] data.

3. I said to Crile that no one would have fallen on his sword for his numbers. We were in the ballpark in our 1967 [NIE] estimate of force structure. It was adequate to mount Tet but didn't give them second-strike capability.

4. I also called George's attention to the actual 1967 NIE estimate. He said he had it. I said, "You are doing precisely what you accuse the United States government of doing—grabbing numbers out of context."

Carver explained that "in the 1967 estimate we made it clear that we had been underestimating certain categories in the past, and with all categories the enemy amounted to 500,000. . . . I tried to make it clear in *prose*: a complicated structure the aggregate size of which was in the 500,000 range, but *not 500,000 soldiers in the field.* . . ."

None of these comments that Carver insisted he made to Crile turned up in Crile's memo of their conversation. In any case, why, twelve days before the broadcast and after the documentary was already "locked up" (Crile's phrase), did Crile decide to interview Carver?

"I had urged Crile to get in touch with him, and he did," said George Allen. "Because although I was Carver's deputy, this phase he led himself: He himself went to Saigon, and he played the principal negotiating role. But Carver," added Allen, "was much more . . . policy-oriented. . . . He was a guy who always saw the glasses half full, I saw the glasses half empty. For CBS's purpose, I conclude by the fact that they didn't interview him at length and didn't use him was because they concluded that the half-empty glass was more amenable to the outlook they wanted to convey."

"The question of whether George Carver should or should not have been in the film as opposed to George Allen is a judgment call," said Crile. "Ultimately I went to George Carver because I wanted to touch base with him, but George Carver was on paper, George Carver's positions were on paper."

But why bother interviewing Carver, a reporter asked Crile, when it was already too late to include any revelation he might offer? "Well," said Crile, "why the hell not?"

"I think Crile wanted to see my general line," said Carver himself.

"Maybe if it was congenial he would snip in something. I think," Carver added, "they were trying to technically cover their flanks on any charge that they had not talked to me."

The "co-ord," when the film would be transferred to videotape, was scheduled for Friday, January 15, eight days before the broadcast. Two days before the co-ord, on a Wednesday, Adams wrote a note to George Crile:

> George:
>
> I think that *without* fail and *right away* we should send an errata sheet to correct the mistaken quotes from the Meacham letters (the ones mentioning Davidson and Danny Graham).
> As of this moment the press release is embargoed—therefore no harm done. But after January 20, we might get into trouble if, say, the *Times* quotes our misquotes. . . .

Klein was working in his editing room when Carolyne McDaniel burst in. She was very disturbed. "What's the problem?" said Klein.

"Sam has read through the script of the film and has discovered misquotes," she replied breathlessly. After Klein was able to calm her down, Carolyne explained that Adams had discovered erroneous information embedded in two questions asked by Wallace. Obviously, answers to questions containing incorrect information were invalid. Both of those questions were in Act 5, the final act of the program. One contained an erroneous piece of information about General Davidson, the other about Danny Graham. Carolyne said that Adams told her he intended to draw up a "disclaimer," going on the record to say that he discovered the errors before the broadcast aired, in case the questions were not corrected.

"Please, just relax," Klein told her. He kept pleading with her to be calm, telling her that he would take care of the problem. But he explained to her that only George Crile was empowered to decide what specifically should be done. He said to her, "Just give George a chance."

Sam Adams walked in. Adams was distressed. He confirmed to Klein that he had reviewed both the Davidson and Graham "problems" in the Meacham letters and that indeed both questions in the film had to be changed if the program was to be accurate. Adams explained in detail to Klein what those problems were. And then, in a conversational aside, he added something that struck Klein like a hammer. He said he had learned that "Davidson is as healthy as a clam." Klein could not believe his ears.

How could Davidson be well when throughout the making of this documentary Crile had assured and reassured Klein and everyone else that Davidson was a terminal cancer patient, too ill to be interviewed? Klein held his tongue; he had a more pressing problem to contend with. He left Adams and, several minutes later, walked into the cul-de-sac of editing rooms where he was working on Kent Garrett's broadcast. He heard a commotion coming from the 210A editing room. He entered and found there Anne Cadel, the *CBS Reports* graphic artist; Terry Robinson, the production manager; Phyllis Hurwitz; Carolyne McDaniel; and Grace Diekhaus. After talking to Klein, Carolyne had spoken to Crile in Washington. When their conversation did not convince her that Crile intended to make the necessary changes, at her wit's end, she had gone running to tell Diekhaus. Now Phyllis had Act 5 on the editing machine. She was "rolling" the act in search of the questions Adams said contained inaccurate information. Klein was furious. He had specifically told Carolyne that the solution to the two problems had to be decided by Crile, the producer of the program, and that the unit had to give Crile that opportunity to decide—something he was incapable of doing when he was 200-odd miles away in Washington.

Phyllis located the disputed questions. Klein looked at those segments of the film. He said, "There seems to be a problem." Then he told Grace Diekhaus: "George is the only one who is capable of deciding this. I don't know whether or not the information in those questions is accurate. Let's just wait until George comes in tomorrow."

Diekhaus agreed.

The following morning Crile, back from Washington, came into Klein's editing room. Klein showed him the questions in the film that had so distressed Sam Adams. Crile looked at the sequence involving Davidson and said that the question did contain inaccurate information and had to be removed from the documentary. Then Crile reviewed the other "problem," referring to some alleged misdeed committed by Danny Graham. "It's fine," said Crile. Adams was wrong; the section contained no inaccuracies.

Klein began working on the inaccuracy involving Davidson. Editing at that stage was a tedious process since the negative had already been cut and the various sound tracks mixed. It took Klein a while to make the change Crile wanted. Afterwards, Klein went to talk to Carolyne McDaniel. He was still seething over her actions of the day before, calling the women together to screen the film when he had told her that only Crile could decide what to do about the "problems" Adams had discovered. There were too many people in the vicinity of Carolyne's desk. Klein wanted to speak to her in private. He asked Carolyne to meet him in a nearby empty office, vacated recently by Judy Reemtsma, who had replaced Andy Lack as the *CBS Reports* senior producer.

Klein told Carolyne how distressed he was by her behavior the previous day. Carolyne kept telling Klein: "You don't understand, you don't understand what I've been through. You should have understood."

"I do understand," Klein said. "We all had a difficult time. But there's a difference between right and wrong," he added. "And you should have given George the opportunity."

Carolyne recalled her telephone conversation with Crile. "You know that he wasn't going to do anything," she said.

Klein said, "You had to give George the chance to demonstrate that."

That afternoon Klein had to leave CBS to check the final print of the broadcast, which was being processed at a nearby film laboratory. Crile said he wanted to come along. It was snowing outside, inches accumulating on the pavement, the snow turning gray at the curb, tainted from the exhaust of midtown traffic. Crile and Klein managed to hail a cab and were sloshing up the steep incline of 57th Street between 9th and 10th avenues when Klein said to Crile: "Sam has told me that Davidson is 'as healthy as a clam.' "

Crile was slumped in his seat, slouching so low he could barely peer over the seat in front of him. He did not reply.

They viewed the prints and found them in order. Klein was chatting afterwards with the men who managed the studio. Crile kept silent. Outside they found the snowstorm taking on blizzard proportions. Unable to collar a cab, they took a bus back to CBS.

Around five o'clock Crile entered Klein's editing room. He had reviewed the Graham "problem" again and had decided that there was indeed a misquotation. During the interview with Westmoreland, Wallace had read aloud a segment of a letter that Comdr. James Meacham had written to his wife from Vietnam. Now Crile (thanks to Adams) had discovered that a comment written by Adams or Crile had inadvertently been included in the quote about Graham from Meacham's letter. It was an honest mistake. The question was, how should it be corrected? Crile told Klein what he wanted him to do: instead of actually cutting the erroneous material out of the sound track, Crile wanted Klein to insert a "cutaway" shot of Westmoreland. The camera would focus on Wallace reading from the Meacham letter. Then, at the moment of the misquote, Klein would edit in the Westmoreland shot; the camera would be showing Westmoreland when Mike uttered the misquotation. No one would be able to tell that Wallace was still reading from the letter; instead of removing the inaccuracy from the film, Crile intended to simply introduce a device to distract the viewer.

Klein swiveled on his editing stool and stared at Crile. "There is no way," he said, "that I am going to participate in cosmetically altering the appearance of this film. If you want that done," Klein added, "you'll have to find somebody else."

Crile's face turned white. He got up and left the room. Moments later he returned with Grace Diekhaus. Klein screened the misquote for Diekhaus. "If there's a problem with this track," he said, "I am not going to put in a cutaway. "I'm not concerned with how the problem occurred," Klein added. "If it's a misquote, it does not belong in the film. You can't permit somebody to respond to a question that's inaccurate."

But Crile refused to allow Klein to physically remove the erroneously attributed comment about Graham. Klein refused to cover up the misquote by inserting a cutaway shot of Westmoreland. In the early evening Klein left CBS and went home, the stalemate between editor and producer still unresolved.

The next day was Friday, January 15, a crucial date in the preparation of the broadcast. At 11:30 P.M. the co-ord was scheduled to take place. At that session the film would be transferred to videotape, and once the broadcast was on videotape, no alterations would be made except in the most dire emergency. The actual transfer from film to videotape would be accomplished in a studio across 57th Street, in the CBS Broadcast Center. Before the co-ord, Klein had much work to do. He had to prepare an "air print," sync up his tracks; studio costs were exorbitant, and any remaining problems had to be resolved before the film reached the studio.

Klein arrived at CBS early that Friday morning and took the elevator to the eighth floor. He glanced into Andy Lack's office, but Lack was not there. Klein intended to discuss with the executive producer Crile's refusal to edit out of the broadcast an admitted misquote. Klein was convinced that inserting the cutaway of Westmoreland to cover up the problem was cosmetic—and thus dishonest.

Klein was walking back from Lack's office when he passed the office of Grace Diekhaus. Crile was there, talking to Grace. Diekhaus was sitting at her desk, Crile standing in front of it. As Klein glanced in, Crile beckoned him with a wave of his hand. Klein entered.

"Is everything okay?" Crile said.

"As far as I'm concerned we still have a problem," Klein said.

"Well, I've discussed the problem with [vice-president Roger] Colloff," said Crile, "and Colloff said my way of handling the Graham misquote in the Meacham letter was fine."

Klein paused, then replied, "That's an executive decision. I understand that it's Colloff's prerogative to make it. But," he added, "I think Colloff should actually *see* the problem before he decides what should be done about it." Klein was quiet for a moment. Then he added, "But if that's the way Colloff wants it, I'll have to follow those instructions."

Klein went to his editing room. He began searching for a shot of Westmoreland somewhere in the film that he could use as a cutaway. At this point all he would do was locate an appropriate shot, have it printed up, and tack it onto the end of the broadcast. Once the film was transferred to videotape, he would edit in the cutaway of Westmoreland, disguising the fact that Wallace was reading from the Meacham letter when he delivered the misquote. Klein would insert the Westmoreland shot on Sunday.

While Klein was working on the correction, Crile was taking time from his crowded schedule to write a letter to a key interviewee, informing him officially of a decision that had been made long before. The letter was to Walt Rostow:

Dear Mr. Rostow:

I wanted to let you know that the broadcast we have been working on is now scheduled to be aired Saturday night, January 23, at 9:30 EST. We had hoped to use substantial portions of your interview but in the end did not use any of it. I apologize for this and would like to explain why we made this decision.

1. Our broadcast is essentially a presentation of evidence that we have come to believe represented a conscious effort on the part of General Westmoreland's command to suppress and alter critical intelligence on the enemy in the year preceding the Tet offensive. You said that you knew nothing about the specific incidents that we related to you. In effect, you said that you were not in a position to comment authoritatively on these matters.

2. You should know that we looked further into the charges made by George Allen of the CIA that you had pressured him (and others at the CIA) to prepare a report demonstrating "success" in pacification at a time when the CIA did not believe such a conclusion was appropriate. We were able to confirm Mr. Allen's version of this incident through other sources, one of whom worked closely with you. We chose, however, not to include Mr. Allen's filmed remarks on this matter because it seemed inappropriate to air only this portion of your interview, when we had not asked you to participate for this sole purpose.

Indeed, a source close to the Vietnam project insisted that this Allen-Rostow scenario was the only one Crile ever seriously considered including in the film.

Crile argued that "the American public had been misled about the size of the enemy we were fighting," and defended Sam Adams's role in the documentary, insisting that CBS had relied on Adams "for the exhaustive research he has made available to us," but that "our reliance on him is not in the area of conclusions or interpretations. . . . As you will see, Mr. Adams is only one of a number of voices in the documentary and certainly not the most important."

Crile concluded by telling Rostow that he would not be able to send him the transcript of their interview that Rostow had requested; Rostow was not entitled to one since no portion of his interview was going to be aired.

On the surface this lengthy letter was merely a courtesy, explaining to a high-ranking official why his testimony had been discarded completely. But it was also an indication that CBS was aware of the critical importance of its decision to disregard Rostow's version of events—a decision, according to Crile, he made jointly with Colloff. CBS was answering in advance criticisms of its program that were likely to be leveled after the broadcast aired.

Throughout that evening, Klein kept on preparing the program for the co-ord scheduled for 11:30 that night. He had to assemble all the elements in proper order. At the close of each act he had to insert the black "slugs" that would run while the network broadcast its commercials. He had to ensure that the black leader he inserted for those commercial breaks equaled exactly the length of the ads themselves. The commercials would be cued electronically by computer; the timings had to be absolutely precise. Klein was working in close contact with Terry Robinson, the production manager, who was providing him with the list of commercial lengths and station breaks. There were countless technical details to which Klein had to attend.

At 11:30 P.M. the members of the Vietnam project gathered in the studio in the CBS Broadcast Center where the broadcast would be transferred from film to videotape. Klein and Crile were there, along with Hurwitz, McDaniel, and Terry Robinson. Zigman was still recuperating at home from his operation. Joe Fackovec, the additional editor Klein had asked Crile to hire, was not in attendance either. Klein would handle all the editing chores. The co-ord was a straightforward technical process, conducted for the most part by specialized CBS technicians. The film itself was on reels in a room below. Klein, Crile, and the others simply sat in the studio monitoring the transfer. There was a CBS color expert present; when film goes to tape, there may be a compression of colors, requiring certain adjustments. A CBS director was in the studio, too, along with an assistant director, audio men, and someone operating the chyron machine, which would produce the graphics that had been designed for the broadcast. The transfer was a smooth one. By about 2:00

A.M. the co-ord was over. Now the program was truly air-ready, on videotape, virtually carved in stone. Klein felt relieved. He would have to return on Sunday to insert the Westmoreland cutaway and attend to some other minor details, but effectively the documentary was finished. Finally, he thought to himself, his misery was about to end. Everyone said good-bye. The Vietnam documentary unit ceased to exist, with each member of it drifting off to a new assignment.

On Sunday the weather was arctic, with a gusty wind that startled pedestrians, battering them like a lurking mugger. Klein got out of a cab in front of the Ford building. He ran up the long flight of steps and spun the revolving glass doors, escaping from the wind's icy embrace. He took the elevator to the eighth floor, knowing that this would be the last time he would have to devote his energies to the Vietnam documentary. Today he would insert the Westmoreland cutaway, disguising the fact that Wallace was reading a misquote from Commander Meacham's letter. It was about 9:30 A.M. when Klein gathered all the elements he needed. He filled his arms full of reels and lugged them over to the Broadcast Center, where he found Terry Robinson, the production manager, waiting for him in the studio.

"You're not gonna believe this," she said, "but we have to make some changes."

Klein was stunned. "You must be kidding," he said.

Robinson told Klein that she had mentioned to Andy Lack that changes were being made. She said that after she talked to Lack, Lack and Colloff had discussed the problem. Then, she added, Colloff, Lack, and Crile had had a discussion. The end result was that Klein had to insert a line into the completed documentary. The cutaway shot would be added, but the misquote had to be physically removed from the program, covered by a line of blurring narration. Klein sat there. He could not believe his ears. Wouldn't this film ever be finished?

Crile arrived about two hours later. He walked into the studio but did not utter a word about the line that now had to be added to the program. Klein did not mention it to the producer either. Fifteen or twenty minutes went by before Crile sat down and said to Klein, "You know—we have to make a change."

"I understand that," said Klein. "Terry's explained it to me."

"Colloff says that we should make the change if it's not too much trouble."

"It's a great deal of trouble," Klein said.

Klein knew exactly what he would have to do. He would have to remove the misquote and add a line of Wallace narration to plug up that gap, connecting Wallace's comments before and after the misquote. Then he would insert the cutaway of Westmoreland. The problem was, the shot he had previously chosen would not do now. He had to comb the broadcast in search of a shot of Westmoreland that fit to the microsecond the time gap left by editing out the erroneous information. The cutaway could not be a second shorter or longer. "It's a very big ordeal," Klein told Crile.

Klein labored over the problem throughout the day. Again and again he screened the documentary until finally he found a shot of Westmoreland he felt he could use. He timed that shot—a wide one of Westmoreland simply sitting listening to Wallace—to ascertain the length of the line Crile would have to write for Wallace. Klein would take the comment that Wallace had been making to Westmoreland during the shot he had selected, get Wallace to record the new line of narration, then blend old and new together to achieve a smooth, natural mix. The task took him hours. Then Klein focused on other details that had to be done. He would not actually insert the Westmoreland cutaway and the blended lines of narration until the following Wednesday, four days before the broadcast.

Klein finished his work at about 3:00 P.M. Crile had departed long before. Now Klein had to carry his material back to the Ford building from the Broadcast Center. Before he left that studio, however, there was something he intended to do. He telephoned Joe Zigman at home. Zigman was due back at work after his illness the following day, a Monday. Klein wanted to apprise Zigman of what had been occurring. Zigman had to know; he was the associate producer of the program. Then Klein left the CBS Broadcast Center and plunged into the darkening afternoon. He jogged across 57th Street, juggling the reels in his arms. Sprinting up the steps of the Ford building, he reached the revolving doors and entered one set just as Andy Lack was entering. For a moment the editor and executive producer inadvertently acted out a charade more appropriate to Laurel and Hardy, wanting to stop and chat but unable to decide whether to quit revolving inside the building or outside of it. Lack finally stepped out into the cold winter air. Klein followed him. Lack was wearing a thick overcoat and a hat with flaps covering his head. They stood there staring at each other for a moment, their breath smoking. Then Klein said, "Are you aware of what has happened?"

"I *think* so," Lack replied. He explained to Klein that Crile had not, as he had claimed to Klein, spoken to Colloff about both "problems." All Crile had mentioned to Colloff was the misquote involving General Davidson. He had not uttered a single word to Colloff about the misquote from the Meacham letter involving General Graham.

11

Westmoreland
Fights
Back

ON MONDAY, Joe Zigman returned to work after his protracted illness. That morning Crile called a meeting of his Vietnam unit to tell the others about the changes that had to be made in the documentary. Klein was still troubled over the news Andy Lack had imparted the previous day— that Crile had never informed Colloff of the misquote in the Meacham letter. Klein regarded Crile's failure to tell Colloff as the ultimate abuse of trust in their relationship. Crile began speaking, hesitated, resumed, stumbling as he stated that the alteration had to be made because Colloff had so ordered. . . . Klein's anger was increasing. He started to talk, challenging Crile's version of events, but was restrained by Zigman. "Forget it," Zigman told Klein in front of Crile. "Forget it." Klein kept quiet.

Klein had measured the cutaway of Westmoreland he intended to insert into the film. Later that day Wallace arrived at the sound studio to record the line of narrative that had been written for him. Klein sat with a stopwatch. Wallace hovered over his microphone, peering at Klein through a window in his sound booth. Mike read aloud the line once; his recitation was too lengthy to fit the allotted time. Mike recorded the line a second time, speaking more rapidly.

"You gotta do it again," Klein told him, checking the stopwatch.

Wallace was starting to become agitated. His time was a valuable CBS commodity, and he did not intend to squander it repeating *ad nauseam* Crile's line of narrative. "I'm only doing it one more time," he announced, speaking to Klein in the studio through his microphone.

Fortunately the third time Wallace delivered the line it exactly matched the specified interval. Klein mixed the necessary elements together, ensuring a smooth narrative transition from the original line Wallace had uttered to the new line Crile had written, and then the production manager scheduled time in the Broadcast Center studio for Wednesday. Meanwhile, Klein kept on editing Kent Garrett's documentary, *A Time to Live, A Time to Die.* Zigman would visit from time to time; he knew Kent Garrett, and they liked each other. Zigman would appear at the door. He would utter some epigrammatic witticism about the Vietnam broadcast, then enter and sit down. Hurwitz was still working alongside Klein. With the three members of Crile's unit in the same room, soon one or another would offer some desperate anecdote that in retrospect seemed hilarious. They would recall these stories, their laughter rising and falling. Thus, without anyone ever actually confiding in him, gradually Garrett became familiar with the Vietnam project's problems.

Joe Zigman had a pet phrase. Sitting in that editing room with Klein, Hurwitz, and Garrett, he would say, on occasion after occasion, "I can't believe that George is smelling like a rose."

Wednesday came, and Klein completed his work on the program. Now all Klein had to do was wait for the broadcast, on Saturday at 9:30 P.M. He harbored a premonition—that the end of the broadcast would mark the beginning of the controversy.

Sam Adams may have had a premonition, too. That Wednesday he wrote a letter to Col. Gains Hawkins, the military's Order of Battle specialist whose testimony in the documentary buttressed the charge that Westmoreland had imposed an artificial "ceiling" on the size of the enemy.

A week ago, in his note telling Crile that *"without fail* and *right away"* the misquotes in the Meacham letter had to be corrected, Adams had given Crile his opinion of the program: "I've seen the whole thing now and think it's absolutely superb. No problems at all. . . ." Now, however, in his letter to Hawkins, he called the program "reasonably good," adding: "but, as I mentioned before, there's a major problem: The documentary seems to pin the rap on General Westmoreland, when it probably belongs higher than that. . . . In this regard," Adams continued, "I finally got hold of Komer. He's agreed 'in principle' to see me in a few days—but maybe he'll change his mind after the Saturday show. I'll tell you what he says. . . ."

Hawkins had insisted to Crile during their on-camera interview that President Johnson had to have known the intimate details of the debate over enemy strength because Robert Komer, Johnson's special envoy, was fully aware. Now Adams was calling "the rap" on Westmoreland "a major problem." The premise of the documentary was that Westmoreland had conspired to keep the true size of the enemy from Washington. However, Adams was convinced that the White House had indeed been privy to the essential details of the debate over enemy strength. Thus, either there had been no conspiracy—a possibility which Adams refused to consider—or the White House had to be at its apex. And if the White House was hatching the plot to suppress, clearly the documentary's premise of a Westmoreland-led conspiracy was wrong.

On Thursday morning, in Charleston, S.C., the alleged master-plotter looked more like a Miami Beach pensioner, sitting in his den devouring his ritual breakfast of cereal buttoned with banana slices. Minutes before, Westmoreland had waved good-bye to his wife, bound in the fading gray family sedan for her exercise class. Now as he ate he was watching the CBS news program *Morning with Charles Kuralt and Diane Sawyer.*

Said Sawyer: "It is an axiom of war that, above all, one must know the enemy. On Saturday night the CBS News broadcast *CBS Reports* will show that the American government in Washington was deceived about the enemy in Vietnam—specifically, in 1966 and 1967, deceived about how vast their numbers were. The broadcast is called 'The Uncounted Enemy: A Vietnam Deception,' reported by Mike Wallace and producer-reporter George Crile, who found at the heart of the deception not the hand of the enemy but the American military command." Sawyer then introduced Wallace and Crile, followed by a sequence from the broadcast in which Westmoreland seemed to admit that he did not accept the "McChristian-Hawkins briefing" because "the people in Washington were not sophisticated enough to understand and evaluate this thing. And neither was the media." Sawyer clucked disapprovingly, then introduced other sequences from the broadcast, with Wallace and Crile "selling" the CBS audience on the certainty of their conspiracy premise the way Crile by himself had convinced his superiors at CBS during his several screenings.

The segment was over. Westmoreland glanced down and saw that his hand holding the spoon was hovering halfway between the cereal bowl and his lips, frozen there in midair the moment Sawyer had begun her provocative "promo." Only now his hand was *shaking.* He put down the spoon and reached for the telephone. He called David Henderson, a friend who was a partner in a prominent Washington public-relations firm.

"Dave," he said, "CBS is going to crucify me, and I can't see a damn thing I can do about it."

"After the broadcast," said Henderson, "we'll arrange a little press conference."

The following day, Friday, full-page advertisements appeared in the *Washington Post* and in the *New York Times*. There were the faceless uniformed plotters huddling around their conference table, with the word CONSPIRACY emblazoned across it in thick black letters. The accompanying text read: " 'CBS Reports' reveals the shocking decision made at the highest level of military intelligence to suppress and alter critical information on the number and placement of enemy troops in Vietnam. A deliberate plot to fool the American public, the Congress, and perhaps even the White House into believing we were winning a war that in fact we were losing.

"Who lied to us? Why did they do it? What did they hope to gain? How did they succeed so long? And what were the tragic consequences of their deception. . . ?"

Soon others would be asking the same questions—about the makers of the CBS documentary.

That Friday, January 22, Crile spoke by telephone with Brig. Gen. Winant K. Sidle. It was Sidle who had commanded the military's Office of Information (MACOI) in Saigon in the period being scrutinized by the documentary. Daily, Sidle and his men had journeyed from Westmoreland's two-story "Pentagon East" headquarters at the Tan Son Nhut airfield in suburban Saigon to the Joint United States Public Affairs building downtown. There, in a large auditorium, at five o'clock each day Sidle and his men delivered briefings to the press—the legendary "Five O'Clock Follies," so called because of the recurrent clash of military optimism against journalistic cynicism that turned the briefings into a sideshow.

By late 1967 relations between that Saigon press corps and the military had reached a new low. Newsmen were convinced that the Johnson Administration was engaged in a blatant public relations campaign to demonstrate "progress" in the Vietnam War. Westmoreland had been recalled by the White House—against his will—both in April and in November 1967 to assure Congress and the American people that the war was still winnable.

"Indeed," wrote Peter Braestrup in *The Big Story: How the American Press and Television Reported and Interpreted the Crisis of Tet 1968 in*

Vietnam and Washington, "by 1967 Saigon newsmen felt that West-moreland and the military spokesmen at MACV, under pressure from Washington, were gilding the lily, presenting the war of attrition in black and white terms (United States progress, enemy decline) instead of in the grays that the realities demanded."

The military was equally as skeptical of the journalists' ability to "get the war right." Despite the quantity of reporters actually in-country at the time of Tet, wrote Braestrup, "this large number of accredited 'media representatives' . . . gave a misleading impression." He estimated the "fact-finding" manpower available in Saigon during the Tet offensive as "perhaps sixty newsmen in all," the rest being support staff, free lances, etcetera. Few of those newsmen had any real understanding of the military. "As a result," Braestrup argued, "many newsmen were ill-equipped to understand, let alone question, official or unofficial explanations of military deployments, problems, and progress. They had to learn, in highly unsystematic patchwork fashion, while on the job. . . ." Braestrup added that "the television networks were perhaps the least 'serious' in this respect. Their bureau chiefs were assigned to Vietnam for one year; the reporters came and went on tours varying from one to six months. . . . Of the eighteen-odd network correspondents in Saigon when Tet hit, only half had been accredited four months earlier. . . . Thus," concluded Braestrup, "when the Tet offensive came, there was only headshaking among newsmen as Westmoreland claimed a military setback for the foe. (Months later the Westmoreland judgment became widely accepted, but without retroactive credit to the general.)"

This mutual antagonism between the Saigon press corps and the military was a crucial aspect of the CBS story. The CBS documentary would accuse Westmoreland and his intelligence command of a conspiracy to conceal information on the size of the enemy from the Congress, the President, the Joint Chiefs of Staff, and the American public. Underlying that conspiracy premise was the notion that Westmoreland's motive was to help the Administration convince the American public that the Vietnam war was heading toward a favorable conclusion, and thus help reelect in 1968 a president whose support Westmoreland needed in order to prosecute his war. The military's conflict with the Saigon press corps was the crucible of the debates over the Order of Battle. But CBS chose not to explore that conflict, perhaps because to have done so the network would have had to bare its own archives of the period to public scrutiny and historical judgment, including Walter Cronkite's milestone commentaries, immediately following Tet, which declared that an American victory was now unlikely and that a truce must be negotiated.

Had Crile wanted to take his investigation in this direction, providing an explanation of the military's concern over press reaction to a larger-seeming enemy, an interview with Gen. Winant K. Sidle would have been pivotal. Sidle was the Saigon fulcrum of the seesaw battle between the Administration's boasting and the journalists' skepticism over the progress of the war.

In their telephone conversation the day before the broadcast, Crile informed Sidle that he had "just got word via Ike Pappas [the CBS Pentagon correspondent] and then Jack Smith, the [Washington] bureau chief, that you had told somebody in the Pentagon that you thought there was something you had that we should know about."

Sidle told Crile he had heard that CBS was going to "accuse us of a cover-up. . . ." Sidle recalled the press conference he had delivered on November 24, 1967—MACV's first full explanation of the final National Intelligence Estimate draft, and its altered Order of Battle, to Saigon newsmen. Although the press briefing would not be specifically mentioned in the documentary, in conversations with reporters Crile and Adams would frequently refer to it and previous briefings as proof that the military was engaged in a public relations campaign to minimize the size of the enemy. Crile told Sidle, "I'd love to have you send that on." Surprisingly, he then admitted: "I've only seen the news accounts of that, you know. . . ." Sidle went on to expostulate at length, reading parts of the transcript of that press briefing and providing explanations of it. Crile responded periodically, punctuating Sidle's rambling monologue with skeptical comments and questions.

"I think you gotta see the show and see the whole context of it. You must see it because, of course, Adams is a triggering mechanism here, but Adams is not, by any stretch of the imagination, the key witness or anything," Crile finally told Sidle. "He only picks up the CIA side, which is really not what this story is about. It really is about the people inside [military] intelligence, how they felt about the things that were happening."

"Well," said Sidle, "did you talk to Phil Davidson by any chance?"

Five weeks before, Adams had been told by Col. Edward Hamilton that Davidson was "bouncing around fine." Subsequently Adams had told Klein that Davidson was "as healthy as a clam." Klein had repeated Adams's comment to Crile a few days prior to the telephone call.

"Davidson was—is he dead now?" Crile asked Sidle.

That Saturday, Klein watched "The Uncounted Enemy: A Vietnam Deception." During the broadcast, though, he kept thinking of only one thing: the controversy the program was sure to catalyze. He had seen the advertisement in the New York Times: the plotters huddling around the conference table with the word CONSPIRACY emblazoned across it. He had sensed the excitement at CBS itself. People there were anxious to see the program; no one apart from the Vietnam-unit members and the executives who supervised them really understood its content since the broadcast had been made in semisecrecy. All they knew was that it was as provocative as it was powerful.

The broadcast ended—and Klein's telephone began ringing. Many of Klein's friends telephoned, most congratulating him. His mother called to praise the film. She had been as staunch an opponent of the Vietnam War as her two sons. Like Ira, his friends and family had been against the war in Vietnam. The program aroused in them, as it was calculated to do, passions that had lain dormant for a decade. It ripped open old wounds. The broadcast was compelling; it was convincing.

Westmoreland did not see the actual broadcast. Although his interview with Wallace was a warning that the broadcast would be a hostile one, he adhered to the schedule of engagements inserted on his calendar. The evening the documentary aired he was at a black-tie dinner party at Washington's Hilton Hotel. However, perhaps with the upcoming program in mind, he had done something out of character that week: For the first time in years he had gone to see a movie. The film was *Absence of Malice*.

The next morning Klein purchased Sunday's *New York Times*. He skimmed the bulky newspaper in search of commentary about the previous night's broadcast. Klein kept flipping pages until a large four-word heading attracted his attention. On the bottom of page twenty there was a *Times* editorial entitled "War, Intelligence, and Truth."

The *New York Times* editorial read:

A CBS documentary on Vietnam last night has surprising present pertinence. "The Uncounted Enemy: A Vietnam Deception" showed that Lyndon Johnson was victimized by mendacious intelligence.

Withheld from him was the fact that the Vietcong had twice the 285,000 troops he was told they had just before the 1968 Tet offensive. Those "captured documents" of which he boasted were in truth packed with accurate information—but the summaries he received were doctored, to keep the press from "drawing an erroneous and gloomy conclusion," in General Westmoreland's own words. . . .

Uncritically accepting the gospel preached the previous evening from atop CBS's microwave mountain, the *Times* editorial went on to link the past to the present.

. . . What makes this report more than a matter of history is America's continuing preoccupation with guerilla war elsewhere, notably in Central America. El Salvador is not Vietnam and fortunately the United States' involvement is much more modest. But as policy is pitched to the strength of rival forces there, the reliability of intelligence estimates is as important now as before Tet. . . .

Even after so many years, General Westmoreland still tries to explain away the falsification of intelligence, even to the commander in chief. President Reagan would be well advised to protect himself by finding out how much Lyndon Johnson knew—and when he knew it—about the last war in its most crucial period.

The *New York Times* editorial was an extraordinary one. The upper echelon of *Times*men were notorious for their skepticism of television, burying coverage about the medium in the newspaper's graveyard back pages. At the *Times*, television news was regarded as a glossy copycat headline service whose agenda was set by the *Times* itself. Rarely in its history had the *Times* been so charitable, rendering an instant benediction over a controversial television documentary—suggesting, in fact, that President Reagan might be "well advised" to undertake an investigation to learn what President Johnson did or did not know. It is perhaps significant, in explaining the *Times*'s rush to judgment, that of all the allegations in the documentary, the editorialist chose to focus on the one dealing with the Fourth Estate itself, quoting from the August 20 cable to complain that "the summaries he [Johnson] received were doctored to keep the press from 'drawing an erroneous and gloomy conclusion. . . .' " The Nielsen overnight ratings would demonstrate that the mass audience had paid scant attention to the CBS broadcast (its 9.4 rating would earn it seventy-ninth place among the seventy-nine prime-time programs on network television that week). However, the broadcast seen by approximately 8,000,000 viewers had touched a raw exposed nerve among one segment of the population—the press itself.

That Sunday, January 24, Westmoreland spent hours on the telephone initiating his counterattack. David Henderson, the public relations specialist, had offered to handle his response to the program *pro bono*. The press conference would be held on Tuesday at Washington's Army–Navy Club, near the Pentagon. The ex-officials who rallied to Westmoreland's defense were: Ambassador to Vietnam Ellsworth Bunker, the CIA's George Carver, Lt. Gen. Danny Graham, Col. Charles Morris, and the "terminally ill" Gen. Philip Davidson, Westmoreland's chief of intelligence in Vietnam during the period under examination. Two ex-military officers who had appeared on the CBS program declined to cooperate with Westmoreland. After the broadcast Davidson's predecessor in Vietnam, Chief of Intelligence Gen. Joseph McChristian, sent Westmoreland this bitter cable:

> I've gone over my notes and find that George Crile did tell me that Colonel Hawkins testified that he had been ordered to abide by a "ceiling" established by you. Knowing this unproved allegation, I answered George Crile's question. I'm sorry if my answer hurt you.
>
> As to the allegations in the documentary pertaining to actions that took place after I left Vietnam, I feel that the people who were there should help you refute them. If they cannot refute them, then I think you, General, should determine who the guilty persons were.

The other negative response came from Colonel Hawkins himself:

> In response to your telephone call this date, January 24, the following comments are provided in accordance with your request.
>
> 1. I do not, repeat do not consider that I was quoted out of context on the *CBS Reports* documentary.
>
> 2. I never received any direct orders from you at any time. I was two echelons removed from your level of command.
>
> 3. If my interview with CBS had been shown in its entirety, my remarks would have indicated the soundness of our holdings on the enemy main forces and local forces. My concerns were focused on the political and guerilla categories.
>
> 4. I am sorry if the concerns I carry with me to this day have caused you distress in regard to your integrity.
>
> I have given these remarks careful thought, and I hope that these remarks will clarify our telephone conversation this date.

On Monday morning when Klein arrived at CBS he found everyone ecstatic about the show. Crile was euphoric, Diekhaus was enthused. Only Klein was subdued. "We need more shows like this one," announced Andy Lack. But Klein was not affected by the elation surrounding him; he was not interested in reading the out-of-town reviews of the program. He was waiting for Westmoreland's response. He was waiting, at last, for the opportunity to hear the side of the debate that had been quarantined from the CBS documentary.

While CBS (its documentary awarded a seal of approval by the "paper of record") was complacent in its triumph, a witness whose testimony had been excluded from the broadcast was fuming. On January 26 Walt Rostow sat down and wrote a lengthy letter to the *New York Times*. And as Rostow, in Texas, was writing his letter that Tuesday, a few thousand miles away in Washington, D.C., a scenario was being enacted that could have been torn from a reporter's memoirs of Saigon in the fall of 1967. There, at the Army–Navy Club, was Gen. William Westmoreland, defending his reputation before skeptical reporters. Surrounding him at the podium were the defenders he had been able to muster. As ex-Ambassador to Vietnam Ellsworth Bunker would say afterwards, it was "just like the old days." Lt. Gen. Danny Graham was present, along with a host of ex-officials whose testimony either had not been solicited by CBS or whose interviews had not been filmed for the CBS broadcast. Westmoreland opened his remarks with a reference to the movie he had seen the previous week—one that in retrospect seemed prophetic.

". . . Last week," he said, emotion filling in his throat, "my wife urged me to attend a movie which was my first in five years. The name of that movie was *Absence of Malice*. Although I did not take the movie literally, it did show an innocent man whose life and many others were ruined by the unscrupulous use of the media. Little did I know that within a week a real life, notorious reporter, Mike Wallace, would try to prosecute me in a star-chamber procedure with distorted, false, and specious information, plain lies, derived by sinister deception—an attempt to execute me on the guillotine of public opinion. It was all there," Westmoreland added, "the arrogance, the color, the drama, the contrived plot, the close shots, everything but the truth. . . ." Westmoreland went on to accuse CBS of conducting "a vicious, scurrilous, and premeditated attack" on his character and personal integrity. "In essence," he added, "Mike Wallace, primarily on the basis of material provided by a former intelligence analyst for the CIA, Sam Adams, accuses me of withholding and falsifying important intelligence information to the extent that generated a sinister conspiracy against the national interest. That is a preposterous hoax and will not go unanswered. Thus, I have invited you here this morning to make known the falseness of the accusation and the numerous specific points raised on the program in support of the accusation. . . ."

Westmoreland introduced the officials he had assembled in his defense: Bunker, Graham, Carver, Morris, and Gen. Philip Davidson. He then recounted the steps that led to his alleged entrapment in the CBS project:

1. He had not learned about Sam Adams's involvement in the project until he was actually before the CBS cameras.

2. He had "done no research and had brought no documents" to refresh his fourteen-year-old memory of events.
3. "If I appear excited on the film," he said, "you can see why, because I was ambushed."
4. He had subsequently written a letter to Wallace and "Mr. Creel" (Westmoreland would continue to mispronounce the CBS producer's name for months after the broadcast) in which "I enclosed several contemporary documents to correct my imprecisions. I also recommended additional interviews with other knowledgeable officials such as Ambassador Bunker; Ambassador Komer, who was my deputy for pacification; Mr. George Carver; my former chief of staff Gen. Walter P. Kerwin; and a former head of the CIA who had served in Vietnam, the Honorable William Colby. To the best of my knowledge none of those gentlemen was interviewed. None of my statements on film were corrected, and I received not even the courtesy of an acknowledgment of my letter. . . ."

Westmoreland argued that to include the disputed categories in the Order of Battle would have been to "introduce a substantial jump in enemy strength when in fact there was no increase in combat strength," thus deceiving "everybody, our superiors in Washington, the news media, and the American people. But let me say parenthetically," he added, "[our] headquarters knew about this intelligence, the intelligence community at CINCPAC [Commander-in-Chief, Pacific; to whom Westmoreland reported] in Hawaii, the CIA, the embassy, the ambassador. Even the White House, they knew about the figures, and I refused to include those in the Order of Battle because they did not represent an increase in combat strength. In Saigon, Ambassador Bunker strongly supported me with that concept. . . ." Westmoreland said that "the representations made by Mr. Wallace reflected premeditated malice. . . ."

Danny Graham followed Westmoreland, introducing selected segments from the broadcast in order to critique them. Like Westmoreland, Graham insisted that "all evidence collected by [military intelligence] was reported back to Washington. It was also reported back through State and CIA channels, as Mr. Bunker and Mr. Carver will attest. . . ."

Davidson followed Graham onto the podium, fielding questions from the press. Both he and George Carver also insisted that all the information collected by military intelligence had been funneled to the entire intelligence community plus the White House itself. ". . . We had many, many sharp disagreements as to how some of this should be interpreted," said Carver, "but . . . all that evidence was provided by . . . our military colleagues, so I think the charge that they suppressed evidence falls, clearly, of its own weight." Then Carver dealt with the essential element that the documentary had ignored: the role of the press itself. ". . . I think you gentlemen will be honest enough to acknowledge to yourselves, the media bore a certain measure of culpability. Journalists had to fit what they had to say within a few column inches. People in the television media had to fit what they had to say within a few seconds of air time, and there was a great itch for simplification. Give me the bottom line number. Never mind the complicated details. And this disturbed a lot of reporting, official as well as private, and a certain measure of analysis. And complexity is a very hard thing for the media or for our kind of society to cope with. . . ."

Carver then went on to discuss the National Intelligence Estimate itself, whose final draft the documentary had described as a cave-in by the CIA to military pressures, with the CIA acceding to all of Westmoreland's demands.

"The results of all those discussions and debates," said Carver, "was an agreement hammered out in Saigon, the essence of which was personally hammered out between General Westmoreland and myself in a private session. Our staffs, quite correctly, were at loggerheads, and we had reached what seemed like an impasse. But the general and I talked," Carver added, "and we reached an agreement which neither of us may have thought was ideal, but both of us thought was . . . we could live with, and which would free the president from being beset, as he was up to that point, by conflicting estimates from every element of his official community which produced only confusion not clarity. . . ."

Then Carver dropped a bombshell. "And it was not General West- moreland who dictated that they [the categories described textually in the final NIE draft] be dropped from the Order of Battle, as Mike Wallace said in his rather stentorian tone. It was *I* who suggested that because of the sponginess of the evidence we should describe these, not with the kind of number on which people would fasten and seize and run in to their computers and try to do weighted averages and all the other statis- tical nonsense that you try to do with very soft numbers, but that we should describe them in prose, which was a much better vehicle for describing that sort of thing. . . ."

Carver concluded by saying, "There's a great deal of argument about Vietnam. Nobody claims to have the truth. Anybody who does," he added, "either doesn't know what he's talking about or he's lying. . . ."

That afternoon, Mike Wallace telephoned CBS from Nicaragua to speak to George Crile. Crile was out to lunch, so the call was transferred to Sam Adams. About two o'clock that afternoon, Adams recorded the content of his conversation with Wallace in a memo for Crile. Wallace had asked, wrote Adams, "if there was anything new on the show." Adams told Wallace about a pair of favorable newspaper articles. Wallace then asked Adams "whether there was anymore noise from Westy." Adams replied that as far as he knew, the answer was no. (It wasn't until after the telephone call that Adams learned, from Carolyne McDaniel, about the Westmoreland press conference held that morning.) Wallace wanted to know if CBS was being supportive. Adams replied that as far as he knew, the answer was yes.

Wallace had one final question. "He asked [are] there any other problems?" wrote Adams to Crile. "I said that we were beginning to think that maybe LBJ knew more than the documentary implied he did."

12

The
Controversy
Grows

ROBERT KAISER WAS ONE of the reporters who attended Tuesday's West-moreland press conference at the Army–Navy Club. The following morning his account appeared in the *Washington Post*. Kaiser described how General Graham, during a show-and-tell exercise, had misedited a passage from the documentary. Kaiser wrote that "the clip from the documentary that Graham had showed was edited to cut out [Col. Gains] Hawkins's final words, when he said that the political Order of Battle included 'the Vietcong's political bureaucracy and the guerilla strength.' The guerillas were armed.

"Asked about this use of editing to distort Hawkins's remarks, West-moreland made no reply. . . ."

CBS regarded Graham's sleight of hand, and Westmoreland's conten-tion that he had been "ambushed" in his interview with Mike Wallace, as proof that the two men were still practicing deceptions. Indeed, West-moreland had not been "ambushed"—a term only appropriate to occa-sions when journalists pounce on people without prior warning. West-moreland should have been prepared for a grueling interview session since he knew the interrogator would be Mike Wallace and that the topic would be the Vietnam War. Crile read reporters the letter he had sent

Westmoreland before the interview, spelling out topics to be discussed. Few reporters noticed that the letter was dated the day Westmoreland arrived in New York or that the real purpose of the interview had been buried among a list of other issues. On January 30 Westmoreland wrote a note of "regret" to Crile, informing the producer that he had totally forgotten about receiving the letter and apologizing for failing to acknowledge its receipt at the press conference.

That day Crile telephoned Col. Charles Morris (the director of intelligence production immediately below Gen. Philip Davidson in the military intelligence hierarchy), whom he had interviewed by phone in mid-December but whom he had decided not to put on camera, although he regarded the information Morris had provided him a crucial confirmation of the broadcast. According to Crile's notes of that earlier telephone interview, Morris had confirmed the existence of a larger enemy and that "the American public had been misled." During that previous telephone conversation, with regard to enemy infiltration in the months before Tet, Morris said, "We screwed up and didn't want to say it." After the Westmoreland press conference, however, Crile was reportedly angry over Morris's testimony, which contradicted his notes. He taped a telephone call to Morris on January 30 to resolve the discrepancies.

He asked Morris about the "we screwed up" statement. "We did screw up," replied Morris. "There's enough bad we did over there to where if we just tell exactly what happened as best we can reconstruct it, we'd still be entitled to a knock on the wrist. But it was honest. There was nothing surreptitious about it. And that's what I really resent about the whole thrust of the program is that you said that Westmoreland and Phil Davidson, whom you people didn't even bother to contact, and Charlie Morris, Danny Graham were involved in a conspiracy. That's your word, I believe. Your program's word. A conspiracy to deceive and that couldn't be further from the truth!"

Three days after the press conference, on a Thursday, a *TV Guide* writer met with a CBS source for a lunch at a Manhattan restaurant. During the course of their conversation the source asked if the writer had seen "the Vietnam show."

The writer had not. "Was it a good piece of work?" he asked.

"It was definitely a *powerful* piece of work," the source replied.

"What do you mean 'powerful'?"

"Did you know about Westmoreland's press conference on Tuesday?" the source said.

"No, I did not. I didn't even know the show dealt with Westmoreland."

The source summarized the program's premise that in the year prior to the Tet offensive Westmoreland had led a conspiracy to conceal the true size of the enemy from the president, the Congress, and the American people. "Get a transcript of the press conference," said the source. "More important," the source added, "get a copy of the script of the program. Read the script *before* you screen the show."

"Why read the script first?"

"It was a powerful piece of work," the source said, indicating, by a finality of tone, that the discussion of the Vietnam documentary had ended.

Normally cool and unflappable, the source had seemed inexplicably agitated. The writer decided to discuss the conversation with a colleague, without revealing the source. *TV Guide* already had a script of the broadcast plus a transcript of the Westmoreland press conference. One of the writers was preparing a column item describing the press conference, with reaction from CBS, in the following week's edition of the magazine.

Independently the pair of writers sat down and spent time studying the show's script. Afterwards they conferred, soon realizing that they were in basic agreement over certain problems within the twenty-six-page document. To begin with, from the point of view of print journalists the script was vague in the supporting evidence it mustered to buttress its allegations. The "ceiling" on enemy-strength estimates Westmoreland allegedly had imposed was supported in the broadcast not by hard fact but by murky impressions. Col. Gains Hawkins, the Order of Battle specialist, kept talking about "the message" he had gotten at a crucial briefing with Westmoreland; by "message," however, he did not mean an overt order but some subliminally transmitted insinuation. Gen. Joseph McChristian, the predecessor as chief of intelligence to Gen. Philip Davidson, seemed also to have been at that briefing. But while CBS stated that Westmoreland had suppressed McChristian's report of a larger enemy, McChristian himself offered no testimony in the broadcast confirming that allegation. Again, when asked if Westmoreland had imposed a "ceiling" during the CIA–military conferences on Order of Battle in the summer of 1967, Col. George Hamscher replied, "We can't live with a figure higher than so and so . . . is the message we got."

Who was Hamscher anyway? He first appeared in a section of the documentary that began with Wallace saying: "*CBS Reports* has learned that Colonel Hawkins was in fact carrying out orders that originated from General Westmoreland. Westmoreland says he doesn't recall those orders. But the head of MACV's delegation [to the CIA–military conference at CIA headquarters in the summer of 1967] told us that General Westmoreland had, in fact, personally instructed him not to allow the total to go over 300,000."

CRILE: Wasn't there a ceiling put on the estimates by General Westmoreland? Weren't your colleagues instructed, ordered, not to let
those estimates exceed a certain amount?

HAMSCHER: We can't live with a figure higher—

In their first readings both writers assumed that Hamscher was that
"head of MACV's delegation." However, four pages later in the script
Wallace was referring to "Colonel Hamscher of DIA. . . ." DIA was the
Defense Intelligence Agency which, the writers knew, was the intelligence branch of the Pentagon, based in Washington. Hamscher could
not be both the head of a military intelligence delegation from Saigon
and a representative of DIA.

Later in the broadcast Wallace argued that "the battle between MACV
and the CIA went on for weeks. . . . But in the end the CIA suddenly,
without explanation, reversed its position and gave in to all of General
Westmoreland's demands. . . . It was on [CIA Director Richard] Helms's
authority that the CIA finally accepted Westmoreland's figure as the official estimate to be sent to the president."

GEORGE ALLEN: As I say, I didn't talk to Mr. Helms about why he
thought we should drop our opposition to the MACV figures. But
the *feeling was* [emphasis added], naturally, that it was a political
problem. . . .

HAWKINS: . . . There was no mistaking the *message.*

HAMSCHER: . . . is the *message* we got.

ALLEN: . . . the *feeling* was . . .

By the standards of print journalism there seemed to be an excess of
allegations and a corresponding dearth of hard evidence. Only two documents were dealt with in any detail in the broadcast—Westmoreland's
August 20 cable and the report fom the CIA's Joe Hovey predicting Tet.
Furthermore, it was clear that the program lacked balance. The only two
officials who testified in Westmoreland's behalf were the general himself
and his co-conspirator, Lt. Gen. Danny Graham, whose rebuttal was
limited to a brief denial. Why hadn't the officials who had appeared at
Westmoreland's press conference been included in the broadcast? In particular, the omission of General Davidson seemed inexcusable.

However, in CBS's defense, the documentary was indeed a complex
one. To tell such a convoluted story within the confines of ninety minutes, CBS might well have had to compress and pare; perhaps the pictures

and comments on the screen were merely the tip of an enormous quantity of substantiating documentation interred in CBS's files.

What both *TV Guide* writers agreed on was that Westmoreland's press conference had raised troubling charges about the program and that, on the surface, the evidence provided in the script seemed "soft." The charge, after all, was "conspiracy"—a serious offense. The writers obtained the videotapes of both the broadcast and the Westmoreland press conference. On February 3 they submitted a joint proposal to their editors suggesting an article "on this documentary—the controversy and questions it has raised within CBS and outside." However, the writers added, "we would *not* want to address the essential controversy of the broadcast—the statistical quagmire of troop strength—or even to explore whether Westmoreland was lying or telling the truth. What we want to examine is . . . whether or not [the broadcast] was *right*, was it *fair?*"

That week, articles about the controversy had begun to appear in the national press. *Newsweek*'s Charles Kaiser (Robert Kaiser's younger brother) commended CBS. " 'It was a question of whether we . . . finally were going to come to grips with the nature of the war and the scale of the enemy forces we were up against—or whether we were going to continue this process of self-delusion,' " Kaiser quoted approvingly from CBS witness George Allen's testimony in the program. "By trying to set the record straight," Kaiser concluded, "CBS tackled a key part of that crucial question." The *New York Times* had already accepted the premise of the program in its editorial the day following the broadcast. Now columnist Hodding Carter weighed in, writing in the *Wall Street Journal* that "appalling lies" constructed by "good soldiers" had led to erroneous policy decisions. Carter hoped that he would not learn about similar intelligence deceptions in El Salvador fourteen years too late. The February 2 *Washington Post* featured a column by William F. Buckley, Jr., touting the CBS program as a "truly extraordinary documentary" which "absolutely" established that Westmoreland had withheld vital information on enemy strength. Five days later, again in the *Washington Post*, Philip Geyelin returned to the controversy, lauding CBS for laying bare the "sorry record" of the intelligence community's effort to conceal crucial intelligence. Like others before and after, Geyelin drew parallels with current intelligence deceptions possibly being hatched in Latin America. It was not until Gen. Maxwell Taylor answered the Buckley column with one of his own that the *Post* published a defense of Westmoreland. Taylor voiced his surprise "at how readily a man of Buckley's background accepted the substance of the hatchet job on Gen. William Westmoreland by Mike Wallace . . ." and argued that "there was no concealment of the matter in Saigon" and that it was "well known and aired in Washington." Meanwhile, also in Westmoreland's defense, George Carver was telling the *Christian Science Monitor*: "Not only was [LBJ] aware of the debates, he said, 'Can't you guys get together on a number?' "

Behind the scenes the opposing camps were flexing their muscles. Reed Irvine of the conservative media watchdog Accuracy in Media sent a letter to CBS News president Bill Leonard detailing in five pages his complaints about the broadcast:

> You chose to put together a very serious attack on the character of General Westmoreland and General Graham. You failed to tell your audience of the mass of evidence that casts very serious doubt on the validity of those charges.
>
> Accuracy in Media requests that you honor your obligations under the fairness doctrine and provide air time for the other side of these issues, unless, of course, you can demonstrate that you have in the recent past aired another program or programs on the same subject which told the other side of the story. We are not aware of any such program.

Leonard's reply to Irvine stated that "our broadcast fairly presented a report on events during the Vietnam period which the American people have every right to know. The evidence on which our broadcast rests is solid, including the broadcast statements of numerous intelligence officers.

". . . To state, as you do, that we did present General Westmoreland's side of the question but somehow did not do it succinctly enough to satisfy your tastes thrusts you directly into our editing rooms, a place you surely should not be present. . . ."

Leonard concluded by rejecting Irvine's request for equal time under the fairness doctrine as "totally without merit. . . ."

The letters for or against kept flying. Rep. Paul McCloskey, Jr. (California), wrote a five-page letter to George Crile, saying: "After our telephone conversation on January 26 I had the chance to read both the transcript of CBS's January 23 broadcast and General Westmoreland's subsequent press statement.

"CBS's report is accurate, and General Westmoreland's denials are hollow and misleading. . . .

"Give my regards to Sam Adams," Representative McCloskey concluded. "He is a true patriot."

The 1960s Vietnam legacy was still seething beneath the surface calm. For years the verdict on the war had gone unexamined and unchallenged. Now, suddenly, once again people had to choose sides. Initially, those who had supported the American involvement gathered to West-moreland's defense, while those who had been opposed rallied to CBS.

The letters flew back and forth, providing the warring factions with stacks of testimonials that might prove useful if the controversy boiled over into a court battle. That, of course, was the key question—did Westmoreland intend to sue CBS? However, it was not a question being asked by the press, at least not publicly. After the opening flurry, in which heavyweights had exchanged jabs (with Westmoreland supporters out-numbered in the national press four to one) the controversy evaporated from the newspapers. Editors seemed reluctant to pursue allegations of alleged wrongdoing by one of their own—the respected CBS News divi-sion. Their reporters seemed reluctant to spark further controversy, which might turn the threat of a lawsuit into a reality. It would prove difficult for the press to evaluate the opposing arguments, so elevated was their esteem for CBS, so profound was their contempt for Westmoreland. After nearly a decade and a half, the "credibility gap" was still a yawning, unspanna-ble chasm.

On February 7 the *New York Times* published the letter Walt Rostow had written two weeks before. It read:

> Your editorial on January 24 ("War, Intelligence, and Truth") draws from the CBS documentary of January 23 precisely the conclusion it clearly pro-jected, i.e., "that Lyndon Johnson himself was victimized by mendacious intelligence" in the period before the Tet offensive of January 1968.
>
> The conclusion is false; and those who produced the documentary know it is false.
>
> President Johnson received directly and read voraciously the captured docu-ments to which you refer—not summaries—as well as reports of CIA, State Department, and AID [Agency for International Development] officers in the provinces; prisoner-of-war interrogations; intercepts; and all manner of other basic information. Each week Ambassador Bunker filed a long country-team report covering every dimension of the situation in South Vietnam, military and nonmilitary, which, in retrospect, historians will find exceedingly accu-rate and done with patent integrity.
>
> On the basis of this flow, it was clear by November 1967 that Hanoi planned a maximum offensive effort in the time ahead, including efforts to induce "a great uprising."
>
> . . . Just before Tet, Westmoreland asked President Johnson for permission to cancel the Tet truce in I Corps, put the United States forces on alert, and make special dispositions for the protection of Saigon.
>
> The only surprise at Tet was that the Communists attacked as many as forty provincial capitals. Most of the attacks were on a small scale and easily turned

back. The surprise was not the scale of the VC forces revealed but the bold impudence of the effort. It represented an unlikely diffusion of resources and resulted in a disaster from which the Vietcong (and their political cadres) never recovered. . . .

President Johnson was fully aware of the Vietcong Order of Battle debate, at the center of the CBS documentary. It concerned the size of the logistical and local forces, not the VC main force units nor the North Vietnamese forces. It was at my suggestion that General Wheeler ordered an effort to reconcile the Washington and Saigon estimates at a Honolulu meeting. It was precisely because Order of Battle estimates were so inherently difficult that we relied on the widest possible range of intelligence, never on the Order of Battle numbers alone.

As I indicated earlier, CBS is quite aware of all this from its own research and a three-hour taping session with me on July 24, 1981, in New York, covering all of this and more. The director of the documentary, Mr. George Crile, wrote to me on January 15, 1982, explaining that nothing from that session was to be used and, therefore, CBS was relieved of the requirement of providing me a transcript of the taping. (CBS has every right to make that decision.) His letter included the sentence: "We did not suggest that the enemy's attack at Tet came as a surprise to the White House or to the American military command."

Whatever Mr. Crile's intention, your editorial writer and every other viewer of the documentary had the right to draw a contrary impression. . . .

A few days later the *Times* published a letter from Crile. In it Crile asked Rostow to explain "this apparent contradiction":

General Westmoreland acknowledged in our broadcast there had, in fact, been a massive infiltration throughout the fall in the magnitude of about 20,000 a month. He said he could not explain why the higher numbers had not been included in any official reports (they indicated no more than 7,000). And he said he had been wrong in November 1967 when he used the figure of 5,500 to 6,000 a month on *Meet the Press.*

After our filmed interview General Westmoreland changed his position again. Since then he has maintained that the massive infiltration in the fall of 1967 never took place.

Mr. Rostow, however, in a January 25, 1982, memorandum for the LBJ Library (a copy of which he sent to me), maintains that this massive infiltration in the fall of 1967 did take place and attacks our suggestion that the president didn't know about it. It was, he wrote, "a quite massive invasion of South Vietnam by fresh, regular North Vietnamese units. . . . The infiltration rate may well have been higher for a few months than 25,000. Everyone concerned, including President Johnson, knew this."

The problem is that this infiltration is not registered in any official records. . . .

Crile, in his letter to the *Times*, misinterpreted Rostow's discussion of infiltration in his January 25 memorandum. "What was happening in the autumn of 1967," Rostow had written, "was not an 'increase in infiltration': it was quite a massive invasion of South Vietnam by fresh, regular North Vietnamese units. . . . At least two divisions moved into a position to attack the base at Khe Sanh. The 'infiltration rate' may well have been higher for a few months than 25,000. . . ."

In other words, Rostow was making a distinction between infiltration, which generally consisted of replacement troops for those enemy killed or wounded in South Vietnam, and an invasion of fresh NVA over and around the demilitarized zone in the north. Crile had blurred that distinction by removing the inverted commas around the phrase infiltration rate—punctuation Rostow had used to express his skepticism. Crile's editing (whether intentional or not) of the quotation marks gave the erroneous impression that to Rostow *infiltration* and *massive invasion* were synonymous.

In early February, Crile screened video cassettes of the Westmoreland press conference so that he could, as he had promised vice-president Roger Colloff, rebut the allegations leveled against his documentary by the officials who had come to Westmoreland's defense. It was during that screening that, for the first time, Klein learned of the letter and documents Westmoreland had sent to Wallace and Crile after his May 16 interview, which Westmoreland regarded as a request for a correction. It was also during that screening that Klein heard the CIA's George Carver, in Westmoreland's defense, insist it was he and not Westmoreland who had proposed a crucial compromise at the Saigon conference over Order of Battle. The day after, Adams appeared in Klein's editing room, declaring, "We have to come clean. We have to make a statement. The premise of the show was inaccurate." Adams told Klein what he had already written to Col. Gains Hawkins: that there was a major problem with the documentary; that he believed the conspiracy had originated with President Johnson, and consequently the documentary had been wrong in overburdening Westmoreland with blame. After that, Klein made his decision to discuss three of the documentary's substantive problems with *CBS Reports* executive producer Andy Lack, postponing his scheduled vacation in the process. Those three problems were: Adams's "We have to come clean" statement; the documents and letter Westmoreland had mailed to Wallace and Crile; and Carver's assertion that it was he, not

Westmoreland, who had proposed the compromise that Crile and Adams regarded as a CIA cave-in to Westmoreland's demands. Klein's final meeting with Lack (and *CBS Reports* senior producer Judy Reemtsma) had been interrupted by Mike Wallace, who reminded Klein that he had been merely "cosmetics" in the broadcast, comforting Klein with the closing thought that "at 60 *Minutes* this kind of thing happens all the time."

On Saturday, Ira Klein left New York for his two-week vacation in Florida. In his absence Klein hoped that Lack would initiate an inquiry into the documentary. Indeed, Klein had specifically suggested to Lack that someone from outside CBS News be brought in to act as an ombudsman.

Lack did "investigate" one of Klein's assertions—that Adams had come to believe that the conspiracy originated in the White House and not with Westmoreland. "I called Adams," Lack recalled later. "He said he didn't know what Klein was talking about."

George Crile wrote his rebuttal to the Westmoreland press conference. Crile ended this eleven-and-a-half page document with this comment about Lyndon Johnson's role:

"We knew all along that LBJ was told about intelligence disputes (Walt Rostow told us that but simply said the president wanted them resolved). What remains unclear, however, is exactly what the president was told—by whom and in what manner. I don't think we're likely to get to the bottom of that one." Then Crile added, "Perhaps we should have made some reference to this puzzlement, but beyond this failing I do not at this point have any areas of concern."

Colloff received the memo, read it, and filed it away. Over the days that followed, the controversy over the broadcast seemed to melt away. The newspapers and magazines were directing their attention elsewhere, undisturbed that a discredited general had leveled serious allegations against the most prestigious documentary unit in all of broadcasting. It was during this time that the *TV Guide* writers received approval from their editors to write a story on the dispute between CBS and Westmoreland. They were to jointly research a piece on the fairness and accuracy of "The Uncounted Enemy: A Vietnam Deception"—evaluating CBS's evidence and the ethics of the procedures used to gather that evidence. The subject of their investigation was to be the documentary itself, not the fourteen-year-old debate between Sam Adams and the military.

13

The
TV GUIDE
Investigation

T V GUIDE initiated its investigation of the CBS broadcast early in February. Over the next two months the pair of writers interviewed executives at the network, members of the documentary's production team, ex-officials whom CBS had not interviewed or whose interviews had not been included in the broadcast, and many of CBS's own on-camera witnesses. It was those conversations with some of CBS's own witnesses that the writers found most disturbing. With one exception (Col. Gains Hawkins, who withheld comment), every CBS witness interviewed by *TV Guide* said he did not believe there had been a conspiracy to suppress the true size of the enemy. Even more troubling, not a single one of them could recall being asked during his CBS interview if he believed in the conspiracy premise his testimony would buttress in the program. Furthermore, the version of events that CBS's witnesses gave to *TV Guide* sometimes differed dramatically from their on-camera testimony. Then, three-quarters through the investigation, the writers encountered a source who offered to furnish them the unedited official transcripts of CBS's interviews. Examining those unedited transcripts, it became evident that much of the testimony to CBS had been misrepresented, distorted, or manipulated in order to make the conspiracy tale a more convincing one.

The documentary's distortions began in the very first act when West-moreland, in the spring of 1967, allegedly suppressed the report of a larger enemy presented to him by Gen. Joseph McChristian, the then-chief of intelligence, and Col. Gains Hawkins, the Order of Battle specialist. The scenario started with Westmoreland returning to Saigon after an April 1967 trip to Washington, where, according to Mike Wallace in the program, the general had "used very specific figures to assure the president that the enemy was losing strength, that we were winning the war of attrition," while telling Congress that he "believed we were on the road to victory. . . ." Meanwhile, back in Vietnam, said Wallace, ". . . his intelligence chiefs had come to agree with the CIA's growing conviction that we were fighting a larger enemy. They had been studying the captured enemy documents, and when Westmoreland returned to [his] headquarters, General McChristian and the military's leading expert on the Vietcong, Col. Gains Hawkins, presented him with the bad news. Hawkins began the briefing."

This was the McChristian-Hawkins briefing. During the production of the program Klein had wanted to introduce this "briefing" sequence with still photos of McChristian and Hawkins, but Crile had told him that it was unclear whether both men had been together. In the program, how-ever, the two officers' comments about "the briefing" were intercut.

HAWKINS: There was no mistaking the message.
CRILE: Which was?
HAWKINS: That there was a great concern about the impact of these figures, that—their being higher.
CRILE: They didn't want higher numbers.
HAWKINS: That was the message.
WALLACE: This is the way General McChristian remembers West-moreland's reaction to the briefing.
McCHRISTIAN: And when General Westmoreland saw the large in-crease in figures that we had developed, he was quite disturbed by it. And by the time I left his office I had the definite impression that he felt if he sent those figures back to Washington at that time, it would create a political bombshell. . . .

"The documentary gives the impression that there was a single meet-ing," said Sam Adams. "There were at least two." Adams recalled that he had told Crile before the broadcast, "Look, you're talking about two meetings." In fact, what Crile had done was combine comments about three separate incidents into what seemed to be one pivotal meeting. A review of the unedited official transcripts of both men's CBS interviews revealed the truth.

> CRILE: Now you went to a briefing with General Westmoreland carrying a flip chart, didn't you?
>
> HAWKINS: Yes. This was in the main briefing room at . . . MACV headquarters. . . . The figures I briefed on that particular occasion were the new strength figures on the political OB, as we called it. This is the VC political bureaucracy and the guerilla strength, shown from two operations—Corral and Ritz. . . .

Hawkins went on to say that, from Westmoreland's reaction, he got "the message" that he was to go back and lower his numbers. Hawkins recalled Westmoreland saying, " 'Take a second look at this briefing.' That was the first briefing. 'Take another look at these figures.' "

Hawkins reduced his estimate ("I don't think it was all that smaller") and again briefed Westmoreland (this time accompanied by special ambassador Robert Komer). Again, according to Hawkins, the briefing was not approved.

Hawkins was discussing two briefings he gave to Westmoreland in the J-2 conference room. But McChristian was discussing an earlier and different event. In his CBS interview with Crile:

> McCHRISTIAN: Just before I left Saigon, left my job as chief of intelligence, the reporting had just come in on updating the strength of political Order of Battle, the Vietcong infrastructure. And also on the guerilla strength. I had a cable prepared to go to Washington on the new strength figures, and I took the cable to General Westmoreland because it was a big change that we had been working on and anticipating for some time, but I wanted him to see this before it went in. General Westmoreland was perturbed by this because it was a large increase in strength, and he asked me to leave that cable with him 'cause he wanted to review it. Shortly thereafter I left the country, and I don't know for a fact actually what happened to that message.
>
> CRILE: So far as you know, it, those increases, did not go through?
>
> McCHRISTIAN: So far as I know, I don't know whether they went through or didn't go through. I don't know for a fact what happened to them.

McChristian was telling Crile about a cable he left with Westmoreland, in Westmoreland's office. Hawkins was testifying about a pair of briefings given in the MACV J-2 briefing room. By compressing these three separate events into one "briefing," CBS made it seem as if McChristian were directly supporting Hawkins's testimony. Hawkins was alleging that "the message" he got was that Westmoreland was not going to accept estimates of a larger enemy because of the political impact such as an increased assessment of the enemy might have in Washington. This "message" was key CBS evidence that Westmoreland was bent on suppressing the true magnitude of the North Vietnamese and Vietcong forces—the first step in his "conspiracy." However, Hawkins had flatly stated to Crile (in a segment that was not included in the broadcast) that he had never, at any time, received an *order* to make such arbitrary reductions. His interpretation of Westmoreland's "message" at the briefings was circumstantial and subjective, ripe for contradiction if not confirmed by another source. By placing McChristian's comments about his own cable in the context of the Hawkins briefing(s), CBS was suggesting that McChristian had gotten "the message" to suppress as well. The problem is, McChristian insisted to CBS more than once that nothing he ever submitted to Westmoreland had been suppressed.

> CRILE: Ah, so no one was challenging your numbers, but they were starting to challenge the categories of enemy that you were including.
> McCHRISTIAN: I don't know. . . . They didn't do it while I was there, so I can't address that.

Throughout the interview, time and time again Crile tried to fix McChristian's cable as the catalyst for his transfer back to Washington in late May 1967. But McChristian told Crile that he had received his transfer orders "some time before" he delivered the cable to Westmoreland. "George," said McChristian, "I don't think there was a connection in my trying to increase the estimate because the trend on enemy strength was constantly going up." Instead, McChristian said, he suspected that Lyndon Johnson's special ambassador to Vietnam Robert Komer had instigated the transfer. "Komer came there to take over some of the operations which I had initiated," McChristian told Crile, "and I believe I was looked upon as being in the way of Mr. Komer."

By abusing McChristian's interview, CBS had made it appear that his testimony supported Hawkins's when in fact McChristian had offered absolutely not a shred of evidence of wrongdoing.

TV Guide: Did you have any feeling at any time that you were
   being asked to suppress information?
McCHRISTIAN: No. Absolutely not. I did not.
TV Guide: After your meeting with Westmoreland, did you leave
   with the notion that there was a conspiracy being hatched?
McCHRISTIAN: Absolutely not.

"Until you put people under oath in this situation and ask them questions, you're not going to get the same answers from month to month or
reporter to reporter," Crile told *TV Guide*.

On December 21, 1983, McChristian stated under oath that "no one
ever pressured me to change any estimate of enemy personnel strength,"
that he had no knowledge of whether his higher numbers were connected
to his transfer, and that he had "no personal knowledge of any conspiracy
to suppress or alter intelligence on the enemy in Vietnam."

From the time the documentary aired, Westmoreland began contem-
plating the possibility of a libel suit against CBS. The documentary had
deeply angered him. He summed up his feelings to the *TV Guide* writers
in an interview at his home in Charleston, in late February. "When I
returned from Vietnam," he said, "I was belittled, I was burned in effigy.
I could accept that. I knew I had done the job in Vietnam the president
had asked me to do. I was reviled, I was disparaged, but I could accept
that. At least my children could hold their heads high, knowing that,
right or wrong, I was an honorable man, doing his duty for his country.
But now," he added bitterly, "Mike Wallace has gone on national television and accused me of being a liar—worse, a traitor. How can my
children live with that?"

Westmoreland seemed a mere shell of the jut-jawed general whose
confident face was featured on newscasts throughout the late 1960s. His
eyes teared easily. He slurred some words. He seemed to suffer spasms of
forgetfulness. "What CBS was saying," he said over and over, "was that I
have the blood of American soldiers on my hands." The program implied
that Westmoreland's "conspiracy" had contributed to the United States'
unpreparedness for Tet.

A libel suit seemed to him the appropriate response, but there were
formidable obstacles. Almost all of his friends and former colleagues were
advising against a lawsuit. To begin with, there was CBS itself—an imposing opponent: No case in recent memory against CBS had reached
trial. To discourage Westmoreland, friends reminded him of the lawsuit

against *60 Minutes*, Mike Wallace, and producer Barry Lando filed by Col. Anthony Herbert in 1973. A decade later the case was still mired in the morass of pretrial discovery—motions, responses to motions, responses to responses. CBS could simply stall a Westmoreland lawsuit until the sixty-eight-year-old general dropped dead.

Even if Westmoreland did survive to see his suit reach trial, how would he cope with the extraordinary costs of such litigation? The resources of even Westmoreland's wealthiest sympathizers were puny in comparison to those of the largest communications corporation on earth. Westmoreland, on his frequent trips out of Charleston to fulfill speaking engagements, kept testing the idea of lodging a libel suit, probing for financial support. Meanwhile, the TV Guide writers were proceeding with their investigation.

Act 1 of the documentary focused on the "McChristian-Hawkins" briefing, thus raising the curtain on the "conspiracy." Act 2 documented the next step—Westmoreland's imposing a "ceiling" on enemy-strength estimates at the series of conferences convened by the CIA, in the summer and early fall of 1967, to reach a consensus on the size of the enemy. As Mike Wallace depicted it, the "confrontation took place here at CIA headquarters in Langley, Virginia, at something called the National Intelligence Estimate Board. And the man designated to present the CIA's case was George Allen's protégé, Sam Adams, the man who had first discovered evidence of a larger enemy army."

Interweaving comments from Adams and Hawkins, CBS drew a scenario of duplicity: While secretly agreeing with Adams's higher estimate, Hawkins defended the command position. Wallace then dealt with the "ceiling" itself—the "smoking gun" (Sam Adams's term) proving a Westmoreland-led conspiracy. Here is how Wallace documented an order Westmoreland allegedly gave to his military-intelligence delegation:

WALLACE: *CBS Reports* has learned that Colonel Hawkins was in fact carrying out orders that originated from General Westmoreland. Westmoreland says he doesn't recall those orders. But the head of MACV's delegation told us that General Westmoreland had, in fact, personally instructed him not to allow the total to go over three hundred thousand.

CRILE: Wasn't there a ceiling put on the estimates by General Westmoreland? Weren't your colleagues instructed, ordered, not to let those estimates exceed a certain amount?

HAMSCHER: "We can't live with a figure higher than so and so"—

CRILE: Three hundred thousand.

HAMSCHER: —is the message we got.

Thus, the documentary made it appear that Col. George Hamscher was the head of the military delegation, when in fact the head of that delegation was Gen. George Godding. Hamscher worked for a completely different intelligence organization—the Pentagon's Washington-based Defense Intelligence Agency (DIA). CBS had never asked Gen. Godding for an on-camera interview.

Crile said that he telephoned Godding twice during his investigation. In his on-camera interview with Col. Gains Hawkins, the Order of Battle specialist, Crile told Hawkins, "Godding told us that Westmoreland actually instructed him to keep below a certain number. This was his quote; Westmoreland apparently said this: 'I don't care how you do it, use any number you want, just don't let the total go over 300,000 Vietcong.' "

Godding denied to *TV Guide* that a ceiling had been imposed. If, as Crile claimed, Godding had confirmed the ceiling, why didn't CBS ask him to appear on camera?

The documentary also charged that Hawkins was "carrying out orders" (imposing a ceiling) that "originated from General Westmoreland." But in Hawkins's interview with Crile, he had said *no fewer than four times* that he had not been given a numerical ceiling before the Langley meeting. Hawkins told Crile that he had defended the "command position"—the total of 296,000 enemy estimated in the May Order of Battle.

"Who told you that? Anyone?" asked Crile.

"No one told me. I deduced it. And I defended it willingly. I was not given any specific orders," Hawkins said.

When Crile informed Hawkins that Godding said Westmoreland had told him not to let the total go over 300,000 Vietcong, Hawkins replied, "I'm not familiar with that instruction."

There were undocumented escalations of terminology in the CBS broadcast (Hawkins's "message" became an "order originating from Westmoreland"), and there were quotes out of context. In Act 2, for instance, within the CIA-conference scenario, Westmoreland was seen reacting to Col. George Hamscher's account of a meeting at the Pentagon in August 1967, when military officers allegedly reduced the strength of enemy units arbitrarily to keep the ceiling on the enemy estimates under 300,000 men.

"Now who actually did the cutting, I don't know," said Westmoreland in the documentary. "It could have been my chief of staff. I don't know. But I didn't get involved in this personally."

In fact, an examination of the unedited transcript of Westmoreland's

CBS interview revealed that Westmoreland offered this statement in answer to a question from Wallace about a completely different meeting— one that had taken place in Saigon a month or so after the alleged-Pentagon meeting, when the CIA and the military reached a final compromise on the Order of Battle dispute. By inserting Westmoreland's statement about the Saigon meeting after Col. George Hamscher's allegations about a Pentagon meeting, CBS made it appear as if Westmoreland were admitting that he knew about the Pentagon affair. In his interview with Mike Wallace, however, Westmoreland had explicitly denied any knowledge of such a meeting.

In fact, *TV Guide's* investigation revealed that CBS had enough circumstantial evidence in hand to question whether this Pentagon meeting had taken place in the summer of 1967, as charged, or, as seems more likely, in the spring of 1968, months *after* Tet. The documentary stated that six people attended this meeting, although only one was named: Col. George Hamscher of the Defense Intelligence Agency, who provided the details on camera (calling it "a group grope"). Hamscher thought he remembered Godding and Hawkins. In his CBS interview, Hawkins denied being involved in any such session. When Crile read him Hamscher's description of how "individual units were sliced arbitrarily," Hawkins replied, "Main force units were not cut—to my knowledge. Never, never, never cut. And I was the man who had the pencil." (Adams, in a memo to Hawkins, later admitted he was mistaken when he placed Hawkins at that meeting.)

Godding also denied that he had attended such a meeting. However, Danny Graham (whom both Hamscher and another participant, Major John Barrie Williams, said had chaired that Pentagon meeting) did remember attending such a meeting *after* Tet.

While CBS's evidence for placing that Pentagon meeting in August 1967—almost five months before Tet—was conflicting and confusing, there definitely had been a post-Tet meeting at the Pentagon attended by Graham, Hamscher, and Williams in April 1968. At that time, representatives of the Defense Intelligence Agency (to which Hamscher and Williams belonged) had met with representatives of Westmoreland's military intelligence to reconcile conflicting post-Tet estimates of enemy strength.

"Can you say without hesitation the meeting you are referring to at which you say units were reduced occurred in 1967 and not 1968?" Capital Legal Foundation's Anthony Murray asked the now-Col. John Barrie Williams during his deposition.

"I cannot . . . Whether that was '67 or '68, I can't give you a specific time . . . ," Williams replied.

Could CBS, wittingly or unwittingly, have transposed this meeting to a time eight months earlier, thereby buttressing its chronology of conspiracy?

By mid-March the *TV Guide* writers were in almost constant contact with CBS, either making calls to clear up questions or receiving them from Wallace or Crile, anxious to volunteer information. To its credit, from the beginning CBS had ordered its employees to cooperate with *TV Guide*. Gradually, though, it was becoming clear to CBS that the investigation was uncovering facts that seemed to contradict the broadcast. Some at CBS began to spread rumors of dark motives behind the inquiry. Sam Adams, during this period, wrote a letter to Gains Hawkins:

"George Crile tells me that *TV Guide* is winding up to take a swipe at the show. He's convinced that it's a plot by the publisher, Walter Annenberg, to defend his old buddy, Westy. As yet," Adams added, "the *TV Guide*rs have not contacted me—who, George assures me, will be cast as a villain. You know the old refrain: Okay by me, so long as they spell my name right. . . ."

The writers, in the course of their research, heard that allegation—that the article had been instigated by *TV Guide*'s publisher. They took pains to disabuse CBS executives of the notion. The truth was, the investigation had been inspired by the pair of staff writers who pursued the story independently, with no interference from the editors of the magazine, let alone the publisher. Yet time and time again over the next few months the "Annenberg conspiracy" premise would pop up. CBS seemed to find it incredible that the origin of the article could be complaints from CBS employees appalled at the procedures used to prove the conspiracy.

On Monday, March 15, Ira Klein returned from his two-week vacation in Florida. Carolyne McDaniel told him that *TV Guide* was investigating the broadcast. Wallace had advised her that CBS intended to cooperate fully. Thus, when a *TV Guide* reporter had called asking for Alex Alben's telephone number in California, she provided it. (After *TV Guide* spoke to Alben, he and Carolyne McDaniel conferred by telephone, with Alben summing up the reporter's questions and his own responses. McDaniel typed up that interview summary and dropped it off at Mike Wallace's office. Wallace's secretary forwarded copies to Bob Chandler and Roger Colloff.)

That first day at work Klein was determined to meet with Andy Lack to learn what steps CBS had taken about the "problems" Klein had revealed to Lack before Klein's vacation. He knew Lack was busy producing an instant "special" on Central America, so he waited until the end of the day. Around half-past six Klein entered Lack's office and sat down on a couch. Lack was sitting in front of a television monitor, his head propped on his hand, watching the early "feed" of the CBS evening news. They exchanged greetings. Then Lack said, "Listen, Ira, I simply don't have the time to conduct a thorough investigation."

"All right," Klein said, "if that's the way you feel, it's your prerogative."

They were silent for a moment. Then Klein said, "Did you know that George Allen screened interviews?" Klein explained to Lack how Crile had ushered Allen into the editing room to screen testimony already on film.

Lack looked stunned. "Did you tell me that before?" he said.

"No," said Klein, "we didn't discuss it." Klein had limited his earlier discussions with Lack to the three problems: Adams's disavowing the premise of the program; the Westmoreland "correction" packet; and the Carver-initiated compromise. His purpose had been to give Lack a glimpse of the documentary's glaring inaccuracies. He had not delved into the details of Crile's procedures. His aim had been to set CBS's own internal investigative machinery in motion.

Lack knew that the screening of segments for Allen was a blatant violation of CBS guidelines. He rose from his seat in front of the television monitor and walked over to his desk. He sat down. "Did Sam try to call you in Florida?" he said.

"No," said Klein, "I haven't spoken to Sam."

Lack said that Adams had told him he intended to telephone Klein in Florida. "You know," Lack added, "Sam has the very highest regard for you, but he denies making the statement."

In a telephone conversation, Adams had denied to Lack that he had told Klein: "We have to come clean. The premise of the show is inaccurate." Lack was surprised that Adams had not telephoned Klein. Adams had told Lack he was going to call Klein to clear up "the misunderstanding."

Klein said, "I guess George got hold of Sam."

Lack said, "I guess so."

Klein was disappointed. He realized that CBS intended to take no further action regarding the problems he had brought to Lack's attention.

CBS was a corporation like any other. Other corporate entities sold sacks of potatoes, CBS sold bushels of news. The corporate mentality was the same, crisis management was the same. Be it General Motors, confronted by a Ralph Nader, or CBS News, challenged by Gen. William Westmoreland—the overriding priority of those in authority was self-preservation. It was clear that CBS was going to give the West Point motto a new twist, transforming "Duty, Honor, Country" into "Duty, Honor, *Company.*"

14

More
Errors
Emerge

Finally, on tuesday, Sam Adams telephoned Ira Klein. They talked about trivial matters for a while. Then Adams said, "Spring is coming on. You should definitely come down to visit us at the farm. . . ." Klein realized that Adams was ending the conversation without ever mentioning the "misunderstanding" over his disavowing the premise of the documentary. Adams had not uttered a single word about the broadcast. "Sam," Klein interjected, "I think it's important that we discuss something." He reviewed what Adams had told him. Again Adams agreed that Westmoreland had been overburdened with guilt by the premise of the program.

Crile had been out of town. He returned on Wednesday. That afternoon Klein went to Crile's office. He felt obliged to tell Crile the details of his discussion with Lack before his vacation. He knocked on Crile's door, then opened it. He closed it again when he saw that Crile had visitors. Klein did not learn until later that Crile was being interviewed by *TV Guide*.

Previously the reporters had spoken to Crile by telephone. Now they were conducting a six-and-a-half-hour interview with Crile over two days. At the time, they had not been offered the unedited official transcripts of CBS's interviews, so their questions were based primarily on their independent research. However, they did have the Westmoreland and Graham transcripts, obtained from the interviewees themselves. (CBS guidelines mandated that the subject of an on-camera interview be sent, on request, a transcript of the full unedited interview.) In the course of that conversation it became clear to the reporters that, for a journalist, Crile had a peculiar cast of mind, evidenced by exchanges such as the following:

> *TV Guide:* . . . [McChristian] also told me nothing of his was ever suppressed while he was there.
>
> CRILE: Pardon me. He did not say that the report was blocked?
>
> *TV Guide:* All he said was that he left it with Westmoreland, and that was it. It was left with Westmoreland, and then he left. He was transferred out.
>
> CRILE: General Westmoreland said that he blocked the report.
>
> *TV Guide:* He said that he blocked the report?
>
> CRILE: In the documentary he did.
>
> *TV Guide:* Do you remember that? I don't get that. I don't know where he says he blocked it. Maybe he said that he didn't send it through—. I think we may agree that he didn't send it through.
>
> CRILE: Well, I don't see what the difference is.

When the writers insisted that "blocking" was not necessarily synonymous with "not accepting," Crile told them they were "getting technical in terms of words. . . . Westmoreland is acknowledging that he blocked this. That he wouldn't accept it, that he didn't send it on." Later Crile again accused the writers of "trying to find legalisms in terms of words. . . ." What people actually said, their verbatim accounts in the CBS interviews, seemed less important to him than what he knew to be the truth.

As the interview wore on it became more and more apparent that Crile, like his star witness Col. Gains Hawkins, had a tendency to hear incontrovertible "messages" when others might detect only suggestions whose motives needed to be clarified. Often, when the reporters offered concrete contradictions between the premise of the program and what witnesses had told the reporters, Crile replied with sweeping generalizations, citing the overall context of the times or some other "larger truth" as proof that he was right. He seemed far more comfortable with abstractions than the concrete events elucidated in his documentary.

The reporters asked Crile about George Carver's statement at the West-moreland press conference that it was he and not Westmoreland, as the documentary stated, who had initiated the crucial Saigon NIE compromise. Crile dismissed Carver's revelation. ". . . In the end because Carver comes up with the proposal to end the controversy means nothing," he said. "The fact is he was under orders from Helms that, in the end, if you cannot reach agreement with them, you've got to compromise, because he cannot allow the civilians and the military to be taking a different position. That is ultimately too compromising."

But Crile had no proof of any such order from Helms.

Twice during the conversations, when confronted with statements to *TV Guide* from CBS witnesses that seemed to contradict what they had told CBS, Crile remarked that truth would not really surface until people were placed under oath. "We're walking into a real maze," he said, "in which until you put people under oath and go into the record, you're not going to get to the bottom of it."

After the reporters' second interview with Crile, on Thursday evening, Klein was sitting in the office of an associate producer watching the CBS evening news when Crile walked in. Klein stood up, Crile welcomed him back from vacation, and Klein shook Crile's hand. Then Crile told Klein he had just completed a grueling two-day session with *TV Guide*. "I think Walter Annenberg, the publisher, is behind this thing," Crile said.

Crile was walking out of the room when Klein said, "George, I think we should talk."

Crile stopped. He looked haggard, ashen after the exhausting ordeal with the reporters. "I guess we should," he said.

The producer and editor sat down and began to talk, with Klein reviewing the events that had troubled him about the making of the documentary. Klein kept emphasizing his dissatisfaction with Crile's investigation. Why had Crile waited until shortly before the broadcast to interview George Carver? Even more mystifying and disturbing to Klein, why had Crile *never* interviewed Lyndon Johnson's special ambassador to Vietnam, Robert Komer?

Suddenly Crile lunged forward, saying, "Are you going to talk to *TV Guide*?"

Klein stared at him for a moment. "Are you *afraid* I'm going to talk?" he said.

Crile leaned back in his chair. He shrugged his shoulders, waving his hands to indicate that whether Klein did or did not speak to *TV Guide* really was not his concern. Then he told Klein that it was important that he and Adams meet for a face-to-face chat.

"Whenever Sam is available," said Klein, "I'm here."

The next morning, Friday, March 19, at 10:00 sharp, Crile reappeared in Klein's editing room. "It's important that you talk to Sam," he said.

"Absolutely," said Klein. "I'll be happy to talk to him whenever he comes to New York."

That day *TV Guide* conducted a lengthy in-person interview with Mike Wallace at CBS. Wallace placed a tape recorder in front of him as the interview began.

TV Guide asked Wallace about his understanding of the premise of the program, his view of Sam Adams's role, his relationship with Crile. The reporter was particularly interested in ascertaining how deeply Wallace himself had been involved in the research, preparation, and production of the film. It became clear over the course of the interview that Wallace's involvement had been superficial, not because of any lack of competency but simply because his busy schedule at CBS prevented him from delving deeply into the details of a film whose production had taken more than a year. Ultimately Wallace had had to rely on Crile for his understanding of the story he was narrating.

On Sunday, March 21, almost two months after the broadcast had aired, George Crile finally interviewed a crucial witness to the events in Vietnam. That Sunday Crile telephoned Robert Komer at Komer's Virginia home. It had been Komer who had called Col. Gains Hawkins's second briefing to Westmoreland "Byzantine." It had been Komer who Gen. Joseph McChristian believed may have been responsible for his transfer out of Vietnam. Hawkins was convinced that Komer had been reporting everything to President Johnson. Klein had again reminded Crile the previous Thursday that Komer should have been interviewed for the broadcast.

That evening Klein returned to his apartment to find a message from Crile on his answering machine. Crile wanted him to get together with Sam Adams as soon as possible. There was a note of urgency in Crile's voice, so on Monday morning Klein went straight to Crile's office. Crile said, "I telephoned Komer." He told Klein that Komer had nothing significant to add to the documentary.

"Fine," said Klein. He believed that Crile had only called Komer to pacify him.

On Monday, acting on information from a source, *TV Guide* telephoned George Allen and confirmed that Crile had indeed screened for him, prior to his second interview, testimony from witnesses already on film. The reporters called Crile, who admitted he had screened the material for Allen. That day Wallace spent hours reading transcripts of interviews for the broadcast. One CBS staffer was sitting in his office when he heard Wallace's voice booming: "Where in hell is George Crile?" Wallace stormed past, a transcript in his hand.

TV Guide kept pursuing its investigation, examining the documentary segment by segment. In Act 4 Wallace had charged that the military had suppressed internal reports of increased infiltration during the months before Tet.

> WALLACE: . . . consider what was happening at Westmoreland's headquarters on the very day he left for Washington in November 1967 to tell the American public the enemy was running out of men. On that day a senior intelligence officer, Lt. Col. Everette Parkins, a West Point graduate who planned to make a career of the army, had become so incensed by MACV's refusal to send on reports of an enemy infiltration of twenty-five thousand that he lost his temper and shouted at his superior.
>
> CRILE: Lt. Col. Parkins was fired for trying to get his report through and—
>
> COOLEY: He was relieved from his position. The word "fired," . . . yes, he was.

"It was my *perception,* and the perception of most officers and men in OB Studies [emphasis added]," said Cooley in an affidavit, "that Lt. Col. Parkins was relieved for supporting the higher figures." Cooley, Crile's on-camera source, had no firsthand knowledge of the Parkins "firing." Astonishingly, neither did Parkins. Although Parkins refused to be interviewed by CBS on camera, he did speak to Crile by telephone. Said Crile: "I ran the whole thing out for him, and Parkins muttered, 'That's approximately right.' "

"Crile asked me if I came home from Vietnam early," Parkins told *TV Guide*. "I told him I came home a couple of weeks early, but when I heard the word 'firing,' that was a new one to me. The questions Crile mostly asked," added Parkins, "had to do with strength estimates."

The reporters read to Parkins from the official unedited interview transcript what Mike Wallace had told Westmoreland: that "Parkins said it [his report] had to be sent on, that the infiltration constituted a near-invasion, and Washington should be alerted. Parkins lost his temper, shouted at Colonel Morris. He was fired, his army career destroyed, the report was blocked. . . ."

"No," Parkins told *TV Guide*, "I didn't hear the story till I heard it from you."

Sam Adams said that he also interviewed Parkins, twice. Adams read to the reporters from his chronology those two separate accounts. Neither one contained any mention of what Wallace told Westmoreland: that the report "had to be sent on" or that "the infiltration constituted a near invasion" or that the number of infiltrators was "25,000" or that "Washington should be alerted." Parkins never told Adams that he "lost his temper" or that he "shouted at Colonel Morris" or that "he was fired" or that his "army career was destroyed."

However, Parkins *did* tell Adams what he told *TV Guide*: that the incident with Col. Charles Morris, as far as he was concerned, had less to do with a particular report than with a five-month-old "drastic personality conflict" between the two men. "He and I had not gotten along since the day he walked into the command and had an instantaneous dislike for me," said Parkins. He insisted to *TV Guide* that he did not lose his temper or shout at his superior; Morris, he said, did all the shouting.

Parkins said that after the incident with Morris (which Adams claimed occurred on November 15, 1967), he remained in Vietnam until about January 6, 1968, preparing other reports "with no problems." He said that no one ever shouted at him again, nor did he ever—before or after the incident with Morris—feel he was being pressured to produce lower infiltration estimates. He left Vietnam about three weeks before his tour of duty was over. (Parkins did not resign from the army until five years later, with the rank of lieutenant colonel.) "The rotation was just about normal," he said. His replacement had arrived. "It was pointless," he added, "for two people to be doing the same job."

"Well—I don't really know what the hell I'd say about all that," said Sam Adams. "I would say that everybody *else* said they thought Parkins had been fired. I didn't get into the nuts and bolts of what *Parkins* felt happened."

TV Guide had talked to Col. Charles Morris, the officer who had allegedly fired Parkins. Morris told the reporters what he had already said at the Westmoreland press conference: that the argument was over an order he gave to Parkins to get ". . . a better handle on relating reported killed-in-action to actual killed-in-action or wounded-in-action. . . ." Morris said that the military had a wealth of captured documents, and he asked Parkins "to see if he could detect a pattern between what our people had reported on these operations . . ." and what enemy documents claimed. Morris said Parkins told him it could not be done and he would not try. "No officer in combat tells me he won't try," said Morris, "and for that he was fired." Parkins later would dispute that version of events in a sworn affidavit. Similarly, his subordinate, infiltration analyst Michael Hankins, insisted in a sworn deposition that the Parkins-Morris argument did focus on the methodology used to arrive at a higher estimate of enemy infiltration, developed by Hankins. However, Hankins did not actually hear that conversation, nor did Parkins discuss with him its details.

TV Guide had also questioned Morris's deputy, Col. Lew Ponder, who was in the room at the time of the incident. Ponder confirmed Morris's testimony. Crile said his sources were Cooley, Lt. Bernie Gattozzi, and Lt. Col. David Morgan, none of whom had been present during the incident. TV Guide asked Crile whether, in his conversation with Morris before the broadcast, he had asked about the Parkins firing. Crile said yes. Morris had insisted, said Crile, "that he fired Parkins for not agreeing to carry through a methodology that he wanted to be done."

> TV Guide: You didn't ask him what kind of "methodology," what he meant by that?
>
> CRILE: I told him that the explanation as offered by the other people was that it was in connection with infiltration.
>
> TV Guide: Did he tell you what the argument was over?
>
> CRILE: It wasn't exactly clear to me what he was talking about. He was talking about a methodology. He said, "I had given him orders to observe a certain procedure which he would not do, and anybody who doesn't observe an order gets fired."
>
> TV Guide: Did you talk to Ponder?
>
> CRILE: No.

Later Crile explained why he did not feel obligated to include Morris's version of the Parkins firing in his broadcast. ". . . It's like our earlier discussion about whether the [McChristian] report was blocked or got stopped," said Crile. ". . . Those people who were involved in that business, working with Parkins, and in Parkins's discussions with me—the message was that Parkins was fired for trying to push too hard to get these infiltration estimates through."

The more the TV Guide writers delved into the documentary, the more contradictions they uncovered. In the program, for instance, Wallace charged that Lt. Col. Danny Graham had coerced Lt. Russell Cooley and Comdr. James Meacham into altering the data base of the MACV computer after Tet. "In effect," said Wallace, "they then accused Graham of personally engineering a cover-up. . . ."

> MEACHAM: . . . We didn't like what Danny Graham proposed to do. We didn't want him to do it. At the end of the day we lost the fight, and he did it.

But Meacham also gave Crile information that softened the charge against Graham. For example, the documentary ignored the fact that the decision to alter the data base was made in General Davidson's office, amidst a group of "maybe twenty" people, with both sides presenting their case and Davidson ultimately deciding in Graham's favor. Meacham, who attended that meeting, clearly did not view Graham's act as a "cover-up":

> CRILE: Was it the equivalent of burning government records?
> MEACHAM: No, no. Not at all. It wasn't equivalent to burning any-thing. All—
> CRILE: —destroying—
> MEACHAM: No. I wouldn't say it was equivalent to destroying any-thing at all. . . .

Later:

> CRILE: And why did [Graham] want to do this? What was he worried about?
> MEACHAM: I don't know that I can recall the specific issue. I sup-pose it was that—that the figures were getting too far out of bal-ance at that time, between what we thought was true and what he thought should be true. I think I—it's only fair for me to say at this point, of course, that Colonel Graham had access to lots of dif-ferent kinds of intelligence that we didn't—my section didn't.

Later:

> CRILE: Would it, for instance, have been against military regulations to do that [alter the computer's data base]?
> MEACHAM: No, no. It was certainly not falsification of official rec-ords, if that's what you're asking.

Later:

> CRILE: Now, if that had gotten out at the time, if Secretary McNamara had been told that somebody had gone in and done this to MACV's computers, what would the response have been?
> MEACHAM: Well, I don't know. I mean, you're trying—you're trying

to make something harder than it is here. We didn't like this because we thought our data base was right; we thought we had some fixes back there on some . . . very reliable documents; we'd spent months of our lives working that system; we thought it was okay. We didn't want it fiddled with. . . . Every estimate starts out at the bottom and filters up to the top, and various people can put in their judgment . . . on those things. It wasn't our judgment, and we didn't like it. But I don't think it was hard and fast enough that any one of us could've gone to Secretary McNamara and said, "Danny Graham is tinkering with official records" and made a case that would've been believed.

Nor did Lt. Russell Cooley, in his interview with CBS, charge Graham with a "cover-up." Cooley told Crile that both sides (the one represented by Meacham, the other represented by Graham) were in agreement that the running total in the computer was wrong and should be corrected. After Tet, he said, because of the massive number of enemy killed "we had reduced [their strength] so low it was really beyond, you know, credibility." At the meeting in Davidson's conference room, he added, ". . . The controversy arose whether we would do it now, stop in time where we were and reset the figures, or go back in time, reset the figures, and come forward. The latter was the one chosen, as best as I can recall," Cooley added. "That we did go back in time, reset figures, and come forward."

CRILE: You mean there was an agreement that the way the figures had been carried was wrong and had to be changed.
COOLEY: Obviously. Yeah. That was—that was more than implied; that was very clear.
CRILE: And the question was, "How do you do it?"
COOLEY: Exactly
CRILE: [And] you all said that you should just start the best way, the most honest way is just to start from there and say we were wrong, and let's go with what we think is right now.
COOLEY: Well, the question of honesty . . . came into play if you went back a year or two years in history and started playing with figures. That becomes an—an unacceptable way of doing it. If you want to go back three months and say, "Three months ago we were wrong for the following reasons: we underestimated infiltration; we weren't carrying our units with a correct criteria; or we

blew it," and then you carry it forward, that you can buy. That's basically what we ended up doing, as I recall.

Cooley had told Crile that Graham went back only about three months—"that you can buy," he said. He was not accusing Graham of a cover-up. He was telling Crile that what Graham wanted to do was legitimate, whether or not he and Meacham felt it was logical. In that interview with Cooley, Crile neglected to ask one key question: Did Graham, in fact, ever actually change the data in the computer base?

"To my knowledge, no," Cooley said. ". . . To my knowledge, the data base that was referred to was never changed."

". . . Commander Meacham and Colonel Cooley insist that Graham did alter the record . . ." Wallace said in the documentary, ending the sequence.

During the two months following the broadcast, after an initial spurt of columns supporting the CBS program, the press was comparatively quiet on the controversy between Westmoreland and CBS. While both sides in the dispute kept busy corralling new supporters, the national media—print, television, and radio—apparently saw no purpose in pursuing the story. Then in April the first serious press criticism of the program emerged. In the April issue of the *Washington Journalism Review*, Peter Braestrup published an article entitled " 'The Uncounted Enemy: A Vietnam Deception' A Dissenting View." In the article Braestrup stated that "in essence Mike Wallace and producer George Crile were revising the complex history of the Vietnam War, recycling a tired 1975 congressional minicontroversy over United States Vietnam intelligence and—presto— producing a seemingly brand-new Vietnam 'conspiracy scandal' with Gen. William C. Westmoreland, the United States commander in Vietnam from 1964 to 1968, cast as villain. It was Westmoreland, according to CBS, who kept the bad news from Lyndon Johnson.

"Wallace and Crile, however, skewed the facts. . . ."

Braestrup was an authority on the period; his article should have sparked further discussion in the press. However, perhaps because the *Washington Journalism Review* had only a limited (though influential) readership, there was little reaction from other magazines or newspapers, and none at all in national television news broadcasts. The only detailed response came from George Crile, who sent Braestrup an angry rebuttal.

At the time he wrote his article Braestrup had obtained the script of the broadcast, from which he quoted liberally, plus three interview transcripts: those of generals Westmoreland and Graham and the unused interview of Johnson adviser Walt Rostow. By then the *TV Guide* reporters had acquired the transcripts of several other interviews as well. Time after time they found discrepancies between what on-camera witnesses *seemed* to be saying in the program and their actual testimony. Statements by witnesses that contradicted or even softened an assertion CBS held to be true were left on the cutting-room floor.

Early in the documentary a guerilla analyst named Richard McArthur had testified that in the summer of 1967 he had "found that someone was changing the numbers, the numbers that were reported by the sector advisers in the field."

Wallace returned to McArthur and his claims in the section of the documentary that dealt with the post-Tet period. ". . . General Westmoreland was insisting that Tet was a great victory," said Wallace. "And it was left to his intelligence officers to document that claim by demonstrating massive losses in the enemy's army. It was at this point, in the weeks after Tet, that things began to career out of control at MACV intelligence. Guerilla analyst Richard McArthur told us what happened after Tet when he tried to defend the integrity of his figures."

McArthur returned from a vacation to learn that his guerilla total had been reduced by half. When he complained to his superior, the officer told him: "Mac, lie a little, Mac. Lie a little."

"Shortly after," Wallace concluded, "McArthur was transferred. MACV intelligence, meanwhile, went ahead and produced its first official estimate of enemy strength after Tet. This is that document, sent on to the Pentagon and the White House, listing an enemy reduced to 204,126 men. . . ."

Was the slicing of McArthur's guerilla totals evidence of Westmoreland's deception, as CBS was charging? CBS had heard contrary testimony from two of its own star witnesses, Colonel Cooley and Commander Meacham, both of whom were interviewed *after* McArthur, when Crile already had McArthur's story on film. What Meacham told Crile was that the guerilla category had *always* been used, in the military's complicated bookkeeping system, as "the slop factor."

". . . If we had so many casualties, for example, that we had to assess against our grand total number, and we couldn't—where there'd be some we could attribute to the 325th division, there'd be some we could attribute to another division, and at the end you have a big bunch [of casualties] left over, and you just take these out of the guerillas. This seems arbitrary," Meacham added, "and it is arbitrary, but it's not inconsistent with the way things actually happened because—after a big loss they tended to upgrade guerillas into the regular forces."

Meacham told Crile it was *his* decision to use the guerilla category as a shock absorber. ". . . We'd always done this. I could've probably argued for doing it a different way, but it was my decision to assess this against the guerilla figures."

In a subsequent CBS interview Cooley confirmed Meacham's explanation.

> CRILE: Can you understand the stress of Richard McArthur, the guerilla analyst?
>
> COOLEY: I can understand his distress because it was—a decision made unilaterally without consulting him or—without his input into it. And again, as best I recall, it was taken out of the guerilla figure because they were—theoretically, poorly equipped. They were thrown into battle, into a more conventional, open-hostility environment and therefore would suffer higher losses than the—the better-trained North Vietnamese soldier or a Vietcong. [Cooley added moments later,] The figures—the guerilla figures basically weren't documented in any case. Guerillas were a product of the system and the manner of calculations.

Was there something sinister about the reduction of McArthur's guerillas? McArthur certainly thought so, while Meacham and Cooley clearly did not. Meacham and Cooley's testimony was not included in the broadcast.

15

The
CBS Internal Inquiry

O<small>N APRIL</small> 1 Klein began working on a rush documentary about West Germany. Three weeks later he was editing "Our Friends the Germans" when Mike Wallace entered his cutting room. For a few minutes Wallace and Klein chatted. At the time, the producer of the West German program was working in the room.

"I'd like to talk to you alone," Wallace told Klein.

"It wouldn't be about the Vietnam show, would it?" Klein said.

Klein and Wallace found an empty editing room. They sat down. Wallace impaled Klein with his renowned laser look. "Somebody's been leaking information to *TV Guide*," he said.

"Mike," Klein said, "do you believe what was presented on the screen was accurate?"

"I don't have any reason to believe otherwise," said Wallace. After a pause he added, "Do you believe anything was taken out of context?"

Klein was silent for a moment. All along, Crile had reassured him that Roger Colloff was reading transcripts to verify that the testimony in the program had not been taken out of context. Had Colloff performed the task properly? Klein was still thinking about that when Wallace rose and, without another word, walked out of the room.

Moments later Klein stood up and followed Wallace into the corridor. Wallace was not in sight, but the door to Crile's office was closing. Klein knocked on Crile's door and walked in. Wallace was there, his feet propped up on Crile's desk. Klein sat down on the couch. "What is this all about?" he said. Crile told him that *TV Guide* had telephoned George Allen, asking whether Allen had screened segments before his second interview. Crile said that he had just telephoned Colloff to tell the vice-president that Allen had indeed been in the editing room. (Later Roger Colloff offered this version of his conversation with Crile that day. ". . . Crile called me and said, 'Roger, I've got some bad news for you,' " Colloff recalled. "He was very agitated. I was upset. No, I didn't know at the time that Allen had screened other interviews.")

Wallace then initiated a discussion about the damage that harsh publicity might do to a career. *TV Guide's* article clearly would not be a friendly one. It was unfair if Crile had to shoulder the attack alone.

"What about Ira Klein's career?" said Klein. "What about Joe Zigman's career. What about Phyllis Hurwitz's career? What about discovering what's right from what's wrong?"

Wallace sat there peering at the editor through the half-moon glasses precariously perched on the tip of his nose. His legs came off Crile's desk. He leaned forward and said, "That's right, that's right."

Then Klein started discussing the specific details of the Allen incident. "I was in the editing room," he began, "when George came in. He had George Allen with him. . . ."

Wallace got up and walked out of Crile's office.

Klein and Crile continued their discussion for a few minutes, then Klein departed. He met executive producer Andy Lack in the hall. "Mike came in to see me—did you know about that?" he said.

Lack said that he did know. Wallace had come to see him first. Lack raised his hands in the air, as if to say: What can I do?

Throughout April *TV Guide* continued its inquiry, interviewing in all some forty people (many several times) either involved in the program's production or supervision, or who had participated in the events described in the documentary. By late April the writers had accumulated stacks of taped interviews and a thick file of documents, including not only the official unedited transcripts of the program but other internal documents as well.

At the end of April, Joe Zigman dropped into Klein's editing room to say hello. He sat down and told Klein that *TV Guide* had telephoned him, asking if Sam Adams had been rehearsed a few days before his interview with Mike Wallace.

"Joe, you know that Sam was rehearsed," said Klein. "You were there."

Zigman laughed. "They asked me if Sam was rehearsed on Friday," he said. "I told them no, 'cause it was really on Thursday."

By early May the *TV Guide* reporters were ready to write their article. They informed the editor of the magazine, who had asked them to give advance notice of delivery since, on the basis of the evidence they had uncovered, he was planning to carve out eleven and a half pages of text—the longest article in the magazine's history. Furthermore, the editor intended to run the article as a cover story. He needed to know the piece's delivery date as early as possible so he could plan ahead.

The reporters began assembling their piece, working from a jointly conceived outline and dividing up sections between them. When reporter A finished section A, the reporter would immediately begin section C, while the other reporter worked on section B. The reporters soon realized that even eleven and a half pages (the average *TV Guide* article runs from two to three pages) were insufficient to encompass all of their research. Among others, the "Parkins firing" incident was discarded, along with the "Pentagon slashing meeting" and "altering the data base" sequences.

After the article was written, *TV Guide's* editors sent a researcher to New York from the home office in Radnor, Pennsylvania, and installed her for two days at a midtown hotel. The researcher spent those two days studying the article, reviewing its documentation—playing devil's advocate and trying to find flaws. The article then was submitted to the editors, who made no changes that were not approved by the reporters. Finally it was time to choose a title. The reporters rejected a number of suggestions before accepting: "Anatomy of a Smear."

On May 23 the managers of CBS's 200-plus affiliated television stations were gathering in San Francisco for a three-day conference, to begin the following day, sponsored by the parent network. The annual convention was designed to arouse grass-roots enthusiasm for the network's programs. Many of CBS's top brass had flown in for the occasion. Van Gordon Sauter (the news division's new president) was there, along with such stellar CBS correspondents as Ed Bradley, Andy Rooney, Morley Safer, Bill Moyers, Bill Kurtis, Diane Sawyer, and Harry Reasoner, who would rub shoulders with the delegates at cocktail parties and charm junketing journalists at specially arranged press conferences. Even Dan Rather jetted to San Francisco from New York, anchoring the news from CBS's San Francisco affiliate. Only Mike Wallace was missing. Ironically, Wallace had flown off to Vietnam on assignment from *60 Minutes* to cover the trip of a delegation of Vietnam War veterans attempting to learn more about missing American servicemen and about the effects of the defoliant Agent Orange.

On the morning the conference began, delegates who had arrived at San Francisco's prestigious Fairmont Hotel the night before walked out of elevators and headed toward the newsstand to purchase the morning papers. They were soon wide awake and gaping. There in white letters on a black background was the May 29 TV *Guide* trumpeting its cover story, "Anatomy of a Smear." The cover line, tucked in the upper righthand corner, read: "How CBS News Broke the Rules and 'Got' Gen. Westmoreland." Below were three snapshots—of Mike Wallace, George Crile, and Westmoreland himself. As *San Diego Chronicle* columnist Terrence O'Flaherty wrote a few days later, for the CBS delegates and executives the appearance of the *TV Guide* article at that delicate moment was "like finding a dead rat in the punch bowl."

It was difficult to conceive not only a worse moment but a worse locale. San Francisco's gay population was still seething over "Gay Power, Gay Politics," the controversial documentary about gay influence in San Francisco politics that George Crile and Grace Diekhaus had produced several years before.

The *TV Guide* investigation disclosed:

- CBS set out to prove the conspiracy premise without ever trying to test its veracity.
- CBS did little to investigate the obsessive commitment of its consultant (to whom the network paid $25,000) to proving that conspiracy premise.
- Contrary to the CBS News Standards, CBS rehearsed that paid consultant prior to his on-camera interview.
- CBS allowed the CIA's George Allen to screen segments of other interviews, against its official guidelines.
- CBS was guilty of misediting some interviews and distorting the content of others, while ignoring prospective interviewees who might have refuted its conspiracy premise.
- Sam Adams, the paid consultant, had disavowed after the broadcast the CBS thesis of a Westmoreland-engineered conspiracy to suppress the true size of the enemy.

Over the nine and a half pages that followed, *TV Guide* documented those allegations, adding others in the process. *TV Guide* had located

Gen. Philip Davidson's private physician, who, with Davidson's permission read to the reporters medical records demonstrating that Davidson had been in excellent health during the period of the CBS investigation.

On May 24, the official opening day of the conference, Van Gordon Sauter convened a private meeting of CBS executives in San Francisco. Representing CBS, Inc., were Gene Mater, vice-president of the Broadcast Group, and Ralph Goldberg, the associate general counsel. Representing the news division, along with Sauter himself, were Bob Chandler and Roger Colloff. The purpose of the meeting was to decide what to do about the *TV Guide* allegations. Several options were discussed, including an inquiry conducted by a newsman, but supervised by an in-house lawyer, and an inquiry supervised by outside counsel. Reportedly, CBS chairman William Paley at one point suggested retaining Archibald Cox. But Sauter was convinced that the inquiry had to be "a journalistic not legalistic judgment." Later he told a reporter from the *American Lawyer* magazine: "CBS News had to know whether we were right or wrong. And it wasn't by having some goddam lawyer from Wall Street come in here to find out. That's what *we're* about." At the meeting, Sauter added, "The universal conclusion we reached—including the lawyer (associate general counsel Ralph Goldberg) who was with us—was that it should be done within the news division."

The decision was made to conduct an internal inquiry into *TV Guide's* charges. Sauter that day telephoned Burton "Bud" Benjamin, the CBS News senior executive producer and an experienced documentary maker, to ask him if he would be willing to head that investigation. Benjamin said yes. Throughout the following day CBS executives in San Francisco fended off a barrage of questions from reporters, claiming they hadn't had time to read all of the *TV Guide* article. However, on May 26, the conference's closing day, in his address to the affiliate managers assembled at San Francisco's Masonic Temple, Sauter said that he and another unnamed high-level CBS executive would "thoroughly examine [the *TV Guide*] charges . . . [with] the same vigor and objectivity we bring to our own reporting."

At CBS headquarters in New York, executives were busy dodging the same questions. The day the *TV Guide* article appeared, the newsstand in the CBS lobby ran out of the magazine within hours after it opened. CBS staffers were purchasing tens of copies at a time. Journalists who telephoned the CBS public relations department were read a prepared statement: "The *TV Guide* article raises serious questions that are being reviewed by CBS. Because of the length of the article and the complexity of the subject matter it would be inappropriate to respond at this time."

However, at least one San Francisco reporter who telephoned CBS in New York was told by a public relations person to consider the possibility that *TV Guide* owner Walter Annenberg had a "vendetta against CBS in general and Mike Wallace in particular."

The following morning, May 27, on page one of the *Washington Post's* Style section, critic Tom Shales weighed in with a lengthy article attacking the *TV Guide* piece. However, Shales did not concentrate on allegations in the article. Instead he focused on the owner of *TV Guide*, Walter Annenberg, whom Shales characterized as "a conservative multimillionaire and longtime devoted Republican." Shales expounded at length on Annenberg's ties to both Richard Nixon and Ronald Reagan, recalling recent pro-Reagan editorials written by Annenberg for *TV Guide*. "It was beginning to look as though Annenberg might play for Reagan the same saber-rattling, media-baiting, network-attacking role Spiro Agnew played for Nixon," Shales wrote. "The White House does not like the networks, and CBS is considered by Reagan forces the most 'liberal' of the three.

"Now comes this big, splashy attack on CBS News. . . ."

Both *TV Guide* reporters had flatly denied to Shales that the publisher had participated in any way in formulating or writing the article. Shales printed those denials while hammering home his theme of guilt by association. Shales's column was widely syndicated in newspapers all over the country and would have an immediate impact on other newspaper reporters. CBS was prohibiting its personnel from publicly commenting on the controversy until its internal investigation was completed. Newspaper and magazine reporters who wanted to write about the controversy had only *TV Guide* to talk to on the record. The *TV Guide* writers found themselves defending not the allegations in their article but their own integrity against the accusation that the piece was an anti-CBS ploy devised by their publisher.

On June 3 Bud Benjamin began his internal investigation into the *TV Guide* charges. At the suggestion of a CBS executive, Benjamin's first CBS interview was with the editor, Ira Klein. When Klein arrived at Benjamin's office that day, Benjamin was alone, talking on the telephone. Klein waited outside until Benjamin was finished. When Klein entered, Benjamin said to him: "That was Joe Zigman on the telephone. He just confirmed the rehearsal." [*TV Guide* had claimed that Adams had been thoroughly rehearsed a few days before his on-camera interview with Wallace, in contravention of CBS guidelines that specified all interviews had to be spontaneous and unrehearsed.] Klein explained to Benjamin the details, as he recalled them, of Adams's rehearsal. "Adams was definitely rehearsed. I was in there periodically," Klein told Benjamin. "Wallace was not there, nor possibly even aware of what was going on. . . ." Benjamin spoke to Klein again. This time Phyllis Hurwitz was with Klein. She confirmed Klein's account.

At their first meeting, Klein and Benjamin also discussed other substantive matters, including the packet of official documents Westmoreland had sent to Wallace and Crile after his interview—documents he regarded as a "correction." Benjamin had that packet on the corner of his desk. He asked Klein if Klein had scanned the packet's contents. Klein said that he had. Benjamin agreed that the Westmoreland documents constituted a request for a correction. Klein also confirmed to Benjamin that after the broadcast Adams had expressed doubts about the documentary's premise.

In fact, at that very time Adams was still expressing his doubts. On June 6 he was in West Point, Mississippi, invited there by Col. Gains Hawkins, the Order of Battle specialist who had testified against Westmoreland in the program, to address Hawkins's hometown Rotary Club. Adams explained to reporters from the *Clarion-Ledger* why the broadcast had stopped short of saying Lyndon Johnson had ordered the ceiling on enemy-strength estimates. "George Crile and I had endless discussions on this," Adams recalled, "and I said, 'George, I think you ought to do more to imply that the White House was in on it.' And he said the problem was we didn't have any direct evidence," Adams added. He now believed he did. "Now we have a letter from Walt Rostow saying, 'I told LBJ constantly that we had this flood of guys coming down the trail.' He called it a virtual invasion," Adams said of Rostow's letter.

The truth was, Rostow had said much the same thing in his interview with George Crile—an interview that CBS had discarded as being irrelevant to the purpose of its program.

Benjamin continued his investigation throughout the month of June and into July, interviewing staffers involved in the production and supervision of the documentary, while head CBS News researcher Toby Wertheimer, assisted by Barbara Pierce, studied the transcripts of CBS interviews used in the program as well as other internal documents. Benjamin asked Crile to respond in writing to *TV Guide*'s allegations. Alex Alben was flown back from Stanford University Law School to be interviewed by Benjamin. Officially, Benjamin's report on his investigation was scheduled to end up on CBS News president Van Gordon Sauter's desk. However, CBS insiders were suggesting that the report's final destination would be CBS corporate headquarters. Even before the *TV Guide* article was published, when the thrust of the line of questioning was apparent,

Frank Stanton (president of CBS, Inc., from 1946 to 1972 and alleged to be one of the corporation's largest stockholders) had met with CBS, Inc., president Thomas Wyman to discuss the forthcoming article. After the article was published, sources revealed, Stanton lunched with two-time CBS News president Richard Salant, under whose regime the CBS guidelines for fairness and accuracy had been codified. CBS sources reported that Stanton had told Salant that board chairman William Paley was "fit to be tied." The documentary about drugs in Miami for which Crile had served as correspondent was put "on hold." (Eventually it would be cancelled.) In contrast, reporters were told, Howard Stringer was regarded as "indispensable" because of his position as executive producer of the *CBS Evening News with Dan Rather*. "Every effort will be made to acquit Howard of any blame for the documentary's faults," said a CBS executive.

Meanwhile, Benjamin and his tiny staff kept interviewing, his pair of assistants dutifully taking notes of his conversations with CBS staffers. Some of those discussions included sharp exchanges, indicating that Benjamin was asking hard questions and pursuing the truth with a dogged tenaciousness. *TV Guide*'s allegation that Crile had interviewed George Allen twice, and before the second interview had shown Allen portions of other witnesses' testimony, evoked several of those exchanges.

> CRILE: There was nothing basically wrong with the first interview. This was a personal thing with me. Allen was particularly concerned about ratting on the CIA. He looked like hell, looked guilty, on those questions about the CIA. . . . I felt very badly for what it would do for Allen. No, I didn't tell Andy Lack or Howard Stringer that I did the interview twice. I don't know if they knew. No, I didn't know this was a violation of the CBS guidelines. Was it?
>
> BENJAMIN: How could it be spontaneous and unrehearsed if you interviewed him twice?
>
> CRILE: I honestly was not aware of it being a violation of the guidelines.

And later in that same June 15 interview:

> BENJAMIN: Why did Allen see the other interviews?
>
> CRILE: For the same reason as the second interview. I know it's against the sensibilities of everyone here. . . . I don't think what I

did there was right. Allen was caught in stage paralysis. He felt badly about doing the interview—he felt isolated as if he were a whistle-blower. I wanted to show him he wasn't alone out there.

However, it is clear that at the time Crile showed Allen these segments of other interviews he was fully aware that doing so violated the CBS guidelines. More than a month before Allen's first CBS on-camera interview, Crile had taped a telephone call with Lt. Russell Cooley, in which Crile told Cooley: ". . . in terms of how you appear on the film, you are really terrific. You look good . . . it really is very, very good."

COOLEY: Is there a chance of seeing any of this after it's put together, before it goes on, or—I don't know how you work that?
CRILE: Unfortunately, we're not even allowed by our bureaucratic guidelines to—or rules—to let anybody see anything before.
COOLEY: That's right.
CRILE: Yeah. It's—it's—they're tough as nails about that. I could get basically booted.

Benjamin pursued the theme of the Allen double interview with *CBS Reports* executive producer Andy Lack on June 22:

BENJAMIN: Did you know that Allen was interviewed twice?
LACK: No.
BENJAMIN: Do you agree there was a violation?
LACK: First I would ask why it was done a second time.
BENJAMIN: What about spontaneity?
LACK: If you go back a second time to ask additional questions, that is okay.
BENJAMIN: What if you don't like the way it looks?
LACK: I don't buy that.
BENJAMIN: What if I say I'll screen other material for you?
LACK: [Shakes head no.]

TV Guide's contention that CBS tossed its sympathetic witnesses soft questions produced another exchange between Benjamin and Crile:

BENJAMIN: Were there soft questions for sympathetic witnesses?
CRILE: Allen certainly wasn't an adversarial interview. Hawkins was pretty tough. He was an agonized man.

BENJAMIN: What adversarial interviews were there—Westmoreland, Graham, Rostow. Three. Correct me if I'm wrong.

CRILE: There is a place for an adversarial interview, but why do you want to go adversarial if a person is confessing?

Benjamin pointed out to Howard Stringer, the documentary's executive producer, that in the Allen interview Crile had asked Allen to describe the same incident involving Lt. Gen. Danny Graham eleven times, "to get a better answer."

"Oh, shit," said Stringer.

The sharpest exchange between Benjamin and Crile occurred over *TV Guide's* allegation that Westmoreland had seemed ill-prepared for his interview. Benjamin asked Crile why he (Crile) "found it necessary to send a letter the night before the interview" after he had (according to Crile) "read the same letter to the general on the phone." Crile replied, "I wrote the letter to get on the record and spell it out to Westmoreland."

CRILE: Short of spelling out the accusations I did everything I could.

BENJAMIN: He seemed ill-prepared.

CRILE: There's something more fundamental here. This was the commander of the United States forces talking on a critical issue of the war. We were dealing with a very disturbing report which he blocked. . . .

BENJAMIN: I had the sense that he didn't understand why he was here, that he was not well informed.

CRILE: I have to get back to this. He was wearing the mantle of MacArthur and Eisenhower. There are serious charges.

BENJAMIN: Do you think Westmoreland was somewhat inept?

CRILE: Yes. He seems stupid.

BENJAMIN: Well, if he doesn't come off well, maybe you should have got someone else to defend him.

CRILE: Westmoreland was not the show.

BENJAMIN: He came out as the heavy, George.

Over and over in Benjamin's questioning of Crile there was implicit the assumption that a documentary should be fair.

BENJAMIN: Should we have used more of [Danny] Graham?

CRILE: Graham was not being candid. He was being demonstrably untruthful.

BENJAMIN: Then maybe Graham was the wrong man to interview on camera. . . .

Benjamin was also concerned over Crile's omission of the CIA's George Carver from the broadcast:

BENJAMIN: Would you say that Carver was articulate?
CRILE: He's brilliant. It was going to be Carver or Allen all along.
BENJAMIN: Allen is so tight on camera, you say, so inhibited. And his boss is so articulate.
CRILE: Allen was the most honorable, spoke with force and integrity. I relied heavily on Tom Powers [the author of a book about Richard Helms]. Carver was identified . . . as Rostow's man at CIA. He had a willingness to think intelligence was the piece of paper that can get through the bureaucracy. . . . If Allen had not come on, I would have felt compelled to have Carver on. But Carver was in a terrible position, having caved in. . . .
BENJAMIN: Wasn't that good to have on the show?
CRILE: The CIA story wasn't the story in the show. It was a judgment call. Carver's position was firmly etched in documents in my file. His position flip-flopped. I could have turned the tables and tried to roast Carver.
BENJAMIN: Couldn't you have let Carver tell his story and let the audience decide, which we often do around here, George?

Benjamin did not seem able to understand why special ambassador Robert Komer had been omitted as well. He mentioned Komer to Sam Adams in their June 21 interview:

ADAMS: He would have been a damned interesting interview.
BENJAMIN: What would Komer have said?
ADAMS: This is what Komer would have said. "Of course, we did that stuff. The goddam lying press. Of course we did that. We had to."
BENJAMIN: Might have fortified your case?
ADAMS: Yes.

Benjamin also queried CBS executives about the letter Westmoreland sent CBS after his May 16 interview—the letter he claimed was a request for a correction, the one Crile ignored.

BENJAMIN: Did you see the Westmoreland correction letter?

LACK: I saw it after the broadcast. I had a discussion about it with Crile and Mike and I was told that it had been taken to Colloff. I told them I would have handled it differently. I would have included a line about the letter in the broadcast—"Westmoreland wrote us again after the interview . . ." I think Mike agreed with me. He had some doubts about the way it was handled.

Benjamin also raised the issue in his June 23 interview with Howard Stringer. Stringer, Benjamin noted, "agrees the Westmoreland letter is a correction letter."

Stringer told Benjamin that he had reminded Crile of the CBS guidelines "umpteen bloody times."

Benjamin interviewed Mike Wallace on June 17. About his interview with Adams, Wallace said, "My job was to lead him but I was tough. I asked him some tough questions—about being obsessed, about his story sounding too pat, about being sold out by George Carver. But Adams was our employee, our consultant," Wallace added. "I made handwritten notes before I met Adams, but I told Crile: 'I'm up to my ass. You have to fill me in.' "

Several days after their interview, on June 21, Wallace wrote Benjamin a memo:

Bud:

Just a few random weekend thoughts after that draining day in your office. (And, by the way, I thought your inquiries were sensible and fair and direct.) I remain satisfied that the thrust and the substance of the broadcast were accurate, that a ceiling was imposed and the books were cooked, in a surreptitious way, to portray success or at least progress and the light at the end of the tunnel. And I continue to believe that Westmoreland was aware of what was going on. He may come off as dumb now, in the film and to some of his former colleagues, in retrospect. But I find it difficult to believe that the man arrived at the position he achieved in this country's military establishment without considerable savvy, both political and strategic. . . .

Wallace had reaffirmed his satisfaction with the "thrust and the substance" of the broadcast; however, he seemed less sure about the procedures used to prove the program's conspiracy premise. After noting the activity of the "old boy's Vietnam network" since the broadcast, Wallace went on:

As to some of the journalistic calls made in the course of the production, there is no doubt another producer might have gone about it differently. Some other characters might indeed have made the piece more varied, more a puzzle than a polemic, in the sense that the evidence we adduced pointed unmistakably at "cooking" by the [military] command. But there are surely other journalists who wound up with the same conclusion that CBS News did, most noticeably Thomas Powers of *The Man Who Kept the Secrets* [a biography of CIA Director Richard Helms]. I don't think I've often seen a piece on *60 Minutes* that I didn't believe might have benefited from a slightly different emphasis here, a nuance there, some cutting here, some adding there (all of this in retrospect, mind you), including some of my own. But that's a judgment call, not a failure of integrity or honest reporting. . . .

It is clear from Wallace's letter that Benjamin, by June 17, was dissatisfied with some reportorial techniques Crile had used to prove his premise. It is also clear that Wallace was attempting to draw a distinction between those procedures and the premise of the program itself.

Wallace went on in his letter to reveal what might have been his purpose in writing it. "Which brings me," he wrote, "to the phrase 'excess of zeal,' which I used the other day trying to understand what went on with George."

Apparently Wallace had characterized some aspect of Crile's behavior as an "excess of zeal." Now, after talking to Crile, he was writing Benjamin to explain that damaging characterization.

I talked with [George] for a long time that evening after my session with you. And I came away with a more sensitive understanding of the problems he had faced in getting some of these men on the record. [Wallace added:] I sympathize with the chore Geoge had in drawing them out. [Wallace called it "a delicate chore to get it out of them."]

There were lapses in technique, standards violated in spirit, if not in fact. But I'm persuaded they were not venal in nature. I don't think the truth was violated. The thrust of the *TV Guide* piece was that CBS News had knowingly, consciously smeared Westmoreland. That was the unmistakable message from their cover and their TV ads. But later on, in the piece itself and in the *Washington Post* piece by Shales, both Kowet and Bedell [the writers of the *TV Guide* piece] undercut that thesis themselves. They profess not to have made a judgment as to the validity of the charge of "smear"; they were just looking at the process. And in that process one of them said that the piece fell between the cracks.

Again Wallace was making a distinction between the "process" of the program's production and its content, arguing, in effect, that the *TV*

Guide writers had limited their investigation only to procedures, without attempting to shed any light on the substance of the program itself. The writers had stated in their article that its purpose was not to determine the truth or falsehood of CBS's conspiracy premise, but to examine the methods and documentation used to "prove" that conspiracy charge in the broadcast. The truth was, though, that the writers had discussed far more than procedures. They discussed evidence that CBS had used to buttress the conspiracy charge. Nor could the violations of ethics in using the procedures themselves be relegated to the role of misdemeanors. Whatever journalism is, be it good or bad, it is no more than the sum of its procedures. The only way a journalist using unethical procedures or unfair ones can reach an accurate conclusion is through divine inspiration or blind luck. CBS would never specify which of those two external agents had so miraculously shown George Crile the light.

The truth is, CBS did not have conclusive evidence proving a "conspiracy."

16

The Sauter Memorandum

THE SAME DAY that the *Washington Post's* Tom Shales weighed in with his attack on *TV Guide*, the *New York Times* published a front-page story on the dispute, written by Tony Schwartz. Behind the *Times's* traditional mask of neutrality a reader could detect disapproval of CBS's reportorial tactics. Soon the *Washington Post's* sister publication, *Newsweek*, published a column supporting CBS. (*Time* magazine remained silent, waiting for the results of Benjamin's investigation.) Hundreds of other periodicals merely repeated the *TV Guide* charges or the rebuttals printed in other columns from unnamed CBS sources. Few newspapermen felt the need to pick up a telephone and advance the story by searching out fresh material on their own. Overall the press seemed embarrassed, having to immerse itself in a debate brewed from two volatile ingredients: the Vietnam War and the very nature of journalistic procedures themselves.

Columnists who had counted themselves "doves" in the early 1970s tended to defend CBS, while "hawks" often defended Westmoreland, as if, in the intervening decade, not a single study had been done nor a single book published to sculpt their frozen perceptions into new perspectives. Most troubling of all, the press as a whole seemed incapable of grasping the crucial issue in the debate: Whether or not Westmoreland was "guilty" of the CBS charges, the evidence required to "convict" him on air needed to be no less stringent than the evidence required to convict a genuinely popular figure.

CBS staffers had been asked to remain silent until Benjamin completed his investigation. Instead, CBS executives fed their pet reporters nonattributable comments, which the reporters then took to *TV Guide* for on-the-record answers. The end result was hundreds of thousands of words written in the press without any further light being shed on the controversy. No one seemed to feel any obligation to go beyond the *TV Guide* article (and Braestrup's earlier *Washington Journalism Review* piece).

While Bud Benjamin was conducting his internal inquiry from his office in New York, Van Gordon Sauter, the CBS News president, was trapped in the public eye of the swirling controversy. Every summer the major television networks screen for leading critics their upcoming fall programs. Traditionally the meeting place was Los Angeles. But due to rising costs and growing dissatisfaction with that city's hotel accommodations, that June CBS had taken its press junket to Phoenix, Arizona. There, Sauter was daily bombarded by questions from the press about the CBS investigation. Sauter told the newsmen that CBS was "deeply troubled" by the *TV Guide* charges. However, he insisted that he considered the allegations of ethical violations as "separate from the issues of the broadcast." Many questions to Sauter focused on the identity of "the source" within CBS who had assisted *TV Guide*. Asked if the *TV Guide* article had been prompted by leaks from a disgruntled CBS employee, Sauter replied, according to a press account, that "he didn't know, but that it could have been prompted by leaks from a 'source' who simply cared about good journalism." Sauter said, "I don't believe it was sour grapes by a CBS News employee. Obviously the person—I don't know who he or she is—was disturbed by what was in the documentary." On June 14 CBS Broadcast Group president Gene Jankowski told newsmen assembled at the Arizona Biltmore Hotel: "If we find that we've erred, believe me, you're going to hear about it."

The question on many reporters' minds was—when? Initially Sauter had stated that the results of Benjamin's investigation would be made public "in two weeks." Three weeks and two days after Benjamin began his inquiry, a CBS spokesperson was telling reporters, "It's still being worked on. It's just not completed." Then, on July 10, the *New York Times* reported that Sauter expected to receive the completed report from Benjamin that coming weekend. "Sauter," added the *Times*, "confirmed this week that CBS would make a public accounting." *Variety* reported that "[Howard] Stringer's future . . . may be riding on the outcome. . . ."

George Crile had responded to internal requests for a written rebuttal of *TV Guide* with a massive White Paper, contradicting point by point every allegation in the article. He denied that Adams, as charged, had been rehearsed or that the Allen screening was intended "to influence Allen's answers." To bolster his denials he included portions of CBS interviews and testimonials supporting the documentary from ex-officials. *TV Guide* quoted Crile as saying that if Rostow had told him in the interview what Rostow said in his letter to the *New York Times*, Crile would have included that portion of the interview in his broadcast. In his White Paper, Crile stated that "*TV Guide* has given the false impression that the letter cited in the question to producer Crile referred to Rostow's February 7, 1982, letter to the editor of the *New York Times*. This is not true." In fact, the letter Crile was referring to, Crile wrote, "was *not* the *Times* letter, but a formal memo written by Rostow to the LBJ Library after the broadcast. *TV Guide* either purposefully or through sheer negligence totally misrepresented producer Crile's position," Crile continued. "This misrepresentation allowed the magazine authors to make perhaps their most serious charge—that CBS 'killed' the Rostow interview because it would have upended the thesis of the broadcast. This is a false accusation built on a factually incorrect premise. . . ."

The White Paper was dated June 3. As Benjamin's investigation progressed, the firm, aggressive tone of that White Paper dissolved into a quietly desperate one. Crile's concern over the direction of Benjamin's investigation, and over his own growing isolation, was reflected in a revealing six-page memo to Mike Wallace.

> Mike:
>
> I meant what I said the other day—that I can't apologize to you for getting you into this mess. I can't do it because I believed in the show then and still do believe in it. It doesn't mean, however, that I don't feel badly seeing you dragged unfairly through all of this—you sounded so depressed on the phone.

Crile thanked Wallace for the support the correspondent had given him, adding, "Win, lose or draw in this contest, you have a dedicated friend for life. But that's the future, and there is the spectre of the hangman's knot to deal with first."

The "hangman's knot" was Bud Benjamin's internal investigation.

"I just don't think we can sit back and expect divine justice from the CBS internal review," Crile wrote. Without waiting for Benjamin's report, he insisted, CBS should issue a statement standing by the "substantive points and accusations made in the show. . . ." "I think we should move heaven and earth to try to get the powers-that-be to make up their minds about this question as soon as possible," he added. ". . . I really think it's worth talking to Dan [Rather] about this. It seems to me that this is a clear cut question of what's in CBS's best self-interest and he could be of help."

Crile went on to lay ultimate responsibility for production of the program in the laps of his superiors. "It was my understanding from the beginning that we were all in this together—that it was different from any other show—that questions might be asked—transcripts reviewed in ways that ordinarily wouldn't happen. Presumably," he added, "this is what Stringer and Lack were supposed to have done. They, of course, didn't. . . ."

It was clear that Crile believed Benjamin's "hangman's knot" belonged around Howard Stringer's neck.

"My commission was to go out *with* Adams and prove on film that these people would testify to what Adams told us they had told him," he wrote. "So I did it. . . . In effect, CBS News, as you put it on the phone, bought the Adams thesis. . . . Howard Stringer knew [Adams] was traveling with me to do interviews—sometimes even serving as a kind of associate producer reading back reverse questions."

Crile added, "I think Bud [Benjamin] needs to have you remind him of the realities of the business. He needs to know what an investigative report is. He needs to be reminded who commissioned this show, what they commissioned, who was responsible." Who did Crile think was responsible? "As far as I'm concerned," he said, "everyone did their job on the show, except Howard [Stringer]. And I think you ought to tell Bud that if he has criticisms about the documentary that the person who was primarily responsible for overseeing the show and making sure it was both fair and accurate was Stringer. I say that, Mike, simply because it is (1) true and (2) because Howard is apparently making mischief. And I believe with all my heart that Bud and everyone else ought to know very clearly that there are a lot of people involved in this. If there were failings here—in this explosive documentary which we all understood was going to be controversial—the man who was supposed to protect all of us and watch out for the reputation of the news division was Howard Stringer. And he is bad-mouthing the show. . . ."

Was Crile's accusation against Stringer legitimate? Theoretically speaking, yes; at CBS, the executive producer of a documentary had to accept responsibility for any of its flaws. Practically speaking, however, the charge ignored the realities of making documentaries at CBS. Stringer had had to oversee not only this documentary, but several others in production simultaneously; he could not know the intimate details of all of them. Like Ira Klein, Stringer had to depend on the producer for the details of the story and of the investigation. This dependence was compounded at *CBS Reports* by a hallowed tradition of allowing producers considerable independence in the making of a program. Stringer deserved a share of the blame; he had been an advocate of the documentary, and, realizing its controversial nature and Roger Colloff's relative inexperience in journalism, he should have exercised tighter control. However, Crile was on a solo flight, the captain at the controls of this ill-fated program, and while Stringer bore a measure of accountability, the ultimate cause of the disaster was pilot-error.

On July 7, Crile followed up his memo to Wallace with a letter to Van Gordon Sauter. "Since I haven't been able to talk to you directly about the documentary," Crile wrote, "I am writing now to put some of my thoughts on paper before you make your final ruling. . . ." Crile reaffirmed his pride in the program, his conviction that the documentary was fair and accurate—and his belief that any blame (if the program had flaws) should be borne by his superiors. "As I explained to Mike in a more detailed and admittedly impassioned note," he added, "I produced precisely the documentary that CBS commissioned. . . ." Crile went on to say that "there has been a general atmosphere here that has presumed guilt on my part while denying me even the right to openly defend myself and the show. All I'm told is to wait until Friday to receive your verdict. . . ."

His letter to Sauter concluded with this request: "If, after you and Bud review his report, you have serious doubt about the documentary or about my reporting practices, I would like to know what those criticisms are, and then to have the opportunity to defend the broadcast in person."

The next day, July 8, Benjamin wrote the fifty-nine-page report summing up his investigation of *TV Guide*'s charges. Sauter submitted two copies of the report to CBS, Inc., headquarters, where it was reviewed by Gene Jankowski and Gene Mater, respectively, president and vice-president of the CBS Broadcast Group. Sauter would later confirm to a reporter that retiring board chairman William Paley and CBS, Inc. president Thomas Wyman also read Benjamin's manuscript. Then, on the night of July 14, George Crile got his opportunity to defend his work before Sauter. That evening, Sauter assembled key CBS staffers, including Crile, in his office to discuss a memo he intended to release, revealing the results of Benjamin's investigation. Benjamin was not present at that meeting, attended by Crile, Wallace, Stringer, Colloff, Sauter, and Sauter's deputy, Ed Joyce. Sources later described the meeting as a stormy one, with much shouting, as Crile, Wallace, Colloff, and Stringer all challenged Benjamin's conclusions. Sauter himself characterized the discussion as "long" and "very amiable," "except for a couple of outbursts, one on my part. Everybody had their say," he added.

Sauter had prepared a draft-memo, whose conclusions were debated until the early morning, with Sauter ultimately agreeing, at the insistence of the others, to move up from the bottom of the memo his declaration that "CBS News stands by this broadcast." Then the participants scattered. Sauter went home and went to bed. About 4 A.M., he arose and wrote the memo that was circulated the following day, July 15. The eight-page, double-spaced memo (presumably distilling the essence of Benjamin's fifty-nine-page report) affirmed that CBS supported "the substance of the broadcast." However, Sauter added that "we now feel it would have been a better broadcast if:

"—it had not used the word conspiracy;

"—it had sought out and interviewed more persons who disagreed with the broadcast premise; and

"—there had been strict compliance with CBS News Standards."

What followed was a devastating indictment of the CBS broadcast: ". . . We now believe that a judgmental conclusion of conspiracy was inappropriate," and "there was insufficient effort to seek out and interview more of those who contend there was no deception, particularly given the complexity of the subject matter."

Sauter then went on to detail the documentary's flaws, including the Allen screening ("there was a desire to elicit a stronger interview"), the omission of Adams's role as a *paid* consultant, two journalistic oversights resulting "in material relating to one set of events being connected to another set of events" . . . "four instances of editing . . . contrary to guidelines. . . ." Sauter found only two of *TV Guide's* accusations "unwarranted":

"1. We do not believe the paid consultant was rehearsed for his interview.

"2. He [Sam Adams] has not, as alleged, backed away from the premise of the broadcast."

Other *TV Guide* allegations were left unchallenged, either because of "honest disagreement" among Benjamin, Sauter, and Ed Joyce, or because they were "either inconsequential or too subjective to judge with certainty." Thus Sauter was able to dismiss, without discussing, *TV Guide's* detailed review of such CBS *evidence* as the McChristian-Hawkins briefing and the 300,000-ceiling sequences. Sauter announced the creation of a new position, vice-president, News Practices, to evaluate internal and external complaints. Tacitly admitting Wallace's minimal contribution to a documentary that bore his "signature," Sauter declared that "on projects of a complex and controversial nature, the full involvement and collaboration of the principal correspondent is vital. Future assignments," he added, "will take this essential need into consideration." Most important of all, he stated that CBS was "planning a future broadcast on the issues treated in the original broadcast."

The Sauter memo was distributed to CBS employees (and, at the same time, the press) on its issue date, July 15. That day Klein left CBS to begin editing another project. He felt more sad than bitter. The Sauter memo was a disappointment. His hope, his desire had been that by permitting Benjamin to do a thorough investigation, CBS would tell him, Klein, the details of the Vietnam story he had not learned from Crile. Instead, while the memo kept on defending the "substance of the broadcast," that substance was never explicitly addressed, except to deny that "conspiracy" was the appropriate word. He was even more disturbed by CBS's contention that the full Benjamin report could never be released because it was a privileged "internal document," based on the testimony of witnesses who had been promised confidentiality. Klein, for one, had never expected his revelations to Benjamin to be kept confidential. It had been his understanding that he was speaking on the record and that the Benjamin report would be made public. But after a six-week inquiry all that was filtering through the crack in CBS's documentary was what Van Gordon Sauter thought people should know.

Klein had believed in the CBS tradition—the fearlessness, tempered by fairness, of an Edward R. Murrow. But Murrow was long dead, his legacy tainted by bottom-liners and news-you-can-use types. Finding out who turned over the transcripts to *TV Guide* seemed a more pressing priority in some quarters of CBS than finding out whether this $300,000-plus documentary contained a shred of truth.

In the days that followed, the Sauter memorandum made headlines in hundreds of newspapers across the country, most interpreting the document as a vindication of the *TV Guide* article. At the same time, though, newsmen were congratulating CBS for admitting its errors. There was, however, one major dissenter, Tom Shales of the *Washington Post*, who led off his article ("CBS's Lavish Apologia") with: "CBS has done more apologizing for an outstanding documentary on Vietnam than Richard Nixon ever did for Watergate." Shales's target this time was not *TV Guide* publisher Walter Annenberg but Sauter himself, whom Shales accused of succumbing to pressures from his superiors. "In terms of journalistic authority and reputation," Shales wrote, "CBS News is a giant and *TV Guide* a ridiculously tiny gnat. Why, then, should CBS News have bent over so far backwards to entertain the accusations—in public yet—and risk imperiling the morale and reputation of its own staff in the process? Because, extremely knowledgeable insiders say, Black Rock—CBS corporate headquarters in New York—applied immense pressure on Sauter to do so, for reasons that remain dark and mysterious and, to some within CBS, frightening."

Shales identified the arm twisters as CBS, Inc., president Thomas Wyman and Broadcast Group president Gene Jankowski, with a possible assist from founding father William S. Paley himself. But Shales's explicit assault on Sauter and implicit defense of George Crile and Mike Wallace was a lonely one. And within a week of Shales's intemperate frothing, a *Washington Post* editorial appeared contradicting its own television critic, rejecting Shales's "dark cloud of commercial pressure," while commending CBS for "journalism that is self-confident enough to be self-critical."

The *Los Angeles Times* and the *New York Times* also published editorials commending CBS for its forthrightness. "The lesson here," said the *Los Angeles Times*, "is not only for CBS News but also for all in journalism, whether print or television. The public expects balanced and fair and full reporting in documentaries as well as in news columns. When the credibility of one journalistic enterprise is tarnished, all suffer." The *New York Times*, whose earlier editorial had lavished praise on the program, now declared that "CBS was right to take seriously General Westmoreland's complaints" and called for the network to open the airwaves to "aggrieved viewers." However, while these and other periodicals were congratulating CBS for the Sauter memo, many journalists were demanding to see the report on which it was based, arguing that CBS had promised to make public the results of its six-week investigation, not an eight-page interpretation, reflecting the collective views of Benjamin, Sauter, and his deputy Ed Joyce. Sauter kept insisting that the fifty-nine-page Benjamin report had been prepared as an internal document and was therefore not comparable, say, to the lengthy report written by the ombudsman of the *Washington Post* after its Pulitzer Prize–winning story of an eight-year-old drug addict had been revealed as a hoax.

Few members of the media focused on a crucial contradiction embedded in Sauter's memo. However, to some journalists CBS's repeated insistence on "standing by" the substance of the documentary while admitting violations of journalistic ethics seemed a dangerous precedent. By "standing by" the program, they felt, CBS was asserting that the end justifies the means: If, as Sauter argued, "none of these violations changed the substance of the broadcast . . ." then of what value—or necessity—were sets of journalistic standards when abridging them did not violate the "substance of the broadcast" as well?

In preparing his memo Sauter had clearly considered its implications: Anything he said might be used against him and CBS should Westmoreland decide to turn to the courts for redress.

From the beginning Westmoreland had been considering a court action against CBS and had been restrained only by the prohibitive cost of a libel suit and the difficulties such suits posed for "public figures." He had been seeking advice and had received scant encouragement. Reportedly, among those whose counsel was discouraging were Clark Clifford, of the Washington, D.C., law firm Clifford & Warnke, and noted trial lawyer Edward Bennet Williams. Senators Barry Goldwater and Strom Thurmond also reportedly advised Westmoreland not to sue. It was not until after the *TV Guide* article appeared that Westmoreland got his first truly positive response. Geoffrey Schmidt, a partner in the Manhattan law firm Schmidt, Aghayan & Associates, was the first to advise Westmoreland that a suit against CBS had some chance of success. Reportedly, Schmidt felt that certain Wall Street investment firms might be willing to contribute to Westmoreland's defense, and offered his own services on a contingency basis. He would handle the preliminaries, with an Edward Bennet Williams-type hired later for the trial itself. But those plans were displaced by the advent of Dan M. Burt of the Capital Legal Foundation, who offered to take the case on a *pro bono* basis.

Burt was a self-made millionaire specializing in the arcane and complex practice of international tax law; he had, for the past several years, used the public-interest Capital Legal Foundation as a legal pungi-stick, impaling unsuspecting federal agencies in lawsuits, in service of Capital Legal's "free-market" philosophy. Shortly after the *TV Guide* article he had received a telephone call from a prominent New York Democrat (Burt himself was a registered Democrat), whom Burt would later identify only as "a neoconservative, deeply involved in cultural politics."

"Have you heard about this Westmoreland business?" the caller said.

"What 'Westmoreland business'?" said Burt.

The "neoconservative Democrat" told Burt he had received a telephone call from a "senior executive" at CBS who was outraged over his own network's broadcast and who was sure that if Westmoreland sued, CBS would reach an immediate settlement. Would Burt be interested in taking that case?

"No," said Burt, adding, "but I'm willing to listen."

"Read the *TV Guide* article," said the caller.

That same day Burt did obtain a copy of *TV Guide* but did not have an opportunity to read it until early the following morning. What he read outraged him. "My reaction was, 'I'll be a son of a bitch!' " Later that morning he telephoned the "neoconservative Democrat."

"I can't say that I'll take the case," he said, "but I will consider it."

Soon he received a call from David Henderson, the friend of Westmoreland who had helped to arrange the general's press conference. Burt and Henderson chatted at length.

"I did meet with Westmoreland," said Burt.

Subsequently Henderson sent Burt a videotape of the broadcast, cassettes of the press conference, the official unedited transcripts of Wallace's interviews with Westmoreland and Rostow, plus the packet of "correction" documents Westmoreland had mailed to Wallace and Crile after his CBS interview. Burt read the material and viewed the video cassettes. He then met with two of his attorneys at the Capital Legal Foundation, Pat Embrey and Jim Moody. Embrey and Moody had seen the tapes of the press conference but had not reviewed the transcripts or "correction" packet.

The question was: Should Capital Legal take the case? Embrey was adamantly opposed, arguing that libel suits were not Capital Legal's business and that libel suits in behalf of public figures were carpeted with quicksand. However, the most compelling reason for refusing the case, she insisted, was her conviction, on the basis of what she had seen, that "Westmoreland did it."

"Let's be sure," said Burt. He asked Embrey to take home with her that evening the other material Henderson had sent, including the pair of interviews, and study them overnight. The following morning he called her into his office. "What do you think?" said Burt.

"CBS did it," said Embrey.

Burt telephoned Henderson and told him he was interested in seeing Westmoreland again. Henderson arranged a second meeting. "General," said Burt to Westmoreland, "let's get this straight. I want you to think very carefully. Have you ever done anything that you should be ashamed of— have you ever done anything wrong that I should know about?"

Westmoreland considered the question. Then he said, "No, absolutely not."

"General," Burt said, "I am the toughest son of a bitch who ever lived. If you are lying to me," Burt added, "there will be nothing I can do to save you from utter ruin."

"I understand that," Westmoreland said calmly.

Burt was impressed. He had (his phrase) "cocked both barrels at the general and fired," and Westmoreland's dignity had not even been dented. He decided that Westmoreland had the inner steel he would need to withstand fierce cross-examination at trial, if the case got that far—and he hoped it would not.

It is evident that Sauter's memo on the Benjamin report (not only validating most of TV Guide's charges but going further to disavow the appropriateness of the word "conspiracy") was the glue that sealed the marriage of Burt and Westmoreland. From the day in June that Burt agreed to take the case, Westmoreland and CBS were on a collision course that led straight into court. Burt spent the next few months both studying a course of action and exchanging feelers with CBS over a possible settlement of Westmoreland's grievance out of court. On August 10 Westmoreland sent Thomas Wyman, president of CBS, Inc., a letter outlining those grievances against CBS News and requesting that the network "publish a complete apology, approved in advance by me, in the same manner and the same media in which you advertised the program." Westmoreland also asked for a compensatory payment for the harm he had suffered and "a full retraction, of not less than forty-five-minutes' duration," in which CBS would present "the actual facts and methods of preparation concerning the story you published. The material in this retraction and the production itself must be subject to my complete approval," Westmoreland added.

On August 24 Sauter rejected all of the requests but reiterated an invitation to appear on the follow-up program—a discussion with representatives of diverse views on the troop-strength question. CBS continued its preparations for that program. The format for the show, originally scheduled to be taped on September 8 and televised a week later in prime time, was a panel discussion. Sam Adams described the proposed lineup of panelists in a letter to Col. Gains Hawkins:

My information on the lineup for the panel show:

Chief Moderator: Diane Sawyer (subject to change). The most interesting thing about her is that she knows a lot about the controversy and for the damndest reason. Her current boyfriend is Richard Holbrooke, longtime spear carrier for Robert Komer. As you might expect, Holbrooke knows a lot about what went on.

Questioner A: Peter Braestrup, author of *The Big Story*, a book about how the press screwed up reporting on Tet. Braestrup has also written an article (which I can't locate) critical of the documentary. He's a fair-minded person, however, and therefore not to be feared.

Questioner B: Robert Kaiser of the *Washington Post* (and author of a first-rate book on Russia). Kaiser knows a *lot* about the controversy and is a friend of George Crile, who's briefed him.

Participants:

—You and me.

—George Carver, my ex-boss at CIA. You met him when he visited MACV on July 7–11, 1967, and again when he headed the CIA delegation on September 6–12, 1967. He's convinced nothing untoward happened (in my opinion, because he wasn't aware of all the behind-the-scenes maneuvering at MACV). Strangely enough, Carver and I like one another, although he usually characterizes me as overzealous and something of a nut. As for you (whom he once referred to as "poor old Gains"), he thinks that somehow I've brainwashed you. Carver's an interesting and *very* bright person . . . and not really dishonest.

Fourth Participant: still up in the air. Westmoreland doesn't want to come on, [Gen. Philip] Davidson is waffling, and Danny Graham's in the wings. My candidate, naturally, is Danny since I have the goods on him, having talked to most of his subordinates. (They agree with Bill Benedict's characterization of him that he's "crooked as a snake.")

In early September, General Davidson received a telegram from CBS describing the program. According to Davidson, it read in part: "Please understand that the purpose of our proposed broadcast is not to continue the discussion of the points covered by Benjamin but to shed new light on the issue of substance in the documentary, which is: Were intelligence estimates of enemy strength in Vietnam deliberately reduced or otherwise manipulated?" Davidson had asked CBS for a copy of the Benjamin report. "No member of the panel or guest or journalist in our planned broadcast has seen the report," said the telegram. ". . . The details of production of the follow-up broadcast have not been completed. It is to begin with a summary of the thrust of the *CBS Reports* documentary, then move into questioning of the guests by the guest journalists and perhaps by the CBS News moderator." Davidson had also asked CBS if opening statements would be permitted. "No opening statements are planned," said the telegram, "but we assume questions will elicit comprehensive statements by all parties."

Davidson was particularly concerned over the opening CBS "summary of the thrust of the *CBS Reports* documentary." He told a reporter, "It would seem to me extremely crucial that we have a word-for-word rundown of what this summary of the thrust of the CBS documentary program is. Otherwise, by their interpretation, they can put you on the defensive right off."

The program was scheduled to air on the evening of September 15. In the first week of September, however, both Westmoreland and Davidson notified CBS that they would not appear. Several days later another proposed panelist, Lt. Gen. Danny Graham, also told CBS he would not participate. On September 7, the day before the program was to be taped, CBS announced that it had postponed the broadcast. The following day, in what CBS executives characterized as a last-ditch effort to avert a lawsuit and Westmoreland supporters characterized as a grandstand ploy, Joan Richman, executive producer of the follow-up panel program, sent a letter to Westmoreland offering him fifteen minutes of air time at the beginning of the show "to say what you wish to say in the manner you wish to say it." The offer was unusual but not unprecedented; in 1981, ABC had awarded Kaiser Aluminum four prime-time minutes to rebut statements about the company in an *ABC News* segment. Westmoreland's unedited response would be followed by the panel of representatives from both sides debating the "substance" of the documentary.

Westmoreland's camp rejected the offer of free air time as too little, too late. Even before CBS had mailed that September 8 letter Westmoreland had definitely decided to petition the courts for relief. On September 13, in the United States District Court in Greenville, South Carolina, Gen. William C. Westmoreland filed against CBS, Inc. and four individual defendants (Adams, Crile, Sauter, and Wallace) a $120 million libel suit.

17

Westmoreland Sues

O N SEPTEMBER 13, almost eight months after his first press conference, again Gen. William C. Westmoreland stood at a podium in the Washington, D.C., Army–Navy Club addressing an audience of print and broadcast journalists. However, this time Westmoreland was not angrily denouncing his accusers, but calmly asking for justice, revealing that that very morning his attorneys were filing a libel suit against CBS, seeking $120 million in compensatory and punitive damages. Westmoreland was telling the reporters:

> I am an old soldier who loves his country and have had enough of war. It was my fate to serve for over four years as senior American commander in the most unpopular war this country ever fought. I have been reviled, burned in effigy, spat upon. Neither I nor my wife nor my family want me to go to battle once again.
>
> But all my life I have valued "duty, honor, country" above all else. Even as my friends and family urged me to ignore CBS and leave the field, I reflected on those Americans who had died in service in Vietnam. Even as I considered the enormous wealth and power that make CBS so formidable an adversary, I thought too of the troops I had commanded and sent to battle, and those who never returned.

Finally, I have dwelled at length upon the tremendous bulwark of liberty and freedom that is the First Amendment to the Constitution of the United States. I now feared that public reaction to CBS as the truth came out might lead to weakening of that bulwark through legislated codes of conduct or other attempts to restrain the media. . . .

In three carefully constructed paragraphs Westmoreland had bowed deferentially in the direction of the pair of constituencies most likely to resent his lawsuit: organized groups of ex-Vietnam veterans, who consistently complained he paid scant attention to their predicament and the press itself, which might regard a legal challenge against one of its members as an assault upon the First Amendment, ensuring the freedom of all the media. In the process Westmoreland had also managed to portray himself as an underdog, contesting in court an institution of vast wealth, power, and influence.

Accordingly, I made one final attempt to obtain redress from CBS for the wrong they had done to me, to all the men and women who fought in Vietnam, and to this country as a whole. I sent them a letter, which I give you today, requesting an apology and a public explanation of how and why they had gone wrong. I have also given you today their reply. As you will see, they remained adamant. . . .

Reporters who had witnessed the earlier press conference detected a difference in Westmoreland's demeanor. He was not stumbling over words anymore. After a decade dodging snipers, the general was launching a main-force thrust against the enemy, and despite his disclaimer, the prospect of a decisive fight to the finish was an invigorating one.

It is, therefore, with the very greatest reluctance, and consciousness of the long and bitter legal battle I am about to engage in, that I have advised my attorneys, the Capital Legal Foundation, through their president, Dan M. Burt, to file suit today in South Carolina, my home state, against CBS for libel. At this moment correspondent counsel in South Carolina is filing our complaint against CBS requesting damages for libel. There is no way left for me to clear my name, my honor, and the honor of the military. . . .

. . . The issue here is not money, not vengeance. If I am successful in this case, as I believe I will be, I will not retain any monetary award for my personal use but instead will donate it to charity. . . .

The question before the American people in *Westmoreland* versus *CBS* is not whether the war in Vietnam was right or wrong but whether in our land a television network can rob an honorable man of his reputation. The question is not whether I was a good general or a bad general. The question is not whether we won or lost the war in Vietnam.

The only question is whether CBS had an obligation to be accurate in its facts before it attempted to destroy a man's character, the work of his lifetime. I trust the American judicial system and an American jury will fairly evaluate what I and those in positions of responsibility said and did, and I am pleased to put my reputation and honor in their custody.

It was a well-conceived speech—sharp in its focus, moving and subtly responsive to the concerns of the assembled reporters. Westmoreland had delivered it almost flawlessly, dampening his indignation, sugarcoating his belligerence. In fact, Westmoreland had been exhaustively rehearsed by his attorney Dan Burt, who had written most of the statement himself. Afterwards, it was Burt who fielded questions from the press, allowing Westmoreland only to confirm that, should he win the suit, he intended to donate any money he received to veterans' organizations. Short and thin, Burt had to peer over the podium and seemed tense and uneasy in front of the cameras and microphones. To top CBS executives watching the press conference (transmitted directly to CBS headquarters in New York via a specially placed antenna on the Army–Navy Club roof), the impending court battle between this featherweight and CBS's heralded heavyweight counsel must have looked like a blatant mismatch.

In the complaint filed in Greenville, South Carolina, that day, Burt listed fifteen charges against Westmoreland that he said were "false, unfair, inaccurate, and defamatory." In addition, Burt noted that conspiracy was "a crime punishable by imprisonment and fine."

"CBS will mount a vigorous defense of this lawsuit," replied Van Gordon Sauter, "not only because we see this suit totally devoid of merit but because it constitutes a serious threat to independent journalism in our society." Sauter added that CBS's offer of a follow-up program "still stands." "A fifteen-minute, unedited statement of [Westmoreland's] position and opinions, followed by a balanced and unedited discussion of the issues, would serve the public's interest in this matter."

"There was no opportunity in that fifteen minutes to undo the harm unless CBS admitted they were wrong," insisted Burt. "All [Westmoreland] would have done would have been to dignify a lie."

The controversy had spilled out of the newsrooms and into the courts, where the yardstick used to measure any damage to Westmoreland would be the rules of libel. Supporters of CBS would blame Westmoreland for instituting legal action that might well result in a chilling revision of law. Critics of CBS contended that CBS itself was to blame by airing its sloppy, ill-conceived documentary. Initially, though, the lawyers refrained from joining the debate. Guilt would be decided in the first instance by a jury and ultimately by historians. For the lawyers what counted now were the tactical decisions they could take to milk from the legal system every advantage for their respective clients. It was no accident, for instance, that Burt had targeted his libel complaint not only against CBS, Inc., but a set of individuals as well. Named in the suit were Sauter, Crile, Wallace, and Adams. By isolating individual defendants both from each other and their corporate parent, Burt was creating a potential opportunity to divide and conquer, ready to exploit any differences in the defendants' self-interest, should such differences surface. On a short-term basis he also hoped to inflate CBS's costs, forcing it to duplicate its efforts in behalf of five defendants. Most important of all, perhaps one of those defendants would be forced to secure separate counsel. Rumors emanating from CBS (Burt would develop at least one source inside CBS, at the executive level) indicated that Crile was disenchanted with the Sauter memorandum and livid over the Benjamin report on which the memo was based. He was especially resentful that CBS had compelled him to remain silent during Benjamin's investigation.

"It's one thing to be misunderstood and not have your own defense in the outer world," he explained later. "It's another thing to be closed off in CBS and not be able to explain yourself to your peers. You want to be able to tell CBS people that there is a defense." Crile argued that his enforced silence during the Benjamin inquiry "had disastrous consequences for me, CBS, and the ability of the country to think rationally about the questions the documentary raised. A narrow attack on the process alone got misconstrued as an attack on the substance of the broadcast."

Crile could, however, count on one firm ally throughout: Mike Wallace. Like Crile, Wallace was disturbed by Benjamin's uncompromising stance.

At the time the lawsuit was announced, Ira Klein was working on a documentary series called *A Walk Through the Twentieth Century*. Featuring CBS correspondent Bill Moyers, the programs originally were scheduled to air on CBS's cable service, although produced not by CBS but by the Corporation for Entertainment and Learning. The lawsuit had come as no surprise to Klein. He had regarded one as inevitable, ever since he discovered CBS's own reluctance to investigate itself. Now, he realized, he would not be able to avoid becoming entangled in the legal web of pretrial depositions and affidavits. What he had not resolved in his own mind was his relationship with CBS. He still felt loyalty.

One day Klein got a call from the *CBS Reports* production manager. She told Klein that the CBS lawyers were anxious to reconstruct the uncut "negatives" of the documentary so that they could screen the original dailies and outtakes. "Would it be all right with you if Phyllis helped out?" she asked.

Hurwitz was working as Klein's assistant on the Moyers project. Klein said he had no objection. He asked Hurwitz, who consented to return to CBS to assist the lawyers. Hurwitz spent a week, off and on, at CBS and during that period from time to time she would encounter the CBS general counsel, George Vradenburg III. Vradenburg seemed eager to talk to her. Hurwitz told Klein, who encouraged her to cooperate with CBS in every way. He told her that he was willing to cooperate with CBS, too. It was important that CBS understand what occurred in the making of the film. Soon Klein received a telephone call from a CBS lawyer. They exchanged pleasantries; she told Klein she was just starting to work on the Westmoreland case. Then she asked Klein if he had any CBS documents in his possession. "Absolutely not," he replied.

Twice CBS general counsel Vradenburg asked Hurwitz to meet him. Both times Hurwitz, at Klein's urging, complied. Hurwitz confirmed to Vradenburg that Adams had been thoroughly rehearsed, as *TV Guide* charged. She had not only seen the questions lying on Crile's desk, later that day she had skimmed them. Vradenburg wanted to know from her what had transpired in the editing room. Hurwitz recalled that at times Crile had simply "acted strangely." What, Vradenburg wanted to know, did Hurwitz mean by "strangely"? Hurwitz told him Crile seemed to be under great stress, but she was disturbed; it was clear to her that Vradenburg was trying to tell her what to say if she were ever called on to testify.

After the interview, as they walked toward the elevator, Hurwitz told Vradenburg he definitely should talk to Klein, who could provide precise times, dates, and places of crucial behind-the-scenes events. Vradenburg, in turn, kept telling her how much CBS wanted to speak to the editor, soothingly patting her shoulder. At the elevator Hurwitz turned to Vradenburg. "Look, let's not play semantics," she said. "You write it out, I'll sign it."

Hurwitz returned to the editing room she shared with Klein. She told him she felt abused by Vradenburg, manipulated. It was then that Klein made a fateful decision. He had come forth and spoken to Lack out of loyalty to the Vietnam unit, out of loyalty to Lack himself, out of loyalty to CBS—its tradition, its reputation. Now, however, it was clear to him that the CBS lawyers were more interested in winning their lawsuit than ascertaining the truth about their documentary. It was in late October, after a telephone call from Dan Burt, that Klein first met with Westmoreland's lawyer.

From the moment that Westmoreland filed his lawsuit, George Crile was determined to obtain his own counsel, resisting efforts by CBS to represent him along with the other defendants. Reportedly, Crile first met with John Vardaman of Williams & Connolly, who had counseled him in the past. But Vardaman revealed that Westmoreland had consulted his firm about the case, thus preventing him from representing Crile. However, Vardaman did advise Crile that there was a clear potential for conflict between him and CBS. Crile then turned to Victor Kovner, a First Amendment lawyer whose firm, Lankenau, Kovner & Bickford, represented the *Village Voice* newspaper and public television's *The Dial* magazine. Kovner agreed to take the case. Meanwhile, all the other defendants, including CBS, Inc., itself, would be represented by one of the nation's most prestigious and powerful law firms.

"If a recognition poll were to be conducted, Cravath, Swaine & Moore would surely emerge as the best-known corporate law firm in the country," wrote James Stewart in *The Partners: Inside America's Most Powerful Law Firms*. Cravath was renowned for luring the brightest law students and lavishing its lawyers with exalted paychecks. "A mystique has grown up around Cravath," wrote Stewart, "to which no one firm could possibly measure up. . . ." Among Cravath's blue-chip clients were oil companies (Royal Dutch Shell and Ashland Oil), banks (Chemical Bank), investment bankers (First Boston, Paine Webber, Inc., and Salomon Brothers), plus assorted industrial titans such as Allied Chemical and Bethlehem Steel. Its portfolio of media moguls included not only CBS, Inc., but the *Washington Post* and Time, Inc. But it was Cravath's defense of another prestigious client, IBM, which had most recently reaffirmed its reputation for bulldog tenacity, exhaustive research, and, most of all, an unparalleled mastery of the tactics of delay. In litigation that began in the early 1970s and lasted almost a decade, Cravath had defended IBM in a series of complex antitrust actions until finally, after an expenditure of some $50 million, the United States Justice Department had simply given up and walked away from the suit. CBS general counsel George Vradenburg (himself a former Cravath associate) later explained to a reporter from *The American Lawyer* magazine why he had selected Cravath to defend CBS in the Westmoreland complaint. "I decided not to go the more predictable route, with a First Amendment lawyer . . . because we have to face it: More and more of these cases are going to trial. I wanted a lawyer who could try a case before a South Carolina jury and not seem like a foreigner. So I picked Boies."

In his early years at Cravath, David Boies had taken time off to work on civil rights cases in the South. Later he took a leave of absence to become antitrust counsel to Sen. Edward Kennedy when Kennedy became chairman of the Senate Judiciary Committee. At the age of thirty-four, Boies had played the pivotal role in winning the IBM antitrust action. Now, at forty-one, he was a Cravath partner concentrating on antitrust and securities cases, often lawyering in behalf of CBS. Boies cultivated in the courtroom what one government attorney called an "angelic" demeanor; his blue eyes and curly blond hair reinforced the cherubic image. But Boies's depositions and cross-examinations revealed a sharp intelligence and a steely grasp of the nuances of litigatory technique. Boies had never ever defended a client in a libel case. In that regard—and perhaps only in that regard—he resembled his opponent in the forthcoming Westmoreland lawsuit.

As he never neglected to tell any reporter who neglected to ask, Dan M. Burt had risen from humble circumstances in Philadelphia, a Depression butcher's son whose personality bore the indelible scars of violent street encounters. In his early teens he ended the harassment of a neighborhood bully by planting a knife in his tormentor's side. Later Burt's father moved south and became a charter-boat captain. Characteristically, Burt's most vivid memories of the sea were violent ones. He was fond of telling people exactly how to slaughter a captured shark.

Like Boies, Burt was graduated from Yale Law School near the top of his class. However, his route to Yale had been a far more circuitous one. Tainted by his high school disciplinary problems, he was unable to gain admittance into a prestigious American university. Instead, he commuted to Philadelphia's La Salle College where he demonstrated enough academic promise to earn a three-year scholarship at Cambridge University in England. His "First" at Cambridge (equivalent to our Phi Beta Kappa academic record) opened Yale's doors. However, after Yale Law School, despite his exalted class standing, Burt received no offers from blue-blood law firms such as Cravath. Later he could scarcely conceal his contempt for such firms, symbols to him of class, snobbery, and at the same time a kind of corporate mediocrity, where lawyering was a matter of herding enormous numbers of bodies, buttressed by unlimited finances, into any particular case.

Some suggested that his antipathy toward Cravath was the result less of his indignation over class differences than over a personal insult delivered to him when he was still a student. While Burt was still at Yale he was interviewed by a former Cravath partner, who, instead of offering Burt a job, merely took him out for a drink. The bar they went to had unusually tall bar stools. Burt, who is only about five feet three inches, remarked about their height.

"I guess that's the story of your life, Dan—always three inches too short for the table," the former Cravath partner reportedly said.

During a break in a deposition, Burt would tell David Boies: "I've been waiting to get even for that for the past fifteen years."

However, it was clear that Burt's dislike of the large law firms had deeper roots than some slighting remark about his stature. His hostility was directed at all those who by birth enjoyed special advantages. The irony was, the man who despised the very rich would soon prove adept at becoming one of them. After Yale he opened a successful private practice in Gloucester, Massachusetts, with a plate-glass office window overlooking the blue bay. Soon, though, he was using his cunning to amass a fortune as an international tax attorney, counting among his clients members of the Saudi Arabian royal family and numerous multinational corporations with interests in the Middle East. By the late 1970s Burt was a self-proclaimed millionaire. Then in 1980, at the age of thirty-seven, he gave up some of his lucrative practice to assume control of the fledgling public-interest law firm, Capital Legal Foundation. Capital Legal was one of a handful of business-oriented nonprofit groups; the firm solicited contributions from large corporations and conservative foundations, and often represented them in legal and political battles against the more numerous consumer and environmental public-interest firms that proliferated in Washington during the 1970s.

Soon Burt had managed to make a major nuisance of himself both on Capitol Hill and at the White House. Espousing a "free-market bias," he was challenging businessmen and reformers alike. He took on the Carter Administration, recovering about $1 million of the $4 million in oil company "tribute" that Department of Energy special counsel Paul Bloom had handed over to charities. When the Reagan Administration decided to pay interest due from Poland on United States bank loans, to avert a formal default from Warsaw, Capital Legal sued unsuccessfully to block the United States' decision to pay out $71 million to the banks. Subsequently he turned his attention to Ralph Nader, writing a book in 1982 that accused the Nader consumer-group network of a variety of nefarious practices. "He's rich," Burt said of Nader. "He doesn't understand what happens to the little guy when business is punished."

By 1982 Burt's income from lawyering was more than $600,000 a year. He owned two homes in Washington, an apartment in London (his wife was English), and was building an extravagant summer home on the island of Bar Harbor off the windswept coast of Maine. There seemed no reason for him to detour his sprint toward the "brass ring," heckling various federal agencies while he harvested the international tax bonanza of his private practice. And then he had received the telephone call from that prominent "neoconservative Democrat."

Burt was a mass of contradictions, using his hatred of the establishment to become part of it yet remaining terminally the outsider, uttering gutter epithets one moment and passages from Yeats the next—outrageous and full of rage. Clearly, never in its distinguished history had Cravath faced anyone like him.

For both sides, the case itself was fraught with obstacles. Cravath joined the litigation with CBS already on the defensive; in his memorandum Sauter had rejected only two of *TV Guide*'s allegations (Adams's disavowing of the premise of the program after the broadcast, and his rehearsal a few days before his on-camera interview with Wallace), while admitting that "conspiracy" had been improperly used in the broadcast. (The conspiracy charge, of course, was at the crux of the Westmoreland defamation suit.) Ethically, Sauter had clearly taken the right step when he asked Benjamin, and not an attorney, to conduct the internal investigation, since only a journalist was qualified to judge whether or not a peer had violated the profession's implicit codes and the explicit ones detailed in the CBS News Standards. Strategically, however, for the CBS lawyers the comparative forthrightness of the Sauter memo (CBS had done more recanting than most observers had anticipated) was a liability. The nature of the suit itself—the defendants each being sued separately—presented another potential problem to Cravath. As a mere producer, Crile was expendable, while correspondent Mike Wallace was almost sacrosanct. From the beginning Crile had recognized the divergence of interest between himself and the others, seeking, against Boies's advice, separate counsel to defend him. For months CBS would be unwilling to admit that a potential for conflict existed and that its insurer should pay for Crile's lawyers.

However, the hurdles Cravath had to clear were small ones compared to the obstacles the libel law placed in the path of the plaintiff. Until 1964 the courts had held that defamatory statements were beyond the protection of the First Amendment, leaving the states themselves to define their rules of libel. Generally, though, defamatory statements were legally presumed to be false. The burden of proof was on the defendant; in some states even truthful statements had to be made with pure motives. In 1964, however, the Supreme Court revolutionized defamation law. In *New York Times* versus *Sullivan* for the first time the Supreme Court ruled that even false statements of a defamatory nature were entitled to the protection of the law, so that free speech would not be constrained by the fear of not being able to prove the veracity of a statement in court. As long as the "defamatory" remarks were made about a public official and related to his official conduct, the official could not recover a damage judgment unless he could prove that the statement was made with "actual malice"—that is, with knowledge that it was false or with reckless disregard of whether it was false or not. The Supreme Court described "reckless disregard" as "a high degree of awareness" of the "probable falsity" of the statement. It required the plaintiff to prove more than mere negligence. "Reckless conduct," said the Court, "is not measured by whether a reasonably prudent man would have published or would have investigated before publishing. There must be sufficient evidence to permit the conclusion that the defendant in fact entertained serious doubts as to the truth of his publications." The burden of proving actual malice was on the plaintiff, and it had to be proven with "convincing clarity." Thus, as one observer wrote, "actual malice involves the reporter's attitude toward the truth, not toward the plaintiff."

In 1979 the Supreme Court ruled in *Herbert* versus *Lando* that a public figure suing for libel may inquire into the thoughts and editorial processes of journalists, but this additional ammunition for plaintiffs seemed to have had little impact. Since *New York Times* versus *Sullivan*, few public figures had successfully pursued libel suits against the media. Although about ninety percent (or forty-two out of forty-seven) of the libel trials held between 1980 and mid-1983 resulted in jury verdicts against the press, the truth was that most libel suits never reached that trial stage—a full seventy-five percent of them being dismissed in summary judgment proceedings. And of those twenty-five percent that did reach trial, a majority of the jury decisions against the press were later reversed on appeal. A public figure's task was a formidable one, his chances of winning no better than one in nine. One reason for those poor odds for the plaintiff was that in a libel action truth was an absolute defense.

Under the libel law a reporter could simply gather allegations about a public figure, get his superiors to publish (or broadcast) them, then sit back and pray that the plaintiff's lawyers wouldn't be able to convince a jury that the defamation was false. In *Westmoreland* versus *CBS*, Dan Burt would not only have to prove to a jury that CBS had acted with "actual malice" but that his client was innocent of the charges leveled in the CBS documentary. In this regard, whether CBS did or did not have sufficient evidence (or any evidence at all) when it made the documentary was irrelevant, except in so far as it proved the malice charge. The burden of proof was on the plaintiff—and rightfully so, since without such a heavy burden the press would be unable to fulfill the role of "watchdog" over government so necessary to the preservation of democracy.

Aside from the exorbitant cost of pursuing a libel action and the difficulties imposed by the defamation law itself, Burt had one more liability as he undertook the Westmoreland suit: Gen. William C. Westmoreland himself. Westmoreland was a pariah whom most Americans viewed as unsympathetic, the stigma of Vietnam clinging to him like swamp stench. Burt had to make the aggressor (the plaintiff in the libel suit) seem like the underdog. In order to win his case, Burt would have to change America's mind about Westmoreland. Long before any trial he would have to win the battle of the press, and to do so he would have to obtain the Benjamin report. For Burt, the Sauter memo was "a wedge to open the coffin"; he was convinced that the Benjamin report contained even more damaging confirmation of the allegations made by *TV Guide*.

However, the first clash between the warring legal camps would occur over another crucial issue: the venue of the case itself. Should the court proceedings unfold in New York where the deed (the broadcast) had been done, as CBS argued, or in South Carolina where the general suffered the damage (he resided there), as Westmoreland's lawyers argued? The court's decision on this matter was critical to both sides. Cravath was fearful of having to argue its case before a South Carolina jury. Burt feared that no New York jury would return a verdict favorable to the general who had lost the Vietnam War.

18

The Lawyers Take Control

DURING THE WEEKS that followed the filing of Westmoreland's complaint in the United States District Court in Greenville, South Carolina, the opposing legal teams butted and bumped each other. Through its local South Carolina counsel, Capital Legal Foundation was issuing sweeping demands that CBS surrender the documents used in the preparation of the broadcast. The ultimate objective was to obtain the Benjamin report, which Burt and his lawyers were sure contained evidence he could use to prove "actual malice." On November 1 CBS informed the court that it would *not* hand over Benjamin's study. CBS lawyers declared that the Benjamin report was "privileged material" and that the document was "not sufficiently likely to lead to relevant evidence." Three days later Westmoreland's lawyers filed a motion to compel CBS to turn over their report.

Burt could not match Cravath's resources of money and manpower. While awaiting the court's decision about releasing the Benjamin report, his strategy was to use the press as a painful thumbscrew, squeezing CBS until the network conceded any documents he needed to build his case. Early in the game he played what appeared to be a trump card—some quotes he had obtained from the official unedited transcripts of CBS's interviews. He slipped several of these snatches of on-camera (but un-broadcast) conversations into various court papers; others he fed to report-ers famished for fresh copy. He wanted Cravath to think that he already had the full transcripts of CBS's interviews. If Cravath believed he already had the interviews, he reasoned, it would hand them to him without a contest, "proving" to the public that its client, CBS, had nothing to hide. In fact, though, Burt did not possess any of those interview transcripts. He was bluffing, and it worked. On November 5 CBS's lawyers complied with Burt's request and surrendered all twenty-six hours of on-camera interviews. However, that clash over the interview transcripts—a prelude to the fight over the release of the Benjamin report—was merely a skir-mish. More decisive would be the court's decision on the venue of the trial—whether the lawsuit should be tried in South Carolina, as Burt wanted, or in New York City.

From the beginning Dan M. Burt was gambling that the complaint he had filed in behalf of Westmoreland would never reach actual trial. The decision to file in South Carolina, which had one of the most favorable libel laws for plaintiffs, was designed to force CBS to agree to a quick settlement outside of court. Faced with the prospect of arguing its case before a jury in Westmoreland's home state, Burt hoped that CBS would quit rather than fight.

"If we lose this one and have to try our case in New York, it will give us trouble," Burt admitted. "But if we win, CBS is going to be in even more serious trouble. If CBS has to sit for trial in South Carolina," he added, "they're going to be staring right down the mouth of a rebel cannon."

The suit was filed in Greenville. But throughout the court proceedings that followed, neither Burt nor any of his lawyers was able to resolve for the judge a central enigma: Why was Westmoreland suing CBS in a city 200 miles away from his home? The truth was, should there be a trial, in the time it would take Westmoreland to drive between Greenville and Charleston each day, he could fly to New York City and back again. CBS's lawyers rammed that point home, adding that the individual defendants had too little contact with South Carolina to support any personal juris-diction over them by the Greenville court. CBS also argued in court that the case bore no particular relationship to South Carolina and that, as a matter of logic and law, the case belonged where the broadcast was pro-duced.

The first time Burt flew to Greenville to directly address the judge in court, he realized he had made a terrible mistake. "When I stood up and began talking," he recalled, "the judge was not listening."

Capital Legal Foundation's argument that it would be inconvenient for

Westmoreland to travel to New York fell on deaf ears. It was clear that Westmoreland was out of South Carolina more than he was in it. After CBS requested that the suit either be dismissed or transferred, on November 18 Federal District Judge G. Ross Anderson, Jr., issued an order shifting the site of the lawsuit to the Southern District of New York—New York City. Now CBS was on its own turf.

While Dan Burt was losing his first battle against Cravath in the courts, George Crile was mounting an attack to counter Burt's earlier coups in the press. Crile had kept in contact with some of the broadcast's star pro-conspiracy witnesses, including the CIA's George Allen and Col. Gains Hawkins. Crile had called Allen on the eve of the telecast to tell him that parts of his interview would be aired. A day or two later Crile had telephoned again to ask Allen for his opinion about the program. Allen said he thought, in general, that the broadcast had been a successful one, although he had some misgivings about the way his response to questions concerning CIA Director Richard Helms had been used in the program. He felt uneasy, he recalled later, about statements of his that seemed to imply that Helms's actions had been politically motivated. Then, after the TV Guide article appeared, Allen dined with Crile in Washington. Crile expressed to Allen his concern over the reaction inside CBS to the TV Guide article. He asked if Allen would be willing to write a letter stating his views about the telecast. According to Allen, Crile was concerned about his having shown Allen the segments of other witnesses' testimony. "He acknowledged that he had been aware when he showed me the film clips that that was not accepted practice," Allen recalled. Crile suggested the points Allen should make in his letter and that the letter should be addressed to Sauter. Crile, said Allen, was aware that an internal CBS investigation was underway.

Later Allen wrote to Sauter in support of the program. Crile telephoned him again to suggest he meet with executives of the Lehrman Institute in New York. Crile thought Allen might want to write an article, which the Lehrman Institute would publish, on "the politicization of intelligence." Allen flew to New York and met with officials of the Lehrman Institute. He agreed to write the article but never did. Subsequently, though, he did write an article that was published in U.S. News & World Report.

Crile had more success converting Col. Gains Hawkins into an instant journalist. Shortly after the broadcast, he had asked Hawkins to write out his memoirs of Vietnam: Crile had told Hawkins he felt confident he would be able to place such an article in the New York Times. Hawkins did so, penning a rambling reminiscence of his wartime experience, detailing in the process his relationship with Sam Adams during the events covered by the CBS documentary. However, Hawkins said later, the *Times* turned down the article. Months later, again at Crile's urging, Hawkins revamped that memoir, submitting the revision to the *Washington Post*, whose Robert Kaiser, according to Hawkins, helped reshape the article into a publishable piece. On November 14 the Hawkins article appeared in the *Post's* Sunday *Outlook* magazine. It was entitled "Vietnam Anguish: Being Ordered to Lie (A Mississippi colonel explains how it feels to cover up and to tell the truth)." In the article Hawkins explored the events leading to the "deception" (he did not use the word "conspiracy") described in the CBS documentary. But buried in the middle of the piece was his stunning revelation of his own deception during the Ellsberg-Russo Pentagon Papers trial. Hawkins recalled how, after his retirement from the army, Adams had visited him in his home in Mississippi. Hawkins remembered his irritation at the "persistence" Adams showed probing "for more information on what had gone on behind the curtains in Saigon." He was particularly incensed over the fact that Adams "seemed to suspect General McChristian [General Davidson's predecessor as chief of intelligence]," which to Hawkins "was only slightly less than sacrilegious." Hawkins's irritation soon turned to anger when, at Adams's instigation, he was subpoenaed to testify as a defense witness in Los Angeles at the Pentagon Papers trial. He wrote that his anger at Adams, "who seemed to be charging . . . that the entire gamut of [military] intelligence had been corrupt," was compounded by the fact that he "despised Ellsberg and his partner Anthony Russo." Thus, Hawkins explained, when a pair of army counterintelligence agents showed up on his porch, he told them *there had been no deception* in formulating estimates of the size of the enemy (emphasis added). He said he "stuck by that position throughout two trips to Los Angeles. . . ."

It was possible that Hawkins's admission that "I was committing—or at the very least flirting with—perjury" was the primary reason that the article had been written. The *Post* article gave Hawkins (and CBS's lawyers) an opportunity to ventilate and explain away an event in Hawkins's past that Westmoreland's lawyers might use to cast doubt on his credibility as a witness.

When Burt saw the headline of the article, he ordered one of his lawyers to telephone the *Post*. A day later the newspaper printed a "clarification," stating, "The headline, 'Vietnam Anguish: Being Ordered to Lie,' referred to Hawkins's view of his position. The *Post* did not intend to refer in the headline to any specific officer—Gen. William C. Westmoreland or any other of Hawkins's superiors." To whom the *Post* headline *did* refer would remain a mystery.

Before the federal judge in Greenville decided that the case belonged in New York, there had been a series of hints that CBS might be seeking an out-of-court settlement. Burt had been in contact with several "emissaries," claiming to be speaking in behalf of CBS but operating through third parties. Through one intermediary he was approached by a CBS executive who said he was acting on his own initiative. Then a person who claimed to represent ex-CBS president Frank Stanton (a leading CBS, Inc., stockholder) contacted Burt. In each case the intermediaries wanted to know if Westmoreland's terms for a settlement might vary from his August 25 letter to CBS. Each was told that an apology would not be sufficient; damages must also be paid. CBS refused to consider giving Westmoreland any compensation. Mike Wallace was particularly adamant, arguing that CBS should not consent to pay Westmoreland "even five dollars." In fact, Westmoreland's lawyers were unwilling to accept a settlement that did not include a payment of at least several *million* dollars.

In mid-November, Westmoreland received a telephone call from Gen. Maxwell Taylor who, in February 1982, had written a *Washington Post* column rebutting William F. Buckley, Jr., and supporting Westmoreland. Taylor told Westmoreland he was calling on behalf of a member of the CBS board of directors, a former government official. The board member offered to meet Westmoreland alone, without any lawyers present, to discuss ways the dispute could be resolved. Westmoreland rejected the offer, referring the would-be mediator to his lawyers. Both sides were fearful of looking like losers. Having filed the lawsuit, the Westmoreland camp now could not settle for the apology it could have obtained without going to court. Having won the crucial change-of-venue battle, CBS was less willing than ever to consider paying damages to Westmoreland. The die was cast; CBS was heading toward a trial. Burt's only hope of avoiding a New York jury was to make CBS pay such a steep price in negative press commentary that the network would be forced to negotiate. Likewise CBS would try to make the price too steep for Westmoreland, not only by outspending him but by scaring potential backers away from a cause CBS was convinced was tainted. CBS suspected that the Westmoreland lawsuit was more than merely an attempt by an aggrieved ex-official to clear his name. At a New York luncheon of the National Academy of Television Arts and Sciences in mid-November, Sauter had charged that there were people around Westmoreland who looked upon the lawsuit as "not just the general recovering what he sees as his diminished credibility" but also "as a way of getting back at network news organizations, especially CBS," and broadening the laws of libel as they applied to all news media, print as well as broadcast. Sauter mentioned the right-wing media "watchdog"

Accuracy in Media (AIM) as being intent on "assassinating CBS News." Realizing the harm that too close an identification with the right wing might do to his credibility, after AIM had collected from its members $35,000 in funds for the Westmoreland defense, Burt refused the money, henceforth not only distancing himself from the influence of organizations such as AIM but giving Westmoreland strict orders to stay clear as well. The truth was, from the beginning Burt's relations with the "right" had not been cordial, particularly with those leading conservatives who had argued that Westmoreland should have selected as counsel a law firm more experienced in First Amendment litigation.

However, while Burt was distancing himself from the most visible totems of conservatism, he was mining the conservative financial base for the enormous funds he would need to prosecute his case. By the end of November, funds were running low. To defray the costs of the lawsuit, in December Capital Legal Foundation sent out direct-mail solicitations asking for contributions. Literature that accompanied the mailing said that Capital Legal Foundation had "already spent much of its own money in the case" and that "funds [were] running dangerously low. . . ." A month later, however, that 150,000-piece mailing had yielded only a paltry $15,000. Already Capital Legal Foundation had spent between $250,000 and $300,000 on the case and expected to spend up to $600,000 in 1983. Noting that Capital Legal Foundation's total budget for 1982 was only $850,000, Burt told reporters that "CBS may spend us to death."

Eventually, though, Burt would find the funding he needed from such conservative foundations as Richard Mellon Scaife, the Smith Richardson Foundation, the Fluor Foundation, and the Olin Foundation.

Meanwhile, beginning in early November, Burt and Boies were inundating New York Federal District Court Judge Pierre Leval with paper, pleading, respectively, for or against the release of the Benjamin report. Cravath opposed releasing the report because it was "a privileged, confidential, self-evaluative analysis" and was "protected under the New York 'shield law.' . . ." Cravath argued that the report was "privileged" as "a voluntary, internal self-improvement measure taken by CBS." Contrary to Capital Legal Foundation's "assertion that [Benjamin's investigation] was done 'openly,' " Cravath added, "it was done in strictest confidence— the only way it could be done if it were to obtain any useful information. Its purpose was to determine how CBS's journalistic practices could be improved in the future. . . . CBS took a brave step—and one distinctly in the public interest—when it commissioned the Benjamin study. The study was only possible because of the assurances of confidentiality to those who participated in it. If this study is disclosed, similar self-improvement studies in the future will be made impossible. . . ." Cravath further argued that by turning over the document to Westmoreland, the court would be compelling "CBS to divulge its confidential source information"—confidential sources protected by the New York State "shield law" that protects "both identity and information and [vests] the media with the option to disclose or to refuse to disclose. . . ."

In rebuttal, Capital Legal Foundation contended that Cravath's arguments were inconsistent and contradictory: How could the Benjamin report be an internal self-evaluative document, not meant for publication, and at the same time be entitled to protection under a "shield law" guarding the sources of "a professional journalist or newscaster . . . gathering or obtaining news for publication . . .?" Clearly, the Benjamin report had not been meant for publication, or else CBS would have published it. "The fact that Mr. Benjamin works for a news organization," argued the Westmoreland lawyers, "cannot transform a corporate memorandum into a reporter's privileged source document."

CBS began seeking affidavits to bolster its position. Both *Time* magazine and the *New York Times* refused CBS's requests. However, in mid-January the law firm of Patterson, Belknap, Webb & Tyler, which represented Dow Jones and Company, Inc., publishers of the *Wall Street Journal*, submitted to Judge Leval a set of affidavits supporting CBS's opposition to releasing the Benjamin report. Included were affidavits from Edward R. Cony, vice-president of News of Dow Jones (whose *Wall Street Journal* was itself a defendant at the time in a publicized libel suit); Reuven Frank, president of NBC News; Earnest J. Schultz, executive vice-president of the Radio-Television News Directors Association; and Steven Nevas, First Amendment counsel for the National Association of Broadcasters, as well as affidavits from ABC and *Newsweek*.

In mid-January, Westmoreland supporters counterattacked. The American Legal Foundation, which billed itself as a "nonprofit public interest legal organization," asked the Federal Communications Commission to revoke all of CBS's licenses for its five owned-and-operated television stations, alleging that CBS had violated Commission policy by "deliberately distorting, slanting, and falsifying" its news program, "The Uncounted Enemy: A Vietnam Deception," and "failing to take the required remedial action to correct the distortion." Meanwhile, fed by lawyers from both sides, newspaper reporters kept publishing commentary plus any fragments of documents that arrived in the mail. Burt, in particular, viewed those continuing newspaper reports as vital levers he could use to pry the Benjamin report out of CBS's vault. He had lost the argument over venue. If he did not get the Benjamin report, he confided to a reporter, "we're dead." The way to get the report, he believed, required not only excellent arguments in court but digging through musty archives in search of the hard evidence the program itself had lacked. He still was doubtful that he could win his case before a New York jury. His aim was to fuel the press's curiosity about Benjamin's study, putting added pressure on CBS. The Sauter memorandum had been "the wedge to open the coffin"; he regarded the Benjamin report as the *corpus delicti*, riddled with forensic evidence of CBS's culpability.

In contrast, from the early days of the Westmoreland suit CBS executives had been avoiding public comment. But in January, CBS decided that a change of tactic was necessary. Burt had been beating CBS at its own media game; CBS had to go on the offensive, recapturing in the media momentum it had lost first with the publication of the *TV Guide* article and then with the Sauter memorandum. Reportedly, some of Sauter's superiors felt that the news president's memo had treated the *TV Guide* article too favorably. Sauter was asked to pick a platform from which he could set the record straight. Sauter chose the occasion carefully, selecting as his target audience the most bountiful assemblage of journalists he could find: the annual convention of the Society of Professional Journalists—Sigma Delta Chi—meeting in Philadelphia. Sigma Delta Chi was the nation's oldest media association. Founded in 1909 as a fraternity, it now included on its membership rolls some 28,000 journalists. Its annual Distinguished Service Awards, given each spring since 1931 for "outstanding contributions to newspaper, magazine, and broadcast journalism and to research," were among the profession's most prestigious ones.

Sauter was well regarded by most newsmen. Even though he no longer sipped beer from a can during interviews in his office and now sealed shut his shirt collars with limp bowties, his disarmingly disheveled appearance gave him a certain appeal. Reporters appreciated his blunt, candid comments, often spiced with salty epithets, which were so unlike the vapid, bland slogans that usually slipped from the mouths of television executives. If anyone could convince the journalists that CBS was fighting for a principle—the First Amendment that safeguarded all journalists—it was Van Gordon Sauter. On January 25, in an address to Sigma Delta Chi, Sauter reaffirmed his conviction that "the validity of the broadcast will be sustained in court. CBS will win." Then he added, "But this is not just a CBS issue. The lawsuit has become a rallying point for people who seek to use it as an instrument for damaging the image, spirit, and aggressiveness of the news media. For those who regard an independent, searching press as a threat to what they perceive as traditional values, the case becomes a focus for their campaign. They seek to diminish the voice . . . the calm, objective voice . . . of the media, so they can advance their narrow agendas and shout above those who are committed only to fair and accurate reporting of controversial issues.

"While we are confident of winning this trial," Sauter added, "we know it will be a long and arduous process. And we frankly feel a certain sadness at the prospect of the general, on the witness stand, facing the documents and the testimony that will sustain the CBS position and in the end do irreparable damage to his reputation. But many of those directing and supporting this lawsuit will have achieved their goals regardless of how the general fares. He is merely the pointman in their search-and-destroy mission against the news media. And thus we should not consider this as just a legal matter between a citizen and a news organization. It is part of an ongoing battle waged by those who seek to curtail the freedom of the press in this society. In that context, it is not just CBS, it is all of us. . . ."

Sauter concluded his remarks by defending CBS's decision not to turn over to Westmoreland's lawyers the Benjamin report, arguing that "those who contributed to it were told they would do so in confidence. And that confidentiality is imperative if news organizations are going to conduct exacting post-broadcast or post-publication study of their work. . . ."

Sauter's charge that Westmoreland was "the pointman" for right-wing forces "in their search-and-destroy mission against the news media" was trumpeted in newspapers across the country. Again a disturbing tendency of the press, noticeable from the start of the controversy, became evident. The vast majority of reporters, including representatives of prestigious newspapers, were content to merely echo segments of Sauter's speech, retransmitting his charges of right-wing machinations without testing their veracity. *Los Angeles Times* television writer Peter Boyer was an exception. After the speech he asked Sauter to identify the dark adversaries determined to scuttle the First Amendment. Citing the Westmoreland lawsuit as an excuse, Sauter referred Boyer to CBS vice-president Bob Chandler. (The week before Christmas, Chandler had reassumed from Roger Colloff sovereignty over "soft" news.) Boyer acted on Sauter's suggestion and contacted Chandler. Chandler named AIM and the American Legal Foundation. "Those groups have attacked CBS over the years and will continue to do so," Chandler told Boyer. "But the point [of Sauter's speech] is that on the face of it, it doesn't make much sense for Westmoreland to pursue it himself. So why are they doing this? Obviously, to have something to rally around and to exploit. . . ."

That seemed to be Chandler's evidence: ". . . that on the face of it, it doesn't make much sense for Westmoreland to pursue it himself."

Boyer telephoned Westmoreland, who called the Sauter charge "uncategorically false." He telephoned Dan Burt, who, characteristically, said that if Sauter "would like to make that statement somewhere else, like in a street or alley, I'd be happy to take the matter up with him. Sure there are some people out to get the press, but it's not us," Burt added, detailing the steps he had taken to quarantine himself from both AIM and the American Legal Foundation. "There is no right-wing *jihad.*" Boyer contacted AIM's Reed Irvine, who said he found Burt "a little difficult to get along with" and confirmed that Burt had refused to accept the $35,000 AIM had raised for Westmoreland's defense. Boyer telephoned American Legal Foundation director Mike Carvin, who said, "It's ironic that when their [CBS's] practices are called into question, it's called a 'conservative plot.' But when Mike Wallace investigates shoddy business practices, it's a crusade for truth and justice." Unfortunately, among the hundreds of articles and columns written about *Westmoreland* versus *CBS,* the thoroughness of Boyer's report was a rarity. Fearful of becoming prize exhibits in either side's media circus, their stories turned into propaganda posters, reporters were being manipulated anyway. All anyone had to do was wave a red flag in front of the First Amendment, which guarantees journalists the right to be aggressive, and the press suddenly turned passive.

On March 8, a month and a half after Sauter had addressed its convention, Sigma Delta Chi announced the winners of its 1982 Distinguished Service Awards. Honored in the category of Magazine Reporting were the authors of *TV Guide's* "Anatomy of a Smear." On March 28 Sauter wrote a letter to *Quill,* Sigma Delta Chi's magazine, to "put before the membership and others in journalism some troubling facts about the *TV Guide* article. . . ." Sauter said that the article contained "serious errors," and he detailed "three examples of inaccuracy, each of which vividly illustrates a shocking disregard for the truth." Two of those alleged "errors" embodied familiar CBS denials: that after the broadcast, Adams had not disavowed the thesis of the documentary (a Westmoreland-led conspiracy), and that Col. Gains Hawkins insisted that no statements in his CBS interview had been taken out of context. However, the third "error" Sauter cited was one CBS had not mentioned before. Sauter wrote: "*TV Guide* quoted George Allen [Sam Adams's superior at the CIA] as saying that he 'tried to dissuade producer George Crile from even doing the show, because I thought they were making a mountain out of molehill.' " Then Sauter quoted a passage from the letter Crile had convinced Allen to write to CBS in late June, reaffirming his support for the program. "I am writing to set the record straight with respect to my involvement with the *CBS Reports* program, "The Uncounted Enemy," and the *TV Guide* story, 'Anatomy of a Smear,' " said Allen in the letter. "The latter lifted out of context and tends to distort remarks I made in a telephone interview with one of its writers. I did *not*," added Allen, "attempt to dissuade CBS from doing the show, and I do *not* believe the show made a 'mountain out of a molehill.' . . ."

The charge CBS was leveling against *TV Guide*'s writers was a serious one. Sauter was accusing them of lifting Allen's remarks out of context and distorting them. Had the writers misquoted Allen in their article? Three days after Sauter's letter to the editors of *Quill*, *TV Guide* sent to *Quill* a rebuttal, including a verbatim record, in context, of exactly what Allen had told *TV Guide* in his taped interview:

> ALLEN: I kind of objected and tried to dissuade Crile and company from even doing the show because I thought they were making a mountain out of a molehill. I told them that, you know, this problem of the numbers was only symptomatic of the much larger problem of the tendency of the military and political leaders to self-delusion on Vietnam, or on any other policy issue to which there has become a deep emotional attachment by the people that formulate the policy.

The writers then asked Allen how producer Crile had reacted to that.

> ALLEN: Well, he objected, you know. It would have killed his story, so he didn't use those parts of my interview where we were talking about that.

CBS never again suggested that Allen had been misquoted. However, CBS did manage to get some minor revenge on the authors of the award-winning article. The winners of Sigma Delta Chi Distinguished Service Awards were invited to a banquet in Los Angeles the following June. Sigma Delta Chi had arranged with KNXT, the CBS owned-and-operated Los Angeles television station, to produce an award-winners' montage so that before each reporter picked up his or her award at the podium, a brief film clip documenting the award-winning achievement could be shown. About a week before the award ceremony, KNXT informed Sigma Delta Chi that its personnel would not put together the sequence introducing the *TV Guide* writers.

At the last minute, at extra cost, Sigma Delta Chi had to hire an outside editing crew to assemble that one segment.

19

INSIDE STORY

O N JANUARY 1 Ira Klein had finished editing the hour film in Bill Moyers's multipart (non-CBS) series, *A Walk Through the Twentieth Century*. In February he was offered another film to edit in that same series, beginning in May. In the interim he would be free to work on another project. Through mutual friends he had heard that senior producer Judy Reemtsma wanted him to edit a CBS documentary. On Monday, March 14, Klein telephoned Reemtsma. He admired not only her talent as a producer but her warmth as a human being. They chatted about the proposed project for a while, neither one mentioning a word about the Westmoreland controversy. At the close of the conversation Reemtsma told Klein she would get back to him the following day.

Klein assumed that Reemtsma would have to talk to *CBS Reports* executive producer Andy Lack before officially assigning him the editing job. Reemtsma could not avoid the fact that Klein was a central figure in the controversy. His association with the CBS documentary was becoming a burden; he detected signs that the controversy might eventually eclipse his career. Thus he welcomed Reemtsma's offer of employment and the loyalty she and others whom he considered friends at CBS were demonstrating by inviting him back. Reemtsma telephoned Andy Lack, who in turn called CBS vice-president Bob Chandler. Chandler had no objection to Klein returning to CBS. That evening Klein returned home to find a message from Reemtsma on his answering machine. Tuesday morning he telephoned her. "I'll be looking forward to seeing you next week," said Reemtsma. Klein had been hired to edit the film; he would begin the following Monday. Klein was looking forward to working at CBS again.

Tuesday evening, suddenly, an obstacle materialized to block Klein's path back to CBS, its outline emerging in the midst of a telephone conversation Klein was having with Andy Lack. Lack was cordial; he wanted to know where Klein had been and what he had been doing since he had stopped working at CBS. Klein told him about editing the Moyers film. Lack welcomed him back into the CBS fold, then added this caveat: "If you want to work at CBS now or in the future, it's essential that you speak with our lawyers before you begin working."

"What specifically do they want to discuss with me?" said Klein.

"Well," said Lack, "they're interested in talking about the source of the TV Guide article."

When Klein heard that, he grew furious. "Listen, Andy," he said, "it serves no purpose going on a witch-hunt for sources." Klein reminded Lack that he had come forward to speak to him out of loyalty to the unit, out of loyalty to Lack himself.

"I understand that," Lack replied, "but it's important that you call the lawyers. If you want to work here, then you have to talk to the lawyers."

"That's something I'm going to have to think over," Klein said. He hung up the telephone. A few minutes later the phone rang. It was Andy Lack again. Lack wanted to make sure that Klein had the name and telephone number of the lawyers. On Thursday, Klein found several messages from Lack on his answering machine, each more anxious than the previous one and all asking him to call immediately. Lack had arranged for Klein to meet with Cravath attorney David Boies at 5:00 P.M.

Klein telephoned Lack and revealed his decision: He would not talk informally to CBS's lawyers. He felt it was more appropriate for Boies to depose him. Klein had heard Phyllis Hurwitz's account of what she regarded as a blatant attempt by CBS's lawyers to manipulate her for their purposes. He told Lack that all CBS's lawyers had to do was depose him, and he would answer forthrightly any question put to him.

Lack insisted that Klein talk to the lawyers now, in an informal setting. It was a reasonable request since Klein had been intimately involved in the project. Klein had assumed from the beginning that once he started work at CBS there would be an opportunity to set the conditions for talking to the lawyers. What was upsetting Klein was that there had not been even a hint of any obstacle to his employment until after he had accepted the job on Tuesday.

"I was offered the job, I accepted the job," Klein said. "And now you're telling me that if I don't speak to the lawyers, I can't have the job. You're setting preconditions for my employment."

"What do you mean 'preconditions'? There are no preconditions," said Lack.

"How do you define it?" said Klein.

Lack reiterated that Klein had to talk to the lawyers, adding, "I'll support you in whatever decision you make." He and Klein talked on for a while, then Judy Reemtsma took the phone. "Trust me," Reemtsma said. Klein told her that he had complete trust in her.

That night Klein sat down and wrote a letter to Van Gordon Sauter detailing the chronology of events that were obstructing his return to CBS. On Friday morning he called Judy Reemtsma and told her he had written but had not yet mailed a letter to Sauter explaining his position. Lack got on the phone. Klein told Lack he planned to mail the letter that afternoon. Lack asked Klein to first call Bob Chandler. Klein did. He explained to the CBS vice-president that he would like to talk to the CBS lawyers on the record, that he had no reservations about being deposed by CBS at any time.

"I think that sounds reasonable," Chandler replied. "I don't find a problem with that." Chandler told Klein he would speak to the CBS lawyers and then get back to him.

Klein waited for Chandler's return call, then called Chandler back around 5:00 P.M. Chandler indicated that he had heard about the letter Klein intended to send to Sauter. Klein asked if he was going to be allowed to begin work on Monday. "Absolutely," said Chandler. "We'll be happy to have you back." Chandler added that, during Klein's first week at CBS, he would like to meet with him. Klein agreed. He understood that Chandler would attempt to persuade him to sit down and chat with the CBS lawyers.

On Monday, March 21, for the first time in months Ira Klein returned to work at CBS. On Tuesday, Chandler telephoned. He made an appointment to see Klein on Wednesday. Klein agreed, but the following day, as he walked across 57th Street en route from the Ford building to Chandler's office in the CBS Broadcast Center, he was seething. For as he walked, flitting through his head were flashbacks of a similar journey he had made across 57th Street nearly nine months ago. Then he was going to meet with Bud Benjamin; now he was going to meet with Bob

Chandler. Nine months had passed without any of Benjamin's investigation having been revealed, except for the eight-page Sauter memo which had raised more questions that it had answered.

Klein reached Chandler's office, entered, and sat down. According to Klein, Chandler told him that Wallace was complaining because he had been rehired. Then, Chandler said that the CBS lawyers wanted to talk informally. Klein repeated that he was willing to talk to the CBS lawyers any time, any place—as long as the conversation was on the record, preferably in the form of a sworn deposition.

"The lawyers don't want to depose you," said Chandler. "They're afraid you're going to be a hostile witness."

The irony did not escape Klein. After all his efforts to work within the CBS system, all the days he had spent attempting to get CBS to investigate itself before outsiders did—now *he* was the one who was "hostile." What a peculiar and perverse system it was that had turned him into CBS's enemy—and Crile into CBS's ally. Again it was duty, honor . . . company.

Chandler and Klein reminisced about the past for a while. Then Chandler began to discuss the implications of the Westmoreland lawsuit for CBS—the damage that would be done if Westmoreland obtained a favorable verdict in court. He talked about CBS's credibility, how important it was to CBS's news division. . . . Chandler rose from his chair. He stood there, surveying his office—the same one he had before he had been displaced by Colloff a few years before. He told Klein that he had returned to his old post specifically to deal with the controversy. Chandler, an experienced newsman, had been deprived of the day-to-day stewardship over "soft" news during this documentary's birth. His skepticism toward it had run deep, inducing him to delay approval of the program during the early stages. As soon as Chandler had departed, the problems began. It was CBS vice-president Roger Colloff, the relative novice in news, who had replaced him and had supervised the making of the documentary. Now Colloff was gone. CBS had had to call back Chandler to defuse the volatile spillage that others had left. Undoubtedly, one of Chandler's most delicate tasks would be his handling of Ira Klein.

Chandler mentioned the Benjamin report to Klein, telling him that the report "was only a problem of tone." Chandler again asked Klein to talk to CBS's lawyers. Klein said he would talk to the lawyers only on the record. The meeting ended in that stalemate. Klein went back to editing Reemtsma's documentary. In mid-April, Chandler called Klein again. He told Klein that CBS deputy general counsel George Vradenburg was on the extension phone in his office. Chandler asked Klein if he would be willing to talk to Vradenburg. Klein expressed to Chandler his concern over being characterized as a potential "hostile witness." Vradenburg joined the conversation, advising Klein of the dangers of being deposed without adequate advance preparation. Klein told Vradenburg he did not need any "preparation" to simply tell the truth as he knew it. Klein completed the Reemtsma project at the end of April and left CBS. Subsequently, CBS would attempt to dismiss his substantive disagreements with Crile over the program's production and premise as a mere "personality clash."

CBS began the third week in April with a sad day, soon followed by a bad day. The sad day was Wednesday, April 20, when CBS's eighty-one-year-old board chairman William Paley retired. Paley was going to become a partner in the Whitcom Investment Company, which owned Whitney Communications, which in turn owned a one-third interest in the *International Herald Tribune* newspaper that Paley would represent. However, in turning over command of CBS to president and chief executive officer Thomas Wyman, Paley was not completely divorcing himself from the company he had converted from a group of failing radio stations into a communications giant. He would still keep his office at Black Rock, retaining his pivotal post of chairman of the board of directors' powerful executive committee and serving CBS as a consultant.

Paley could survey with pride his fifty-five-year reign. His record of achievement was unparalleled in broadcast history. He had earned early legitimacy for CBS by wooing away from his competitors such star entertainers as Jack Benny, Red Skelton, and Burns and Allen. But it had been the news division—led by Edward R. Murrow, then Walter Cronkite—that had provided a more durable pedigree. CBS's prime-time magazine *60 Minutes* was the highest-rated program in all of television, and Dan Rather's evening news led all its competitors by a significant margin. Still, within CBS the nostalgia over Paley's retirement was muddied by a nagging doubt: The Westmoreland lawsuit was an inexorable acid, eating away proud CBS's credibility. The damage was exacerbated the day after Paley's departure when public television's *Inside Story* aired the first thorough examination by television itself of "The Uncounted Enemy."

Inside Story's verdict on the CBS documentary was particularly important to CBS because the program's host and chief reporter was a journalist highly regarded by his peers. Hodding Carter's father had been the editor of the *Delta Democrat-Times* in Greenville, Mississippi. In 1946, when the only reward a reporter in Mississippi could expect for raising the subject of race relations was a "necktie party," the elder Carter had written a series of editorials against racism that earned him a Pulitzer Prize. Hodding Carter III, the son, inherited both the editor's chair and the crusading temperament of his father. When Jimmy Carter became president, Hodding Carter followed the newly elected candidate to Washington, becoming best known as the State Department spokesman during the Iranian hostage crisis. The result of Hodding Carter's independent investigation into "The Uncounted Enemy" was crucial to CBS not only because of his credentials as a journalist but because of his politics, too. No one could dare accuse Hodding Carter of being a right-wing dupe, part of the plot to shatter CBS's credibility as a news organization. He was a confirmed liberal-Democrat. Furthermore, he had lavished praise on the CBS documentary when it first aired. On January 28, five days after the broadcast, he had begun his column in *The Wall Street Journal* with: "*CBS Reports* rendered an important public service the other night with 'The Uncounted Enemy: A Vietnam Deception.' Important not simply because it detailed the appalling lies fed to the upper reaches of government and to the American people about enemy strength in Vietnam during the late 1960s, a story told before, but also because it illustrates with sharply etched clarity a continuing reality in government. . . ."

CBS was deeply concerned. *Inside Story* staffers had recently been dropping clues that the program, to be aired that week on public television stations throughout the country, would be a searing indictment of the CBS documentary. Carter told reporters who asked him about his six-week-long investigation that he was going to "eat my words." He conceded that had he known then what he knew now, he would not have written his January 28 *The Wall Street Journal* article. "A little humility is good for me," he said.

"A little humility" from one of the broadcast's staunchest initial defenders meant a lot of headaches for CBS. Hodding Carter was not AIM's Reed Irvine, he was not the American Legal Foundation, he was not Dan M. Burt. Hodding Carter was a journalist of unimpeachable pedigree, of untarnished reputation—and as confirmed a liberal as could be found within the confines of the United States. If Carter attacked "The Uncounted Enemy," CBS's allegation that critics of its broadcast were "pointmen" for the right wing, determined to destroy the First Amendment, would fall flat.

During *TV Guide's* investigation, CBS had told its employees to cooperate with the reporters; no obstacles were to be placed in their paths. "The policy is," said one CBS executive at the time, "to let the chips fall where they may." By the time Hodding Carter undertook his investigation, however, that policy had altered. CBS had dug a yawning moat around its embattled Black Rock fortress. Initially CBS did not respond to Carter's call to lower its drawbridge. Telephone calls were not returned; appointments were broken. Finally, however, under pressure from those who did want to speak out in their own defense, CBS overcame its corporate shyness. Mike Wallace later called CBS's decision to offer Carter at least limited access a "free-the-slaves" movement, giving him and others itching to speak an opportunity to do so. Sauter, who had cancelled one scheduled interview session with *Inside Story*, reconsidered and consented to appear on camera for the broadcast. So did Roger Colloff and George Crile. Mike Wallace was not interviewed on camera, however. Sources at *Inside Story* insisted that Wallace had agreed to appear before their cameras, then had cancelled the interview, citing scheduling conflicts. Wallace would later insist that it was *Inside Story* that had avoided interviewing him, despite his repeated efforts to go on camera. Carter and his staff interviewed not only the men from CBS but some principal "pro-conspiracy" witnesses who had appeared in the broadcast, including Col. Gains Hawkins and the CIA's George Allen. Carter and his staff also interviewed key ex-officials whom CBS had excluded from the program, such as Gen. Philip Davidson, Westmoreland's chief of intelligence; George Carver, George Allen's CIA boss; and Gen. George Godding, the head of the military delegation at the August 1967 conference on Order of Battle.

It was the tone of Carter's questions to the CBS interviewees which convinced the network that the program would not be a friendly one. As the *Inside Story* air date drew near, producer Rose Economou found herself spending more and more time on the telephone answering questions from CBS, cataloguing CBS's complaints, and dealing with data CBS wanted her to include to cast the broadcast in a more favorable light. Ultimately, calls from Crile and Wallace became so frequent that Economou kept on her desk a pair of handwritten signs, one with Crile written on it, the other with Wallace. When either Crile or Wallace telephoned, she would hold up the appropriate sign so that her co-workers would know she was engaged in a marathon conversation. CBS's concern over the Carter program peaked the day prior to the broadcast. Cravath counsel David Boies had been deposing, under oath, Gen. George Godding, the head of the military delegation to the conferences held at CIA headquarters in Virginia during August 1967. During the course of that deposition, Godding (who had been interviewed by Crile but had not been asked to appear on camera) seemed to confirm CBS's allegation that he had been operating under an artificial "ceiling*" on enemy troop strengths. CBS knew that *Inside Story* had interviewed Godding for the broadcast. Both Boies and Wallace telephoned *Inside Story*, insisting that Godding's revelation during his deposition be included in the program. *Inside Story* chose not to do so; their program was about the evidence CBS possessed at the time it produced the documentary—the standard by which reporters judge their peers' work. The libel law considered "truth" as an absolute defense. Carter, in contrast, was doing a program not about the law but about journalism, in which the only defense is a reporter's decent regard for the evidence he has managed to assemble.

The telephone calls from CBS to *Inside Story* staffers persisted until the last minute. On the eve before the broadcast, *Inside Story* production personnel were still making changes, fine-tuning the focus of their program.

Meanwhile, on the afternoon of the broadcast (the program was scheduled to air in most cities on Thursday, April 21, at 8:00 P.M.), Federal District Court Judge Pierre Leval finally ruled on Westmoreland's lawyers' motion to compel CBS to turn over the Benjamin report. CBS had argued that the document was a "privileged one," while Westmoreland's lawyers denied that any such privilege existed. In his decision, however, Judge Leval did not rule on the supporting theories advanced in court papers by either side. What apparently convinced Leval was a comment Burt had made to him in oral argument. Burt had pointed out to Leval that the Sauter memo had relied on the Benjamin report for its conclusions; by releasing the Sauter memo, he added, CBS itself had forfeited any privilege protecting the report. Leval, in his decision, focused on that argument. Whether or not such a privilege for internal investigations undertaken by news media did or did not exist, he said, in this case CBS had waived any such privilege by publishing the Sauter memorandum.

Leval wrote: ". . . CBS has not treated the Benjamin report as a confidential internal matter. It has relied in public statements on the fact of the Benjamin investigation and on the conclusions expressed in the report for public justification of its broadcast. . . . CBS cannot at once hold out the Benjamin report to the public as substantiating its accusations and, when challenged, decline to reveal the report, contending that it is a confidential internal study utilized solely for self-evaluation and self-improvement. . . ."

As a public figure, Westmoreland was obliged to prove that CBS had aired the documentary knowing that its premise was false or recklessly disregarding whether it was true or not. However, in order to ascertain that evidence of "actual malice," the courts had previously ruled that plaintiffs had to be allowed, under certain conditions, access to reporters' files and even their "state of mind" during their inquiry. Because the

Benjamin report had studied the making of the documentary, Leval said, it "may well lead to evidence of degree of care for accuracy, concern for truthfulness, and possible bias, prejudgment, or malice." He also noted that Westmoreland was suing CBS not only for broadcasting the documentary that he claimed defamed him but, as a separate count, for publishing Sauter's memorandum which repeated the alleged libel. "The Sauter memorandum implies that the Benjamin report supports its conclusions," the judge wrote. If the report did not, Leval added, it could be "important evidence of the necessary element of malice."

Dan Burt was elated, promising to continue his efforts to compel CBS to turn over "everything relevant to whether or not CBS libeled General Westmoreland," including any notes Benjamin had taken during the course of his investigation. Sauter replied, "Sometimes I think the plaintiff's lawyers want to open our desk drawers." Cravath returned to court to ask Leval for permission to have an appeals court rule on the issue of a constitutional protection for self-examinations undertaken by news organizations. Leval denied permission to appeal. By issuing the Sauter memorandum, he reiterated, CBS had waived any such privilege, if one existed.

To some, Leval's decision seemed oppressive. The National News Council warned that his ruling would have "a chilling effect" on a beneficial trend among news organizations to critique their own work. Others, however, denied the existence of any such "beneficial trend." Beyond a handful of highly publicized instances of thorough self-examination, they argued, most of the news media still "stonewalled" whenever their reporting was challenged. Meanwhile, most lawyers specializing in First Amendment cases were taking a position midway between, saying that while the decision might indeed have an undesirable, chilling effect on news organizations' internal investigations, Leval was clearly right on the law. By publishing the Sauter memo, CBS had forfeited whatever constitutional protection of the Benjamin report existed. David Boies told Leval that CBS would turn over the Benjamin report early the following week.

Leval's decision was only the opening blow delivered to CBS that Thursday. Hodding Carter's *Inside Story* was scheduled to air at 8:00 P.M. That morning the *New York Times* published an article previewing the program. The writer of the *Times* article, Frank J. Prial, reported the conclusion of the forthcoming broadcast, along with comments he had obtained from Hodding Carter. Carter told Prial that the *Inside Story* investigation had not uncovered new information about the military operations in Vietnam but had turned up "a lot of old information that was not included in the documentary."

Carter mentioned that Crile and his staff "either did not talk to or did not include interviews" with Gen. Philip Davidson, Gen. George Godding, and Walt Rostow. "If you're going to make a case that there was a conspiracy at the highest levels of military intelligence," Carter added, "then you have to go to the highest levels and allow the chief conspirators to talk." Prial revealed that in the broadcast Carter would say that CBS officials told him they "couldn't reach" Davidson because he was ill. "The show was fifteen months in the making," Carter would tell his audience. "That seems like time enough to reach almost anyone." Contacted by *Inside Story*, Davidson said he had gotten married during that period, had been "playing lots of tennis," and was accessible. Prial reported that Rostow, when contacted by *Inside Story*, "scoffed at the conspiracy theory and insisted that President Johnson had known all along about the varying figures."

Prial had also asked CBS for comment but had been told none would be given until after the *Inside Story* broadcast. "Mr. Wallace," added Prial, "was interviewed for three hours by *Inside Story* but declined to appear on the screen."

That afternoon, a CBS source said, Wallace telephoned A. M. "Abe" Rosenthal, editor of the *New York Times* and a social acquaintance of Wallace. Wallace complained to Rosenthal that, by publishing Prial's article before Prial even screened the broadcast (review cassettes were not available due to last-minute revisions), the *Times* was both publicizing and prejudging the truth of Carter's allegations about the CBS documentary. Reportedly, Wallace was also deeply disturbed by Prial's statement that he had sat for a three-hour interview with *Inside Story* but had refused to appear before their cameras.

The *Inside Story* edition aired that evening was indeed damning to CBS's prestige and credibility. *Inside Story* found investigating the documentary a much more difficult task than it had anticipated. Originally this broadcast had been scheduled to open *Inside Story's* new season of programs, but it had to be postponed. The deeper *Inside Story* probed, the more complex and convoluted events became. Staffers had to assemble and evaluate documentary evidence, schedule interviews, and contend with fickle cooperation from CBS and pressure from both sides in the litigation to tailor the program to fit a particular viewpoint. The program that aired that evening showed traces of last-minute stitching—a technical unevenness. Nevertheless, it was a fascinating, because rare, case study of a television journalist examining television journalism. Of particular interest was *Inside Story's* use of interviews with key officials, whom CBS had ignored, in order to demonstrate the balanced and fair documentary CBS could have put together but had not. For example, *Inside Story* showed intelligence chief Gen. Philip Davidson, a Westmoreland supporter, confirming that although he was healthy during the period when the documentary was being made, CBS never contacted him. George Crile was seen next, telling Hodding Carter: "You probably talked to him [Davidson] by now, I assume. What is it that Davidson has to say that we should have included in there?" Cut to Davidson replying: "Just to set the record straight, neither General Westmoreland nor anybody else in a position of authority over me ever gave me any order, any directive, any hint, any indication to manipulate enemy-strength figures, to minimize enemy-strength figures, or to suppress them, nor did I ever give any such order to the people who worked for me."

Hodding Carter: "That's what the man says. You don't have to believe him, but if you want to make the case that CBS did, that 'there was a conspiracy at the highest level of military intelligence,' he deserves a hearing."

Throughout his program Carter kept hammering home one theme: the importance of fairness and accuracy, which differentiate the premise of a reporter from the propaganda of a publicist. Implicit was a critique of a misguided "advocacy" journalism in which just because a reporter/producer *thinks* something is true, it *must* be true. Crile kept challenging Hodding Carter to demonstrate that he had omitted crucial testimony from "The Uncounted Enemy" by failing to include in his broadcast certain key officials.

What, Crile asked, would the CIA's George Carver have been able to contribute, had he been interviewed on camera by CBS, "that was significant, that would have changed the picture of the whole story?" On camera, Hodding Carter had Carver "answer" the question, contradicting the documentary's charge that it was Westmoreland who had proposed the final Saigon compromise over Order of Battle figures. "Where in the interview, from the reading of it," continued Crile, "do you find Rostow making points that should have been included because they challenged the thesis of the broadcast?" On camera, Walt Rostow insisted: "We had from communications intelligence quite adequate information on the movement of North Vietnamese forces. We could track them from their bases down the Ho Chi Minh Trail. . . . We knew the regiment, the battalion numbers. They were coming down, and they had to be dealt with." And George Carver explained to Carter that he had personally communicated all of the information about these troop movements to Rostow, conferring with him almost daily. Finally, Rostow stated he had passed on all such information to the president.

Hodding Carter challenged the CBS documentary's intimation that the Tet offensive was a disaster for the United States because Westmoreland had deliberately underestimated the size of the enemy. "The president," Mike Wallace had said in the CBS program, "had been alerted to the enemy's intentions [to attack], but no one had been able to inform him of the enemy's capabilities." Carter quoted from a recent article in the *New York Review of Books* written by Truong Nhu Tang. "Tet proved catastrophic to our plans," the former North Vietnamese minister of justice had written. "It cost us half our forces. Our propaganda transformed this military debacle into a brilliant victory."

Col. Gains Hawkins, a CBS "pro-conspiracy" witness, told Carter on camera: "I have never subscribed to the conspiracy theory." And Sam Adams, the program's paid consultant, told Carter that although he believed the military plotted to deceive the *public* about enemy strength, "I find it less plausible that there was an intention to deceive the president."

Carter concluded his program with a stern reminder that without fairness and balance journalism may become indistinguishable from vigilantism. He said, "CBS is entitled to its opinion, but we are entitled to a more balanced presentation. Even if you are sure of guilt, there is a vast difference between a fair trial and a lynching. It's a distinction that was badly blurred when CBS made 'The Uncounted Enemy: A Vietnam Deception.'"

CBS executives were distressed by the program. By confirming on film the allegations leveled in the *TV Guide* article, the liberal-minded Carter had sapped the sanity out of CBS's contention that it was being pursued by a right-wing mob intent on immolating the First Amendment. Carter's program, with its large audience of professional journalists, was likely to further erode support for CBS in the press. The mere airing of the program itself, its focus on a controversy already mired in litigation, struck some at CBS as unseemly. There was a notion prevalent, not only at CBS, that once a dispute entered the realm of the courts, journalists who attempted to analyze it or comment on it without striving for absolute neutrality were breaking some unwritten covenant—ripping apart the interlocked arms of a united press defending its constitutional rights. If journalists could not come to CBS's defense, they should at least have the courtesy to keep quiet. No one was more incensed by the program than Mike Wallace, whom Carter had described in the program as a central witness who "was not available to our cameras." It was that sense of outrage, primed by the Frank Prial article in the *Times*, that Wallace had communicated earlier that day in his telephone call to *Times* editor Abe Rosenthal.

The following morning, Friday, April 22, readers of the *New York Times* editorial page noticed, in the bottom right-hand corner, an item that struck many as extraordinary. In its Editor's Note department, the *Times* published a five-paragraph apology for the Prial article that had appeared the previous morning. "Nothing in the *Times* account suggested that the criticism of CBS by *Inside Story* was fresh, substantive, or otherwise newsworthy," the Editor's Note item said. "Nevertheless, the *Times* devoted some 700 words to *Inside Story*, displayed across six columns at the top of the page. By its length, the *Times* article seemed to imply that the criticisms of CBS were fresh or newly substantiated. By the *Times's* standards of news judgment and fairness, the article was too long and too prominently displayed."

The Editor's Note had been written at the direction of Abe Rosenthal. Sources at the *Times* said later that subordinates had unsuccessfully tried to convince Rosenthal to at least delay the Editor's Note criticizing Prial's article until after Rosenthal saw the *Inside Story* broadcast. Rosenthal's Editor's Note stirred up almost as much discussion in the press as the Carter broadcast itself. Many journalists were puzzled as to why Rosenthal had taken such an unusual (although not unprecedented) step.

"Had the *Times* story been too long?" asked *Time* magazine's Thomas Griffith in his "Newswatch" column. "Over on the food page, critic Craig Claiborne often gets as much space to describe the place and circumstances where he discovered a fish sauce. Was there nothing new in Hodding Carter's critique? It added about as much, or as little, to public knowledge as had the original Westmoreland broadcast." Griffith added that CBS had largely relied on evidence from Sam Adams, who "had previously made his case elsewhere and often: in congressional testimony, in court, in a *Harper's* article. To this old story CBS added the engrossing dramatics of witnesses defending themselves. . . ."

Rosenthal revealed to Griffith his "naive astonishment" at the reaction his Editor's Note had provoked. He said that he had not meant to suggest that *Inside Story* offered nothing new but that the *Times account* had offered nothing new. "The wording," he said, "may have been unclear in my stumbling way." He denied any personal hostility toward Hodding Carter ("I don't know him well enough to dislike him") or that he had succumbed to pressure from CBS. Griffith quoted Mike Wallace as saying, "Can you imagine me trying to pressure him?"

Hodding Carter could. The *Chicago Sun-Times's* P. J. Bednarski wrote that Carter, while in Phoenix a few days later for a preview of upcoming public television programs, "suggested sarcastically that it is Wallace's friendship with *New York Times* editor Abe Rosenthal that caused the paper to essentially retract a preview story it ran. . . ." Contacted by Bednarski, Wallace said, "I'd like to see him say that to my face."

In the days that followed, Carter and Wallace had much to say to each other, not face-to-face, but through newspaper-reporter intermediaries. Wallace took the offensive, charging that *Inside Story* had misedited interviews with Sauter and Crile while discarding completely Roger Colloff's interview. Carter replied that Wallace's criticisms were a "parody" of those made by Westmoreland, *TV Guide*, and others about the CBS documentary itself. What disturbed Wallace most, however, was Carter's statement in the program that Wallace had not been "available for our cameras." Wallace insisted that it was Carter who had cancelled a scheduled interview, that Wallace had told *Inside Story* he was willing to reschedule later, but that no one from *Inside Story* had subsequently contacted him to set up another interview. He said he had eventually sent a telegram to Carter complaining about the treatment given him but had received no response from Carter. Meanwhile, *Inside Story* staffers insisted that Wallace had consistently stymied them in their efforts to interview him on camera.

While Wallace and *Inside Story* were debating in the press, behind the scenes CBS was applying pressure to obtain the exposure Wallace claimed he had been denied in the program. Negotiations between CBS and *Inside Story* executive producer Ned Schnurman went on for weeks, with *Inside Story* offering Wallace air time to respond to the program. According to Wallace, his conversations with Schnurman were initially "cordial," until he happened to read a press release from *Inside Story* describing its broadcast as a show that "brave reporters refused to take on." The release angered Wallace by reiterating that he had absented himself from the broadcast. However, sources at *Inside Story* insisted that negotiations between Schnurman and Wallace foundered over *Inside Story's* bottom-line proposal: unedited air time followed by a panel discussion. "If those terms were good enough for you to offer Westmoreland," *Inside Story* told CBS, "they're good enough for us to offer to you." The negotiations ended without Wallace appearing on *Inside Story*.

By the time those negotiations ended, the dispute between *Inside Story* and Wallace had long vanished from the newspapers, squeezed out by a much more important story concerning the controversy between Westmoreland and CBS. Five days after the Hodding Carter broadcast, on Tuesday, April 26, CBS complied with Judge Pierre Leval's order and turned over to Westmoreland's lawyers the Benjamin report.

20

The Benjamin Report

From the moment in early June that senior executive producer Burton "Bud" Benjamin agreed to conduct an internal investigation of "The Uncounted Enemy," reporters were told by CBS that the purpose of the inquiry was to examine the charges leveled by *TV Guide*. CBS reiterated the limited parameters of Benjamin's study in Sauter's April 26 written statement accompanying the release of Benjamin's fifty-nine-page report. "That report," said Sauter, "reflects on the findings of a relatively narrow inquiry, conducted over a short period of time, which basically focused on whether certain internal rules and procedures have been violated in the preparation of the documentary, as alleged by *TV Guide*. . . ."

Sauter's "basically focused" was a carefully chosen phrase. On page one of Benjamin's report he indicated that while examining *TV Guide's* charges was the *primary* focus of his investigation, it was not the *exclusive* focus. "The core of this report is a point-by-point examination of the charges leveled by *TV Guide*," he wrote. *"But it goes beyond that. It includes an examination of the charges made in the January 26, 1982, news conference called in Washington by Gen. William C. Westmoreland* [emphasis added]." Few reporters would note Benjamin's opening description of his mandate, embracing not only the allegations raised by *TV*

Guide but the charges of Westmoreland and his five supporters at the Army–Navy Club. During that press conference the thrust of the testimony had dealt not with the techniques used in making the documentary but the truth (or falsity) of the program's premise of a Westmoreland-led conspiracy. Benjamin defined his role in the examination as "reporter," as opposed to "judge, jury, prosecutor, or defense attorney. My aim," he said, "has been to get the facts."

Sauter's press release had emphasized that Benjamin's inquiry had been "conducted over a short period of time. . . ." It was clear, however, that the six-week investigation had been an exhaustive one. Benjamin and his pair of assistants had screened the broadcast repeatedly and interviewed thirty-two subjects (fourteen in person, eighteen by telephone). "While we read all of the unedited interviews for the broadcast, we did not screen the film of these interviews," Benjamin said. "Howard Stringer, the executive producer, and Andrew Lack, the senior producer, both expressed the view that we should screen these rushes. To do so would have delayed this report by several months, and I do not believe it would have changed the findings as far as the *TV Guide* charges are concerned."

Later, critics at CBS would fault Benjamin for deciding not to view the raw interview footage. It is difficult to understand, however, what light such screenings would have shed on his inquiry. In evaluating both the *TV Guide* allegations and charges made at the Westmoreland press conference, Benjamin was not judging whether or not witnesses were *convinced* but whether the evidence they had offered was *convincing*, because it had been honestly presented.

Benjamin listed eleven major charges from the *TV Guide* article, adding that "some of them contain subcharges, and so the overall total is higher." He dealt with each allegation in the order *TV Guide* had offered it, beginning with *TV Guide's* summary of the premise of the program. For comparison, Benjamin quoted the summary offered by George Crile in his White Paper: "that in 1967 American military and civilian intelligence discovered evidence indicating the existence of a dramatically larger enemy than previously reported; . . . that instead of alerting the country, United States military intelligence under General Westmoreland commenced to suppress and alter its intelligence reports in order to conceal this discovery from the American public, the Congress, and perhaps even the president."

"Now that I look at it [the statement in his own White Paper]," said Crile, "I would put a period after the words 'intelligence reports' and eliminate the rest of the sentence."

Apparently Crile was no longer convinced that he had proved that

United States military intelligence under Westmoreland had concealed the discovery of a larger enemy from the Congress, the American public, and the president.

Benjamin devoted almost four and a half pages of his report to discussing CBS's decision to discard the interview of Johnson Administration adviser Walt Rostow in its entirety. Crile, Wallace, Colloff, and Adams defended the decision. However, Howard Stringer told Benjamin that "in retrospect" he would have allowed air time for Rostow, "even though at the time they convinced me Rostow was wandering off target." Andy Lack said flatly that Rostow should have been included in the broadcast. Benjamin then took the Rostow incident a step further. "Walt Rostow," he wrote, "was considered the closest source on what the late president knew. Was there any thought of hearing from LBJ himself?" Benjamin recalled the series of interviews given by Johnson to CBS in 1969—interview programs which, although he did not mention it in the report, Benjamin himself had produced, with Stringer his researcher.

"Crile says that he had turned this over to researcher Alex Alben," wrote Benjamin. "Alben says he called the LBJ Library in Austin [Texas] and was told they didn't have any of the outtake film. The matter was apparently dropped.

"The film was in-house. 'They could have had a viewing cassette in two days,' says CBS News archivist Sam Suratt.' "

Ira Klein, of course, was prepared to testify that Alben had given him those outtakes—the "trims" of the film—to review and that Alben himself had a transcript of the program. Benjamin proceeded to quote five statements from President Johnson's interview that contradicted portions of the documentary.

Benjamin also devoted considerable space to a *TV Guide* allegation the Sauter memo had not even mentioned: that the McChristian-Hawkins briefing sequence misrepresented statements from both officers by combining their comments about three separate incidents into one pivotal meeting. Benjamin said, "From our reading of the unedited transcripts, there were clearly two meetings woven into one" and indicated the possibility of "the third meeting to which *TV Guide* refers."

Benjamin added, "Nowhere in his interview with Crile did McChristian say that any of his estimates were 'suppressed,' " nor, although "pressed repeatedly in his interview with Crile," did McChristian ever concede that his transfer was linked to enemy-strength estimates.

In an interview with Klein, Benjamin had revealed his uneasiness over Crile's use of hypothetical questions in some interviews. He had singled out the McChristian interview in particular, which began with a series of hypothetical questions, with no mention of Westmoreland. Subsequently Crile had inserted into the documentary answers to those "hypotheticals," making it seem as if McChristian were specifically commenting on Westmoreland's conduct. In his report Benjamin quoted this exchange from the McChristian interview:

> CRILE: In a time of war, when you're talking about enemy-strength estimates, what are you thinking, General McChristian, when you confront your responsibility?
>
> McCHRISTIAN: Well, I feel this way, that decision-making in time of war not only involves the lives of the people on the battlefield but involves the future liberty of your people at home, and that there's no place—and that's why the West Point motto has "honor" in it—there's no place for an officer in any executive department of government, much less the military, who cannot conduct his public duty honorably.

"This comes from the unedited transcript . . ." said Benjamin. "It is in answer to a hypothetical question continuing a whole series of hypothetical questions. . . . It is not an answer to a specific question about a specific action."

(Later, in an affidavit, McChristian would swear that he complained to Crile, two or three days after the broadcast aired, in a telephone conversation, that "I was upset with the way my reply to hypothetical questions had been edited.")

Sauter had also ignored *TV Guide*'s charge that CBS made it appear Col. George Hamscher was the head of the military delegation at the National Intelligence Estimates conferences in August 1967. "The juxtaposition of the lead and then Hamscher coming up on the screen gives the impression that he is the head of MACV," Benjamin agreed.

"Eight seconds later," Crile explained to Benjamin, "Hamscher is identified as one of the troubled members of the MACV delegation."

"The question should be asked," wrote Benjamin, "would not the head of the delegation also be one of the members?" Benjamin pointed out that Hamscher was "a light colonel stationed in Hawaii. He was not even a part of MACV. . . ."

Some of Benjamin's most pertinent comments would not find their way into his final report. Referring to Crile's white paper rebutting *TV Guide*, Benjamin would note that Crile's explanation of Sam Adams's rehearsal for his interview with Wallace was "not responsive." "If gave [sic] him questions and rehearsed," wrote Benjamin, "then his answers not spontaneous [sic] and unrehearsed."

"Questions to friendly witnesses are selected to support thesis," Benjamin noted. "Answers are similarly selected."

However, Benjamin also noted that "George Crile has been very forthcoming about supplying us with material—even material not beneficial to him."

Of *TV Guide's* allegation that Crile's superiors had not exercised proper supervision over the producer's work, in his final report Benjamin said that the magazine had "provided no supporting data to prove its charge." He said that "Roger Colloff went far beyond what a vice-president with extensive managerial functions normally does on a broadcast. . . ." Benjamin absolved senior producer Lack from any responsibility for the broadcast and said Mike Wallace told him he was not as "involved with the Vietnam broadcast as he is on *60 Minutes*," adding that Wallace was "hardly uninvolved. . . . He attended some screenings, adjudicated some creative disputes, and conducted four interviews for the broadcast. . . ." Benjamin neglected to discuss what role, if any, executive producer Howard Stringer had played in supervising the documentary.

Benjamin concluded his examination with a summary of the broadcast's eleven "principal flaws":

- The premise was obviously and historically controversial. There was an imbalance in presenting the two sides of the issue. For every McChristian there was a Davidson; for every Hawkins, a Morris; for every Allen, a Carver.
- A "conspiracy," given the accepted definition of the word, was not proved.
- The double interview of George Allen.
- The screening of interviews for Allen.
- Sam Adams not being properly identified as a *paid* consultant.
- Journalistic oversight which permitted two McChristian-Hawkins meetings to appear to be one meeting.
- Journalistic oversight which permitted General Westmoreland to discuss one meeting which was then cut into a sequence about another meeting.
- Other violations of CBS News guidelines.
- The coddling of sympathetic witnesses.
- The lack of journalistic enterprise in trying to find General Davidson or in checking out his "illness."

- Imprecisions in the handling of the Hamscher introduction and in the *Meet the Press* matter involving Westmoreland's "correction letter."

Having confirmed most of *TV Guide*'s allegations while flatly rejecting none of them, Benjamin added a crucial comment.

> . . . *TV Guide* may have been wise in not challenging the premise of the broadcast. It seems odd, to say the least, for the magazine to launch an attack of this dimension and still say of its investigation: "Its purpose was not to confirm or deny the existence of the 'conspiracy' that CBS's journalists say existed." The reason for that may be that even today military historians cannot tell you whether or not MACV "cooked the books" as the broadcast states. The flow of definitive information is painfully slow and may never be conclusive.

The implication was clear: If *TV Guide* had been wise in not challenging the premise of the broadcast, CBS would have been equally as wise had it not advanced that premise in the first place. Benjamin had concluded that the CBS premise was not only "not proved" but perhaps unprovable. CBS was in serious trouble.

Since mid-July, when Sauter made public his eight-page memo, the press had been avidly awaiting the Benjamin report on which Sauter's conclusions were ostensibly based. Demand for the fifty-nine-page document was so heavy, a spokesman told a reporter who telephoned late on the day of its release that CBS had had to order another printing. The next morning, Wednesday, April 27, newspapers across the country carried lengthy articles, many front-page, blaring Benjamin's revelations and conclusions. A few reporters felt that Benjamin had "nitpicked" the documentary to death, but the vast majority regarded Benjamin's study as the definitive verdict on the CBS documentary. If there had been lingering doubts about the allegations leveled at the documentary, the Benjamin report eliminated them.

For CBS, however, the report was far more than a public relations disaster. Van Gordon Sauter had been cited as a defendant in Westmoreland's lawsuit for repeating in his memo the "libelous" statements of the original broadcast. In ordering the release of the report, Judge Leval had said it "may well lead to evidence of degree of care for accuracy, concern for truthfulness, and possible bias, prejudgment, or malice. . . . If the Benjamin report does not say what the Sauter memorandum says it says," Leval had ruled, "it could be significant proof of malice or recklessness on CBS's part in issuing Sauter's statement. . . ." In sum, the Benjamin report and the Sauter memo had to be consistent with each other.

". . . I find a strong line of consistency between the memo and the report," Sauter told *Washington Post* television critic Tom Shales.

But was there a disparity? A comparison of the two documents revealed several:

1. Sauter's July 15 memo said there was "honest disagreement" over *TV Guide's* allegation that CBS tossed sympathetic witnesses soft questions. Benjamin stated flatly that there was a "coddling of sympathetic witnesses."

2. Sauter said, ". . . It would have been a better broadcast if it had not used the word 'conspiracy.' " He also said, "We now believe that a judgmental conclusion of conspiracy was inappropriate." However, Benjamin's critical assertion that the conspiracy "was not proved" was missing from Sauter's memo.

3. Sauter stated in his memo, "We do not believe the paid consultant [Sam Adams] was rehearsed for his interview." Benjamin said, "This charge . . . is open to question."

4. Regarding the Westmoreland "correction letter" and documents, Sauter stated, "It remains a judgmental decision whether a Westmoreland memorandum included within these documents would have served to clarify the general's position." Benjamin, in contrast, cited "imprecisions" in the way both Col. George Hamscher's introduction in the documentary and "the *Meet the Press* matter involving Westmoreland's 'correction letter' " were handled. Sauter made no reference in his memo to the Hamscher introduction, presumably lumping that topic plus the "300,000 ceiling" and Col. Everette Parkins's firing (all of which Benjamin dealt with in depth) among those allegations which were "either inconsequential or too subjective to judge with certainty."

5. In explaining why CBS, in the face of so many violations of its guidelines, continued to "support the substance of the broadcast," Sauter wrote in his memo that "seven retired military officers and a former CIA agent came forward on the broadcast to support the premise that these figures were intentionally manipulated. They presented compelling evidence that the enemy-strength figures had been distorted under pressure from more senior officers."

Benjamin, however, never suggested that CBS's on-camera witnesses had presented "compelling evidence"; indeed, although he offered no definitive judgments, in the sections of the report dealing with the Mc-Christian-Hawkins briefing, the 300,000 ceiling, and Parkins's alleged "firing," Benjamin's own investigation cast doubt on the accuracy of the scenarios CBS had constructed. Benjamin's only comment regarding the witnesses assembled by CBS to buttress its premise related to the difficulty of eliciting their testimony. "To get a group of high-ranking military men and former Central Intelligence agents to say that this is what happened [the military "cooked the books"] was an achievement of no small dimension. These were not fringe people but rather prototypical Americans." However, Benjamin did not venture an opinion on the validity of their testimony.

"The Benjamin report," Sauter emphasized to reporters after the document was released, "was one of several resources utilized in the evaluation of the broadcast reflected in my July 15 statement."

Two days before the Benjamin report was made public, CBS had convened a meeting in New York at which Sauter and the lawyers cautioned some of those involved in the controversy—including Crile, Wallace, and Lack—to avoid talking to the press about either the lawsuit or the Benjamin report itself. After the report was published, however, those at CBS who felt abused by Benjamin's study began quietly and anonymously to express their discontent to the press. Benjamin's report was accused of being "unfair" and "inaccurate." Soon criticism of Benjamin himself started surfacing. He was disparaged for being a "purist," "literal-minded," and "fundamentalist." His own "forte" was "historical documentaries"; he had "never produced the kind of controversial, ambitious piece that 'The Uncounted Enemy' was. . . ." It was true that none of Benjamin's documentaries had been "controversial" enough to generate a libel suit against CBS. However, as producer of the CBS series of documentaries that were aired for nine years under the banner of *20th Century*, Benjamin had proved himself adept in the use of eyewitness interviews, of which Crile's program was an assemblage. In fact, Bud Benjamin was largely credited with having adapted for television documentaries the use of "eyewitnesses" to authenticate a script's narration. No producer in all of television had credentials more formidable than Benjamin's. Nevertheless, it was not long before the criticism of Benjamin from within CBS became more explicit.

Wallace publicly rebuked Benjamin for not appreciating the degree of difficulty of Crile's assignment: convincing ex-military intelligence officers to come forward. "These men were not your traditional whistle-blowers," he told Connie Bruck of *The American Lawyer* magazine. "They were coming forward more in sorrow than in anger, and they had nothing to gain from it."

Crile disputed Benjamin's judgment that the broadcast lacked "fairness and balance" in terms of "people or time on camera." He argued that Benjamin's 8–2 ratio of supporters of the program's premise versus opponents was misleading because the eight supporters cited by Benjamin were members of the military and thus on Westmoreland's side. Benjamin, of course, had pointed out that, aside from Westmoreland and Danny Graham, only those military men (Cooley, McChristian, Meacham, McArthur, Hamscher, Hawkins) whose testimony could be used to support the premise had been put on camera.

In deposition, Howard Stringer would dismiss many of Benjamin's "principal flaws" as "technical violations" of the CBS standards. He did not agree with Benjamin's conclusion that the "conspiracy" was not proved. "I believe that the evidence in the broadcast was sufficient to give us reason to use the word in the context in which it was used," Stringer said, adding that ". . . good men disagree."

Stringer, Colloff, and CBS vice-president Chandler in their depositions tried to walk a tightrope, careful not to fix their seal of approval on Benjamin's "principal flaws" while avoiding any answer that might be construed as criticism of a respected colleague. Privately, though, within CBS, the report was causing turmoil. CBS executives, especially at the corporate level, were appalled by the revelations. Some urged that Crile be fired, but that option was discounted; if Crile were cut loose, CBS would no longer have any control over his comments. Crile had been arguing that he had done the documentary his superiors had commissioned him to do and that CBS shared responsibility for any of its flaws. Soon, however, an occasion arose which provided those who wanted Crile publicly reprimanded an expedient excuse to do so.

21

The McNamara Tapes

"**F**ROM THE BEGINNING," George Crile told a reporter, "the biggest mistake I made was not personally defending my own work. I held back because I was told by CBS News executives not to say anything. I had complete faith in the documentary and considered the *TV Guide* article so irresponsible that it did not occur to me that CBS would not attack the charges made. I should have launched a massive counterattack myself against *TV Guide*," Crile added, "which was compulsively guilty of all the things they accused us of by misrepresenting our transcripts and people they claimed to be quoting."

But the Benjamin report reinforced Crile's isolation. After reading the results of CBS's own internal investigation, few reporters were willing to listen to Crile's rebuttals. Most reporters were now convinced that serious violations of fairness and accuracy had been committed in the preparation of the program. While acknowledging in their stories that CBS still stood by "the substance" of the broadcast, they were leaving the debate over what actually had transpired in Vietnam to the lawyers.

During this period, increasingly Crile was physically isolated from CBS as well. He had been assigned to film a documentary on the Sandinista revolution in Nicaragua. Although CBS had already postponed indefinitely the Miami drug trade broadcast in which Crile had served as correspondent, there was speculation that CBS wanted to demonstrate that Crile could produce a flawless program on a controversial subject. CBS assigned a veteran documentarian to supervise Crile's work on the Nicaragua program, reviewing every inch of footage he brought back. Crile had already undertaken two trips to that troubled Central American country. He had returned from his first visit, CBS sources revealed, with some 65,000 feet of film. Still, after his footage was screened, he was sent back to Nicaragua to shoot more, accompanied by a new camera crew. By mid-June, after his second visit to Nicaragua, he had accumulated over 100,000 feet of film. CBS told him to return to Nicaragua a third time. CBS had scheduled the documentary for August when congressional debate over United States aid to Nicaraguan rebels fighting the Sandinista regime would be at its height. However, Crile's third journey to Nicaragua was destined to be indefinitely postponed. Instead, within a few weeks, Crile would be in limbo.

In September 1982 Capital Legal Foundation had formally asked CBS to surrender all copies of any audiotapes made for the Vietnam broadcast, and to identify and describe any that had been used and then reused or destroyed. The request was part of the sweeping discovery process, due to extend until December 31, 1983, by which the plaintiffs hoped to uncover documentary evidence of "actual malice." A few months later, in a conversation with Dan Burt, Ira Klein mentioned that Carolyne McDaniel had told him that Crile had taped interviews with ex-Secretary of Defense Robert M. McNamara. Klein told Burt that, at least four times, Carolyne had urged him to listen to the McNamara tapes, going so far as to tell him they were in Crile's bottom left-hand desk drawer. Klein had not listened to the tapes. He told Burt that he did not think Crile knew that Carolyne had listened to them.

In January, Burt asked David Boies if any such tapes of McNamara existed. Boies replied, Burt said later, that none had been made. On January 12 Burt wrote Boies a letter: "May I inquire as to whether or not you are certain that Mr. Crile did not tape-record any of his conversations with Mr. McNamara? While you have not furnished us with either copies or transcripts of any recordings of those interviews, we are concerned that such recordings and/or transcripts may nevertheless exist."

Boies did not answer Burt's letter. An associate of Burt's telephoned McNamara, who insisted that his conversations with Crile had been off the record and had definitely not been taped. Burt sat on the matter for almost six months. Then, on the morning of June 10, he telephoned Harriet Dorsen, an associate of Crile's counsel Victor Kovner. Burt reminded Dorsen of a telephone conversation Dorsen had had in January with Burt's associate Pat Embrey. According to Embrey, Dorsen had said then that no McNamara tapes were ever made. Following Burt's June 10 telephone call, Dorsen wrote him a letter, insisting that she had told Embrey that tapes *had* been made "of the prebroadcast conversations with Mr. McNamara and Mr. [Bernie] Gattozzi" but had, "to the best of [Crile's] knowledge, in the ordinary course of events, been reused or lost." Dorsen said she had told Embrey that "at the time the litigation began, when Mr. Crile assembled all of his files for his attorneys, these tapes no longer existed. . . ."

After talking to Dorsen, Burt telephoned David Boies. According to Burt, Boies said he did not know anything about any McNamara tapes. "Look," Burt recalled saying, "I am going to depose Carolyne McDaniel on that point. You'd better call her right now and find out what she knows." Burt added that Boies might be able to refresh McDaniel's memory if he reminded her that Crile had kept the tapes in the bottom left-hand drawer of his desk. Several hours later, said Burt, Boies called him back. There had been audiotapes, Boies said, but they had been inadvertently destroyed. Capital Legal Foundation lawyers spent the weekend of June 11–12 preparing a letter to Judge Leval, asserting that CBS had surreptitiously taped an interview with McNamara, later destroyed the tape, and then improperly concealed those facts in formal trial proceedings. Burt wrote in the letter to Leval that he believed "more than five" audiotapes of interviews had been made during the preparation of the broadcast and subsequently destroyed. He accused CBS and other defendants of supplying him "with false and misleading information concerning the materials destroyed."

Reached by reporters on Monday, June 13, Boies denied Burt's charge in the letter to Leval that the erasure of the audiotapes constituted "destruction of critical evidence," arguing that a McNamara tape and at least one other had been reused in the ordinary course of business. Boies also said he had never denied to Burt that McNamara had been taped.

The controversy over the tapes was further fueled on Tuesday when newspaper accounts across the country carried McNamara's angry reaction to the revelation that Crile had taped conversations with him. McNamara said it would have been "entirely unethical" if Crile had, as charged, made an audiotape, without his knowledge or consent, of what had been an off-the-record conversation. "I hope that isn't standard CBS practice," he added.

It was not *accepted* CBS practice. The CBS News Standards specifically prohibited any employee from taping telephone conversations without prior consent.

CBS furthered the controversy when its lawyers revealed that some of the "destroyed" tapes had suddenly been located. Boies told Judge Leval that Crile had found tapes he had made not only of interviews with McNamara but others as well. Crile had also taped conversations, almost all off the record, with former Under Secretary of State George Ball, former army Chief of Staff Gen. Matthew B. Ridgway, former United States delegate to the United Nations Arthur Goldberg, and others. The McNamara interview, Crile admitted, had indeed been recorded without McNamara's knowledge, even though the conversation was a confidential one.

McNamara was not the only one angered by Crile's surreptitious taping of conversations. Reportedly, William Paley was also enraged. Sources said that Paley himself contributed to a decision made at the highest levels of CBS on Wednesday, June 15. On that day CBS suspended George Crile, with pay, for taping conversations with McNamara and others without authorization. David Boies told the press that Crile had been "suspended from editorial responsibilities" for an indefinite period—an action, Boies added, which CBS viewed "as serious disciplinary reaction." Crile had not, however, been dismissed. CBS also released through Boies a statement apologizing to "a number of individuals" whom Crile had tape-recorded. The statement added that "while the appropriateness of such taping is debated within the journalistic community, it is forbidden by CBS News policy unless specifically authorized by the president of CBS News or his designee. In these instances such authorization was neither sought nor given."

That same Wednesday, in a sworn affidavit, Crile added the names of Lt. Bernie Gattozzi, Lt. Russell Cooley, and Brig. Gen. Winant K. Sidle to the list of taped telephone interviews. Crile said he had recorded the conversations with Goldberg, Ball, and Ridgway on the same cassette following the end of the McNamara telephone conversation and kept the tapes in his desk alongside other tapes. Meanwhile, he said, he was also using tapes from his desk on other assignments, including the interview with Ricardo Morales—the ex-CIA operative in Miami whose story he had thought might make a documentary—that had consumed thirty-eight cassettes. The Morales tapes he had stored "at home in a trunk with other materials which do not relate directly to any current projects at CBS." It was in that trunk, the previous weekend, Crile explained, that he had discovered "a tape containing part of the conversation with McNamara and the conversations with Ball, Ridgway, and Goldberg." He had located the Sidle tape "in a space behind one drawer" in his office at CBS. He said he had undertaken the search for tapes at the urging of his attorneys, who told him that Burt had said "a witness was prepared to testify that the [McNamara] tape was kept in the lower left drawer of my office desk." Concerning his suspension, Crile told *Washington Post* television critic Tom Shales, "I'm too stunned right now to know really what to think."

Crile was not the only one baffled by CBS's decision. The basis for the guideline against taping without prior permission was not an ethical caution but a legal one: State laws widely varied on the legality of telephone taping. However, in New York State, where Crile did his taping, recording calls without permission was not unlawful. With regard to the ethical issue, news organizations themselves could not agree on the propriety or impropriety of taping, wherever legal, without prior consent of the interviewee or a superior. Some reporters felt that taping an on-the-record telephone interview was the electronic equivalent of taking notes; they argued that as long as the subject did not ask to go off the record, the tools a reporter employed were his concern only. Taping, many insisted, produced a verbatim account of a conversation far more accurate than note taking. Others argued that reporters had the right to tape even off-the-record telephone conversations without telling a subject they were recording. The issue, then, they insisted, was not whether the information was recorded but whether the information was kept confidential. Telling a subject the conversation was being taped, they argued, might have a chilling effect, the equivalent of a policeman warning a suspect that anything he said might be used in court against him.

In contrast, the opponents of taping believed that not warning a subject he was being taped was an unnecessary deception—a kind of audio entrapment. Interviewees, they said, somehow had an inherent right to have their conversations with reporters recorded in a form which permitted them to change their minds or reevaluate their comments or even issue denials. In any case, there was a consensus that even reporters whose news organizations proscribed taping without prior permission regularly violated those internal guidelines. Many journalists suspected that CBS's suspension of Crile over what they regarded as a minor infraction of etiquette was merely masking an ulterior motive.

"We are very disappointed at CBS News management's overreaction to what is really a commonplace practice," said Crile's attorney Victor Kovner.

Five days after Crile was suspended, Burt deposed Carolyne McDaniel on the subject of the "surreptitious" audiotapes. She recalled that on the day of the McNamara taping, Crile had asked her to obtain for him a blank tape from the CBS stockroom, informing her that "he was going to tape the conversation with Mr. McNamara." She said that afterwards she was cleaning Crile's desk one day when she noticed the tape in a drawer. She listened to it, without asking Crile's permission beforehand. It was the only audiotape made for the broadcast to which she had listened, aside from tapes that Crile himself had given her to transcribe. She had played back the McNamara tape, she said, because NcNamara "had been a household word during my college days, and I was very curious about hearing Mr. McNamara in a private telephone conversation." She also confirmed that she had told Ira Klein she had listened to the tape. Klein had told Burt that McDaniel had "urged" him to listen to the tape, "at least four times."

> BURT: Did you urge Mr. Klein to listen to the tape?
> McDANIEL: No, I did not. I did not urge Mr. Klein to listen to the tape.
> BURT: Did you ask Mr. Klein to listen to the tape?
> McDANIEL: No, I did not ask Mr. Klein to listen to the tape.

Later:

> BURT: Ms. McDaniel, do you recall having mentioned the tape to anyone other than Mr. Klein?
> McDANIEL: You mean the existence of the tape?
> BURT: The existence of the tape.
> McDANIEL: I can't remember mentioning that to anyone other than Mr. Klein.

Burt asked her whether, on the McNamara tape, she had heard Mike Wallace's voice.

> McDANIEL: Again, keeping in mind that I jumped from place to place on the tape, I recall not hearing Mr. Wallace on the tape.
> BURT: Why did you jump from place to place on the tape when you listened to it?
> McDANIEL: Because it was not a particularly interesting interview.
> BURT: Even though you had not heard the tape before?
> McDANIEL: Correct. It was not interesting to me.

Burt believed the McNamara tape had interested McDaniel, that it contained material that did not support the program's thesis, and that

Crile had thus intentionally destroyed it. "Then why," he asked, springing the trap he had set, "did you mention it to Mr. Klein if it was uninteresting to you?"

McDaniel seemed suddenly uncertain, replying only that "in the context of whatever conversations we had, which I can't recall, it seemed an appropriate thing to do."

That afternoon Burt began an exhaustive interrogation of Crile on the same topic. During the deposition of McDaniel, Burt asked her how she had identified the tape in Crile's drawer as being the one with the McNamara conversation on it. "Did you read the tape, read the cassette housing?" he asked. "Yes," McDaniel replied. "Well, I read—I do not remember how it was labeled, but I remember I could identify it as the McNamara tape." Later in that same deposition, Burt asked McDaniel if she had read the labels of other tapes in Crile's desk. She replied that she had. "Can you recall what the labels said?" Burt asked. "No, I cannot," McDaniel replied, "other than the McNamara."

Burt raised with Crile the issue of how the McNamara tape was identified. Crile told Burt that he "apparently did not mark the cassette which included the conversations with George Ball, General Ridgway, and Arthur Goldberg, as well as Mr. McNamara. . . ."

The logical question was: How could McDaniel identify the McNamara tape if Crile had not marked it? Perhaps she heard another McNamara tape. The lawyers on both sides would save the contradictions and discrepancies that emerged in depositions for the trial itself.

Crile stated that his second conversation with McNamara had been recorded on two cassettes, but that he had been able to locate only the cassette that contained the end of that interview, followed by the interviews of the other ex-officials. Crile could not recall taking any notes of that McNamara conversation. Burt asked Crile why he taped that conversation with McNamara.

CRILE: I wanted to have as accurate a record as possible of the conversation.
BURT: Did you tape your in-person interview with Mr. McNamara?
CRILE: No.
BURT: Why did you not tape it?
CRILE: . . . I was using a notebook, and that seemed to be adequate for the task at the time.
BURT: When you taped Mr. McNamara's phone conversation, was there a notebook on your desk?
CRILE: I don't recall. I presume so.

BURT: Was there a pen on your desk.

CRILE: I don't recall.

BURT: Do you customarily work with a pen and paper on your desk, sir?

CRILE: There is customarily a pen and paper on or in my desk.

BURT: Then why did you decide to tape your phone conversation with Mr. McNamara rather than take notes?

CRILE: . . . I used the tape recorder as a backup in the event that Mr. McNamara might be talking faster than I could keep up with my pen and paper.

BURT: Did Mr. McNamara talk any faster on the phone than he did in person?

CRILE: I don't recall.

"When the McNamara tape issue arose," Crile told a reporter, "it looked like a new violation. My reputation already had taken a terrific beating, and with a huge lawsuit pending, CBS just preferred to keep me out of the public eye."

CBS was, indeed, intent on keeping Crile "out of the public eye." Crile's most recent violation of the CBS guidelines offered CBS an opportunity to resolve a troubling dilemma. Crile's documentary, "The Battle for Nicaragua," was still scheduled to air in August. It was clear that any broadcast about such a sensitive topic as the Sandinista regime in Nicaragua by so controversial a producer would only generate fresh controversy. On July 8 CBS killed the Nicaragua documentary, citing as its reason Crile's suspended status.

"What happens is that it goes into the scrap heap, to put it bluntly," said vice-president Bob Chandler. "George Crile is so totally intertwined in the thing, we can't very well place him on suspension and then use the material."

Crile told the *Los Angeles Times* that he was heartbroken over the decision. "I thought it was a terribly important project," he said. "I was trying to give people an understanding of what the government is that the Reagan Administration is opposing and what forces inside Nicaragua the CIA claims to be representing."

With his documentary junked, Crile was totally quarantined from the CBS editorial process.

Of course Crile and McDaniel were only two of many witnesses who, by the beginning of August, had been forced to endure exhaustive depositions presided over by one set of lawyers or the other. From CBS, Capital Legal Foundation had interrogated, along with Crile and McDaniel, Stringer, Colloff, and Wallace; plus George Allen, Sam Adams's ex-CIA boss. Cravath had deposed Westmoreland, General Godding, Colonel Morris, Lieutenant Gattozzi, and several military-intelligence analysts it felt could support the premise of the program.

The depositions themselves served several purposes, apart from simply eliciting new information. The lawyers conducting them endeavored to get on the record statements from witnesses which at trial, under cross-examination, could be compared with other testimony, yielding crucial contradictions. Using the metaphor of a bridge game, the depositions were opening bids calculated to force the opponent into prematurely showing his strong suits. Assertions by a witness that could be refuted by documents or other testimony already in a lawyer's possession were sometimes left unchallenged, saved for the trial itself. Meanwhile, witnesses at the pinnacle of their professional careers were regularly being struck dumb by early senescence, a sudden amnesia that often left them unable to recall, when pressed, anything much more substantive than their own names. "I don't recall" became a refrain that echoed over and over, not only in response to questions about momentous occasions but minutely trivial ones, too. The forgetfulness, of course, was a tactic. Each witness had usually been thoroughly prepared beforehand by his respective counsel. A journalist found it difficult to distinguish between this intensive preparation and a "rehearsal"; in the pretrial stage, spontaneity was something that both sides strived to avoid. An official record was being compiled. Reality would intervene only when, at trial, that record was tested in the crucible of cross-examination. In a sense the discovery process was a parody of the broadcast itself. The crucial difference was, in the closing act of this drama, it would be a federal judge and not CBS who decided what testimony should or should not be included. It would not be Mike Wallace versus Westmoreland, but David Boies versus Dan M. Burt.

Journalists familiar with the deposition process viewed it with undisguised cynicism. From time to time word filtered out of CBS that one or another of its executives felt depressed over having to corroborate every comma of the documentary. Many journalists privately sympathized with the dilemma. The prevalent notion, in some journalistic quarters, was that having to swear under oath that one was telling the truth was a perfectly legitimate excuse for evading it.

Yet the depositions were fascinating, not only for the occasional, if unintentional, admission on someone's part of a fact that seemed to confirm the argument of the plaintiff or of the defense, but for the hints of trial strategy that emerged. The burden, of course, was on Westmoreland to prove not only "actual malice" but that the alleged conspiracy had not occurred. CBS would argue that, despite its flaws, the documentary had been conceived and executed in "good faith" and that the conspiracy, whether or not proved in the documentary, had actually taken place. An additional CBS tactic surfaced during the deposition of Howard Stringer. Burt had asked Stringer for his recollection of the thesis of the broadcast.

STRINGER: . . . A conspiracy at the highest levels of military intelligence to suppress and alter critical intelligence.

BURT: Did this conspiracy to suppress and alter critical intelligence include General Westmoreland?

STRINGER: It was not so stated in the broadcast. I believe General Westmoreland is not a member of military intelligence.

Stringer went on to argue that "the thesis of the broadcast refers to what high-ranking intelligence officers did" and not to what Westmoreland did. General Westmoreland, he pointed out, was not a high-ranking intelligence officer.

BURT: I'm asking you to tell me whether you believe the broadcast suggests that General Westmoreland was part of a conspiracy to suppress any intelligence information with respect to troop strengths in Vietnam.

STRINGER: I do not believe the broadcast suggests that he was involved in the conspiracy—a word that is used only once and in reference only to a conspiracy at the highest levels of military intelligence.

Later:

BURT: Does the broadcast as a whole permit a reasonable person to conclude that Westmoreland was part of a conspiracy to suppress information on enemy-intelligence estimates?

STRINGER: . . . I do not believe reasonable people watching this broadcast would conclude that we said that General Westmoreland was part of any conspiracy.

Other CBS witnesses offered the same explanation of the thesis of the broadcast: The program had not accused Westmoreland of having participated in the conspiracy. Who, then, were the alleged conspirators—CBS's own on-camera witnesses: Cooley, Meacham, McArthur, Hawkins . . . nearly everyone except Westmoreland.

It was one thing to read that David Boies had told a magazine writer: " 'Westmoreland may find it difficult to prove that he was defamed by the program.' He [Boies] points out that the word 'conspiracy,' which was used only once in the program, was not tied to Westmoreland but to high military-intelligence officers." However, it was quite different to hear respected executives of television's most prestigious news division offering that argument. If the CBS executives were right, then almost every print and television reporter who had commented on the program had been fooled. So had the CBS executives themselves. Not one of them had ever attempted to correct a reporter's "misconception" about the Westmoreland-led conspiracy. Not one of them had ever suggested that the target of the program, the "chief sinner" (Sam Adams's phrase), was anyone other than Westmoreland himself. One could sympathize with the plight of men caught in a libel suit; one could understand why they might not be able to recall in deposition minor events that might prove embarrassing. It was more difficult to comprehend why, to serve a litigator's purpose, newsmen would so casually disregard logic.

Taking depositions from "hostile" witnesses was only one part of the complex discovery process. "Friendly" witnesses had to be interviewed as well, their comments edited by the lawyers into coherent sworn affidavits. The warring legal camps were also conscripting fresh recruits. Sam Adams was still a paid consultant to CBS, scouring the country, attempting to convince ex-military intelligence analysts and ex-CIA officials to support the documentary in court. CBS had leased a room for Adams at New York's Plaza Hotel. He had an expense account. He was still taking notes for his epic Vietnam tome. Cravath was sending out safaris of four or five lawyers at a time; Capital Legal Foundation had a lone lawyer or two on the same mission. The process was tedious and costly. Ex-officials had to be located, then lured into the controversy, reassured that their testimony was indispensable. When the offer of the carrot was rebuffed, there was always the stick. Looming over them all was the threat of a subpoena compelling them to cooperate if they refused to do so voluntarily.

However, the search for testimony to document each side's case was no more critical than the quest for documents themselves. In particular, unearthing documents was crucial to the Capital Legal Foundation. The burden rested on Westmoreland to demonstrate that the alleged "conspiracy" did not occur. In order to refute that CBS charge, Burt and his attorneys would have to reconstruct what did transpire. Using the Freedom of Information Act as a lever, Capital Legal Foundation was prying open file cabinets abandoned in government warehouses since the Vietnam War, seeking physical evidence from the army, the CIA, and the DIA. CBS, too, was engaged in a massive search for cables, memos, and reports. Cravath was particularly eager to locate any scrap that could substantiate the documentary's charge that Westmoreland had imposed an artificial ceiling on enemy-troop strengths. If Cravath could find cables confirming that allegation, Westmoreland's lawyers would be hard pressed to prove there had been no conspiracy. Late in August, CBS obtained a document that almost convinced Dan Burt to quit the case.

It was a constant struggle to dredge up the funds Capital Legal Foundation needed to pursue its discovery of evidence. Recently Burt had begun to delegate to his associate counsel David Dorsen (a cousin of Kovner associate Harriet Dorsen) the task of deposing witnesses while he canvassed for money. Now, suddenly, his concerns had been compounded by a document that the CIA had delivered to CBS. CBS's lawyers were telephoning reporters, telling them that CBS had in its possession a cable proving the charge that Westmoreland had conspired to suppress information on enemy-troop strength. Around 5:00 P.M. on Tuesday, August 23, Mike Wallace had personally telephoned *New York Times* editor Abe Rosenthal to tell him that CBS had found "the smoking gun."

Dated September 10, 1967, the cable did indeed seem devastating to Westmoreland's case. It was from George Carver to his superior, CIA Director Richard Helms, summing up the status of Carver's Saigon trip to resolve the differences over enemy strength that had kept the CIA and the military at loggerheads in the Order of Battle conferences that summer. "So far," wrote Carver, "our mission frustratingly unproductive, since MACV stonewalling, obviously under orders. Unless or until I can persuade Westmoreland to amend those orders," Carver added, "serious discussion of evidence or substantive issues will be impossible."

Carver recounted for Helms the litany of difficulties his CIA delegation, which included Sam Adams, had faced since arriving in Saigon on September 8. On September 9 General Davidson and his staff had devoted the entire day to a briefing on the military's estimate, "which widened rather than narrowed our differences," Carver said. The briefing continued the following day, but Carver said his attempts "to clear the atmosphere" all failed. "My remarks seemed well received but had no influence on the behavior of General Davidson and his subordinates."

Carver summed up those first three days in Saigon: "Variety of circumstantial indicators . . . all point to inescapable conclusion *that General*

Westmoreland (with Komer's encouragement) has given instruction tantamount to direct order that VC strength total will not exceed 300,000 *ceiling* [emphasis added]. . . . This order obviously makes it impossible for MACV to engage in serious meaningful discussion of evidence of our real substantive disagreements, which I strongly suspect are negligible."

Carver said that he hoped to meet with special ambassador Komer and Westmoreland on September 11, when he would "endeavor to loosen this straightjacket. Unless I can, we are wasting our time," he added. "If I can budge Westmoreland, this whole matter can be resolved to everyone's satisfaction in a few hours of serious discussion. If I cannot, no agreement is possible."

Carver's statement that all indications "point to inescapable conclusion that General Westmoreland . . . has given instruction tantamount to direct order that VC strength total will not exceed 300,000 ceiling" was crushing. It was an unmistakable echo of the broadcast's premise, this time uttered not by CBS's paid consultant Sam Adams nor by his ex-supervisor George Allen, but by the CIA official whom Westmoreland's lawyers regarded as a star witness in their behalf. When Burt heard the contents of that cable, he was stunned. If CBS had "the smoking gun," he would have to bite the bullet. He tried to contact Carver. Carver was away from Washington, in Portland, Oregon; he could not be reached. While Burt's associates were attempting to learn more about the cable from CBS, Burt arranged a meeting with Westmoreland. He was considering telling the general that he could no longer, in good conscience, serve as his attorney. By the time Burt met with Westmoreland, however, Capital Legal Foundation had ascertained that the cable was only the first of a series of five that had been turned over to CBS. However, it was hard to imagine that anything contained in the other four could mitigate the damage done by the cable CBS was releasing to the press.

The meeting between Westmoreland and Burt was an intense and emotional one. Westmoreland, Burt said later, was "heartbroken" when Burt informed him he was considering quitting the case. As the confrontation wore on, though, Burt began to have second thoughts. The distraught Westmoreland insisted over and over that he had not imposed any such ceiling. The meeting ended. Burt was wavering; perhaps Westmoreland was deluding himself, but clearly *in his mind* there had been no artificial limitation on the size of the enemy. By then Capital Legal Foundation had obtained the other four cables.

The second pair of cables from Carver to Helms, both dated September 12, offered Burt scant encouragement. One was the text of a joint assessment by analysts from Washington-based intelligence organizations of enemy strength. (The representatives of three Washington-based agencies who had traveled to Saigon had met to formulate a unified position in opposition to MACV.) In the other cable George Carver reviewed for CIA Director Helms the events of September 11 and 12, which he said were "full of action and behind-scenes scurrying in MACV, but have produced little movement. At present we are at an impasse. . . ." Adams had managed to get the military's guerilla figures "appreciably raised." But when Carver "stressed that our substantive differences were probably not great and could swiftly be resolved if we could proceed [to estimate] category by category, without any weather-eye on the total," General Davidson had "angrily accused me of impugning his integrity, since he had assured me he had no predetermined total. . . ." The implication to Carver was that Davidson indeed had within his head a ceiling which the military would not exceed. Carver was pessimistic that the stalemate could be resolved. "We have reservations for Thursday, September 14 (putting us in Washington September 17) . . ." he told Helms. The probable final meeting in a mission seemingly foredoomed to failure was scheduled for September 13, when Carver and Westmoreland would sit down face-to-face for the first time.

Nothing in the first three cables could have prepared Helms for the message he received from Carver dated September 13. "Circle now squared," the elated Carver began, "chiefly as a result of Westmoreland session (and perhaps Komer dinner). We now have agreed set of figures Westmoreland endorses. Mission seems on verge of successful conclusion, though final Ts to be crossed tomorrow."

Carver explained to Helms how the day had begun on a depressing note. "On morning September 13," he wrote, "General Davidson advised me Westmoreland meeting would do nothing but formalize our impasse since Westmoreland would not accept our position."

Before the face-to-face conference with Westmoreland, Carver met with General Davidson, Westmoreland's deputy Gen. Creighton Abrams, plus special ambassador Komer and General Sidle. This gathering began, Carver reported, with Davidson giving a "rather biased account of proceedings, noting our impasse on figures, saying he thought our paragraph written to avoid quantifying irregulars unacceptable and outlining his draft cable by which General Westmoreland could advise General Wheeler (chairman of the Joint Chiefs of Staff) of our inability to agree."

Komer had insisted previously that in the final estimate no specific numbers should be assigned to the shadowy Self-Defense categories of the enemy "on the grounds," Carver had told Helms, "that the press would add all figures together and, hence, quantifying the irregulars would produce a politically unacceptable total over 400,000." Now Davidson was saying that the paragraph Carver had written describing the SD and SSD was unacceptable. Komer followed Davidson, recommending acceptance of the military's position but "acknowledging logic in some of Washington's views." Thus, by the time that conference ended, nothing had transpired to suggest that Davidson's warning that morning had been anything but prescient. Still, Carver had to carry the charade to its climax. He proceeded to meet alone with Westmoreland himself.

Carver outlined his case for Westmoreland, reviewing "history and context whole estimate, the Saigon discussions, and the rationale behind each of the joint Washington representative figures. . . ." He "also took up quantification paragraph, indicating that Davidson had quoted out of context and showing way we thought it met both Washington and MACV needs. . . ."

Then Carver awaited Westmoreland's response, convinced that Westmoreland would merely rubber-stamp Davidson's obstinate rejection of the CIA's proposals. Thus Carver was astonished when, instead of agreeing with Davidson, Westmoreland agreed with him. "Westmoreland most cordial and receptive," wrote Carver in that fourth cable. "Said he agrees with most of my observations and could see the clear logic behind both sets of figures, which were really not that far apart." Westmoreland also saw the CIA's rationale behind the quantification paragraph, which Davidson had so vehemently opposed. He "had no problems with it, though he would want to take a final look at it in writing. . . ." Westmoreland asked Carver to arrange a meeting between the Washington-based and Saigon-based analysts "to review the evidence once again and see if we could resolve our differences." Carver told Helms that at the meeting of the two opposing teams of analysts he "took Westmoreland at his word, usurped the chair, and announced that all constraints on totals were off, and we could settle down to serious discussions of evidence and issues." After four hours of "brisk discussion" Carver emerged with an agreed set of figures, which Westmoreland promptly endorsed. "On the whole," wrote Carver, "I think we can live quite comfortably with the above figures. . . ."

Carver had begun the series of cables to Helms convinced that the military was operating under a ceiling imposed by Westmoreland. The morning of that decisive Carver-Westmoreland meeting, Davidson, the chief of intelligence, had advised Carver that the Westmoreland session "would do nothing but formalize" the impasse, "since Westmoreland would not accept our position." However, in a face-to-face private meeting, after personally evaluating Carver's analysis Westmoreland had rejected the recommendation of his own intelligence chief and had re-moved all obstacles blocking a compromise. If anything, a reading of the text of the *five* Carver cables (the fifth, written September 14, confirmed the previous day's accords) instead of only the *first* tended to exonerate rather than convict Westmoreland of the CBS charge. If there had been "stonewalling," as Carver indicated in his first cable, all it had taken was a meeting with Westmoreland himself to end it. Reporters to whom CBS had sent the first cable but not the other four felt deceived. "Circle now squared," Carver had begun the fourth cable. Indeed. The "smoking gun" had spun a full cycle and was now aimed squarely at CBS.

22

The
Truth
Defense

IN EARLY OCTOBER, Dan Burt released to the press the letter that Sam Adams had written to Col. Gains Hawkins shortly before the broadcast, revealing that the documentary had "a major problem" in seeming "to pin the rap on General Westmoreland." Burt cited Adams's criticism of the program as a crucial proof of "actual malice": Adams, he said, "didn't believe the broadcast was accurate" before it aired. "He was their consultant," added Burt, "the man they turned to for much of the story. He had a responsibility to advise them accurately."

On October 14 Burt was blessed with another bonanza. Judge Leval ordered CBS to turn over to Capital Legal Foundation the notes Bud Benjamin had used to prepare his report. A week later Cravath's David Boies asked Judge Leval to reconsider. Leval did, deciding that instead of handing over Benjamin's papers *carte blanche* to Capital Legal Foundation, CBS should submit to the court each item for which it asserted a First Amendment protection with an explanation in writing why such a privilege was justified. Rather than assert a privilege for each individual item, Cravath began sending to Capital Legal Foundation any documents it did not intend to deliver to Judge Leval.

Among the first batch of liberated Benjamin "notes" was a pair of volatile memos: Crile's irate June 1982 letter to Wallace complaining about the Benjamin investigation and the lack of support he was receiving from Benjamin, Van Gordon Sauter, and Howard Stringer; and Adams's letter to Crile revealing that shortly after the Westmoreland press conference he had informed Wallace of the documentary's major problem. Meanwhile, Burt was seeking an extension of the pretrial "discovery" process. At the beginning of November, Leval granted him an additional two months, until December 31. (It was later extended to February 28, 1984.) Then, probably in the summer of 1984, CBS would file a motion asking Judge Leval to dismiss the case in a summary judgment. Both sides would argue before the judge, who would then decide whether there was sufficient evidence of "reckless disregard of the truth" on CBS's part to warrant a jury trial. The summary judgment motion would be absolutely critical for both legal camps. David Boies knew that the vast majority of libel suits against the media were dismissed in summary judgment; Dan Burt knew that those libel suits against the media that did survive summary judgment often resulted, in trial, in favorable decisions for the plaintiffs.

Throughout the fall, with the summary judgment looming ahead, the pace of the attorneys' preparations was quickening. The focus of both law teams' efforts was increasingly on "truth," an absolute defense in a libel proceeding initiated by a public figure. Bud Benjamin's conclusion that CBS had "not proved" its charge of conspiracy in the program was not germane to the truth defense. All that mattered, in regard to the truth defense, was whether or not the alleged conspiracy had actually occurred. If Capital Legal Foundation could not prove the negative, Westmoreland's complaint would be dismissed. Cravath's task was to frustrate Westmoreland by papering over with persuasive arguments the documentary's glaring omissions and misrepresentations.

It was late afternoon on a Thursday in the middle of November. Outside the office building towering over Chase Manhattan Plaza in New York's Wall Street financial district, a torrential rain was transforming sewer-stopped streets into canals. Gusts of wind were mugging the unfurled umbrellas of pedestrians sprinting toward the subways. The wind whipped sheets of rain downward while lifting off carelessly fitted hats. Fifty-seven stories above the torrent and the torment, however, the massive, multitiered office of Cravath, Swaine & Moore was the eye of a hurricane—cool, dry, hermetically insulated.

Compared to Cravath, Dan Burt's Capital Legal Foundation (set in a once-proud Washington, D.C., neighborhood that turned seedy and unsafe at nightfall) was vodka poured out in a paper cup. Cravath was a smooth sherry served in a glass whose fragile-seeming stem could not be shattered by a sledgehammer. The reception room, with a warren of corridors wending off at odd angles, was a museum of delicately carved furniture arranged in sparse elegance. Thick carpets muffled even the soft-spoken comments of employees padding by. Dan Burt could not have lasted a day at Cravath. His furious energy, which turned the offices of Capital Legal Foundation electric, would have been considered a violation of Cravath's drawing-room decorum. Burt's impatient shouts, sometimes turning his female staffers to tears, would have been silenced by some senior Cravath partner's raised eyebrow. Burt was the strutting, posturing warlord over a band of legal guerillas; Cravath was the Royal Horse Guard, its attorneys handpicked from the most prestigious law schools. It was David versus Goliath, and on this day Cravath had suffered a casualty.

That afternoon Capital Legal Foundation had deposed Mike Wallace. Earlier, in April, Wallace had been questioned for two days, but then his interrogator had been Burt's associate, attorney David Dorsen. Now for the first time Wallace had faced Burt, and in the battle of wits Burt had wounded Wallace. Wallace had told Burt that during his interview with Bud Benjamin he had discussed the definition of the word "conspiracy," arguing to Benjamin that the word did not necessarily connote an unlawful act. Benjamin's dictionary definition of "conspiracy" used words such as "illegal," "treasonable," "treacherous," "crime," and "fraud."

However, in the deposition that afternoon Wallace admitted to Burt that if *Benjamin's* definition was the yardstick, the program's conspiracy allegation had not been proved. Wallace's comments distressed Cravath's attorneys. Now, after Wallace's admission, at trial Burt could ask a jury to decide whether or not CBS's "conspiracy" charge implied unlawful activity. If that was the case, then not only Benjamin but Wallace, too, was on record as having stated that CBS had not proved the premise of its program. Boies attempted to lead Wallace back over that same cratered path, trying to coax him into amending the damaging statements.

Several hours later, Boies was sitting in his spacious office, strain and fatigue in his face. But while this particular day had been as dark as the slate-gray sky beyond his fifty-seventh-floor window, Boies had had his moments in the sun. Here were some of those brighter moments:

COL. GAINS HAWKINS: . . . if you picked up something you couldn't ignore, you had to take something out. It could not go over 300,000.

PIKE COMMITTEE INVESTIGATOR GREG RUSHFORD: I believe the
military knowingly disseminated false information. . . . I think it
is reasonable to conclude there was a conspiracy.

CAPT. KELLY ROBINSON: The reductions were arbitrary and not justified by the available evidence.

MAJR. JOHN BARRIE WILLIAMS: . . . the numbers were played with.

COL. GEORGE HAMSCHER: The term ceiling was used, and it seemed
very clear to me and everybody else that it was in fact General
Westmoreland who had set the ceiling.

Boies had been as resourceful at extracting allegations in defense of the
documentary as Burt had been in locating officials eager to rebut the
program. The question was, had Boies found the hard evidence needed to
transform these opinions into fact?

Of all the depositions he and his subordinates had taken so far, Boies's
most significant triumph had come during the testimony of Gen. George
Godding. Godding, head of the military delegation to the conference
held in August 1967, had allegedly defended there a total of slightly more
than 297,000 enemy, including approximately 39,000 political cadre.
However, Boies had introduced a cable from the CIA's George Carver to
his superior Richard Helms written a month or so *before* Godding had left
for those August meetings, indicating that the military's actual estimate of
political cadre was slightly more than double Godding's figure. Why,
Boies had demanded from Godding time and time again, hadn't anyone
informed *him* that the numbers he was defending were outdated? Godding had not been able to explain the discrepancy.

"Either Godding was told and he's lying about it now to protect himself," Boies was telling a reporter in his office that Thursday, "or he wasn't
told, which means for some reason they were cutting him out. There's no
innocent explanation," Boies added, "of why they didn't tell the head of
the delegation."

Following the deposition, Burt had obtained from Godding an affidavit
"correcting" some of those inconsistencies. In that affidavit Godding
claimed to have been misled by the Order of Battle documents Boies had
thrust in front of him, supplying answers to Boies's questions "by deduction and not by recollection." In fact, Burt insisted, contemporaneous
documents indeed suggest that Godding had been confused during the
deposition. A "viewgraph" (a chart displayed from a slide projector) existed, demonstrating the exact figures Col. Gains Hawkins had actually
used at that August meeting to defend the military's case. It clearly
showed that the military had increased its estimate of political cadre from
39,000 to a range of 83,000 to 92,000.

Yet Boies cited Godding's testimony as an example of the kind of evidence Cravath was seeking. "What we will be doing in terms of the 'truth defense' is attempting to show that this was not an honest disagreement among reasonable men," he explained, "but it was a conscious and knowing deception. If you buy, for example, what was said at the Westmoreland press conference," he added, "you had honest people reaching different conclusions, and that is not what the broadcast said. What the broadcast said is that it was dishonest people reaching dishonest conclusions for political purposes."

To Boies the post-Tet letters written in March 1968 by Comdr. James Meacham to his wife were also strong supporting evidence of manipulation and falsification. Typical of the Meacham letters, two of which had been excerpted in the broadcast, was this passage: "The types from DIA were here and badgered me endlessly trying to pry the truth from my sealed lips. They smell a rat but don't really know where to look for it. They know we are falsifying the figures but can't figure out which ones and how."

Recently Meacham had signed a sworn affidavit in behalf of Westmoreland stating that the program's conspiracy charge was false—and that he had told Adams and Crile it was false before his CBS interview. He stated that his "numerical estimates of enemy strength took only a few days each month." The rest of the time he devoted to producing other sorts of studies. He reaffirmed that his letters had dealt mostly with studies not involving Order of Battle numbers adding, "my letters expressed my frustration at having to do work (such as some of our studies) that I thought was silly, or a waste of time; they expressed my pessimism about the war; they expressed my personal dislike for some of my superiors. . . . I never intended that the harsh language in those letters be taken literally." Indeed, Lt. Russell Cooley, Meacham's subordinate, and a CBS supporter, warned Crile both in his CBS interview and a subsequent telephone conversation not to place too much emphasis on the dramatic, menacing tone of many of Meacham's letters. "That's Shakespearean drama," Cooley told Crile in the telephone conversation. "He was that way throughout the whole tour. Nothing was ever right for him over there; he never liked anything or anybody. Thus—these grand words. You know: 'The imperialist war machine has done it again.'" Boies was arguing that the letters had become an embarrassment to Meacham, the military correspondent for the *Economist* magazine, and that "he just wanted to run away from [them] as far and as fast as he could." However, the fact was that Meacham had also been the military correspondent of the *Economist* at the time he had asked his ex-wife to give Sam Adams the letters for Adams's in-progress book on Vietnam. Furthermore, there was nothing in Meacham's sworn affidavit that contradicted anything he said in his interview with *TV Guide*—or, for that matter, in his on-camera interview with CBS. Boies would attempt to support Crile's interpretation of the Meacham letters and refute Meacham's own explanation by buttressing the defense with testimony from other ex-military officers.

In late December, both legal teams held press conferences 20 minutes apart, in the same Washington, D.C., hotel, disbursing to the press bulky packets containing sworn affidavits each had collected. Along with testimony from CBS on-camera witness George Allen, Cravath now had statements from two other ex-CIA officials. Richard Kovar, a 30-year CIA veteran who from 1962 to 68 was on the executive staff of the CIA's Deputy Director for Intelligence, said he found himself, during the CBS broadcast, "cheering aloud much of the time and wanting to weep the rest of the time. For the very first time," he added, "I realized with painful clarity that what we had all been involved in was not some abstract academic process but a train of truth versus falsehood that led directly to the debacle of the Tet offensive." Another former CIA official, John Moore, stated that he had "become convinced that there was a conspiracy or cover-up among various elements of the intelligence community, including persons from MACV, CIA, and DIA, to distort and to suppress intelligence information" prior to the enemy's Tet attack. Moore added that he had left the CIA in 1970 "because I could no longer stand being in a bureaucracy which was lying to our government and public."

However, no matter how honest or heartfelt their belief in the premise of the CBS program, the fact was that neither Kovar nor Moore had first-hand knowledge of the events described in the documentary; they were not "players," in the sense that Sam Adams and George Carver were; they were steps removed even from the vantage point of Carver's deputy George Allen, who had characterized his own role as "peripheral." Far more relevant to the truth or falsehood of the CBS conspiracy premise were the affidavits CBS had taken from Saigon-based military intelligence analysts, some of them convinced that Westmoreland's intelligence command—particularly Danny Graham—had engaged in arbitrarily suppressing projections of enemy strength in order to keep the total estimate artificially low.

In a sense, in fact, Cravath was expanding CBS's case by extending the methodology of the documentary itself, compiling comments and documentation confirming that certain officials *below* the actual command level were convinced that some sort of deception involving enemy-strength estimates had occurred. Burt would parry the testimony of CBS's lower-ranking military men with contrary assertions by their superiors, some of whom CBS had interviewed but had not asked to go on camera. Burt's witnesses would insist that no such deception had ever taken place; like Meacham, some would swear that they had told Adams and Crile that there had been no conspiracy. By December, four of the documentary's "pro-conspiracy" witnesses—McChristian, Meacham, Hamscher, and Parkins—had sworn under oath that they did not believe in the conspiracy.

In the documentary, CBS had neglected most of the high-ranking officials who had actually made the decisions about which CBS's own on-camera whistle-blowers had no first-hand knowledge. Similarly, David Boies would be offering few decision makers in CBS's behalf. Virtually everyone who actually participated in the decisions taken in 1967 and 1968 was going to testify in behalf of Westmoreland. Dan Burt's stack of affidavits would surely be sought after for, if nothing else, the value of their signatures to future autograph collectors. Among those who signed affidavits denying the premise of the program were ex-CIA Directors Richard Helms and William Colby; ex-Secretary of State Dean Rusk; ex-Johnson adviser McGeorge Bundy; and, most crucial, ex-Secretary of Defense Robert McNamara. All had expressed their willingness to testify for the plaintiff at trial. Colby had called the Adams-led "attempt to quantify every element of the Communist threat in South Vietnam . . . foolish and futile. There was a general belief among people at CIA that Mr. Adams had taken a legitimate dispute among members of the intelligence community and distorted it," he added. Rusk said he depended not on one source of intelligence but on a whole array of reports that crossed his desk each morning. He had been "aware that within the military itself there were different views on the strength, capabilities, and intentions of the North Vietnamese and Vietcong forces. I was also aware that among the various institutions and individuals supplying intelligence information" there were differing views. "In the summer and fall of 1967," he added, "I was generally aware" that the military "and the CIA differed in their interpretation of intelligence information . . . especially about the strength and composition of the Communist forces in Vietnam."

Robert McNamara was the ex-Secretary of Defense to whom Westmoreland had reported. In a sworn affidavit, McNamara testified that he had told Crile during an interview that the CIA-military debate had not been about the size of the enemy, but about which categories of the enemy should be included as part of the military threat. McNamara stated that, during the period being examined, he was briefed regularly by the military, and weekly (every Monday) by the CIA's George Carver, on intelligence in general and the Order of Battle debate in particular. "It is inconceivable to me" that the military "arbitrarily reduced estimates of enemy strength as a result of this or any other debate," said McNamara. He called Westmoreland an "honorable man of the highest integrity" who "served his president and his country honorably and honestly." McNamara said he was prepared to testify in Westmoreland's behalf at trial.

However, Burt would be relying as much on documentation as on testimony. Capital Legal Foundation's exhaustive search, primarily through the Freedom of Information Act (which could have yielded the same data to George Crile) had turned up documents that put in doubt the charges leveled in the broadcast. CBS's dilemma was summed up in the argument over the Helms "cave in" cable.

Thomas Powers, in his biography of Richard Helms, *The Man Who Kept the Secrets*, reported that on September 11, 1967, Helms had sent a cable to Carver ordering him, at any cost, to reach an agreement with Westmoreland—effectively telling him to "cave in" to the military's demands. Powers had interviewed Helms, but according to Helms's sworn affidavit, had not asked about such a cable. Sam Adams had been Powers's primary source about that cable. Adams had also told Crile about the cable; George Allen, in a deposition, had indicated that such an order had been given. Furthermore, Boies had obtained from a longtime CIA official named Richard Kovar an affidavit which stipulated, according to Boies, "that he [Kovar] did not personally see the cable, but he knows of the cable, and that everybody at that point knew what the instructions were. . . ." However, Boies added, "We don't have that cable." In early November 1983, Boies had taken a deposition at the CIA during which, he said, "the CIA people testified that when Helms left office he threw away all his cables."

While Helms may have disposed of his cable originals before he left office, copies of many of them still existed at the CIA. CBS and Burt both had in their possession Helms's responses to the cables Carver had sent from Saigon in September charting the military's change of heart from early obstinacy to easy agreement, once Carver had met face-to-face with Westmoreland alone. In none of those responses to Carver's cables did Helms issue any instruction remotely resembling an order to reach an agreement. In fact, Helms's cable to Carver dated September 11—the date of the alleged "cave in" order—merely said, "Agree you should remain until you have had session with both Westmoreland and Komer. Please let me know outcome, and please clear with me your departure from Saigon. In other words, team should not, repeat not, leave for Washington until we give approval." He gave Carver that approval two days later.

Thus Boies had no cave-in cable, relying instead on the testimony that one had existed of three ex-CIA officials—Kovar, Allen, and Adams, none of whom had ever seen the alleged cable, nor were in a position to know firsthand any of Helms's decisions. Burt, in contrast, had the series of Helms's replies to Carver, none of which even hinted at any instruction to cave in. And Burt had something else: He had an affidavit from Helms swearing that he did not recall sending such a cable or issuing such an order, and testimony under oath from Carver swearing that he had never received such a cable or any such order. Nevertheless, Westmoreland's burden still remained: As the plaintiff in the libel suit he would have to prove first to the judge and then to the jury that the premise of the CBS program was false.

In his July 15 memo Van Gordon Sauter had conceded that the use of the word "conspiracy" in the broadcast had been "inappropriate"; in his fifty-nine-page report Bud Benjamin had concluded that in the documentary "a conspiracy, given the accepted definition of the word, was not proved." But even if CBS had failed to prove its premise, historically was the charge nevertheless true? In part the answer depended on the premise of that CBS broadcast. What was that premise?

"The question of whether Westmoreland is the subject of the defamation depends on what the broadcast says," said David Boies. "I think the broadcast, insofar as it relates to the substance of the issue, was a very very cautious one. I think the broadcast did not nearly go so far involving Westmoreland as the evidence would have supported, so that I think it is quite consistent to argue that Westmoreland was *not* specifically singled out with respect to the conspiracy charge in the broadcast sufficiently to allow him to sue for defamation," Boies added, "and at the same time, even if he were, the evidence establishes the factual truth that he *was* involved."

If Boies was correct and the broadcast did not include Westmoreland as part of the conspiracy, then why did hundreds of reporters write that the premise was a Westmoreland-led conspiracy? Boies offered the explanation that most of those reporters had never seen the broadcast itself but merely parroted allegations made by others. Boies's argument might impress a court. "There is a difference," he rightly pointed out, "between what [a plaintiff] has to prove in a libel case and what he has to do to satisfy a responsible reporter." The problem was, those reporters who did see the broadcast before they wrote about it assumed that Westmoreland was the target of the CBS investigation. For example, Peter Braestrup published his *Washington Journalism Review* article while the *TV Guide* writers were completing theirs, yet the perception of the CBS premise was the same: a Westmoreland-led conspiracy. Besides, a television documentary is more than the sum of the words in its script; Westmoreland was the glue that bound the program's sequences together. Every decision was laid at his doorstep; Wallace's verbal accusing finger was always wagging in Westmoreland's face. Wallace's admonition to Westmoreland that he bore responsibility for whatever had occurred during his "watch" merely reinforced a premise viewers had already absorbed from the images on their screens: witnesses leveling charge after charge and Westmoreland having to defend himself against the accusations. The high-ranking military intelligence officers to whom the documentary's tease referred were not humble peons in the military pecking order, such as Lt. Col. Russell Cooley and Lt. Richard McArthur, but the commanders of the two military intelligence departments, Col. Charles Morris and Lt. Gen.— then-Lt. Col.—Danny Graham, their superior, chief of intelligence Gen. Philip Davidson—and the supreme commander, Westmoreland himself. The documentary *did* charge Westmoreland with engineering a conspiracy to suppress and alter the size and nature of the enemy, through his intelligence directorate. The question was: Did the evidence support that charge?

"Did the president of the United States not know of the controversy?" Hodding Carter asked the CIA's George Allen [presented as a pro-conspiracy witness in the CBS documentary] in his interview for *Inside Story*.

> ALLEN: I don't know whether the president knew. I don't know what he was being told.
> CARTER: Did people who you knew to be in the highest realms of the White House know about it?
> ALLEN: I think there was an awareness at the highest staff levels of the White House, yes. And I think there was an awareness at the top of the Department of Defense as well.
> CARTER: About the controversy?
> ALLEN: About the nature of the controversy, yes.
> CARTER: About the differences?
> ALLEN: Yes.
> CARTER: About the varying interpretations of strength of the enemy forces—of one kind or another.
> ALLEN: Yes—yes.

The contemporaneous documentary evidence indicates that George Allen was right: Early in the dispute the details of the controversy between military intelligence and the CIA were made available to those men in authority throughout the Washington intelligence community. (Whether Congress was kept properly informed or not was irrelevant; responsibility for doing so belonged not to Westmoreland but to McNamara, Rostow, Helms, etcetera.) The fact is that Westmoreland's superiors, both military and civilian, were kept fully informed not only about the nature of the dispute over Order of Battle but about the raw intelligence data that had fueled it. Beginning months before Col. Gains Hawkins gave his first "briefing" to Gen. Westmoreland, in May 1967, the cable traffic between Saigon and Washington had been buzzing with McChristian/Hawkins's revised estimates for the Viet Cong irregular forces. The CIA, in Saigon and Washington, knew, as did Generals Brown (DIA) and Peterson. By early June, at the latest, Admiral Sharp, Westmoreland's ultimate superior, was fully informed of the intelligence finds. By July 10, a month or so before the crucial August CIA–military conference, not only had the details of the dispute been fully disseminated along the Washington-Honolulu-Saigon intelligence axis, but the dispute over the size of the enemy manpower-pool had ended. There was no longer any substantive disagreement over the totals of the enemy force in South Vietnam. Adding up all categories, the figures on both sides totaled over 400,000. (Only Sam Adams was arguing for 600,000.) The question was: Should all of those categories be included in the official Order of Battle? In particular, did the Self-Defense and Secret Self-Defense forces—hamlet "home guards" composed mostly of older men, women, and children—have a significant enough military potential to be counted as soldiers? In the documentary CBS had obscured the crux of this debate by using the terms "VC" or "troops"—designations that described fully armed, fully trained, uniformed military units.

The United States military in Vietnam had 200 or so analysts in the field and had primary responsibility for Order of Battle estimates. When the CIA proposed to include those estimated 120,000 home guards (SD and SSD) in the Order of Battle summary of its 1967 National Intelligence Estimate, the military protested. Up to then those hard-to-quantify enemy organizations had been lumped in with guerillas and political cadre. If the CIA sliced out the SD and SSD and quantified them separately in its estimate, the military argued, the press would assume that the enemy army was 120,000 men larger than anyone had previously thought. And neither Westmoreland nor his intelligence chiefs believed that those shadowy home-guard units posed a serious military threat. Adams and his disciples did.

In document after contemporaneous document, the military's concern was reported:

July 7, CIA Saigon station chief Louis Sandine to Richard Helms:

". . . including Self-Defense as part of the enemy military strength figure . . . gives the total strength figure a probable error of at least plus or minus five percent. . . ."

July 9, George Carver to Helms: ". . . Davidson agreed that our substantive disagreements on facts neither major nor unresolvable. Chief problem was political and representational. . . ."

August 19, Robert Komer to Carver: ". . . I cannot see case for including vague estimates of low-grade part-time hamlet Self-Defense groups, mostly weaponless, in new Order of Battle. . . . MACV is determined to stick by its guns, and you can well imagine ruckus which would be created if it came out, as everything tends to on Vietnam, that Agency and MACV figures were so widely different. Any explanation as to why would simply lead press to conclude that MACV was deliberately omitting SD/SSD category in order to downgrade enemy strength. Thus credibility gap would be further widened at very time when in fact we are moving toward much more valid estimate. . . ."

August 19, Gen. George Godding (reporting on a briefing he gave to Gen. Earle Wheeler, chairman of the Joint Chiefs of Staff) to Generals Davidson and Peterson (the intelligence chief of CINCPAC): ". . . General Wheeler concurred in the MACV approach that the SD and SSD not be included in the overall total figure. . . ."

August 20, Gen. Creighton Abrams, Westmoreland's deputy, to Gen. Earle Wheeler: ". . . From the intelligence viewpoint, the inclusion of the SD and SSD strength figures in an estimate of military capabilities is highly questionable. These forces contain a sizable number of women and old people. They operate entirely in their own hamlets. They are rarely armed, have no real discipline and almost no military capability. . . .

"The press reaction to these inflated figures is of much greater concern. We have been projecting an image of success over the recent months, and properly so. Now when we release the figure of 420,000–431,000, the newsmen will immediately seize on that point that the enemy force has increased about 120,000–130,000. All available caveats and explanations will not prevent the press from drawing an erroneous and gloomy conclusion as to the meaning of the increase. . . ."

August 29, Ambassador to Vietnam Ellsworth Bunker to Walt Rostow: ". . . [CIA's] experts appear insistent on bringing out an estimate which will make enemy strength 430,000 to 490,000 instead of the range centering on 298,000 developed by MACV. CIA does this chiefly by adding to strength figures some 120,000 so-called SD and SSD forces which are not organized military units at all. . . . I need hardly mention the devastating impact if it should leak out (as these things so often do) that despite all our success in grinding down VC/NVA here, CIA figures are used to show that they are really much stronger than ever. . . . This is inevitable conclusion which most of press would reach."

September 10, Carver to Helms: ". . . Root problems, as we all recognize, lie much more in political public relations realm than in substantive difference. . . ."

September 11, Carver to Helms: "I presented my thoughts on the public relations problem. . . . Komer then launched into an hour-plus monologue reviewing his and Westmoreland's problems with the press, their frustrating inability to convince the press (hence the public) of the great progress being made, and the paramount importance of saying nothing that would detract from the image of progress or support the thesis of stalemate. . . ."

The documents indicate that the controversy was not over, as CBS had said, "the nature and the size of the enemy we were fighting" but which categories of that enemy had enough military potential to be included in the Order of Battle. The military insisted that the SD and SSD home guards were not an effective military threat; Sam Adams argued that the SD and SSD were. But within the CIA there were those, like Carver, who disagreed with Adams, taking the middle position that while those home-guard organizations should be described and roughly quantified, they should not be listed as soldiers in the Order of Battle. In its efforts to justify excluding those disputed categories from the Order of Battle, was the military attempting to suppress their number from officials in Washington? The contemporaneous documents provide persuasive evidence to the contrary. *At least* Helms, Carver, Peterson, Brown (the Defense Intelligence Agency), Wheeler (chairman of the Joint Chiefs of Staff), Rostow, McNamara, and Secretary of State Dean Rusk all knew the general details of the debate over estimates and of the impasse over the Self-Defense organizations. And that same upper echelon of the intelligence community was also fully informed about divergent estimates of other Order of Battle components, such as the number of political cadre. Captain Kelly Robinson accompanied Col. Gains Hawkins to a briefing that Hawkins gave Westmoreland in May 1967, on the new, higher estimates for enemy guerillas and political cadre. After the briefing, Robinson (a political-cadre specialist) recalled in an affidavit, Hawkins told him that "the MACV command would not accept such a high estimate because of concern over how the press and public would perceive that figure." However, the documentary had charged that Westmoreland had conspired to conceal intelligence not from the press (unlikely recipients of classified intelligence), but from his superiors. Yet less than a month and a half after a May 23 memo prepared by the CIA stated that "the number of Vietcong political personnel, listed as 39,000 in the OB, may be well over twice as high," the CIA's George Carver, in a cable that CBS had in its possession before the broadcast, was telling Director Helms that the military (Generals Davidson and Peterson, plus Col. Gains Hawkins) was supporting his figure of 80,000 political cadre "as [a] good estimate."

The military was not attempting to conceal the size of the enemy but to prevent the press from purveying to the American public (and their congressmen) "the gloomy and erroneous conclusion" that the enemy was far larger than had been perceived. The military felt that if the new figures were lumped with those of the enemy's full-time fighting force, it would give a false impression of the enemy's true battlefield strength. It was the military's skepticism of the press's ability to get a story right, justified in part by the press's distortion of war news, that was at the root of the controversy. In a written comment that was not included in the final draft of his report, Bud Benjamin asked, "Did the broadcast give any time to support the military view that press reaction *was* a valid concern?" The answer is: No.

Should, in particular, those home-guard Self-Defense forces have been included in the monthly official tally of enemy troops? The experts are still debating that issue. "If you have ever seen anybody with a leg blown off after tripping over a 105 shell that has been put in by some villager who is Self-Defense or Secret Self-Defense, you are goddamned right they are a military threat," said CBS-supporter Maj. John Barrie Williams (a Pentagon Vietnam-desk analyst) in deposition. However, Williams was unable to offer any enlightenment as to how a mine planted by an organized guerilla or a North Vietnamese soldier could be distinguished from one planted by a member of the Self-Defense forces. Williams agreed with the Westmoreland lawyer who pointed out that "nobody wore any T-shirts saying who they were." "We lived in a world of numbers, that you had to quantify everything," Williams had stated earlier in his deposition.

Or, on the other hand, was the military right in their assessment of the military potential of those Self-Defense forces? What about the 600,000-man army Adams said existed? Where was that army at Tet when less than 100,000 enemy turned up for their all-out Armageddon? If the enemy's inflated estimates of its own secret strength, upon which Adams largely depended for his extrapolations, were accurate, why didn't the popular urban uprisings the North Vietnamese had counted on during Tet ever occur?

And where is the evidence of the massive infiltration—an additional 125,000 uncounted enemy—that CBS said took place during the five months preceding Tet? Carver, Helms, Colby, Rostow, and McNamara, among others, all denied that any such infiltration occurred. The evidence suggests that the infiltration reports CBS said were suppressed were a series developed by a lone analyst. Lt. Michael Hankins, the Order of Battle Studies Group infiltration analyst, said he had been asked by his superior, Col. Everette Parkins, to use a new methodology that Parkins had developed for estimating infiltration. The higher estimates produced by that methodology were rejected not only by Col. Charles Morris, the Director of Intelligence Production, but by analysts in Danny Graham's Current Intelligence, Indications and Estimates Division. The information Hankins used in his extrapolations was available to Graham's men as well. Only his methodology was unique. Hankins's superiors insisted that, when tested against top-secret communications intelligence monitored by the National Security Agency, Hankins's estimate proved to be wrong.

Hankins, it turned out, had never told Adams that he believed his estimates had been rejected for other than innocent reasons, nor had he given Adams specific numbers for the amount of enemy infiltration in the five months preceding Tet. When Adams, researching his books, had contacted him, Hankins had refused to provide any information. CBS, on the other hand, had never contacted him.

Indeed, in the fall of 1967, five North Vietnamese divisions had moved across the DMZ (demilitarized zone separating the two Vietnams) near Khe Sanh, but the entire Washington intelligence community (including George Allen) had been fully apprised of those movements by military intelligence. But CBS insisted that the program had been discussing *infiltration* not wholesale *invasion* of the northern provinces by fully equipped North Vietnamese divisions.

Adams, in estimating enemy troop strength at 600,000 men, had not known about that alleged "massive infiltration." Thus, if the lone military intelligence analyst was right, Adams's estimate would have had to increase by 125,000, bringing his total to 725,000 enemy troops or sixty-five percent of the total Allied force in Vietnam at the time. If that was the case, again where was the evidence of that awesome enemy army at Tet? Why wasn't the enemy able to mount an anticipated "second wave" of powerful assaults? Why, after Tet, did the enemy never again demonstrate a capability of attacking in larger than battalion strength?

There was indeed the basis for an illuminating television documentary detailing how military intelligence engaged in a dispute with the CIA in the year leading up to the Tet offensive in an effort to prevent the press from reaching what the military regarded as the wrong conclusion over the size of the enemy. However, that was not the documentary that CBS aired on January 23, 1982. The CBS documentary had charged a Westmoreland-led conspiracy. Just as the military had anticipated, although fifteen years delayed, CBS had gotten the story wrong, by relying on a paid consultant whose account of events was tailored by his own bias, by allowing a producer to avoid or discard interviews with those who might have been able to rebut the documentary's premise, and by ignoring documents in its own possession which tended to cast doubt on that thesis.

Whether or not Westmoreland would be able to meet the burdens (proper ones, if the press is to be free to criticize official conduct) placed on a plaintiff by the libel law, whether or not he would prove to the satisfaction of judge and jury that he had not conspired, was something that the court would decide. However, whatever the ultimate disposition of the case, the lawsuit had had an undeniable impact on the institutions that should have been central to the documentary but had been ignored: the media themselves. Some press observers saw beneficial aspects resulting from the litigation, with news media exercising stricter restraint over reporters by requiring more proof, under tighter supervision, before allegations could be published or broadcast. Others felt a chilling effect, with the media turning timid and fearful of exercising their constitutional right and obligation to monitor and challenge the conduct of the officials who govern both us and our national policies. However, one thing was certain: If a chill was settling in, it was CBS and not Gen. William C. Westmoreland that had left the door ajar.

Index